The Child in the
Physical Environment

WILEY SERIES IN DEVELOPMENTAL PSYCHOLOGY AND ITS APPLICATIONS

Series Editor
Professor Kevin Connolly

The Child in the Physical Environment

The Development of Spatial Knowledge and Cognition

Christopher Spencer
Mark Blades
Kim Morsley

Department of Psychology, University of Sheffield

JOHN WILEY & SONS

Chichester · New York · Brisbane · Toronto · Singapore

Library of Congress Cataloging-in-Publication Data:

Spencer, Christopher (Christopher J.S.)
   The child in the physical environment: the development
of spatial knowledge and cognition / Christopher Spencer,
Mark Blades, Kim Morsley.
        p.   cm. (Wiley series in developmental psychology and its
applications)
    Bibliography: p.
    Includes Index.
    ISBN 0 471 91235 2
    1. Space perception in children. I. Blades, Mark. II. Morsley,
Kim. III. Title. IV. Series.
    [DNLM: 1. Child Development. 2. Cognition—in infancy &
childhood. 3. Environment. 4. Orientation—in infancy & childhood.
5. Space Perception—in infancy & childhood. 6. Spatial Behavior—in
infancy & childhood. WS 105.5.C7 S745c]
    BF723.S63S64   1989
    155.4 12—dc19
    DNLM/DLC   88-37038
    for Library of Congress   CIP

British Library Cataloguing in Publication Data:

Spencer, Christopher
   The child in the physical environment: the development of
spatial knowledge and cognition.
   I. Children. Cognitive development
   I. Title II. Blades, Mark III. Morsley, Kim
   155.4 13

ISBN 0 471 91235 2

Printed and bound in Great Britain by Bath Press, Ltd, Bath.

Contents

v

Series preface

The female digger wasp *Bembix* digs a small burrow in the ground in which she lays her eggs. She then carefully covers it up so that it is effectively invisible. Having done this she makes a reconnaissance flight in the immediate vicinity of the burrow before departing on a hunt for prey, an activity which may well take her more than a 100 metres away. Once a suitable prey has been caught she carries it back to the burrow as food for her young when they hatch. But how does she find her burrow again? In an elegant investigation made 50 years ago Tinbergen and Kruyt showed that the wasp makes a representation of landmarks in the vicinity of the burrow during the reconnnaissance flight just prior to the hunt. The animal needs to know about the position of its burrow which entails knowledge of its spatial environment. As has been shown experimentally if the environment is not interfered with, the humble digger wasp is remarkably good at finding its way about.

On quite a different scale the Puluwat, a people living in the Caroline Islands of the Pacific, are noted for their extraordinary navigational skills. Without benefit of modern navigational aids or any scientific equipment the Puluwat master sailor navigates with great accuracy between hundreds of islands in the various conditions which are encountered at sea. Gladwin (*East is a big bird: Navigation and logic on Puluwat atoll*, Harvard University Press, 1970) who studied under a master sailor concluded that many categories of information are integrated into a system where the various and diverse elements supplement each other to achieve the astonishing accuracy and reliability typical of these sailors. There are countless other examples both remarkable and unremarkable of animals and people finding their way about in space. What these serve to show is the fundamental importance of knowing the environment and being able to get around in it. The fact that spatial skills and knowledge of the environment are commonplace, though reflected in different ways in different species, underlines

vii

the importance for the individual organism; for successful adaptation they are vital. In fact in the first edition of *The Origin of Species* Charles Darwin speculated on there being what he called an instinct for orientation.

Geographical orientation takes a number of forms. For example, we are able to walk in a straight line, we can maintain a sense of direction should we have to make a detour from the usual route, we can follow, that is read, and make maps of varying degrees of sophistication. These abilities require the involvement of various sensory modalities, movements and conceptual skills. Spatial and environmental knowledge engages an extensive range of widely different capacities ranging from the individual's body image and its relationship to immediate extra-body space to how the environment is represented in the mind. In turn these issues are related to important and fundamental psychological questions such as how knowledge can control action. Knowing one's relations to space and place underpins many common but vital abilities such as: knowing where you are, searching for an object, recalling a scene, giving directions, estimating the shorter of two routes, imagining a scene described in words, getting about in the countryside and in the city.

Of course knowledge of this kind is not formally taught, yet we do expect all children to acquire considerable competenence on these and related abilities and capacities. So what is known about the development of these capabilities and what implications does our knowledge have for educational and other practical matters? The authors have collected together a great deal of recent material which they have critically reviewed. This is now presented as a coherent and cohesive picture of the state of our knowledge of the child in relationship with his physical environment. This knowledge has implications for children with particular disabilities. For example, how do blind children learn about their physical environment and how is their knowledge of environment represented and accessed for action? Can children use maps, and do these symbol systems differ fundamentally from other symbolic acitivities which the children master?

In writing this book the authors have performed a most valuable and timely service. They have brought together material scattered across a wide range of literature and often written with different readers and specialists in mind; in so doing they have plainly demonstrated both the importance and generality of the underlying scientific questions and the applied significance of research in this area. The book will be of interest not only to developmental psychologists and educationalists but also to many others concerned with children and with designing environments for children.

KEVIN CONNOLLY

Acknowledgements

Our Series editor, Kevin Connolly, must stand first in our acknowledgements: for it was he who first conceived of this volume, and who persuaded three environmental psychologists to write for a developmental psychology series, to bring several thriving but separate literatures together. He and Wendy Hudlass, for Wiley, offered support and suggestions throughout in a civilized and yet persuasive fashion. And the manuscript benefiited from the tactful word-processing skills of Gay Rich, Anne Clifton and Julie Watson. We are also indebted to Geoffrey Beattie for some of the illustrations, and Len Hetherington and John Porrill for assistance with photography.

The Economic and Social Research Council has supported much of our recent research; and we are extremely grateful to the Council, and to other sources of finance, in particular, the Nimrod and Glavin Trust, the Nancy Balfour Trust, the Richard Newitt Fund, the Sir Richard Stapley Educational Trust, the Family Welfare Association, and the Singer Foundation.

Our work would not have been possible without the cheerful and enthusiastic support of the children, parents and staff of Mushroom Lane Nursery School, Tapton Mount School, and Lydgate First School, all in Sheffield; Ladywood School at Grimethorpe, and Rise Park Infants School, Nottingham.

Three names appear on the cover, but as the bibliography will show, other members of the research group have contributed considerably; we would like to acknowledge the work of Zhra Darvizeh, Nigel Harrison, Debra Murray, Clare Tyerman, Marie Weetman, Jill Dixon, Susan Mitchell, Julie Wisdom, Jayne Travis, Anita Hill, Barbara Dryhurst and Susan Easterbrook. Kate Baybutt has been our friend and guide to the work of mobility training, and Torgny Ottosson to the use of maps in orienteering. We have benefitted enormously from enjoyable and stimulating discussions with Tommy Gärling, Gunilla Torrell, Lynn Liben, Gary Moore, David Canter, Alan Dodds, Chris Eiser,

Peter Stringer, Arne Yngström, Reginald Golledge, Jaan Valsiner, Simon Catling, Malcolm Lewis, Mary Jefferson, Pia Bjorkild, Giovanna Axia, Anne Beer and, in times now sadly past, Henri Tajfel.

Introduction

The need for a book on the development of spatial knowledge, and the child's changing environmental needs

Students of animal behaviour have long realized the importance to a species of spatial knowledge—knowledge about the location of self with respect to the world, and about the interrelationships between places and objects. Only recently has developmental psychology, together with environmental psychology, devoted much energy to the study of the development of spatial knowledge in humans, and to their spatial needs. This book will survey the considerable recent literature in a way that will be of interest both to students of child development and to those specialists in education and in design who are attempting to produce a better fit between child and environment.

Consider familiar animal behaviours such as food gathering, pairing, avoiding predators, cacheing the young: basic to all of these and other central survival behaviours is the efficient use of space—itself dependent upon spatial information storage and handling. Clearly therefore it is a high survival value process—and one which, with other cognitive skills, will be developed in its essentials relatively early. In a species such as our own, where for a variety of reasons care and dependence are prolonged, the full range of skills necessary for individual survival do not need to come into play for several years; yet the anthropological literature furnishes us with examples of youthful expertise in exploitation of the environment that can seem amazingly precocious to us as settled and urbanized individuals: for example, the Inuit boy fending for himself in Arctic Canada for trial periods from the age of 7 years; the Qualandar child gaining recognition for himself as an independent performer touring rural areas of Pakistan; the Australian Aboriginal youth going walkabout in the Nullabor (see, respectively, Brody, 1981, 1987; Berland, 1982; Lewis, 1976).

Maybe it is because the majority of psychologists are themselves children of relatively undemanding and protective settings that, when propounding theories of development of environmental skills, they have tended until recently to stress the young child's relative incompetence with relation to the environment. Similarly, educationalists have underestimated children when they have considered the appropriate time to introduce into the curriculum such spatial information using skills as map use and map making. Only in the last decade or so has the trend gone the other way. Following on the heels of other 'discoveries' of the competence of infants, environmental and developmental psychologists have realized relatively recently that the child's environmental competence has been underestimated.

As with all such trends and re-evaluations, there is a temptation to overstate; clearly, much *develops* during infancy and childhood. Many aspects of knowledge are sketchy and many demands made upon, for example, memory for a route, result in the child failing to react efficiently to the situation. The child, even more than the adult, is open to distorted, partial and highly stereotyped images of places not known through direct experience. It is this process of development of environmental skills and knowledge that is a central concern of this book. A second concern is the implications and applications of these changes when considering questions about for example: the special problems experienced by the blind and the mentally handicapped in coming to terms with the word, and the special needs of the young with relation to the environment; (these are issues where the architect and planner should be able to turn to developmental psychology for guidance); the implications for the safety of children in cities, and elsewhere; and finally, how we can more effectively introduce environmental knowledge and skills into the curriculum at appropriate ages, so that the child may know and use the environment efficiently and effectively, and do so in safety.

Research on the child's understanding of the world about him or her, and the development of spatial competence, has reached a stage where a book is needed to draw together the diverse material—from child development, environmental psychology, behavioural geography, education, and artificial intelligence. Most of the work published has only limited cross-referencing to work in each of the other traditions. Much is potentially applicable: within special education, for instance, there is much 'pure' literature that is immediately relevant to the mobility education of the young blind child, and to the independence of the mentally handicapped. More generally, the work has implications for planning and architecture, and for road safety—taking into account the child's needs and skills with relation to the environment. Finally, such research has come to challenge assumptions within primary education, and has led to practical work designed to develop the child's understanding of the world from the pre-school years onwards.

The reader will find that this book is structured into three parts, of unequal length. Part 1 is designed to make available to the reader whose principal interest is developmental a brief account of recent non-developmental research on the *processes of environmental cognition*. After asking what is involved in the awareness of the environment, and what implications the study of environmental cognition has for the understanding of behaviour, the first section reviews relevant research from environmental psychology, cognitive psychology and artificial intelligence.

This review summarizes some of the main themes in environmental cognition research—for example, how individuals acquire an environmental image. We discuss how this image is often labelled as a 'cognitive map' and the problems inherent in such labelling—not least the way in which 'map' emphasizes the aspect of place knowledge, at the cost of ignoring other aspects such as the individual's feelings and attitudes towards the environment. We describe some of the different methodologies that have been used to assess individual's environmental knowledge and briefly describe the comparative importance of each of these, with a note about the potential of approaches from artificial intelligence to be useful in providing insights into the mental representation of the environment. We also mention topics such as individual differences in cognition and the possible factors that might influence these differences.

This review of current topics in the first part provides a background for Part II, the main part of the book: *the development of environmental cognition.*

While Part I is concerned with aspects of a fully developed environmental cognition processing system, Part II reviews research on how such a system develops during childhood. We use an expanding scale—geographical scale that is—as the framework for the review. The child's awareness of close body space is our first topic, with, as a special focus, individual differences in spatial skills. Immediate and interpersonal space-skill development is considered next, and we ask how spatial cognition is linked to the development of other cognitions. Geographical-scale space has provided a particularly rich field for research with children, and we devote space to the development of cognitive maps, the child's ability to estimate distances and directions, the use of landmarks, the learning of routes, and the assembly of this knowledge in such a way that the child can efficiently navigate through large-scale areas.

The child's understanding and knowledge of distant places is next; and we compare this with social psychology's account of the development of stereotypes and prejudices about other peoples.

One source of information about places, both distant and close, is the map. Educationalists have long considered that its abstract and systematized presentation of spatial information should not be introduced until the middle-school years; and yet we are able to present evidence to show that much younger children have the ability to understand maps and can use them to start to learn about the world.

The final part of the book, Part III, *on applications of environmental cognition research*, considers three distinct areas where the material already dis-

cussed is of applied relevance. Chapter 10 is concerned with the spatial cognition
of special populations: what research has indicated about the spatial skills of
the blind, and the implications this has for orientation and mobility training.
(The spatial needs of other populations, such as the mentally impaired, is also
briefly discussed.)

Chapter 11 considers the implications of the developmental research on cognition for environmental and geographical education: challenging some of the
educationalists' assumptions; describing the move within education to place
'graphicacy' alongside numeracy, literacy, and articulacy as 'the fourth ace in
the pack'; and evaluating programmes of environmental education, designed to
heighten children's awareness of their everyday world, its buildings, settlements
and the natural world.

We go on to ask how, in the light of all the foregoing accumulated evidence,
one can more knowledgeably plan for children's needs and safety. What are
these needs, and how do they change as the individual develops? What, indeed,
do children do all day? What are their private worlds? Why do many adult-
oriented neighbourhood designs fail to cater for younger needs? Indeed, can
one plan cities for multi-age-group usage? And, finally, in this chapter, how can
planners and politicians take into account the child's needs and competencies
when planning a safer environment?

There is, we conclude, a need for more child-centred environmental research.
The signs are encouraging; and the gains from the research reviewed are both
applied—as described in Part III of the book—*and* pure, as Parts I and II indicate. The separate sub-disciplines of psychology concerned with children and the
environment (developmental, educational, cognitive, social, and environmental)
are at last beginning to influence each other, and to realize the real value of the
innovatory approaches of other research areas: artificial intelligence, geography
and the planning disciplines.

Part I

Processes of Environmental Cognition

CHAPTER 1

Environmental cognition: a conceptual and methodological review

The child's understanding of the world, the child's behaviour as shaped by that understanding, and the environmental needs of the developing child are the principal concerns in the main body of this book. There exist many excellent accounts about the child's knowledge of, and integration into, the *social* world and indeed this has long been one of the major fields of developmental psychology. But the child's interactions with the *physical*, geographical, world has received less attention within developmental psychology, despite evidence from environmental psychologists that has indicated that the physical world is not simply a neutral background for social interactons and individual development, but has a profound influence in suggesting, shaping, facilitating, and sometimes preventing behaviour. For example, few theories of child-rearing practice ever give more than the briefest description of the family's everyday environment; few accounts of pupil–teacher interaction devote any space to the physical setting of the classroom, the school, and the community. But environmental psychologists would rightly maintain that by omitting such features from published papers—and indeed from the research design itself—developmental psychologists are reducing the predictive power of their hypotheses.

We need to know about the everyday settings of the child's development and we need to investigate how the child develops an understanding of those settings. Therefore our main concern becomes that of environmental cognition—the basic processes (to be discussed in Part I of the book) and their development through childhood (the topic of Part II).

In this book we take the position that studying the individual's environmental

Figure 1.1(i) and Figure 1.1(ii)   How much does physical setting affect well being? Two schools in the same city, comparable in size, identical in school programme: yet one would predict important differences ranging from intangible 'ethos' to much more measurable variations in school performance and well-being, related to the architectural style and overall setting.

images is a worthwhile part of psychology's enterprise that can contribute to the exploration and prediction of the individual's behaviour. This is clearly the case so far as species other than humans are concerned and there already exists a large comparative and ethological literature concerned with other species' use of space [see Ellen and Thinus-Blanc, 1986 for a general review of the ethological literature]. Such studies include classic laboratory experiments like Tolman's (1948) work with rats in mazes, which led to his hypothesis that a rat may build up an overall view or 'cognitive map' of an environment that it has experienced (see Olton, 1979), as well as early studies in more natural settings such as Tinbergen's (1951) experiments concerned with the sand-wasp's use of landmarks for locating its own nest. Other research has taken place in large-scale experimental environments, e.g. Menzel's (1973) study of chimpanzees' ability to relocate hidden food, or has tracked animals in their natural habitat (e.g. Fabrigoule and Maurel, 1982). However, we limit our review to the research with humans and only note in passing that the work with other species may have the potential to contribute to an understanding of the role of spatial memory in the evolution of early hominids. McKinnon (1978) has suggested that the need to form elaborate cognitive maps for hunting and foraging may have been a crucial stimulus for the evolution of greater intelligence, but as yet the evidence from ethological research, as well as from studies by anthropologists and archaeologists is far too sparse to provide supporting evidence for such an interesting speculation.

The importance of efficient spatial cognition in everyday life can be made manifest by considering the diversity of one's relations to space and place: knowing where one is; being lost; anticipating a trip; searching for an object; recalling a childhood scene; giving directions to a stranger; estimating the shorter of two possible routes; discerning different neighbourhoods in a city; ignoring one's own intuitions in order to rely on a map or compass; deciding where to live; planning vacations, or conceptualising a scene from a novel or a newspaper report. This list could be extended indefinitely—suffice to say that any such list will include instances of real and imagined places, places known from the past or in the present, places directly related to some action or activity and others that are more contemplative. Any discussion of the individual's understanding of space could take as many perspectives as there are different examples of spatial awareness, but we emphasize the skilled nature of human spatial activity and consider individuals as active processors and users of the knowledge that they have about spatial relations and layouts. In other words, the focus is on how individuals encode environmental information and how they carry out actions and plans on the basis of this stored information. As Byrne (1982) has suggested, one of the central challenges for environmental psychology is an explanation of how, with a natural, untaught, and universal skill, the individual can successfully retrieve and manipulate information from a complex and potentially huge memory store of knowledge about the world.

How does an individual learn about the environment?

Although an individual can obtain environmental information indirectly (e.g. from maps, photographs or verbal descriptions) the source of nearly all environmental knowledge is the individual's own direct experience of the world. This experience is gained from movement and travel through the world and there is indeed some evidence to suggest that large-scale environmental information is encoded in ways that facilitate travel, as well as being a consequence of such travel (see Kuipers, 1982; Gärling, Böök, and Lindberg, 1984a). From experience in the environment the individual can build up a knowledge of where places are in the world and a set of attitudes about those places. This knowledge may be very subjective—it is clear that attitudes and feelings will depend on the individual's predispositions, and also that the understanding of spatial relationships, or where places are located, will depend on the amount and type of experience and the intentions and learning strategies of the individual. Controlled studies of how individuals acquire information about novel environments are difficult and, in general, attempts to elicit precise data are often restricted to small areas and concentrate on limited aspects of environmental knowledge (often just the subjects' abilities to determine the direction and distance of target places). For example, in a series of experiments Lindberg and Gärling (1981) asked adults to walk a path through a maze-like series of uniform corridors and then tested each subject's ability to estimate the distance and direction of several places along the path. Some subjects were blindfolded during the walk and others had to perform other tasks at the same time so that Lindberg and Gärling were able to discuss the effects of these manipulations on the subjects' encoding abilities. Gauvain and Rogoff (1986) allowed 5-, 7- and 8-year-olds to explore a small layout of rooms. Some children were instructed to try to remember the layout, and others simply had to lay a long ribbon through the rooms. The different experimental instructions did not affect the performance of the younger and older children but the 7-year-olds who placed the ribbon remembered more than the children of the same age who were specifically instructed to learn the layout. The latter tended to draw or describe the layout as a list of rooms and ignored their interrelationships. Gauvain and Rogoff (1986) suggested that, at least at the age of 7, children's deliberate attempts to memorize a layout resulted in them using a strategy more useful for learning lists of information than for learning spatial relationships.

The above experiments have been described as examples of studies that have focused on the encoding stage of learning about the environment. In each case the experimental manipulations influenced the subjects' recall of the environment. However, such studies are comparatively rare and although occasional experiments have taken place in buildings (e.g. Gärling, Lindberg, and Mäntylä, 1983) or during an actual road journey (e.g. Carr and Schissler, 1969), most have taken place in small and restricted environments. As yet we know very little about the factors that affect the automatic learning that takes place in every environment, and very little about the intentional strategies that individuals adopt when making a deliberate effort to learn or remember a particular route or place.

The concept of the cognitive map

Most empirical work has concentrated on eliciting environmental knowledge that the individual has already acquired—this knowledge is often described as a 'cognitive map'. In the following sections we discuss both the concept of the cognitive map and some of the environmental methodologies that have been used to elicit an individual's cognitive map. We also point out the bias towards describing an individual's environmental knowledge mainly in terms of its *map-like* qualities so that other aspects of environmental experience have been largely ignored.

To talk of a *map-like* representation is a tempting metaphor when the most frequently used *physical* representation of spatial relations is a cartographic map. Unfortunately there are at least three immediate confusions involved in using a label such as 'map'. First, and most simply, the term has been used extensively in phrases that describe a wide range of heterogeneous phenomena. Indeed, the geographer Graham (1982) has said that the term 'mental map' (often used as a synonym for 'cognitive map') is perhaps one of the most unfortunate in the literature, having been applied to everything from an individual's freehand street map of a neighbourhood to textbook illustrations expressing the environmental preferences of whole groups of people [e.g. the towns and regions within their country that young Britons or young Malaysians would consider when seeking a job—see Gould and White, (1986)].

Secondly, the word 'map' has tempted many investigators to compare the cognitive maps that have been produced from experimental procedures (see below) with a cartographic map and measure the cognitive map for accuracy against this 'standard'. This involves an unquestioned assumption by the investigator that his or her street plan, road map, or ordnance survey map is a true representation of the reality of the world. But a moment's thought [or any good cartographic textbook, e.g. Muehrke (1978)] should prompt the consideration that any part of the real world can be represented in any number of ways—there is no 'standard' and any single cartographic map is no more than what Downs (1981a,b) has called a 'metaphor' for the world itself. To give a frequently quoted example—both the London Underground map and a London street map will include all the subway stations, but the spatial relationship between any two stations will not necessarily be the same on both maps. Each map selects different aspects of information from the world to present to the viewer, in other words each is a different metaphor of the same area. Not dissimilarly, each person's own knowledge of the environment is a metaphor for that environment based on that person's knowledge, experience, and needs in the environment. Rather than using any arbitrarily selected cartographic map as a standard, it may be better to treat the comparison of a cartographic and cognitive map as the comparison of two metaphors and with all the caution that implies.

Thirdly, the frequent use of a term like 'cognitive map' may lead to the impression that there really is a 'map' in the head. This is obviously not the case literally, but the casual use of the term map is often a barrier in attempts to understand the mental representation of the environment. Rather than considering such knowledge as a 'map' (however convenient that shorthand is) it may be more useful to view spatial abilities and representation in the sort of terms used by Liben (1981). She differentiates between *spatial products*—the external products that individuals can generate from recalling environmental information (e.g. sketch maps or verbal descriptions); *spatial thought*—the mental manipulation of spatial information (e.g. planning a route or imagining the view behind our heads); and *spatial storage*—which refers to the cognitive representation of the information and how it might be coded in memory (e.g. as propositions or stimulus–response connections, etc.). The last category might also include the processes that act on the memory store—the processes controlling the acquisition, storage and retrieval of environmental information. It is these processes that are the focus for researchers but, of course, such processes can only be inferred indirectly from interpreting individuals' performances in experiments that measure the ability to generate 'spatial products' or test their 'spatial thought'. Any number of experimental techniques have been used to elicit individuals' knowledge and some examples, with particular reference to children, are mentioned below.

Development of environmental cognition

Before moving on to methodologies, some comments are necessary on an issue that is inseparable from the concept of 'cognitive maps': this is the development of environmental cognition. Development can be taken to mean either the development of knowledge, which comes with increasing experience of a new environment, or the development of a child's ability to learn about his or her own environment. It goes without saying that someone who has lived in the same area for a number of years will know more about that area than someone who has recently moved into the area. The question is how and in what ways does the environmental representation become richer in detail, and with particular reference to children—how do children develop an understanding of their environment? It may be that an adult learning about a novel area and a developing child learning about his or her environment progress through the same stages of knowledge. Such an assumption must be treated with caution because obviously an adult in a new area has had previous experience to make

Figure 1.2   Landmarks. Not just orienting guides for the traveller, but according to much research, the points from which separately experienced aspects of space are articulated into a coherent schemata.

assumptions about any new environment. None the less, the idea that the development of an individual's environmental representation may be similar for both children and for adults in novel areas is often tacitly assumed in the literature. Perhaps the predominant reason for this assumption is the influence of Siegel and White's (1975) theory.

This theory describes the development of the environmental representation in children in the following way. First, children remember landmarks, which are places of particular interest or importance for them. Once landmarks are established, information about routes can be related to them, and children can then form what Siegal and White call 'minimaps'. These minimaps may be accurate and internally consist of images of limited areas, but children may not necessarily appreciate the relationship between a number of different minimaps. The final stage is the coordination of all the different minimaps in an overall and complete representation of the environment. In other words, Siegal and White suggest that the individual's spatial knowledge develops through a number of distinct stages (landmark recognition, route information, and minimaps) into a complete mental recognition of the environment. Siegal and White (1975) drew on a large number of different studies for empirical support for their theory and, in general, their evidence favoured their description of developmental stages. Any number of experiments since the publication of the theory have also shown support for the theory, both with children and adults in new areas. Typical of the studies with children are those that test different age-groups of children who live in the same area and which find that older children have reached a higher stage than younger children (for just one example see Cousins, Siegal, and Maxwell, 1983). More often with adults the same group of subjects is tested a number of times after increasing periods of experience in a novel environment (e.g. Evans, Marrero, and Butler, 1981). Both kinds of study indicate that an individual's knowledge generally progresses through a recognition of landmarks, route knowledge, and then to some comparatively complete appreciation of the environment.

However, despite the general acceptance of Siegal and White's (1975) theory, some aspects of it should be treated with caution. Most of the results from the supportive experiments have come from studies that used 'indirect' methods to test subjects' memories of the environment (e.g. drawing sketch maps or estimating distances) and the use of such methods is discussed more fully below. Studies in which children's environmental cognition has been tested directly (e.g. by re-walking an actual route) suggest that young and even pre-school children can remember a great deal about places that they have experienced even after a single exposure to those places. For example, Cornell and Hay (1983) took 5-year-old children on a walk through a university campus and found that these children were quite capable of re-tracing the route without any mistakes after only walking along it once. Similarly, Darvizeh and Spencer (1984) took 3-and 4-year-old children on a novel walk through a typical urban environment (see Chapter 5) and found that many of these children could find their way correctly along the route several days later. In the latter experiment other children of the same age also walked the route, but had specific landmarks pointed out to them. This improved their ability to re-trace the route at a later date.

To place these results in the context of Siegal and White's (1975) theory they have suggested that children's memory of an environment develops through a number of stages, and that only after landmarks are known can routes be remembered accurately. This implies that route knowledge is only possible after repeated experience in the same environment. But the studies by Cornell and Hay (1984) and Darvizeh and Spencer (1984) demonstrate that children can remember a route after only a single walk along it. In other words, route learning may take place immediately and is not always dependent on a preliminary stage of landmark learning—in fact Cornell and Hay, in contrast to Siegal and White, argued that route knowledge may be based on the memory for a continuous sequence of environmental scenes. But this suggestion may undervalue the importance of specific landmarks because Darvizeh and Spencer showed that children's memory for a route could be significantly improved when their attention was drawn to appropriate landmarks along the way. Rather than viewing children's developing knowledge in fixed stages it may be more appropriate to consider children's ability in terms of their ability to apply efficient strategies for selecting appropriate information from the environment. It is clear that even young children can remember a lot about a simple route after one exposure to it, but they may be less proficient than, say, older children or adults, if they do not realize the benefits of noting effective information as they move through the environment.

Methodologies

In this section we will try to summarize some of the methods that have been used to elicit environmental knowledge. As Evans (1980) has said, the central methodological issue of all environmental research is the problem of 'how to externalise the individual's mental map of the environment'. Most approaches to this problem rely on 'laboratory' methods to assess the individual's knowledge and we will group these according to whether individuals have to rely on *recall* of a previously experienced environment (e.g. giving a verbal description of a place) or *recognition* of an environment (e.g. selecting photographs of places that they know). Testing individuals' knowledge of real environments can rarely control for their experience in that environment—except, very broadly, by taking into account how long the person has lived in that environment. Some experimenters have tried to overcome this difficulty by presenting subjects with films or a series of photographs, treating these as equivalent to experience in an actual environment, and then testing the subjects' memories for the information included in the films or photographs. There are also, of course, the direct ways of testing environmental knowledge; for example, asking subjects to walk a route or find a place.

A few general comments about the multitude of methodologies are necessary. First, any method makes specific demands on the subjects' abilities and will influence both the results obtained and the interpretation of those results. If a subject is asked to draw a sketch map this may demonstrate that the subject has a 'survey' knowledge of an area or has an appreciation of the special relationships of many different places in that area. The same subject could also be asked to give verbal directions between two places and this would indicate an ability to use the same information in a 'sequential' manner. Such results can be informative about the ability to extract and use their spatial knowledge, but it has to be remembered that these are 'spatial products' (see above)—they may have limited value in aiding an understanding of the individuals underlying mental representation or 'spatial storage'. This is rather an obvious point to make, but unfortunately it is not made often enough or explicitly enough made in much of the literature.

Secondly, most methods also make particular demands on a subject additional to the recall of environmental information. For example, asking individuals to draw sketch maps automatically involves not only the ability to draw, but also assumptions by both the subject and the experimenter about what constitutes a map and what subset of information it is appropriate to include therein. Thirdly, some methods may be more appropriate than others for particular groups of subjects. This point is especially important with regard to studies involving children. Asking young children to draw maps or give verbal descriptions is a fairly ineffective way to assess their environmental knowledge. Again this is a rather obvious point, but there is no doubt that the failure to utilize appropriate methods has often led to the underestimation of children's ability. Good examples of this are the experiments discussed above, with reference to Siegal and White's (1975) theory, which have shown that children who are asked to perform a realistic test (re-tracing a route) in a real environment often perform much better than would be expected from other tests. Any task that confounds environmental performance with other skills (whether drawing, verbalizing, estimating distances or direction, etc.) should be treated with some caution. This caution should apply equally to studies involving children and those involving adults. Having made these general comments, some of the advantages and disadvantages of particular methodologies can be discussed.

The 'laboratory' methodologies are numerous. The most basic approach that can be used to find out about an individual's recall knowledge is simply to ask questions, which can be precise ('where is ...?', 'how far is ...?', 'how big is ...? etc.') or more general ('describe a place you know', 'where do you most like to spend time?' etc.) Such recall methods have been used since the pioneering studies of Lynch (1960), who studied individual's responses to a novel city area and found that his subjects tended to agree on the 'elements' of the city image. It was these 'elements' that Lynch then formalized to describe a city in terms of districts, edges, paths, and landmarks. Lynch asked for descriptions after the individuals had experienced the new area, which had the advantage, by working through memory, of selecting out the key features in which he was interested. Other studies have compared what subjects describe after a journey with what they were looking at during the journey—for example Carr and Schissler (1969) used a camera strapped to a person to record exactly what they saw as they drove along a highway. This film record was then compared with the descriptions of the route that the subjects made after completing the journey.

The advantage of allowing individuals to make free responses to general questions is that they have the opportunity to select and describe places of interest or importance to them, and such descriptions are likely to be rich in information beyond the purely factual details of where and what a place is. Hart (1979), working with children in a small town in New England, was able to get them to describe areas that were 'favorite places' or 'secret places' or 'scary places'. (This aspect of the environment—the attitudinal or emotional response to the environment—will be discussed in much more detail below). On the other hand, free responses are inevitably subjective, difficult to qualify, and difficult to compare across different individuals, and the technique demands a degree of verbal fluency thath is beyond the ability of, say, very young children.

As well as asking general questions, it is also possible to focus on a particular aspect of environmental knowledge and ask subjects for a specific verbal description. The most obvious example is asking individuals for a description of a particular route. On one occasion we asked about 100 students to write a description of a very familiar route between their hall of residence and the city centre, as if they were giving detailed directions for an out-of-town stranger to follow. Although it was interesting to compare those students who used libraries and bookshops as landmarks in their description with those who used only pubs, there were so many different approaches to giving the directions that it was difficult to draw any general conclusions. Perhaps the most unexpected finding was how many of the descriptions were technically wrong, and if followed exactly the user would soon have been lost. We say 'technically' wrong because no doubt in practice most users would have easily overcome the misdirections as they actually walked along the route (e.g. an instruction like 'first left after the traffic lights' could be ignored if first left was obviously a minor cul-de-sac; instead the user could assume that the indicated turn was the first major road on the left). In other words, the students who carried out the task often made a number of tacit assumptions about the supposed user's ability to interpret the instruction and therefore also about the user's own general environmental knowledge. The same often applies in more realistic situations of direction giving [e.g. Klein (1982) and Wunderlich and Reinelt (1982) stopped people in the street and asked them the way to particular places]. In other words, the data from studies of direction-giving is often more informative about the assumptions that underlie communication, than it is about environmental knowledge—in fact Wunderlich and Reinelt also analysed the directions they collected in terms of the social interaction that was taking place between the direction-asker and the direction-giver.

Other methods relying on the individual's recall involve asking subjects for direction and distance estimates. (These will be discussed in more detail in Chapters 6 and 7 and are therefore only mentioned briefly here). These include a number of variations. Subjects can be tested in a laboratory by being asked to imagine they are standing at place A in the environment, facing place B; they are then requested to point to where place C would be. Alternatively subjects can do the same task in the environment itself, pointing from where they are to an unseen target. If a number of judgements from different places are made for the same target, it is possible to work out where the subject thinks the target is. These procedures have the advantage of being comparatively simple to carry out; they can also be adapted for working with even very young children (e.g. Conning and Byrne, 1984); and they provide qualifiable results (usually measures in degrees related to the subjects accuracy), which allows comparisons between individuals or groups of subjects.

Distance estimates are less easy to achieve—both adults and children find it difficult to make absolute judgements (e.g. in yards or miles). Subjects can be told to assume that some given standard (e.g. a line painted on a board in the laboratory) represents the distance between two given places in the environment and can then be asked to mark on the line the proportional distance of other pairs of locations (so that a pair of locations that the subject thought were half as far apart as the given standard places would be marked as half the length of the line). An obvious problem with this method is that it assumes not only the ability to estimate distances, but also to make comparative judgements and scale these on the provided standard, and it istherefore particularly inapplicable for research with children. None the less, effective use can be made of distance judgements using a technique called 'multidimensional scaling' (MDS, see Baird, 1979). For example, an experimenter can select a number of target places from an area known to an individual who can then be asked to estimate the distance between all possible pairs of targets. If this data is analysed by multidimensional scaling the subject's estimates can be converted in a two-dimensional map including all the target places. This technique can produce maps that are comparable to maps of the target places drawn directly by subjects.

The use of sketch maps has been one of the most frequent methods of testing environmental knowledge (e.g. Pocock, 1976) and it allows subjects the opportunity to include whatever information they want to put on the map. This can be both an advantage, because subjects may include unexpected places and detail, and a disadvantage, because subjects who know more about an area than they actually draw must select from their store of knowledge. This selection will include what the subject considers important and the experimenter can have little control over the selection criteria applied by the subject. Having said that, it is often surprising how the majority of sketch maps (or at least those illustrated in the literature) are remarkably similar. This is not to say the content of maps, even from subjects in the same area, will be identical, but rather that the style of drawing and choice of symbols, labelling, etc., will be similar. Not surprisingly, especially given that most experimenters only work with urban populations, most sketch maps mimic, however poorly, the style of a typical street or town map. In other words the request 'draw a map' usually prompts a response from the subject in terms of a pseudo cartographic map. This undoubtably biases the kind of information that subjects express about the environment and restricts it to particular categories of physical features, such as roads, rivers and salient buildings—we have yet to see a sketch map thath includes houses, gardens and rows of shops. Similarly, a pseudo cartographic map does not allow subjects to indicate their response to and attitudes about the environment, (see below). There are also other drawbacks to the use of sketch maps: few people can draw consistently to the same scale, so variations in an individual's map may reflect drawing ability rather than environmental knowledge, and several studies have shown a correlation between graphic ability scores and the quality of drawn maps (e.g. Murray and Spencer, 1979, Evans, 1980). Therefore, sketch maps, being so subjective, are not easy to analyse, and comparisons between different subject's maps are difficult.

Any method requiring graphic ability, such as a sketch, is clearly inappropriate in experiments with young children who will not have the necessary drawing skills. To avoid a task that involved drawing, Spencer and Darvizeh (1981b) gave 4-year-old children elements (such as roads, houses, cars, trees, and buildings) with which to make a picture of a route they knew. Other experimenters have asked children to make models. Siegal and Schadler (1977) gave 5-year-old children a model of their classroom and all the classroom furniture. The children were asked to arrange the model until it corresponded with the real classroom, and many of them were able to do so. Nevertheless, even constructing a model requires some ability beyond simply memory for the relevant environmental information [for example Liben, Moore, and Golbeck, (1982) found that pre-school children could reconstruct their actual classroom, by replacing the real furniture, better than they could make a scale model of it]. Models can be useful, but given the practical problems involved in using them (such as the number of items that can be reasonably included) they are limited to small areas.

The above methodologies test recall memory, but it is also possible to examine recognition memory for environmental features. For example, Doherty and Pellegrino (1985) tested children's knowledge of their own neighbourhood by showing them more than 200 photographs of scenes from both the neighbourhood and from similar areas. The children had to say whether or not they thought the photograph was taken in their own neighbourhood. In another experiment, Dale (1971) showed children an aerial photograph and a map of their own village and asked the children to describe what they could see on them.

A frequent problem for environmental research is often the experimenter's lack of control over subjects' experience, and many reports have to assume that the individuals taking part have had equivalent experience (usually on the grounds that they have lived in the same area for the same length of time). There are many inherent difficulties in such an assumption; some individuals may travel more widely or more frequently than others; may use different forms of transport; may always travel alone or in a group (consequently paying more or less attention to their surroundings); may make more use of maps; and so on. These kinds of differences are inevitable in any group of people, but because of such variations, both comparisons between individuals, and generalizations about environmental memory and behaviour, are difficult to make. Several methods have been used to overcome the problem of individuals' differential experience—usually by controlling subjects' exposure to specially constructed environments or by attempting to simulate actual experience of real environments. Specially built environments may include: layouts of objects on the floor of a room (e.g. Liben, 1982); a small model 'town' for children to walk through (e.g. Herman, 1980); or a group of small rooms (e.g. Hazen, Lockman, and Pick, 1978). Using such constructions may allow the experimenter to vary any number of factors: length of time in the layout; angle or order of viewing it; type of experience within the layout; the number of times that the subject experiences the layout; the amount of additional information or the type of experimental instructions that which are provided for the subject, and so on. Most experiments involving special or artificially built environments are concerned with particular aspects of spatial learning (How do subjects learn the pattern of objects in a layout? Do particular instructions help or hinder the ability to remember spatial locations? Does the order in which the subject encounters items in the layout affect recall of those items?). Such questions are particularly related to studies of what might, for convenience, be called spatial cognition, rather than environmental cognition *per se*. Studies of spatial memory provide important insights into the cognitive strategies and processes involved in spatial reasoning, but as our main emphasis in this book is concerned with environmental understanding we only refer to the particular studies that throw light on some aspect of environmental cognition. [For an overview of the research into all aspects of spatial cognition, see Cohen (1985).]

Video images and photographs are sometimes used to simulate the environment. For example, Allen, Kirasic, Siegal, and Herman (1979) showed subjects a series of photographic slides that had been taken along a route through a town. The children were then asked to select the slides that they thought would most help them to remember where they were on the route—adults were more likely than younger subjects to choose scenes associated with turns or intersections along the route. Allen (1981) also used a 'simulated walk', with several different age groups, to discover how subjects would subdivide the walk into segments (e.g. park, campus, residential area, etc.) and to find what features marked the boundaries of each segment. The use of photographs has the advantage of controlling the subjects' experience of the 'environment' and is particularly useful for investigating issues such as the ones just mentioned (selecting scenes or group scenes along a route) because reference can be made directly to the photographs of the scenes. On the other hand, it always has to be remembered that a series of slides or even a videotape present a very restricted view of the world compared with the richness of experience of moving within an environment.

So far this description of methodologies has concentrated on what we have called the 'laboratory' procedures, for the simple reason that they take place in that setting. In fact, a surprisingly small proportion of environmental research had been conducted in the environment beyond the laboratory. This in itself is not automatically a criticism, because much of the relevant research is concerned with cognitive processes and strategies operating on the individual's memory for the environment, and these can be examined in the laboratory. On the other hand, it is difficult to study learning processes without taking subjects into the real world (videos, slides, and small layouts are not usually realistic substitutes). Furthermore, it may be that many laboratory methods, which often involve particular task demands, underestimate the same individual's potential performance in the actual environment. A demonstration of this is provided by Cornell and Hay's (1984) experiment: young children viewed a novel route either by walking along it, by watching a videotape of the walk, or by seeing a slide sequence of views along the route. The children were tested using the same stimuli that they had experienced in learning the route, and at each choice point along the route they had to indicate the correct turn. The performance of the children who walked the route was significantly better than the children who experienced either the slides or the videotape. Results such as these emphasize the need for caution when assessing individuals' and, perhaps, especially children's learning abilities on the basis of laboratory tests.

Most of the research carried out in the environment has involved pointing tasks [e.g. Anooshian and Young (1981)] had children point to landmarks near their home, which were not directly visible), or walking novel routes [e.g. Heft, (1979)] had adults walk a route through a Biological Reserve and varied the type of landmarks placed at turns and intersections to find out how the saliency of the landmarks influenced the subjects' memories for the route.

With time (patience and good weather!) quite intensive work can be carried out in realistic situations. Golledge, Smith, Pellegrino, Doherty, and Marshall (1985) examined an 11-year-old boy over five successive days. He was asked to walk the same route each day and each time was asked: to describe his strategy for learning the route, and aspects of the route that he particularly remembered: to give directions along it as if to another child: to draw a map of it: and to watch a videotape of the route and say what action was necessary at each of the choice points. In this way Golledge *et al.* were able to describe the child's route learning over a period of time. Another example of intensive work is that of Ottosson (1987) who examined children's ability to use large-scale maps to follow a number of routes round their school and was able to interpret the children's performance from their errors and by recording what they said during the task.

Other studies have observed behaviour as it occurs. For instance, when studying adults' map-reading abilities during orienteering Ottosson (1987) spent a lot of time running behind the orienteers and making detailed commentaries about their behaviour. Psathas and Henslin (1967) recorded the messages and instructions sent between taxi cab drivers, and analysed these both for the style of the message and for the information about places and route planning that they contained. Passini (1984) had adults try to find their way round a shopping precinct and, while they were doing so, to provide a protocol (i.e. a verbal description of what they were doing and how they were doing it). From the protocols he was able to describe the trend plans and strategies of each individual as he or she attempted to get to specific parts of the building complex.

More-general studies have tried to capture the richness of the environmental behaviour in a number of different ways. Torrell and Biel (1985) asked 6- and 10-year-old children to keep detailed diaries of all their outdoor activities; these provided an insight into the amount of time that the children spent outside, the sort of activities in which they were involved, and how far they travelled in their neighbourhoods. In another study Moore (1986) had 9–12-year-old children take him on 'field trips' round their own neighbourhoods, and from extensive interviews was able to describe the pattern of their outdoor activities and the factors affecting these activities, such as the attraction of the local parks; the availability of accessible areas for playing games such as football; the excitement of 'dangerous' places like the local electricity substation; and parental restrictions about avoiding areas of busy traffic or wherever there might be a danger of 'strangers'. Perhaps the most detailed study of children ever carried out in natural conditions is by Hart (1979) who lived amongst the children of a New England town, almost like an anthropologist, taking part in their activities and spending long periods of time with them. No summary can do justice to the wealth of material that Hart collected. Apart from the vivid portrayal of children's life out of doors, such a study should also serve as a reminder that so much research is concerned only with a tiny proportion of children's real-life experience and activities.

To conclude this survey of the methods—we mention just two brief points— first it should be clear that the methods appropriate for different settings (laboratory or in the environment) are often quite different. Sometimes this is unavoidable, sometimes it often seems more a matter of experimenters' convenience. Studies that attempt to combine a range of methods, and examine individuals both in the real world and with laboratory tests (e.g. Cousins *et al.*, 1983; Golledge *et al.*, 1985), are to be applauded, but are unfortunately rather few and far between. Secondly, this summary of methods is by no means exhaustive, but more-detailed listings of the main approaches are available in many other sources (e.g. Craik, 1970; Evans, 1980, Golledge, 1987, Stokols, 1972).

The potential of artificial intelligence for studies of environmental cognition

At this point it is appropriate to discuss the potential of artificial intelligence (AI) research for environmental research. AI is not so much a method, but is rather better described as a particular approach to any psychological research. It is an approach that has already made a significant impact in psychology (see Boden, 1987) and has been a focus of debate in geography (see Couclelis, 1986). As yet AI has only had a limited influence on specifically environmental research, and very little on issues related to child development. None the less, we will outline the principles of AI and its potential as a research approach. AI assumes that an analogy can be made between the way individuals mentally process information and the way that a computer may be programmed to process the same information. This has led to two particular approaches in the literature; one might for convenience be called the use of simulations, the other can be more properly labelled AI. Such a categorization, although not wholly justified in practice, will allow us to define and give examples from the relevant research.

Simulations are usually based on protocols or data that are obtained from studies of people. A good example of a simulation based on a protocol is that by Hayes-Roth and Hayes-Roth (1979), who showed an individual a map of a town (which included features like shops, offices, services, etc.) and a list of errands (to buy vegetables at the grocery shop; to order books at the bookshop, etc.). The subject had to use the map to plan a route that permitted the errands to be carried out and at the same time he was asked to provide a verbal description of how he or she was attempting the task. Hayes-Roth and Hayes-Roth analysed the description and from this analysis were able to write a computer program incorporating the kinds of strategies that the individual reported using. This computer simulation produced an effective route. In another experiment Mc-Namara (1986) collected data about adults' ability to remember the spatial relationships of a layout of objects. The subjects made consistent errors and McNamara inferred the cognitive processes that might have led to such errors. He was then able to incorporate these processes in a computer program that simulated the performance of the experimental subjects. Simulations are usually based on protocols or data obtained from experiments with people. In other words, the simulation is produced *after* the empirical studies have been carried out.

In contrast the emphasis of much AI research is on the definition of a problem that requires a solution and then on the design of a program that solves the problem. Although the program writer may, and often does, consider how a person would solve a similar problem, this is not necessarily crucial. What is crucial is designing a program that will successfully solve the given problem. In other words, in AI research the problem is solved *before* any studies with people are undertaken. The successful computer program can then be treated as one of the possible ways of solving the problem. If the problem is also one that people solve then it is worth finding out if people solve the problem in the same way as the computer program by comparing people's performance with the program's performance on the same tasks. This might be clearer with an example:

Elliott and Lesk (1982) designed a computer program that could find a route between two points on a street map. In other words it could successfully plan a route between any starting place and any destination on the map, and in doing so, it selected the shortest route between those places. Obviously, people also plan routes using street maps, but do they do so in the same way as this particular program? In general the routes planned by car drivers did not match the routes selected by the computer program, because the shortest route often involved an excessive number of turns and drivers preferred slightly longer routes if these included a reduced number of inconvenient turns. In this case, the program and the drivers were using different strategies to plan the routes, but on the other hand, if the program and the drivers both selected exactly the same routes this would be an indication that both were using similar processes or strategies. As we know the processes used by the program (since these were deliberately written into it) then the similarity of performance by program and person allows us to infer that the same processes were used by the person. In other words, the AI approach can contribute to an understanding of the mental processes used by individuals in solving problems. Having said that, it must be admitted that AI applications in the area of environmental research are both limited in number and limited in scope (because few studies have gone beyond the stage of designing a successful program to the stage of comparing the programs with human performance). None the less a number of programs have been written to solve problems similar to the ones faced by individuals in the environment. McCalla and Reid (1982) designed a program (called ELMER) to learn information about a hypothetical city, and plan trips through it. Riesbeck (1980) produced a program (McMAP) to interpret typical spoken or written route directions (the kind that might be elicited by asking for directions in a strange city) and to extract the crucial spatial information from them. Kuipers (1978, 1982) has modelled some of the processes that may play a part in the formation of cognitive maps, in a program called TOUR which incorporates various strategies for learning, classifying and moving through a given environment. As the AI approach develops and as programs are compared with human performance, we should gain more insight into the processes of environmental cognition.

Feelings, attitudes, and the mental map

We now turn to a topic mentioned earlier—the role of feelings and attitudes in the formation of an individual's cognitive map. Very few studies have been concerned with this aspect of cognitive maps, and even these few have only included adult subjects. However, there is no reason why the same approach and methodology could not be used with children to study their feelings, and the development of those feelings, towards their environment.

Calling the image a 'cognitive map' and then being surprised that few, if any, of one's subjects represented anything in their sketch maps but knowledge (of places, names, routes, distances, etc.) is perhaps churlish. Yet, although clearly such knowledge—that places exist, of how to reach them, and so on—is basic to the individual's development of travel plans, so also are the 'feeling' components of the environmental image. Places attract, repel, are felt to be friendly, anonymous, hostile, etc. Intuitively, one's actions are guided by more than just the knowledge component of the image, but few studies have bothered to encourage people to represent the affective side. Lynch, here as in other matters, is a pioneer. He argues (Lynch, 1960) that the city's 'legibility'— the ease with which its structure enables us to read it and thus find our way around—is linked to its aesthetic attractiveness: the more memorable in one sense, the more memorable in the other. Cullen (1971) has gone further, in his essays for designers on how to create townscapes, he argues that one can give visual coherence to the buildings, streets, squares, and places of the urban environment in a way that will attract, give a sense of excitement, of mystery, of anticipation, of possession.

There is a phenomenological tradition within geography which is concerned with the individual's experience of place: Tuan (1980) for example discusses the origins of 'rootedness'—a state of being 'unreflectively secure and comfortable in a given locality'; Porteous (1985, 1986) has campaigned for a 'sensuous geography' in which the importance of smells, sounds, and other sensations would be recognized in the individual's feelings for places; and Lowenthal (1985) has indicated how important to our response to places is our awareness of their continuity through history. Hart (1979) in his study of New England children has a fascinating section describing their feelings about their play places—favourite places, places where they felt good, disliked places, and creepy, scary places.

All of this material represents major evidence of what conventional 'cognitive mapping' studies omit, and thus of how powerful determinants of behaviour and response to the environment may be missed by the environmental psychologist. The phenomenological geographers draw heavily upon literary and artistic sources: they quote autobiography, poetry, film, and other means of recreating a sense of place in a most wide-ranging, erudite, and thoroughly enjoyable way. We cautious psychologists have been trained—however much we intuitively accept such arguments—to seek for empirical evidence; and in this area there is little available. Some have doubted whether one *could* impart rigour to this area; for example, Riley (1979) doubts whether such work could be used by designers to create better habitats. The phenomenologists might draw some wry comfort from Goodey and Gold's (1987) observation, that even the findings of the *empirical* tradition within environmental perception research is largely ignored by design professionals. Against this observation one can set counter-examples, such as the series of detailed empirical studies by Purcell on what perceptual features of man-made and natural environments affect aesthetic and preference responses. Purcell, an architect, has developed his model in the pages of professional planning journals (e.g. Purcell, 1987).

In their major review of empirical research on environmental perception, Saarinen and Sell (1980) argue that behavioural geographers and environmental psychologists have tended to select concrete, easily measurable units of analysis, and have neglected 'abstract, symbolic or elusive items like feelings or sentiments'. Similarly, Evans (1980) has cautioned that an overemphasis on the physical aspects settings *per se* may ignore the symbolic meaning places have for people.

When writers from the empirical tradition, such as Evans, stress that the individual's behaviour in, and response to, the environment relates as much to his or her feelings and sentiments as they do to his or her knowledge, then we are challenged to include satisfactory measures of these.

One step in this direction has already been taken with a mapping language specifically for capturing the affective qualities of the city image. The geographer, Wood (Wood 1973; Wood and Beck, 1976), devised a mapping system to capture, on a cartographic base, the affective qualities of the city image. His system, 'Environmental A', has proved simple enough for his relatively unmotivated teenage subjects to use, yet rich enough in impressions elicited to demonstrate strong and consistent differences between the images of cities that, subjectively, one feels to be considerably different from each other. Newcomers to an area, without special knowledge of the area to be mapped, were able for the first time in the literature, to set down in map form their impressions of a city. This highly promising system, although reported by Wood himself and noted in secondary sources, has seldom been used since its initial invention: another reflection of the above-discussed neglect in the literature of the symbolic and affective aspects of environmental perception.

Environmental A was designed for a project on 'the micro-development of cognitions of urban space' in 15–19-year-old American tourists, who were spending a week in each of London, Rome and Paris. Images of these three cities were obtained from the subjects before their arrival, at several points during their stay and after the trip. Subjects first generated a basic cartographic map by means of a simple network or skeleton of interconnected points; and then, using a series of overlays, they represented their knowledge, impressions, and feelings about all the places, routes, and areas that they had mapped, together with any general attributes that they associated with the city and its component parts. Each of these were to be shown on the overlays by means of a small symbol, drawn from the vocabulary of Environmental A. Most of the symbols were ingenious and sometimes witty pictograms: for example, a hammer represented a factory, a skull and crossbones stood for 'Danger: you feel hostility in the air'; and a sleeping eye was 'restfulness: here you feel relaxed'. Attribute symbols were to be used as qualifiers and descriptions of the more factual elements and if the 100 symbols for places, 31 symbols for routes and other lines, 11 area symbols, and 53 attribute symbols proved inadequate to express any idea, then subjects could invent extra symbols.

Wood's studies showed that such a vocabulary is sufficiently restricted to make comparisons and analysis practicable, whilst apparently giving subjects adequate freedom and range of expression. In a further study (Spencer and Dixon, 1983), we found this also to be true of older subjects; further, we found that the use of a vocabulary of symbols served to trigger a wider range of feelings than did a comparable checklist of adjectives.

Devlin (1976) included in her list of the factors that influence the learning of cognitive elements, not only the obvious perceptual factors of visual distinctiveness, and the individual's frequency of exposure to a place, but also the more subjective factor of a place's potential or actual usefulness to the individual. Indeed, the majority of places noted on her subjects' maps could be regarded as this kind of 'functional landmark', such as the maternity hospital (the subjects were young servicemen's wives), popular restaurants, and car-washes.

Wood's subjects, the pioneer users of Environmental A, were tourists who spent no more than a week in each city to be mapped. As has been argued elsewhere (Spencer and Weetman, 1981), the major weakness of such short term studies of the urban image have been precisely that they have traced only short periods of development, and studied only transient populations. Furthermore, as has been argued above, such studies (with the exception of Wood) have concentrated entirely on the development of the structure of knowledge about the city, without taking account of the parallel development of feelings.

Yet initial feelings about the places and sub-areas of the city are likely to affect the individual's subsequent patterns of use of the city, and hence his or her developing knowledge of it, just as initial impressions and attitudes have been shown to affect the course of social interaction between people (e.g. Cook, 1979). Furthermore, one would predict that, as routine journeys bring greater familiarity with the city over time, an increasingly detailed factual knowledge will come to modify the initial affective map [again, parallels can be drawn with person perception studies, (e.g. Warr and Knapper, 1968)].

The Spencer and Dixon (1983) study represented a first attempt to investigate the development of the affective urban image among intending long-term residents of the city (i.e. those who would have a considerable investment in learning about it), over the initial three months of residence [the length of time that our earlier study (Spencer and Weetman, 1981) had indicated in the period in which the long-term structural urban image is formed]. We found that the main characteristics of the subject's 'affective map' of the city had already stabilized after three weeks' residence. The first few hours' impressions may derive from the confirmation or contradiction of people's expectations about the city; these may be quickly supplanted by a new or modified set of feelings as the individual increases not only his or her knowledge, but also his or her involvement with places in the city. Not surprisingly, individual activity patterns explained many individual differences in places included and described. But we were also able to demonstrate that, above these, conserval images of particular city areas and features emerged.

Individual differences

One of the most obvious findings from the studies of the affective components of cognitive maps are the individual differences in attitudes to the same area. Of course people's attitudes will vary according to their expectations, familiarity, particular past experiences and their demands of the environment. This is no more than saying that any individual's cognitive map—both the knowledge-based component and the affective component—will be subjective. This is something that should always be considered, not least because so many experiments are concerned with isolating particular factors and for this reason tend to compare two groups of subjects (who differ only in that factor) in order to produce quantitative results and determine how significant that factor is. However, what is sometimes in danger of being ignored is the range of individual differences in environmental cognition.

Canter (1983b) has emphasized the need for environmental psychology to develop a theory of place evaluation, and has stressed the purposive nature of people's experience of place: 'place evaluation is defined as the degree to which a person sees a place as helping to achieve that person's goals at various levels of interaction with that place'. For example, by analysing questionnaire data, the researcher can identify those aspects of a sociophysical environment that contribute to the individual's responses to that place. Canter demonstrated how this can be applied to describe satisfaction with both large-scale settings (residents of a housing estate) and small-scale settings (nurses in a children's hospital ward). There are now specific scales available to measure an individual's range of environmental competence and sensitivity (such as the Environmental Response Inventory and the children's version, CERI, which will be discussed in Part II).

Individual differences in cognition may arise from variations in the individual's interaction with the environment. Hart (1979) showed that environmental knowledge was directly related to individual children's activity range: parents allowed boys greater freedom of movement than girls and therefore they were

Figure 1.3   Valued environments. Phenomenologists have critized mainstream environmental cognition research for ignoring the clear evaluations people make; and have asked what makes 'places' distinctive, memorable, and important for the individual.

much more knowledgeable about their neighbourhoods. Other factors that influence individual's environmental interaction have been studied—these include; the differences between car owners' and pedestrians' cognitive structuring of the city (e.g. Canter, 1977); the degree to which an individual feels involved in the neighbourhood or the immediate locality (e.g. Newman, 1972); or different individual's perception of the risks associated with various parts of the city or the same parts of the city at different times of the day (see e.g. Hough and Mayhew, 1983, on the fear of crime).

Other differences may come from the individual's own background and experience. Murray and Spencer (1979) were able to demonstrate that the variety of environmental experience in an individual's lifetime affected his or her cognitive mapping skills. Certain 'expert groups' like architects, designers, hoteliers, and others whose business is creating particular 'ambiences' may have a different sensitivity to environmental features; certainly the literature on communications between architects and their clients indicate just how far apart these groups can be in summoning up images of as-yet-unbuilt environments! (McKechnie, 1977b). 'Expert' knowledge will usually come from specific training and practice (e.g. in the case of architects or navigators, etc.), but also an individual's own past experience may generate increased sensitivity to the environment. For instance, Devlin (1976) found that experienced travellers were able to build up a set of expectations about a typical town and could use these expectations to understand better a novel town.

In summary, we cannot ignore individual differences—so great may be the effect of cognitive style, training, and previous experience on the individual's environmental cognition: yet the reader of Part II, where we review in detail the published literature within the developmental psychology tradition, will find very few researchers therein who pay any attention to individual differences.

Conclusions

We have summarized some of the issues related to environmental cognition and behaviour and we have tried to pick out just a few of the themes and methodologies that have influenced this area of research—many of these will be elaborated on later in the book. These issues include *how* the individual's image of the environment develops—an issue that, as we have stressed, has mainly been limited to accounts of place and route knowledge in the cognitive map—and needs to be expanded to include affective and subjective factors in the person's perception. We have discussed the concept of the cognitive map, and theories describing how it may develop in children. Although generally helpful in elucidating the development of environmental cognition, we have pointed out the need for more detailed consideration of such concepts and theories not listed of the methodologies that are available—some of these may be more useful than others. Obviously, different methods will produce different results and these have to be treated with care when trying to use them to infer the person's mental image of the environment, otherwise it may be too early to think of this image in spatial terms if a particular method requires a subject to draw a map or in sequential terms if the subject has to give a series of directions. As we have pointed out these are 'spatial products' and we have, as yet, little idea of the underlying cognitive representation. This is one aspect of the research where approaches adapted from artificial intelligence may be particularly fruitful. Interconnected with such methodological and theoretical issues are questions such as the role played by individual differences in environmental perception—most of the research has emphasized group and average results, and the differences included as experimental variables are usually age, sex, or experience. So far, other factors that may influence an individual's cognition (e.g. particular expectations, or specialist experience) have only been specifically considered. Similarly the interaction between direct environmental experience (i.e. moving through an area) and indirect knowledge (from verbal information, from maps and photographs, etc.) has not been considered.

In the other chapters of this book we will be concerned with describing the results from a large number of studies—sometimes critically—but inevitably the form of study and the particular experimental results will determine the topics written about, but it should be borne in mind that many topics have hardly been written about at all!

CHAPTER 2

Routes, directions and action planning

Environmental information: spatial or sequential? Network or vector?

How is information about the environment stored? Readers familiar with recent debates within cognitive psychology may experience a certain feeling of *déjà vu* as we recount some of the discussions in environmental psychology. Much early debate within environmental psychology was on the nature of learning and retention of environmental information; and, in particular, whether the organizing principle was the sequence/string or spatial/overall location.

Take the case of an adult learning the layout of a new area: we can pose the question thus. Does the individual first learn a set of routes, with landmarks and nodes as the linking devices, and only slowly develop an overall concept of an area's spatial organization? Or, rather, do the landmarks and their relative positions come first (as would be the case if one was granted an initial overview of an area), with routes then filling in the details?

Posed this way, it sounds as if there are two clearly different systems of (at least initial) representation, either of which might be applied to the same area. Now, it is true that in classifying the kinds of sketch maps people draw (the external representations of these internal representations?), Appleyard (1970) and Pocock (1976) both developed typologies of 'mappers' that divide individuals into predominantly sequential and predominantly spatial—a reflection, perhaps, of the two proposed processes. Both writers acknowledge that individuals also vary considerably in the complexity of map they draw; and that the more complex a map is, the less easy it is to assign it to the spatial or sequential category.

How far does the empirical evidence bear out the concept of consistent individual mapping styles? This could have the implication, perhaps, that these would reflect differences in styles of information processing.

Studies by Byrne (1982) and by Spencer and Weetman (1981) have shown that individuals are *not* in fact consistent in their style of mapping, but, rather can switch between styles according to the particular task in hand; if, for example, the situation (or experimenter) places more stress on describing a route, then the drawn product is, perhaps not surprisingly, more sequential than spatial.

We would propose that what appears true of mapping—the externalization of cognitive representations—may be true of the cognitions themselves: i.e. that we are not dealing with clear alternatives, between spatial and sequential, between analogue and propositional, or—to use Byrne's terminology—between network and vector; but rather that task and occasion determines type of representation.

Byrne has used the terms 'vector maps' and 'network maps' to distinguish the two styles in operation, suggesting that they:

> differ chiefly in whether they need to encode horizontal vector distances (e.g. 'A is *n* units South South East of B') or only topological connectedness (e.g. 'B is next after A on the route to C')

So, a network representation would consist of a series of strings: programmes for movement along routes, and a set of propositions (these would not necessarily be stored in verbal form), which would include both physical locations and instructions for changes of direction. (We would add to Byrne's definition the thought that such strings might include instructions for *not* changing direction—our own analysis of the protocols of route-instructions recorded under everyday conditions on the street indicate how frequently people stress a predominant landmark, saying that one should carry on straight past it, thereby giving reassurance that one will know one remains on the right route.)

The reader will have appreciated that casting the 'cognitive map task' in these terms makes it immediately accessible to computational modelling: a topic of sufficient importance to merit separate treatment below, where we consider the potential of the artificial intelligence approach to spatial information.

Points on the program specifying changes of direction are thus, for Byrne, potentially choice points, and these become the nodes whence strings become branched; with as its eventual end, the linkage of routes into a complete network.

A network map may thus achieve complexity without preserving accurate information about distances or directions (Byrne likens it in this to the schematized London Underground maps) whereas a *vector map* would, of its very essence, encode information about directions and distances.

Now, although what lead Tolman to consider that maze-running rats developed cognitive maps was the demonstration of vector knowledge, there is so far less evidence from the literature that humans are major users of such accurate vector maps. Indeed, in many studies, subjects show a tendency to assume, for example, angles of street intersections to be right angles (e.g. Pocock, 1976) and to be considerably in error in estimating distances, often overestimating distances along routes that pass many points of interest, compared with routes that are uniform and dull.

The majority of such experiments, showing a tendency towards network rather than vector maps, have, it should be noted, been conducted in urban settings, where, it could be hypothesized, route knowledge is at a premium, and *precise* directional and distance knowledge are less important, travel being constrained and supported by city structure, and the presence of direction signs.

There exists some anthropological evidence (e.g. Lewis, 1976) of human precision in estimating directions to salient locations across open country; although, as inspection of Lewis's raw data indicates, some individuals are considerably better than others, even among a population such as the Australian aborigines where one might presume that accurate vector maps would be at a premium.

Such individual variability makes any extravagant claims for a human sense of direction seem implausible. Baker (e.g. 1981) has been a modern-day champion of the idea that humans might, via a magnetic sense, have direct awareness of compass directions; his results have attracted both considerable interest and controversy (e.g. Baker, 1987). This is not the place to discuss the hotly disputed experimental details of these studies, or the comparative neuroanatomy of biomagnetic 'organs': suffice it to say for our purposes that, whereas migrating and homing birds make major reliance upon such a sense (e.g. Wiltschko and Wiltschko, 1985), humans may at most have a minor additional source of directional information, which is clearly overlaid by many more immediate and learned cues to direction. Many of these learned cues are not necessarily used at the level of awareness.

Much of the strongest evidence on the nature of the environmental image, and how it is acquired, has come from research with children, which will be reviewed in later chapters.

Acquisition of environmental information

So far, we have discussed information already held; we must now look at the acquisition processes and see how they relates to the activities concurrent with learning. How do we learn about places?

Much of cognitive psychology's research on human memory has lead to the development of theories in which existing knowledge plays a central role— theorists have used terms such as schemata, frames, scripts, plans, prototypes; but all are basically knowledge structures based on past experience, with which new information interacts in perception. Information elicited from memory frequently indicates that schemata expectations have shaped it.

Brewer and Treyens (1981) have suggested that there are five ways in which schemata could influence memory performance—including memory for places:

1   *Encoding schemata* could determine which objects are looked at and encoded in memory (focusing either on schema-relevant information, or on discrepant information).
2   *Frameworks*: schemata may serve as a framework for the selective retention of information.
3   *Integration*: information from the schema may be recalled along with new information. Integration may be so complete that the subject does not distinguish the episodic from the schema-based information; alternatively, the two may remain distinct.
4   *Retrieval*: schemata may be used to guide the search for information in memory.
5   *Communication*: schemata may influence the subset of information selected for answering a query, giving instructions, etc.

Data supporting these hypotheses are provided by Brewer and Treyens' study (1981). Under a plausible pretext, subjects sat in a graduate student's room and were later asked to describe the contents and their location in the room. Memory scores were correlated with schema expectancy (which the experimenters had previously assessed) and saliency. Subjects related this room to other such rooms they had known; they confidently recalled 'typical' objects that had not in fact been there.

The acquisition of cognitive maps of environments larger than a room has received only limited study. Gärling and his co-workers (e.g. Gärling, Böök, and Lindberg, 1984a,b) have studied the learning of medium-scale areas— for example, passages within a building—and shown that acquisition is fast and forgetting is slight. He argues that acquisition is intentional and requires effortful processing; basic to his approach is the assumption that information may well be acquired in connection with the formation and execution of travel plans. This is especially so at the initial stages of learning an environment (Thorndyke and Hayes-Roth, 1982) and the specification and revision of such early travel; the execution of plans leads to the acquisition of new information about the environment by direct observation.

Relation of spatial images to the self

When we come to describe theories of the ontogenesis of spatial images, the concept of egocentricity of the very young child will be discussed. The literature on adults also contains discussions of spatial reference systems which have the individual as their base.

Recent cognitive theories have hypothesized that the locations of objects with respect to one's body coordinates may be represented directly, in propositional form: book-in-front-of-self, window-to-right-of-self. Yet, as Hintzman, O'Dell and Arndt (1981) point out, such a representational system would require that the relational terms of many propositions be changed as one rotated. And to keep the representation up to date as one moved through space would demand a major computational effort, to monitor and update all such self-related propositions. Nor do these authors' own experimental data support an alternative hypothesis of mental rotation, which they had presumed might involve work thus:

> Suppose a person is instructed to imagine facing first in one direction and then in another. In the process of relinquishing the first orientation and establishing the second, does the relationship between the self-image and the cognitive map pass through a trajectory of intermediate states?   (p. 151)

No such rotation or other kind of sequential search could be supported by their experimental data.

Just and Carpenter (1985) have also examined mental rotation in solving spatial problems. Their research links traditional psychometric tests of spatial ability with computer-simulation models of problem-solving by high- and by low-spatial-ability subjects. They demonstrated a range of strategies used by their subjects in solving the same psychometric cube-matching tasks.

1 Mental rotation around standard axes, external to the object
2 Mental rotation around task-defined axes.
3 Comparison of orientation-free descriptions—invariant with the object's orientation in space.
4 Perspective change—in a coordinate system that includes both the observer and the object, with the observer deciding which 'view' to take of the object.

Research on the recognition of objects that have previously been seen from a different perspective has been used by Marr (1982) to demonstrate the existence of an implicit coordinate system. This consists of at least an implicit origin and some directional axes. Yet, in the case of some very familiar shapes (e.g. the outlines of countries), there would seem to be a usual and expected orientation: presented another way, subjects are unable to recognize them (Rock, 1973). Such examples indicate that the mental representation of *some* objects contains an implicit reference to a coordinate system extrinsic to the object.

Palij, Levine, and Kahan (1984) have suggested that if it is possible to specify the orientation of a subject's cognitive map with respect to his or her body, then one can predict whether a given task (say to locate a given target point) will be easy or difficult.

To summarize: the Just and Carpenter findings, from subjects' self-reported strategies, indicate that even in relatively simple spatial tasks there are a variety of approaches brought to bear; that these relate to traditionally measured spatial ability differences; and that some individuals employ a coordinate system including themselves while others do not. Individual strategy differences in spatial problem-solving are beginning to attract research interest (see review by Kyllonen, Lohman and Woltz, 1984). Self-relational strategies, for working with larger spatial arrays, through which one could walk, become unwieldy, and would, as Hintzman *et al.* indicate, involve major computational effort. Yet one can, as Palij *et al.* did with their experimentally instructed subjects, induce particular orientations in the individual's cognitive map of, for example, a small route.

Indeed, returning to object level, if an object has more than one major structural component, then each can be represented within its own local frame of reference—with a separate cognitive coordinate system for each part of the complex object (Marr and Nishihara, 1978). Might not such a system of multiple coordinate systems enable the individual to handle the complexities of geographical-scale space? A further, overarching coordinate system would then be required: in other words, one would have an hierarchical approach to context.

Just such a hierarchical approach has been proposed by animal-learning theorists, Nadel, Willner, and Kurz (1985). They characterize the 'traditional notion' of environmental context as 'simply a collection of unrelated cues competing for associative strength' (perhaps rather a harsh judgement on more recent work in the area); and instead propose that the objects and events comprising an environment are internally represented *both* as individual entities and as things contained within a spatial framework.

The excitement of their position lies in their linking it (O'Keefe and Nadel, 1978, 1979) to a specific brain system. They have proposed that the hippocampus is a central part of the cognitive mapping system: a neural ensemble of elements that individually represent things experienced in the environment, whose interconnection 'amounts to an internal map, enabling the organism to behave as if it had direct access to a roughly veridical model of the environment' (Nadel, Willner, and Kurz, 1985). The internal mapping system would be sensitive to unexpected stimuli, and permits a constant updating of the model. By generating predictions, the mapping system provides the basis for detecting the unexpected.

This is not the place or occasion for a review of the extensive neurological, pathological, and behavioural evidence adduced by O'Keefe, Nadel and their colleagues in support of their position [see O'Keefe and Nadel (1979) for their reply to critics]. Suffice it to say that their account begins to tackle, at a physiological/system level, many of the features noted earlier in the chapter. O'Keefe (1985), for example, has begun to consider whether hologram-like processes, operating in the dentate granule cells, enable the animal to compare current and stored images of the environment.

The role of environmental cognition in route-finding

Chapter 1 devoted space to descriptions of the environmental representations held by the individual—and the factors that may cause them to vary—on the assumption that these perform a key guiding and enabling part in orientation, navigation, and the individual's use of space.

In this chapter we now examine that assumption, and review way-finding theories as they relate to our earlier discussion. We adopt, with Passini (1984), the perspective that way-finding is spatial problem-solving. In contrast to the more traditional static view of spatial orientation, this view sees it in terms of information processing, decision making, and translation of decisions into actions. *Information* in this case consists of both the set of environmental stored information, and the immediately perceived environmental information; with inferential information resulting from subjects' actions upon both other sources.

Decisions can conveniently be described as a hierarchy, with overall goals; translations of these into action plans, consisting of behaviourally described sub-goals; and, as subcomponents of the action plan, specific actions. (We could, of course, continue the hierarchy further on, into the motoric domain, seeing the plans for specific body movements, etc.)

Once analysed in terms of its components, even a relatively simple way-finding task will be found to be solved by many sub-processes. Passini (1984) recorded way-finders' descriptions of their routes and their actions as they walked through urban shopping malls: some subjects recorded more than 100 discrete decisions in completing a task taking 20 minutes.

Analysis of such protocols indicates how *responsive* rather than thought-through and pre-planned is such a decision process: people have often only global and vague initial plans, with a few general decisions, and a number of specifics as initiatories. Particular problems are then tackled as they emerge: Passini observes that generally a new plan is formulated only after a previous plan has been executed. One might argue that progress through a shopping mall—his research setting—might well serve to emphasize this sequential ordering of plans, and the absence of overlapping plans. We need further data from contrasting settings to see how far we can generalize his observation of 'the strong tendency to deal with one problem or sub-problem at a time, and not to solve problems in parallel or simultaneously' (p. 69). Having indicated that we can begin to analyse way-finding into its component decision processes, we now need to see how the process relates to the stored and immediate environmental information.

Passini has offered one model, Gärling a somewhat different one (Gärling, Säisä, Böök, and Lindberg, 1986)—although perhaps their language differs more than their substance. Passini argues that the execution of decisions and of plans can be seen as a *matching-feedback* process, where matching relates the expected object image to the perceived object. Where there is a match, feedback sets the action part of the decision in motion; where there is a mismatch, it leads to further problem-solving. Gärling also sees environments as both posing problems and offering means for their solution; he has examined travel at urban and single-building scale.

We would like to suggest that the assumptions of the Gärling model reformulate some of Passini's observations, and extend it. Here we offer only a summary of the model.

1 Travel plans are integrated parts of those action plans requiring travel.
2 The components and properties of the environment are represented in memory in a way that facilitates travel.
3 Travel plan execution develops the accuracy and extent of cognitive maps.
4 Travel plans entail several hierarchically-organized stages of information processing—accessing information from store, from media such as maps, and from the direct observation of the environment.
5 Maintenance of orientation, by recognizing places, keeping track of one's location when moving about, and anticipating features in the environment, may appear to be an automatic process, but can be shown to be a continuous updating process.

Böök and Gärling (1980a,b; 1981a,b) elaborate item 5 above and provide a model of how orientation is maintained during actual locomotion. Empirical studies have been conducted, controlling subjects' direction, speed, and distance of travel in a small scale environment. These demonstrate that orientation is maintained by a process of continuous updating of position relative to reference points—and that by superimposing distracting tasks on to the updating, one can easily interfere with the process.

Formation of travel plans

Hayes-Roth and Hayes-Roth (1979) suggest that people employ a locally-minimizing distance heuristic (lmdh) in developing a travel plan: a rule stating that the nearest location from the start point will be chosen first, then the nearest location from there, and so on until the complete order is specified.

Gärling, Säisiä, Böök, and Lindberg (1986) have found supportive evidence for such a heuristic and its role in planning: their subjects were frequently shown to work out least distances before working out the route (though this was clearly not the only constraint at work).

Note that, in the original Hayes-Roth and Hayes-Roth experiments, the experimenters had presented their subjects with a graphical representation—a map of a fictious town—and had imposed a time constraint upon their 'running errands' in this hypothetical setting. One cannot imagine experimental conditions (subjects aware of the need to appear logical and efficient to the experimenter; mode of presentation that emphasizes distance and other spatial properties; minimal distracting cues; no affective information, etc.) more likely to produce greater tendency towards lmdh. But what would happen in real life, with subjects confronted with decisions about travel around a familiar setting? As soon as Gärling works—albeit in a laboratory-based, 'what would you do if' situation—with locations from a town that subjects had lived in for at least a year, the heuristic becomes a less complete descriptor. And Evans and Pezdek (1980) have shown that short-term memory representation of an actual environment can be importantly different from that obtained from a map: a real place is unbounded, is four-dimensional (perception may be extended over long time spans), and the perceiver is usually within, and at ground level, rather than above and abstracted.

Presson and Hazelrigg (1984) have further showed that the conditions under which subjects learned about the environment can be crucial for ease of read-out in travel planning: when subjects had learned a route by the indirect, symbolic means of a map, then judgements about directions were relatively easy when standing in the actual environment *in the map alignment*, (and relatively difficult if the judgement was not aligned with the learned map direction). No such alignment differences were found in the judgements of those who had learned the route by more direct experience.

Information encountered *en route*—even where the route is experienced directly—perhaps in the form of a plan—cities and individual buildings may have publicly accessible maps and location plans, from which the individual has the possibility of assimilating information. This information can be incorporated in a previously developed environmental image and may influence the individual's action-plan. Even when 'correctly'-aligned, and decorated with supposedly helpful 'you are here' arrows, translation between mapped and experienced scenes may prove difficult [see studies by Levine (1982)]. If the best-designed, simplified, and aligned 'you are here' local maps pose problems for users, then one must expect even more problems still with conventional cartographic maps (with no such observer-location devices) when these are used in the course of navigation. The use of maps represents a curiously under-researched area; and yet it has considerable theoretical and practical implications. We therefore review research on both adult and child use of maps in navigation in Chapter 8.

Way-finding: an ecological perspective

A consistent theme among those doing empirical work on route-following is that most environmental learning via navigation involves the coordination of information gained at successive vantage points, and/or built up over successive encounters with the environment—successive representations, in contrast with the simultaneous representation afforded by a map.

Gibson's (1979) approach to perception, although unorthodox in many respects, is sufficiently influential among those considering way-finding that we should consider it here. As Heft (1983) further refines it, the Gibsonian-ecological view is that way-finding involves the perception of information over time.

The information used for way-finding is described by Heft as 'an invariant sequence of transitions between vistas', revealed as the individual follows a route. Heft sees this successive nature of environmental information use as challenging 'the standard view, according to which perceptual input is considered to be temporally discrete'. The information specifying a route is a set of relational changes over time comparable with the perception of a melody.

Gibsonians identify 'the standard view' as constructivist: sensory input from the environment is supplemented and enriched by knowledge already possessed by the perceiver. Perception is mediated by cognitive processes. The environment that is perceived is a 'mental construct', according to Moore (1979).

In contrast, Gibson argues that the information available to the perceiver is sufficiently rich as to specify objects, events and the extended layout of the environment: 'As an observer moves along a path, what is perceived is a succession of vistas: each succeeding vista occluded by some barrier, which, as the observer moves past, gradually reveals the next vista'. Heft (1983) has shown that subjects who see a filmed series of transitions between vistas, clipped from a film of a journey, score as well as those who had seen the complete film on a series of tests of route knowledge, both groups being superior to a group who had viewed the complete film *minus* the transitions.

Now, Gibson's descriptions of way-finding and mobility through the environment are based on visual processes. Does this mean that we would need a completely separate theory of mobility in the blind—or can research on blind mobility throw light on basic processes guiding all mobility?

Strelow (1985) suggests that, by supplementing Gibson's explanation of visual guidance, by other perceptual and cognitive considerations, one can produce a comprehensive theory of mobility—even given that there are 'many idiosyncratic features of travel skill by the blind'. Visual guidance of locomotion, according to Gibson's early accounts (1966) included at least nine different sub-skills: starting, stopping, backing up, steering, aiming, approaching without collision, steering among obstacles, and pursuit and flight. Given this list—which has subsequently been added to—it seems unlikely that a single process underlies all.

Mobility of the blind indicates (as we shall argue in Part III) that mobility is not necessarily a visually based process—although it undoubtedly receives considerable visual input in the case of the sighted. The blind can use, and formal mobility training can extend, 'obstacle sense'—the awareness of the presence and locations of local objects, based primarily on the use of echoes created by the individual himself. [Strelow and Brabyn (1982), showed that blind individuals could establish and maintain an accurate travel path parallel to and one metre away from a wall.] Other non-visual cues—sounds, smells, texture, etc.—are also efficiently used by the blind, and a range of artificial sensors has been developed, with the particular aim of giving the blind pre-view of spaces and obstacles ahead (e.g. Warren and Strelow, 1984).

None the less, it assumed by many writers (see review by Warren, 1984) that the blind—especially the long-term congenitally blind—inevitably have characteristic deficits in spatial perceptual and conceptual abilities, and, as a result, require formal teaching in the spatial concepts that sighted children develop through everyday interactions with the environment. Thus, it is usual practice to *teach* relationships such as front, back, left, right, above, below; and topographical concepts, such as hills, boundaries, etc. For a description of current teaching practices, see the major handbook for this area, edited by Welsh and Blasch (1980).

Performance differences by the blind could, logically, arise simply because their lack of vision reduced the input of information, or because they have developed a basically different conceptualization of space. Strelow (1985) argues that, although there is undoubtedly an important informational deficit element, blindness does interfere with spatial-cognitive abilities: 'Compared to the sighted, the blind rely more on sequential, egocentric information than on information taken in by parallel processes'.

But is vision necessary for building up the overall schema of an area? Recall that, as Strelow reminds us,

> The problem of how purposeful travel is possible when goals are out of sight, was at the heart of the classic debate on the principles of spatial learning between theories of cognitive maps and theories of response learning.   (p. 239)

We have already mentioned the idea of propositional coding of spatial information, which could be seen as a lineal descendent of response-learning theories; the main problem with such propositional storage is the need to update and change relationships as one travels through space.

Thompson (1983) has shown that *continuous* visual monitoring is *not* necessary in 'visually guided' locomotion in the sighted: he concludes, on the basis of empirical evidence, that locomotor control involves a time-limited memory for the perceived location of goals (he allowed his subjects brief prior glimpses of a layout); and that there was a complex cooperative interaction between motor control and the memory of the distance of a target. Motor plans would have to be powerful and more complex in order to support lengthy, efficient travel by the blind. Gibson's account, mentioned above, attempts to do without map concepts—but, as Strelow's review indicates, it is not clear that this attempt is successful, because both schemata *and* motor plans may have map-like qualities by specifying distances and directions between their elements. Strelow suggests that in mobility one must see perception and cognition working interactively with, in some tasks, perception being uppermost (e.g. in obstacle avoidance by the sighted) in others, cognition predominating (e.g. travel by the blind) and with some further tasks requiring both processes (e.g. locating and recognizing a place). Gibson's account must therefore be seen as incomplete.

Analysis of directions as a source of insight into environmental information storage and recall

Can analysis of the directions given to a stranger provide an indication of the search through spatial memory, and indeed of the way this spatial memory itself is organized?

Such directions, as part of one of the commonest forms of exchange between strangers, have received some attention within psychology and linguistics; but, in the main, this has been because of the light they shed on the nature of the exchange, and upon the participants' negotiation of a frame of reference.

Thus, for example, Psathas and Kozloff (1976) only offer an analysis of: 'The basic elements of a set of directions without which the set would not be recognized as adequate by those who give and receive directions' (p. 111). Their method is expressly phenomenological—aimed at giving a description that will 'enable us to understand our experiences'. Having collected a large corpus of examples, they then 'resist any idea of reducing it by explanatory formulations', or relating it to the circumstances under which the encounter took place—which is exactly what we would require for our purposes.

For semiotics, the end goal is to discern the phases of direction-giving: defining the situation; providing information and instructions; and ending the set. Each phase is described, with its various constituent elements, but no attempt is made to relate the selectivity of information preferred to any strategy, or to the total data set potentially available to the direction-giver. Nor is there any analysis of the way errors give clues to the mode of storage (see, for example, Psathas and Henslin, 1967).

Somewhat closer to this chapter's concerns is the work on directions conducted by cognitive psychologists within the AI tradition. Kuipers (1978), for example, has discussed the representation of knowledge of large-scale maps, and the use of such maps in the formulation of directions in travel plans. Given its AI origins, it is not surprising that the main emphasis of this work has been on *optimal* representation and use of spatial information.

Riesbeck (1980) has examined the natural language processing of *written* directions, and argues that, at first reading, there does not need to be much spatial reasoning going on at all. For someone who will be able to carry and consult the directions on the journey, the first consideration is the *clarity* of the directions, rather than the development of a spatial plan from them. Identifying the crucial elements in the description guides the process of asking for further information if unclear. In other words, Riesbeck's concern is more with the receiver's comprehension than with the speaker's production of instructions.

Research into directions from the perspective of the direction-giver would be of considerable benefit in giving insights into the formulation of action-plans. Directions are closer in format to such plans than the majority of sketch-maps, distance estimates, etc. which, as noted earlier, have been the principal research tools in environmental cognition research. We should not expect directions to be any more veridical than the sketch-maps and distance estimates: as Passini (1984) has argued, we have an apparent contradiction. People are able to find their way with some accuracy, despite their inaccuracies in spatial representation. Such discrepancies indicate that a simple read-out from stored information is not the only determinant of travel: the information underlying travel plans does not normally *need* to be entirely accurate, as it is constantly checked against current information as the traveller moves through the environment.

In a small-scale study of our own, we have begun to examine not only the protocols of instructions given in the street (to an experimenter who pretended to be from out of town) but also to relate these instructions to the travel plans that the direction-givers were themselves using to navigate through the same area (Buckler and Spencer, unpublished study). We found systematic differences in the directions given which related to the direction in which the speaker was facing: differences, in other words, between those who are themselves about to go along the route, and those who have just completed it. Similarly, Moar and Carleton (1982) found a direction of travel effect: they found that spatial judgements from memory tended to be more accurate in the direction of travel along the routes than in the opposite direction.

A deterministic corrective?

Lest all the research reviewed so far leads us to assume that an entire account of orientation, mobility and route choice can be given in terms of cognitive and perceptual factors within the individual, it is perhaps salutory to the psychologist to see that a whole literature on route choice exists which takes no direct cognisance of these individual-centred factors.

The planning community has developed a series of mathematical models of traffic flow and of pedestrian behaviour (Hill, 1984). Thus, for example, a general interaction model known as a 'gravity model' has been used to predict average flow of pedestrians on the pavements (sidewalks) through a central business district. Haggett, Cliff, and Frey (1977) describe the model thus: 'Interaction is more likely between two pedestrian generators if the generators employ or have more pedestrians individually; with interaction decreasing as a function of distance between these generators'. Which, being translated, means that flow between A and B is predictable from knowing how many pedestrians there are at A and B, and how far apart they are. Upon such a basic prediction, one can then build up additional factors, e.g. time of day, number of restaurants and shops within 100 feet of the route, etc. (see, for example, Pushkarev and Zupan, 1975).

Such models are calibrated by using current, empirically corrected data; and, if used as predictors to guide planners, tend to lead to self-fulfilling prophecies. More important to our present argument, the data they work with derives from observations of pedestrian numbers at points on routes, and has perforce to make its assumptions about pedestrian route-choice on the basis of this aggregate data of observed flow. There is no direct questioning of individuals about their routes, let alone empirical investigation of the factors that lead the individual to choose between several possible alternatives.

Our point is that we, as psychologists, should be aware that it is possible to develop adequate (if conservative) models of pedestrian and other traffic behaviour without taking any psychological data into account. Does this perhaps supply a useful corrective to our studies?

Should one in fact go further, and see such behaviour as being so predictable from a knowledge of environmental factors that one could see the behaviour as *primarily* environmentally determined? Certainly, many of the planning disciplines have made deterministic presumptions about human behaviour, and have used concepts such as 'sociofugal' and 'sociopetal areas', and 'defensible space'. But others (e.g. Franck, 1984) have argued that physical determinism of behaviour, in its strong sense, cannot be accepted, because it ignores genuine choices made by the individual.

Articles, indeed whole treatises, have discussed determinism within behavioural geography and environmental psychology [see, for example, Spencer and Blades (1986) on similarities and differences between the two areas]; this is not the place to enter the debate.

Suffice it to say that the actual form of the environment should be included in all considerations of interaction with the environment, for either directly or through its defining of the individual's cognitions, it will exert a major influence upon behaviour. Thus, for example, a building's layout will determine its legibility, which, in turn, will directly influence the ease with which people plan routes through the building—and may also affect their feelings towards the building as a place [see, for an empirical demonstration, Weisman (1981)].

Perception of distance

The perception of distance, as a field of study, predated by a long time the emergence of environmental psychology, taking its place within mainstream psychophysical estimate studies (e.g. Teghtsoonian and Teghtsoonian, 1969).

More recently, subjects' estimates of distances in geographical-scale space have been used as a technique for the investigation of cognitive representations. It has been argued that distance estimates do not suffer from the distortions found in sketch maps and in narrative accounts (e.g. Evans, 1980). Clearly, distance estimation does not rely upon the graphic and expressive skills. It has, however, other major drawbacks as a basis for reconstructing individuals' cognitive maps.

We first briefly review the use that distance estimates have been put to, and then evaluate their claims.

Studies of distance perception have included: studies of visually estimated distances—where estimates are based upon information that is simultaneously available to the observer (as it is in the majority of psychophysical experiments); studies of the perception of traversed distances—which take place over the duration of travel, require sequential processing of information and add duration to the set of cues for distance (e.g. Sadalla and Magel, 1980; Sadalla and Staplin, 1980a,b); and, finally, studies of cognitive distance at city, regional, or larger scale—where information does not principally accrue as a result of the individual's travel, but is acquired through a variety of media (e.g. Cadwallader, 1976; Evans and Pezdek, 1980). Evans and Pezdek (1980) have stated that humans have moderately accurate, accessible knowledge about geographical scale settings (e.g. across town) and can also give relatively accurate distance and locational estimates at both the smaller scale (e.g. buildings on campus) and the macro scale of their country.

However, Lee (1962, 1970), one of the pioneers of perceived distance research, sees perceived distance as an important cost factor in route-planning. His studies alert us to the fact that distance estimates are apt to be swayed by non-metrical factors, such as whether the routes to be compared are towards or away from the centre of town; what mode of travel the subjects habitually use over the routes; how far the routes are through varied areas, and how many points of interest there are on them (echoes here of psychophysical judgements of segmented and unsegmented stimuli, or judgements of filled and unfilled time periods); plus also the linearity versus complexity of the routes, and so on [see the review of such factors by Pocock (1976)]. Such factors may be shown to operate even when subjects' estimates are based upon apparently more objective information sources, such as maps: Thorndyke (1981) has shown that 'map clutter' can be a powerful source of distortion in distance estimates. This observation holds true whether the subjects are working from memorized maps, viewing the maps directly, or recalling knowledge of their country's geography. Thorndyke suggests, on the basis of his empirical finding, that perceptual and memorial processes of distance estimation are similar: in both, subjects are presumed to scan a perceptual image of the route from the starting point to its end, and that this visual scan is converted into a judgement of magnitude by means of an internal timing of the scan. Clutter demands attention, increases scan time, and results in an overestimate of distance. Similarly, number of turns and intersections on a walked route, could occupy processing time (Sadalla and Staplin, 1980a,b).

By now, the reader's confidence in distance estimates as an uncomplicated and preferable route into the investigation of cognitive representations may well have been shaken. But worse still, Cadwallader (1979) in an important but seldom cited study has shown that individual distance estimates are unstable across different methodologies, even at the ordinal level of measurement; hence no simple relationship can be expected between physical and cognitive distance.

Secondly, Cadwallader has shown that distance estimates are both *intransitive* and *noncommutative*. Subjects are quite likely to say that distance 1 is longer than distance 2; 2 is longer than 3; and 3 is longer than 1; and they are also capable of estimating the distance from A to B as being different from that from B to A. (Only in one-sixth of estimates in Cadwallader's study were the A to B estimates exactly the same as the B to A estimates; most pairs of estimates revealed a difference of somewhere between 10 and 40%.)

The intransitivity and noncommutativity of estimates indicates that people 'do not possess cognitive representations of the physical world that have the mathematical properties of a metric space ... Any internalized spatial representation of the physical world will be highly complex' (Cadwallader, 1979, p. 574).

Salisbury (1985), writing about distance measurement in China, and the flexible *li*, suggests that 'The Chinese *li* is the only unit of measurement that varies in accordance with its difficulty. An uphill *li* is only half as long as a downhill *li*.' Officially, Salisbury may be right—but the empirical evidence seems to indicate that all (perceived) distances are pretty flexible!

Layout, legibility, and the ease with which individuals process and use information about the large-scale environment

What factors about the environment might, then, facilitate environmental information processing? Is there evidence that some settings are easier to learn than others? A study by Weisman (1981) examined the relationship between ease of orientation and four architectural variables: interior signing; the possibility of seeing outdoors; architectural differentiation between the areas of a building; and overall plan configuration. Appleyard (1970) has discussed the importance of physical distinctiveness for both one's orientation and one's aesthetic response to the city. Evans, Smith, and Pezdek (1982) have confirmed Appleyard's observation that the building features that predict how well subjects recall places include: the amount of movement around the building; sharp, distinctive contours; large relative size; complex shape; and high use and thereby familiarity. Additional building characteristics that were found to enhance recall were: the presence of natural features around the building; uniqueness of architectural style; and ease of pedestrian access.

Zannaras (1976), in one of the few city-level studies, has shown that city structure (and especially the arrangement of land use in the city) has a more important role in determining how subjects will remember the city than do any of the range of personal characteristics included in her study (including length of residence and other measures of city use and experience). And Evans, Fellows, Zorn, and Doty (1980) have shown experimentally how colour-coding the interior of a complex building aided visitors' travels through the building and enhanced their recall and recognition memory of the building after their visits.

Such studies indicate that there is indeed likely to be an important relationship between physical layout of the environment and the ease with which individuals can develop useful cognitions of that environment. The research, in addition to its theoretical importance, can also have practical benefits for those wishing to facilitate visitors' use of buildings and other places—see Gärling, Lindberg, and Mäntylä (1983). Sime (1988) describes the ways in which such research may be of benefit to such diverse areas as fire safety research and the relocation of older people.

Here, as in previous aspects of this discussion, we note that just as environmental information can derive from direct or secondary experience, so such facilitating factors can be either direct or secondary: the simple and distinctive layouts referred to above, being an example of direct facilitators; well-designed layout plans being an example of secondary facilitators. Bartram (1980), for example, has shown how a schematic map produces a better comprehension of spatial information than does a conventional map, or ordered listings of spatial information.

Direct experience begins to build upon such a prior, secondary source of information: there exist a number of studies on the microgenesis of spatial cognitions in which subjects have longer and longer interactions with a place (e.g. Foley and Cohen, 1984; Spencer and Weetman, 1981).

Schouela, Steinberg, Leveton, and Wapner (1980) in one such study have described the changes of cognitive organization of a small university campus over the course of students' first six months of residence. Not surprisingly, they found that the representation becomes progressively more differentiated and integrated; but they also stressed the importance of a salient anchor-point as the organizational principle at all stages. Herman, Kail, and Siegal (1979), also working at campus level, and Spencer and Weetman (1981), working at whole-city level, found that spatial knowledge was rapidly structured in the first three weeks of residence, with further significant increases occurring up to a three-month plateau at three months. Only in those tasks demanding an abstractness and flexibility in the use of the cognitive map will individuals with even longer residence be found to be superior (Siegal, Kirasic, and Kail, 1987).

Residence in other, similar, settings provides a frame of reference for structuring a new city or area. Devlin (1976) showed how frequently-relocated wives of service personnel rapidly established their cognitive maps of yet another new small town—with functional landmarks located within days (the maternity hospital being high on their list). And Murray and Spencer's (1979) study of domestic-airline pilots confirms Devlin's conclusion, that individuals frequently forced to establish new roots, develop certain skills in cognitive-map development which others, living in one or two places in a lifetime do not possess.

A similar point can be made about way-finding and use of the natural environment (Kaplan, 1976): prior acquaintance with other rural areas helps individuals to 'read' the landscape.

The natural environment and human needs

The reader may have noticed that there has almost always been an urban backdrop to the research in environmental psychology reported so far—whether it be studies of cognitive maps or of route-finding; and were this book to be a more general review of other areas currently researched within environmental psychology, this trend would continue: urban settings predominate in studies of residential satisfaction and environmental stress, for example. But little or no research exists on the natural environment and its effect on behaviour.

Some psychologists, such as Olivegren (1974), have stated their belief in our species' need for contact with the natural world; and phenomenological geographers have documented this theme with numerous quotations from literature (e.g. Tuan, 1978).

As we shall discover in the second section of the book, developmental psychologists have been more alert to the natural environment's role in fulfilling the child's needs than have those psychologists studying the needs of the adult. One honourable exception to this has been Rachel Kaplan, who has researched everything from the psychological benefits of gardening (1973) and exploration of the wilderness (1976) to the importance of natural features for the well-being of city dwellers (1983). She has demonstrated what others in the planning disciplines have merely intuited: that residential satisfaction can be related to the perceived adequacy and availability of *nearby* natural resources (Kaplan, 1985). In this last study the subjects were residents of multiple-family housing projects at both high and low densities in nine city districts. They responded to questionnaires about the kinds of natural areas near their home, and whether they felt them to be adequate. Large open spaces played a relatively minor role in determining satisfaction; more important was the individual's opportunity to grow plants; and most important of all were the availability nearby of trees, well-landscaped grounds, and places for walks.

Many previous studies of residential satisfaction have indicated the important role played by such *social* factors as perceived similarity among neighbours, friendliness and social networks, and demographic characteristics of the area; and *physical* factors including adequacy of upkeep of dwelling, and availability of services. All of these factors clearly contribute: in this context, can natural environmental features be shown to be more than a pleasant extra amenity? Moore (1979) had offered a tentative earlier indication: prisoners whose cell windows gave a view of natural areas were shown to develop fewer illnesses than

Figure 2.1   Value of the natural environment. Studies of environmental appraisal show that even inner-city areas are more positively evaluated where planting occurs.

those without such a view. We clearly need many more such empirical studies to test the feeling that many share intuitively: that the natural environment may be a major contributor to psychological well-being. Indeed, environmental psychology is only just beginning its exploration of human needs in general: there are promising developments, for example, in considering the meaning of home (e.g. Korosec-Serfaty, 1984; Sixsmith, 1986); and as we shall see in Section 3, research on the child's environmental needs is now proceeding apace.

Images of distant places

Tourist destinations, places one would consider moving to for a job, countries and peoples seen to be in need, allies and enemies, exotic lands and the world's trouble-spots: all are places the individual will know about less from personal experience than from indirect sources. In studying these images and their origins, environmental psychology makes common ground with the social psychology of prejudice: stereotypes of places and of people transmitted by the individual's ambient culture and by the use of the available media. Victorian missionary hymns and early geography primers (on the 'How the World Works for Us' model), travellers' tales and artists' impressions—our forebears' sources of images—have been supplemented and partly replaced by travel brochures, television series set against foreign backdrops, and coffee-table books.

Early research in behavioural geography included survey research on knowledge about and preferences for other parts of one's own country: Gould and White (1986), for example, constructed maps in which areas of equal preference were joined by contour lines, to provide what they termed 'mental maps' (confusingly, given the subsequent use of the term 'cognitive map' within environmental psychology). Some sociologists have used similar techniques to study perceptions of social inequalities (e.g. Bell and Robinson, 1980).

Since the study by Maistre (1970), there have been isolated attempts by geographers and others to assess the effects of mass media on the individual's perceptions. Analysis of the content of newsmedia indicates how selective is the coverage of events, with disproportionate amounts of attention paid to local and non-national stories: in Walmsley's (1982) phrase, 'the media set, through their news reports, an agenda of spatial information for mass consumption'. This gate-keeping function of the broadcasters, journalists and editors is then further compounded by selective processes to do with the individual audience member: selective perception, according to prior interests, and cognitive dissonance processes, to deal with discrepant information.

Indeed, if one interviews people immediately after a news broadcast, as Nordenstreng (1972) showed, little memory remains of the content of that news. He identified four factors predictive of retention of an item: prior interest in the topic; the concreteness of the news item; audience ability to identify with the item; and comprehension. Reviewing further empirical evidence, Walmsley (1982) adds four more factors, all of which are presentational characteristics: most important is the frequency of repetition of an item; the item's position in the bulletin's running order; the amount of time devoted to the item; and the use of pictorial material in its presentation.

One frequently used explanatory tool, potentially important in developing an audience's understanding, is the use of simple maps. Gilmartin (1985) has suggested that the choice of map-projection can affect audience perceptions: her examples are drawn from a comparison of newspaper maps published to illustrate a single news story—the 1983 incident in which a Korean airliner was shot down. Audience evaluation of the conflicting accounts given at the time of the aircraft's intended and actual flightpath could well be affected by the type of map-projection used.

Not all media-derived impressions of distant places come from the news media, of course; much incidental information comes from the settings of television and film drama. A more purposive use of media to affect perceptions is to be found in the brochures produced by travel firms and by countries' tourist agencies. Geographers researching holiday-makers' reasons for choice seem agreed that the 'image' of a potential tourist destination must be important (Mercer, 1971); but, as Dilley (1986) suggests, we have little available research on the means by which such images are formed. Britton (1979) has offered an account of the major promotional campaigns that were aimed at making many Third-World places seem desirable and accessible tourist destinations. Dilley, noting that pictures occupy more than three-quarters of the space in tourist brochures, conducted a content analysis of pictures drawn from national tourist-office publicity material. In his sample, cultural themes were most frequent (local inhabitants in costume, entertainments, old buildings), a categorization that shades into the next most frequent—landscape. The cultural message is used 'to convince the potential tourist that the country has many unusual and fascinating examples of human cultural activity, past and present; that the pageant of human life is older, more varied or just different from at home'. Landscape themes, he sees as designed to stress the scenic attractiveness of the country, together with an indication of wildlife the tourist might see. Recreational facilities were the third most frequently used theme—with a stress on participation in familiar sports in beautiful settings, rather than stressing exotic local sports. Finally, service illustrations seem to have two rather opposite messages—that unique gastronomic (etc.) facilities are available, but yet that being abroad is not threatening by its strangeness. Dilley's own pilot studies in Canada show that public images of popular European and Caribbean destinations are quite close to those being promoted in the brochures; but more distant countries, such as India, South Africa, and New Zealand, 'are perceived by many in ways which might surprise their tourist authorities'. Clearly, we gain our images from a range of sources, and accord more credibility to some rather than to others.

We shall return to these and other studies in Chapter 9, where we consider how children develop their concepts of distant places.

Environmental cognition: the contribution from artificial intelligence

We have already seen how environmental psychology, developmental psychology, and behavioural geography have all initiated studies of environmental cognition from the particular premises of their respective sub-disciplines, and are now beginning to converge. A fourth research tradition—that of artificial intelligence—has recently entered the field, and contributions on cognitive maps, landmarks and route descriptions, and route planning are now frequently appearing in the AI and cognitive psychology journals. Cross-fertilization is well underway; for example, one of the papers most cited in the recent environmental psychology literature is Kuipers' discussion of the 'map in the head' metaphor (1982)—a paper in a mainstream environment and behaviour journal, written by a computer scientist working at the MIT Artificial Intelligence Laboratory, and which itself cites key papers from all three other research traditions. Similarly, mainstream geographical journals have begun to carry articles on the applicability of AI to geographical problem-solving (e.g. Smith, 1984; Couclelis, 1986).

Provided the somewhat arrogant imperialism of some proponents of AI does not alienate other workers who have been in the field of environmental cognition rather longer, the conceptual fillip of the computational approach will shortly begin to be noticeable in all three research approaches. [An early sign has been the paper by Golledge *et al.* (1985)—geographers publishing an article on AI and children's cognition in an environmental psychology journal: research we shall discuss in Section 2.]

To oversimplify, research in AI has two traditions—the *cognitive* approach, where the procedures constructed to solve a given problem are constrained so as to embody what psychology has discovered about human cognitive (and perceptual) processes and structures, and the *engineering* approach, which has no such constraints, and whose goal is the production of programs and machines to solve problems by 'reasoning', as in expert systems, machine translation, robotics and computer-aided learning (Dehn and Schank, 1983).

Kuipers (1982) has indicated how AI has been applied to our area: 'an information processing model describes the cognitive map as a complex data structure and a set of associated procedures that exhibit a certain input–output behaviour' (p. 212). The 'data structure' corresponds to a person's knowledge store. A sequence of observations from the perceptual system is received by the cognitive spatial description; these are assimilated to the data structure—either by extending it or by changing it.

So, how would a traveller learn a new route? He or she would start with an empty cognitive spatial description; his or her observations would consist of a sequence of sensory and motor descriptions. Kuipers labels these 'views' and 'actions', although, recalling mobility in the blind, 'views' need not be visual—they could be auditory, tactile, olfactory images, or propositions. Actions include 'rotate' (recording the angle of rotation) and 'travel' (reading the distance travelled).

The traveller creates a link between each perceptual view and the action taken there to continue along the route; moves on, creates a further link between the previous view/action pair and the new view; and so on, to provide a complete route description. This complete description can be followed independently, or reviewed mentally in the absence of environmental prompts. (Associationist psychologists of yesteryear might enjoy this revival of their fortunes within AI!)

Where the traveller is less attentive, Kuipers suggests that only the 'view/action' links will be formed, with no linking of these pairs to the new view ahead: this will provide a route description sufficient for environment-prompted travel, but inadequate for mental review, or for the anticipation of landmarks.

Such partial descriptions can still be meaningful and useful. Where views are aggregated, linked by actions that involve only *rotation*, then the result will be a *place description*. Places and paths are recognized to be topologically connected when they are seen to share a particular view; and a network of places and paths, linked by topological relations of connection and order, can be created from the sequence of views and actions, and these networks used to solve route-finding problems. (There already exist well-established network search programs.)

Distance and direction information can be derived from the information provided by the action descriptions (rotation and distance of travel). Artificial intelligence research in visual recognition, and cognitive psychology studies of mental imagery both have made available techniques for just such analyses.

Clearly, we are at the beginning, not at a final description: concepts of routes and places in the AI literature are as yet primitive compared with those in the rest of the literature reviewed; the association principles so far described only lead to an asymmetrical route, since the stored links support retrieval from beginning to end, but not vice versa. And yet the approach already offers a powerful framework for modelling route-learning, following, and interrogation.

What makes it particularly appropriate is that AI works in terms of *heuristics* as well as *algorithms*. Whereas the algorithm is a '*finite* set of rules which gives a sequence of operations for solving a specific type of problem' (Knuth, 1973), heuristics are problem-solving rules that do not specify exactly how to solve an entire problem, and do not guarantee success (Dehn and Schank, 1983). Now, the majority of solutions to everyday problems that humans use are heuristics, not algorithms: most of our choices are made in contexts where one can, if necessary, recover from errors at less cost than would be incurred by *precisely* pre-specifying one's course of action. Indeed, most problems are not sufficiently well-defined to allow one to formulate an algorithm to solve them; if they were, and yet had any degree of complexity, the number of steps in one's algorithm would become impossibly large.

Artificial intelligence, early in its development, started working on programs that could reason, by heuristically guided trial-and-error search and other techniques. It has conducted research into understanding, with applications to intelligent translation, natural language understanding, situation interpretation, etc. Artificial Intelligence has become concerned with defining the kind of knowledge people have, and learning how it is stored, accessed, used, and acquired; complete with beliefs and expectation about social rules and about normal human behaviour.

Now, as Dehn and Schank (1983) remind us, 'AI, even human-intelligence-oriented AI, does not share the research goals of human-intelligence research within psychology'. Yet the results of AI research may well be of considerable relevance to environmental cognition research, both in terms of actual findings, and as a mental discipline, tightening one's definitions and reasoning about the area.

Thus, for example, Smith, Pellegrino, and Golledge (1982), after reviewing the AI approach, conclude that many important aspects of spatial decision-making cannot be understood unless the decision-maker's representation of the world is explicitly represented. The researcher would examine his or her knowledge structures and the processes by which the structures are constructed, accessed and modified; and the only way to perform such highly detailed modelling would be via AI programs.

Could it work? Smith (1984) reviews a number of projects designed to construct a computational process model of how decision makers access cognitive maps to make route choices; and has himself been involved in a study that inferred production system models of sequential decision-making from observations of individuals searching an area (Smith, Clark, and Cotton, 1984). A separate model was derived for each of the 60 subjects in their study, and was shown to be related to that individual's cognitive representation of the task.

What of the future? Artificial intelligence research is beginning to tackle the control problem—which of the potential actions should a system perform at each point in the decision-making process. Hayes-Roth's (1985) 'blackboard control systems' do not simply solve problems; they know something about how they solve problems, why they perform one action, rather than another, and are able to adapt to meet the demands of changing situations. Hayes-Roth uses as her example a route-choice with time constraints problem, in which one's traveller has to fit in as many shopping tasks as possible, prioritizing these and weighting these against location; fit in a movie; and collect the car before the park closes. Indeed, route choice, so long just the concern of environmental researchers, seems now to have become a central challenge to many working in AI (e.g. Elliott and Lesk, 1982; McCalla and Reid, 1982; McDermott and Davis, 1984; McNamara, 1986). Such research is not only important for that field's conceptual development, but also has practical applications in, for example, automatic vehicle guidance.

Conclusion: the origins of spatial skills and understanding

From research at the leading edge of AI to research of humbler mortals studying, for example, pedestrian movements in cities, there is much current interest in seeing how cognitive representations of space translate into route descriptions and action plans. In most of these studies, we are aware that a highly skilled performance is taking place. For the rest of the book—and in particular, in the next seven chapters, we shall be concerned with how these skills develop throughout childhood.

Part II

The Development of Environmental Cognition

CHAPTER 3

The development of environmental cognition: from body-image onwards?

The origins and development of those spatial skills described in their adult form in Part I is our main concern in this, the central section of the book. We shall examine the whole range of space-related cognitions, from the child's developing body-image, through the location of objects in close space and the understanding of geographical-scale space to the emergence of concepts about distant places.

Here, as in all areas studied by developmental psychologists concerned with cognition, there are a number of intellectual traditions at work. Liben (1981) has offered an excellent summary, which we propose to follow.

The empiricist position is that psychological concepts of space are derived directly from experience with physical space—with, at its most ideal, psychological space being isomorphic with physical space.

The nativist position, in contrast, is that psychological concepts of space are determined directly by innate factors in the organism: various theorists linking these to broad structures organizing spatial experience—O'Keefe and Nadel (1978), for example, have contended that the hippocampus is predisposed for a Euclidean framework. Others have offered descriptions of specific sensory receptors, dedicated to the detection of particular spatial features (e.g. Hubel and Wiesel, 1959). For a general review of this approach, see Frisby (1979).

The constructivist position—espoused in one form or another by the majority of workers in the developmental field—holds that psychological space is actively construed by the individual. Inherited and experiential factors interact, but, importantly, each individual develops anew the cognitive structures used to organize spatial experience.

The complexity of construction underlying what appears to the experiencer as the simple percept of space fascinated philosophers well before psychology's emergence: Descartes found 'no intelligible connection between ideas of the mind and their supposed external causes'; Locke held the position that 'primary qualities' of objects, such as number, were in the object, but other percepts may involve our reasoning and inferring them; and Berkeley stressed the role of experience in our understanding of space—thus, for example, we learn to estimate distance by learning that a faint, small object is a great distance away. Few philosophers, however, considered the ontogenesis of spatial understanding; and it has perhaps been psychology's major contribution to the debate that much empirical evidence on its development has been gathered, with the 1908s being a particularly active period of research.

The reader will notice in this part of the book that developmental psychologists have adopted approaches that differ somewhat from those employed by environmental psychologists, whose work was discussed in Part I: not only are different methodologies sometimes necessary because of limitations in the young child's expressive competence (a topic we shall return to several times), but the underlying approach is subtly different, informed as it is by the whole Piagetian and post-Piagetian approach to the study of cognitive development.

It is clear that, when working with children instead of adults, it may be necessary to replace environmental psychology's usual methodologies of investigation, reliant as they often are on skills such as model building, drawing, or description. Instead, one may have to infer cognitions from direct observation of the child's behaviour in space. Indeed, Siegal (1981) notes pointedly that kindergarten children who could not build a table top representation of their classroom, none the less 'were never seen bumping into walls in this classroom'. We cannot avoid, however, noting that the observation of behaviour in space is no more a direct route to understanding the individual's spatial representations than is investigating the latter from a child's sketch map of an area.

Piaget and Inhelder (1956) have argued that behaviour in space and representation of space are in fact very different. Piaget makes the distinction between 'practical' space (the capacity to act in space) and 'conceptual space' (the capacity to represent space). The capacity to act and move intelligently through space may well occur before—and in the absence of—the capacity to represent that space. We do not presume that the child 'solves' the problem of maintaining upright posture when walking, at a cognitive level: equally, the young child can locomote through space without conscious thought. (Similarly, one does not have to postulate that animals are cognizant of spatial information, although their intelligent and efficient movement through space argues for some form of stored spatial information.) As Liben (1981) notes, much of the literature, when discussing 'spatial representation' fails to distinguish between such *spatial storage* and the *spatial thought* that individuals can have access to, can reflect upon, can manipulate, and, when the occasion arises, can perhaps report to an experimenter.

The reader will realize that specific research problems should dictate the kind of research methodology employed; similarly, the child's level of expressive ability determines what methods are practicable. None the less, in the literature one may find similar research methodologies being used to investigate very different aspects of spatial awareness. Thus, for example, Piaget, Inhelder, and Szeminska (1960), Hart (1981), and Spencer and Easterbrook (1985) have all asked children to produce representations of their school and home. Piaget used the representations to examine children's ability to use such abstract spatial concepts as reference systems and conserve distances; Hart used the technique to investigate children's knowledge of home area; and we, in our study, were concerned with the child's informal mapping techniques.

In the sections to come, we mention a variety of ingenious techniques that have been used, particularly in work with the youngest age groups. It is important to be aware that not all writers are careful in limiting the claims that can be made about internal representations from evidence drawn from external behaviour.

A sequence of frames of reference?

This part of the book is organized from smallest to largest scale: not just as an organizational convenience, but also, in considering the development of spatial knowledge and skills, as a reflection of the infant's and child's expanding awareness. But is it, as some have claimed, a developmental sequence in the full sense? Does the child first achieve an integrated image of body layout (with much effort expended in body-part coordination); then extend this frame of reference to the immediate world (with the focus being now on object location); and then proceed outward from this to consider the spatial interrelationships between objects and places (as the child begins active movement through space)? Belief in such a sequence has been particularly strong among those working with young blind children [see the review by Welsh and Blasch (1980)]; but, as Pick and Lockman (1981) point out, it is clear that the individual does *not* have to achieve complete mastery of the first frame of reference before working on the next. Indeed, some individuals continue refining these well into adult life: consider, the intricate body–object skill of juggler or musician and the heightened tracking skills of orienteer and hunter. In their review, Pick and Lockman (1981) argue that, when these are fully operational, the individual can call upon a *multiplicity* of reference systems. Some life-tasks call forth an egocentric frame of reference; others an allocentric frame; still others may demand a geocentric frame; and many tasks implicate several frames of reference.

(They define a frame of reference as 'a locus or set of loci with respect to which spatial position is defined'.)

Although there demonstrably exist a multiplicity of interacting spatial reference systems (Pick and Lockman in fact are able to present evidence for there being at least two egocentric reference systems) in the fully competent individual, this does not in itself solve the developmental question: whether it is necessary to establish a working frame of reference at one level before moving outward to the next—with the implication that if, for example, a child lacks a fully integrated body-image he or she will find difficulty in relating objects to self, and objects to each other with the effect continuing outward to full spatial competence.

We shall review each stage/frame of reference in the following chapters, including, where available, evidence that bears upon this developmental question.

To anticipate, the case for a relationship between body-image and other broader spatial skills seems non-proven: see below, and Chapter 10, (where we discuss the issue with relation to the body-images of blind children). There does seem a clear age-related trend from egocentric responding to allocentric responding on a spatial task (see Acredolo, 1978) though when this shift occurs varies dramatically with task type, and the availability and salience of environmental cues, and there is very little work linking competence and skills at personal and local-geographical-space level with those in dealing with broader navigational abilities. There are, however, a number of important, stable, individual differences in spatial skills—as discussed. Thus, most object-to-object positioning tasks demand an allocentric frame of reference: working on a jigsaw puzzle would be an example. But an egocentric frame of reference is presumably also implicated in the very processes that enable the child to coordinate manipulative movements to select and rotate these jigsaw pieces.

Similarly, as Acredolo (1976) has shown, children use the geocentric frame to gain additional information about the relative locations of objects, even when this information could be directly obtained from the allocentric frame: they use the landmarks incidentally provided by the surrounding room to help solve object–object problems.

The concept of a body-image: the original and central frame of reference?

One school of thought about orientation and spatial awareness sees the developmental process as building outwards from the child's earliest and closest domain—the body—to space around the self, and then to broader geographical space: not just as a personal-historical sequence, but as a series of skills and competencies whose achievement depends on the earlier stages. Clearly, much of the neonate's activities are self-related, and it is in the earliest months that coordinations between limbs, between eye and hand (and between will and action?) begin (see, for example, Bruner and Connolly, 1974).

Discovering what image of the body the neonate possesses is clearly a matter of inference; and many writers about 'body-image' and its importance in development have conducted their enquiries with much older children, as we shall see below.

Cratty and Sams (1968), in a paper that has been very influential in the mobility training of the blind, have argued that there is a clear relationship between body perceptions and the child's competence in movement; effective movement in other words depends on the child having an adequate body image. Similarly, other early influential writers on spatial orientation, Howard and Templeton (1966), implied that the body provides the basic reference frame: one relates the position of objects to the body, and uses the apparent movement of these objects with relation to the body to monitor one's movement through the world. Kinesiologists such as Aust (1980), concerned with the study and improvement of human motion, may lay much stress upon body image. Aust writes that 'if a client has little or no conscious awareness of the relationship of his parts, such as his head to the whole of his body, he cannot be expected to align his body parts properly in an attempt to gain and maintain vertical alignment'. She further argues that an inaccurate body-image can be 'as debilitating as a lack of body image'.

Warren (1984), in reviewing work with the visually handicapped, states that it is widely accepted that the blind infant has greater difficulty in establishing a body image than does the sighted infant.

It is instructive to note this stress upon the body image by those writer–practitioners who, like Aust and Warren, work with those individuals whose mobility is impaired, whether through blindness or another cause; and to compare this with the absence of mention of body-image among those writers describing the active movement and exploration of non-handicapped children (take, for example, any of the authors cited in the next chapter). For these latter researchers, it is not so much that the concept of body-image is denied, it is simply not discussed. The process of normal development in their subjects has proceeded past the point where such an image presents any problem.

We find, for example, that Piaget (1929) stresses the importance of walking for children's understanding of space beyond themselves; which as Bremner and Bryant (1985) point out, is to ignore the importance of the crawling and pre-crawling periods in developing spatial concepts, although Piaget, in fairness, may have implied other active movement when writing about walking.

What then of the concept of body-image itself? There has been a useful disentangling of interlocking concepts by Warren (1984) (note that, again, it is a writer concerned with the blind who offers the best review). He discerns in the literature three ways in which the concept has been used.

1 'Body-image' as meaning the child's *knowledge* of body parts and their interrelationship (e.g. Hapeman, 1967).

2 'Body-image' as some form of 'mental picture' of one's body in space (e.g.
  Siegal and Murphy, 1970). Some investigators (e.g. Mills, 1970) have used
  the term to imply both 1 and 2.
3 'Body-image': the psychoanalytic use, referring to the differentiation of the
  ego from the external world.

An earlier discussion of what probably should best be seen as a cluster of
concepts was offered by Frostig and Horne (1964), who differentiated:

1 'Body-image' as the person's subjective feelings about the body (e.g. attractive, too tall, etc.)—a usage familiar in clinical discussions of, for example,
  anorexia; and in social psychological theorizing about self-concepts.
2 'Body concept' is the term Frostig and Horne use to describe the individual's
  learned knowledge about the names and functions of body parts.
3 'Body schema' is their term for a continually changing, usually non-
  conscious, awareness of one's position in space, derived from propriocon-
  ceptive cues, etc.

The reader will see to what a variety of images similar terms have been applied;
and how easy it would be to assume a direct relationship between them because
they share the same name, without offering evidence. We have, for example, in
the literature on the blind, those proponents of what one might label the strong
determinist 'body-image for mobility' position, Cratty and Sams, devising a test
'of blind children's body image' that contains five components:

1 'Body planes': the child has to identify front, back, sides, etc., of his or her
  own body; and then place objects in relation to these planes.
2 Identification of body parts.
3 Body movement—whole body and limb movements.
4 'Laterality': the child has to indicate his or her own right and left, and to
  place objects on own right and left.
5 'Directionality': the child has to identify left and right sides of objects and
  other people.

Others, in using this basic procedure, have extended it—for example, Hill and
Blasch (1980) lay stress in the identification of body parts section to the everyday functions of each part.
    Now, while such a test as that devised by Cratty and Sams may well be
useful to those concerned with teaching the blind child about the body, it is
a considerable further step to say that it is these aspects of body knowledge
whose presence or absence determines spatial competence. It might be argued
that spatial competence is more likely to be indicated by either the 'mental picture of one's body in space', from Warren's list, or Frosting and Horne's 'body

schema', than by a naming of parts. If a child has considerable difficulties in differentiating left and right, up and down (note, we say 'differentiating' them, rather than being able to use the terms correctly: we discuss the development of spatial terms elsewhere), then it would certainly seem worthwhile investigating the implications of these difficulties further. Direct access to 'body schema' is clearly not possible for an investigator, who must make inferences from behaviour. If this behaviour includes linguistic competence, as revealed on the Cratty–Sams test, then access is made easier; but there remains a need to test empirically the relationship between all these various images of the body. We take up these points in the discussion of the spatial cognition of the blind child in Chapter 10, where we offer some preliminary evidence to suggest that the 'knowledge of parts' view of body-image is not by itself predictive of blind children's performance on mobility achievement tasks. We can conclude this section by observing that the centrality of 'body-image' (as some form of integrated scheme of one's body in space) to the early stages of spatial competence remains entirely plausible, but as yet is undemonstrated, and is perhaps impossible to prove.

Spatial abilities: individual differences in childhood and into adulthood

Are there stable individual differences in performance on tasks that have some spatial component? Is there a general spatial factor, or are there identifiable separate spatial abilities? Everyday and anecdotal psychology would in general hold that spatial ability differences exist: what is the psychometric evidence? Do any differences that may exist relate to identifiable differences at neurological level? Could one relate them to environmental factors? And how far are there any sex-related differences?

We give only a brief review of the current thinking on these questions [for a full review, see McGee (1979), or Eliot (1987)], and place our emphasis on such evidence as exists for the development of any such differences through childhood and into adulthood, and conclude with a suggestion that not all observations reported in Western studies are universally applicable.

Early psychometric studies identified a *spatial factor*, which has variously been described as 'being adept at judging concrete spatial relations' (McFarlane, 1925); 'the mental manipulation of shapes' (Kelley, 1928); and 'the ability to obtain and the facility to utilize, spatial imagery' (Koussey, 1935). Recent factor-analytic research has demonstrated the existence of at least two sub-factors: *spatial visualization*—the ability mentally to manipulate, rotate, twist, or invert a pictorially presented stimulus object; and *spatial orientation*—the ability to comprehend the arrangement of elements within a visual stimulus pattern, without becoming confused by changes in orientation of the stimulus. Although there is considerable agreement on the existence of these sub-factors, McGee (1979) notes that 'after 70 years of psychometric research, there is still vast disagreement about just how best to classify standard tests of spatial abilities.' (One despairs of one's subject!)

The majority of predictive validity studies have tested the relationship between spatial test scores and performance at school or at work (and have found respectable, or better, correlations with technical and manipulative subjects and tasks). In addition, Hills (1957) has shown that both spatial visualization and spatial orientation are more closely related to mathematical performance than are measures of verbal ability.

Closer to our present interests, several studies have investigated the relationship between measured spatial abilities and other aspects of orientation—although here the psychometricians do not seem to have been keen to get out of the laboratory: the majority of studies have related spatial orientation to Witkin's field dependence/field independence (1950) and to several Piagetian tasks with a spatial component: perspectives, water level, tracks, geometric forms and house plans (Tuddenham, 1970). Of the 350 or so studies reviewed by McGee (1979), only one related measured spatial ability to real world spatial orientation. Berry (1971), the cross-cultural psychologist, found higher spatial abilities generally among Baffin Island Inuits than among members of the Temne tribe in Africa, and related this to a 'directional sense ... fostered by extensive travel during hunting'. (1971). One further study is commented upon by McGee is Morey, Alexander, and Walker's (1965) work with their 'Road Map Test of Direction Sense', where the person being tested has to describe which way turns are to be made on a schematic printed map. McGee speculates that 'spatial ability may enter into [this] task of directional sense–map reading', but the authors do not help one further, save to indicate a male superiority on the Road Map Test, which increases into the teenage years.

Sex differences have been widely reported in measured spatial abilities [and indeed have been shown to be the underlying, explanatory factor in the published differences on other tests—for example, the field dependence/field independence tests (see Sherman, 1967)].

The usual summary statement is that there are little or no sex differences in spatial ability found during the early years, with a male superiority beginning to emerge some time between the ages of 8 and 12 years (e.g. Maccoby and Jacklin, 1974), strengthening in adolescence and persisting into adulthood. Indeed, male superiority on tasks requiring spatial abilities has been found to be 'among the most persistent of individual differences in all the abilities literature' (Anastasi, 1958; Buffery and Gray, 1972; Eliot, (1987); McGee, (1979). Educationalists have noted the implications of this finding—for instance, in the field of mathematics: Smith (1964), for example, devoted a whole monograph to this topic, and suggested that boys had a greater ability to perceive, recognize, and assimilate patterns in what he calls the conceptual structure of mathematics. The recent major literature review by Linn and Peterson (1985) uses recently developed meta-analysis procedures to make overall inferences from nearly 200 studies and sub-studies, and concludes that:

> Sex differences in *spatial perception* as measured by, for example, the water-level test, exist by age 8, and persist across the life span; though the sexes are differentially affected by the promptings offered in instructions given by experimenters.
> *Mental rotation*, as measured by, for example, Shepard's rotating figure test, was also found to be easier for males than for females, although the effect here is smaller.
> *Spatial visualization* was found to be equally difficult for most males and females: tasks usually consist of complex, multi-step manipulations of spatially presented information, which involve some analytic strategy.

Carter, Pazak, and Kail (1983) have presented evidence that the sexes, whether measured at 9 years, 13 years, or in adulthood, do not employ different algorithms or strategies for processing spatial information. Hence, we shall have to look elsewhere for an explanation of the reported sex differences in test scores.

Yet one may not be able to conclude, on the basis of these Western studies, that one is dealing with a universal. Monroe, Monroe, and Brasher (1985), in a longitudinal study of 6–12-year-old Logoli children in Kenya, found a trend opposite to that found by the majority of Western studies: male superiority existed in early childhood, but disappeared towards adolescence.

Unlike many other psychometricians, these authors related their findings back to the everyday lives of the children they were studying. Thus, for each child in the sample there were four measures of environmental experience: free-time distance from home; directed distance from home; proportion of free time; and object manipulation. Spatial ability test scores were found to be related to age, years of schooling (for girls only), object manipulation, and (for boys only) directed distance from home.

Further evidence comes from the Berry (1971) cross cultural study already referred to, where there were no male–female differences found in the Inuit sample, whereas among the Temne sample, males had higher scores on the spatial ability tests than did females. Berry (whose subjects were all adults) suggests that ecological demands explain the results: unlike the Temne females in Africa, the Inuit females share equally with the males in hunting through the Canadian Arctic.

McGee (1979) cautions that, although Berry's results seem to suggest the importance of experiential factors in the development of spatial skills, cross-cultural differences are not necessarily environmental, particularly when the groups under study are from long-isolated populations.

If experiential factors can have a significant effect upon spatial skills, then, one might argue, systematic training should show some effect upon test scores on spatial orientation and visualization. There exists a small, and somewhat contradictory literature on this matter within educational psychology (e.g. Brinkman, 1966; Thomas, Jamieson, and Hummel, 1973). Some of the studies have been explicitly concerned with determining whether training could reduce male–

female differences in spatial ability test scores. McGee (1979), for example, found no evidence for such an effect of training on a mental rotation test.

Could the development of sex differences in spatial ability, then, be related to hormonal or neurological differences? Peterson (1976) has shown a complex relationship: in her adolescent samples, the less androgenized (less masculine) subjects had higher spatial scores than the more androgenized males; but females with high androgen levels had higher spatial scores than females with low androgen levels. She speculates that there might be an optimal estrogen–androgen balance for the full development of spatial abilities.

There exist many more studies on the neurological correlates of spatial ability, and of their implications for sex differences: work in this area comes from experimental studies of hemispheric specialization, and from brain-injury-deficit studies.

Work in the former suggests that the right hemisphere is specialized for spatial processing; and that males have greater hemisphere specialization than females (see summaries in, for example, Kinsbourne, 1978). Studies of brain injuries confirm that insults to the right hemisphere are more likely to result in spatial deficits than are those to the left (e.g. Stiles-Davis, Sugarman, and Nass, 1985).

A final thought: take any of the well-tried psychometric or developmental tests of spatial ability, and you will find sex differences reported. As subjects themselves know the cultural stereotypes, could we be dealing with a self-reinforcing phenomenon—in which females further underperform on spatial tasks because they have lower expectancies of successful performance? Meehan and Overton (1986) tested this hypothesis, and conclude that expectancies play a partial role, but only a partial one, in contributing to female performance on spatial tasks.

CHAPTER 4

The location of objects and self in space

In this chapter, we come to the area which has—of all those discussed in the book—perhaps evoked most interest on the part of cognitive developmentalists, and which, when analysed, is found to comprise a range of problems:

What does the neonate see and understand of the world immediately around him or her?
How egocentric is the child, both then and later, as his or her mobility increases the possibilities of interactions with the world?
How does the child come to coordinate perspectives?
How do spatial concepts develop, and how does this process relate to their accurate use in language?

Among the topics we consider are movement through space as a factor in the location of objects, and keeping track of one's relationship to a place as one moves. We will make reference back to Chapter 3, and Pick's observation about the multiplicity of frames of reference used by the individual in object- and place-location tasks. We will look at the role that landmarks can play even in immediate space; leaving the discussion of the child's use of landmarks in the broader, geographical-scale environment to subsequent chapters.

Searching for objects is a task that well illustrates the way spatial competence develops, and has as a result received much attention from developmental psychologists. We review some of the literature, looking at the searching process itself; its status as a logical task; then as a process that relies upon mnemnoics, even in the very young child; and one that illustrates how, through into adulthood, context can be used as a strategy for spatial memory. We also ask if different modality effects can be demonstrated in spatial memory, and examine possible cultural differences in abilities and strategies. Throughout the chapter, the reader will note the ingenuity and care with which developmental psychologists have framed their experimental methods so as to address this variety of research questions.

The neonatal view of the world

We have seen, in Part I, how fully competent humans (and animals) perceive organization in their environment; are able to relate objects and events in that world; and to invest them with meaning in terms of these spatial relationships. How does the world appear to the newly born and the very young infant? Is there also a coherence for the young (even given all the obvious points about neonatal visual acuity, and the unfamiliarity of objects and events), or does the individual have to develop cognitive structures for interrelationships through interaction with the world?

Gibson (1966, 1979), as we have already indicated, holds that the perceptual system is attuned, *from birth* to relational information that remains invariant even through the transformations brought about by the perceiver's movement. Piaget (Piaget and Inhelder, 1956), as also noted earlier, argues the constructivist position, contending that young infants perceive unconnected images well into their second year, when abstract schemes for perceptual construction are forming.

Ingenuity is required to gain answers to the questions from such a debate, especially when working with the neonate. Thus, for example, Bower (e.g. 1975) indicated the likelihood that the young infant was capable of relatively high-order expectations, when he demonstrated that such infants had an expectation of an object's tactile presence when they reached toward a point where they, visually, perceived the object to be. Similar ingenuity of method has characterized much recent work with very young children: for example, Stern, (1977) reported that neonates can discriminate between various facial expressions shown by a familiar adult. Antell and Keating (1983) have shown that infants, during the first week of life, can abstract differences between two- and three-element displays from visual arrays that varied in contour density. And Antell and Caron (1985) showed that one- and two-day -old infants can discriminate a difference in spatial relationships between two simple geometric forms (such as a cross and a square).

Demonstrating that neonates are sensitive to relative location as in this last experiment adds weight to the view that the world of the newborn is more organized and more objective than implied by Piaget and, as Antell and Caron suggest, 'the gap between perceiving and knowing is not as formidable as initially envisioned within the Piagetian frame' (p. 22).

Piaget and his legacy

Developmental psychology's approach to cognition of the environment, as to the majority of its fields of interest, has been and continues to be considerably influenced by the pioneering work of Piaget and his associates; similarly, as we discuss in Part III, educational thinking about the development of spatial and geographical concepts has placed much reliance upon Piaget's statements about the child's capacities at particular ages and stages.

Here, the author of a book such as the present one is faced with a dilemma: whether to devote appreciable space to outlining Piaget's many observations and investigations in the relevant area, and showing how these were to lead Piaget to extend his general theory of development to the child's conception of space and understanding of the geographical-scale world; or whether, assuming a familiarity with much of this work by anyone chancing to read a monograph in a developmental psychology series, to risk reducing to almost caricature-like summary the Piagetian position, in one's eagerness to discuss the large body of research that has been stimulated by, reacted to, and extended the founding father's ideas. We have chosen to take this latter risk.

In Piaget's theory of development, knowledge of an object does not consist of having a fixed mental copy of the object, but of effecting transformations on its image, and an intelligent act is centrally one of coordinating operations, derived from the individual's internalization of his or her own actions. Even at the earliest, sensorimotor level, a child engages in activities that include uniting, ordering, and introducing correspondences; with later, the tool of language becoming available to express and explore the more advanced logical relationships between objects.

As we have already seen, when earlier contrasting Piaget's position with that of J. Gibson, a ready-made object or world knowledge is not assumed. From the sensorimotor stage onwards, the child's thought structures develop in the very process of the 'construction of reality'; whilst, at the same time, this intelligence structures reality. Piaget gives as an instance that objects at first have no permanence to the infant; the universe consists of moving tableaux which appear and disappear with no fixed location; but, with the coordination of actions, a 'schema of the permanent object' develops. The infant now searches for an object after it disappears, and knows that it continues to exist, in that he or she knows it to have a spatial location even when outside the perceptual field. During the sensorimotor period, Piaget sees the infant also becoming able to coordinate positions and changes of position, with the possibility of a return to the point of departure, and of the use of alternative routes to get to the same point.

One Piagetian term that has suffered much misrepresentation is that of *egocentrism*. Piaget argued that, in the period of pre-operational thinking (from about 2 to 7 years), the necessary condition for operational development is a decentring from the child's own actions and own point of view: and by egocentrism, Piaget meant nothing more than the absence of such cognitive decentring. The neonate does not distinguish his or her own point of view from other possible points of view: he or she is centred spatially, causally and temporally on his or her own body. By progressive decentring, the young child comes to appreciate that he or she is one element in the universe of objects, and of spatial and causal relationships. The egocentric child, when asked to predict how a display (for example, the three mountains table-top task) will appear from another's perspective, attributes his or her own perspective to the observer, wherever that observer takes up a stance.

Piaget and Inhelder (1956) describe the next transitional stage as preconceptual: children appear to make some effort to predict the other's response, linking this to some characteristic of the display, but may easily revert to an egocentric perspective. As children come to demonstrate understanding that different observers must have different perspectives, they attempt to coordinate the display's spatial relationships in order to predict these viewpoints. Errors at this stage (e.g. reversals of left and right) do not detract from this demonstration of the effective understanding of others' perspectives.

At the concrete operations stage (from about 7 or 8 years of age), the first operational structures take form; and Piaget lists the following spatial operations as the basis of representative space that characterizes understanding at this stage: the partition and addition of parts, placement and displacement, and measuring (as a synthesis of partition and displacement). His researches indicated that topological intuitions about space precede projective and Euclidean (or metric) representations. Topological spatial relations are concerned with the properties of a single object or configuration, and do not locate these objects within a global reference system. Such a location, together with the appreciation of changing points of view and the measurement of distances become possible as projective spatial concepts are constructed; with the development of Euclidean spatial concepts in late childhood, the individual can operate a reference system that is independent of any particular point of view.

Hypothetico-deductive operations, going well beyond the experience gained in interaction with the world, characterize the next stage—that of formal operations, which Piaget dates from about 11 or 12 years of age: the child can reason with verbal material alone, without concrete referents, and can begin to construct theories about the world that he or she can see how to test by systematically varying the hypothesized factors. The corresponding development of the child's beliefs about the physical, geographical scale world in Piaget's theory is dealt with in Chapter 9.

Piaget's legacy to developmental psychology has been to offer a massive explanatory structure for understanding the child's cognitive development. It is rich in descriptions and illustrations, rather than in the kind of experimental tests that psychology has come to regard as the norm (one could imagine the tenor of the editor's letter of rejection if a previously undiscovered Piaget manuscript were to be submitted anonymously to any of the major journals). And indeed, many have been the methodological critiques of his work: thus, for example, recalling Piaget's three mountains task, subsequent research has shown that perspective taking is considerably influenced by changing materials and presentation [Liben (1982), reviews such studies]. For example, by using familiar materials, or by making displays more distinctive, or by allowing the child to rotate the display, researchers have been able to demonstrate good perspective-taking ability by even young children. The view has also grown (see Cohen, 1985; Liben, 1982) that children may actually have very good representations of their spatial world, but are unable to cope with the extraneous demands of the tasks used by Piaget. They understand their world, but fail to demonstrate this because they cannot model in a sand tray, or draw anything accurately, or give a recognizable verbal description. They may also be searching the experimenter's gnomic instructions for hidden meaning.

Siegal (1981) has argued that we need to develop new tasks that place less demand upon the child's expressive abilities than did the Piagetian tasks; but Liben (1982) cautions that performance on any task always involves the child in cognitive manipulation, and thus one must be careful when inferring spatial competence from any single task. And indeed, one must reiterate Piaget and Inhelder's (1956) argument that behaviour in space (be it free or constrained by an experimenter) and representation of space are very different.

Egocentricity and its critics

In view of the foregoing discussion about the challenged legacy of Piaget, we must now begin to outline—or indeed seek—the present consensus within developmental psychology. Where, for instance, stands the concept of egocentricity? The critique has been both methodological and conceptual.

Since the early 1970s, there has been such a wealth of experimentation in the field of early spatial cognition that, as Newcombe (1982) argues in her review, it has become a semi-autonomous sub-field of developmental psychology. It has demonstrated the importance of affective and social variables in the child's spatial performance: Acredolo (1982), for example showed that 9-month-old children who were made to feel secure in an environment, showed their ability to make objective rather than egocentric searches for objects. The usual laboratory settings can be moderately stressful for an infant, and this factor amongst others may influence their tendency to make egocentric responses. In other words, the laboratory cannot be assumed to provide a neutral research setting [and this point is also relevant to the rest of developmental psychology: for a highly critical review, see Bronfenbrenner (1979)].

But the main conclusion to be drawn from the research on egocentricity goes beyond this methodological point. As Presson and Somerville (1985) summarize it, we are now seeing a reconceptualization of egocentricity. The prevalent view has been that the infant begins with the egocentric coding system, to be replaced toward the end of infancy by an objective representational system. Presson and Somerville see the accumulating empirical work as supporting an alternative view, which 'emphasizes changes in the nature of children's developing uses of spatial representation, rather than changes in the form of stored representation' (1985, p. 1).

The very term 'egocentricity' has been used with a number of applications (Houssiadas and Brown, 1980). Piaget first applied it to describe 4–7-year-old's *behaviour* and *spatial thought* (rather than *stored spatial information*). He then extended the term's use to the infant's interactions with objects in space: here, 'egocentricity' refers to the logic inherent in the coordination of overt actions.

More recently, the term has been used rather heterogenously: purely descriptively [e.g. Bremner and Bryant (1985) in describing a *response* that maintains a fixed relation to the infant's body], and as a partially explanatory *coding system* (e.g. Butterworth, 1977). It has been seen as the early, inevitable reference system, or as one available coding (e.g. where a task involves relating an object to the self).

The evidence bearing on the current debate about egocentricity has two foci: the localization of objects, and perspective taking. We will briefly summarize some of the main points from what is now an extensive literature.

How the infant locates objects

Whereas adults and older children may base their searches for objects on knowledge of relative positions, or more complex reference systems, infants do not always search at the location where adults would start their search. Thus, the classic Piagetian demonstration is of an infant searching at the location (A) where the object was previously found, even though the infant had observed it being hidden this time at a different point (B). This is referred to in the developmental psychologist's shorthand as the $A\overline{B}$ error of Piaget's Stage IV (1929); and has come to be investigated by a range of techniques—some of which keep the infant stationary, changing object positions, and others of which move the infant.

Acredolo (1978), for example, had the infant initially respond to an event several times on one side—the training period—after which the infant is moved through $180°$ for a test trial. When the infant responds in the same way on the test trials as on the training trials, these responses have been described as egocentric, in that they maintain a fixed relationship to the infant's body. Rieser's (1979) version of the methodology was devised to establish how young infants deal with events that recur at a particular place: his subjects lay beneath a display of four doors, at one of which occurred an interesting event. Rieser then rotated the infant through 90°, and observed their direction of gaze. Six-month-old infants responded egocentrically, save in those conditions where gravitational cues were available, or where landmarks were placed on the correct door and on the one opposite.

Studies based on such paradigms do not enable one unambiguously to separate interpretations based on the egocentric/allocentric coding distinction, and those that interpret the observed behaviour as learned responses—an altogether more conservative interpretation.

If one adopts a procedure that eliminates the training element, then one comes closer to eliminating the learned response interpretation: Acredolo (1979), for instance, hid an object either left or right of the infant, and who was then rotated by 180° before being allowed to search. Testing infants in their own homes convinced Acredolo that they were able to use familiar landmarks from their surroundings; but the same children relied on an egocentric frame of reference in an unfamiliar setting.

Presson and Ihrig (1982) went back to the experimental details of the Acredolo experiments and found that in her experiments, the infant could never be said to be truly without landmarks—the child's mother and the experimenter both in effect provided objective reference points: the only trouble being that they were unreliable references because they moved round the table as the infant was rotated. Thus, the poor infant, deprived of familiar, reliable landmarks, came to give responses that were the same as if he or she had been responding egocentrically! The reader will not be surprised to come across experiments in future that manipulate all possible combinations of cues—infant, object, gravity, mother, experimenter, and the surrounding world. We can, however, leave the story here, having demonstrated that very young infants are capable of using non-egocentric frames of reference, even if on occasions one has to look closely to realize it; and that developmental changes reflect changes in the way spatial information is used by infants. [In parenthesis, we note, with some concern, that as developmental psychology becomes more aware of the importance of the experimental context, it is still capable of a certain cavalier attitude towards its data: for example, in the Presson and Ihrig (1982) study above, 'thirty infants provided scorable data. Five other infants were tested, but not included due to fussiness'! (pp. 700–1).]

Perspective taking experiments as evidence for egocentricity?

Egocentrism has been also described by Piaget and Inhelder (1956) in much older children than we have just been discussing—7-, 8- or 9-year-olds—because they will often tell the experimenter that another will see an array (the three mountains, etc.) from the same perspective as they do. Piaget and Inhelder state that the child does not understand that the terms left and right, before and behind, are relative to the viewing position. Early follow-ups (e.g. Laurendeau and Pinard, 1970) replicated the finding; but more-recent studies show that the task performance depends crucially upon the materials used: the greater the abstraction of materials, the more difficult the task.

Huttenlocher and Presson (1979) claim that the typical experimental task (selecting the appropriate photograph of the array) interposes an extra interpretive task. Success demands 'a large measure of symbolic understanding about what a photograph can convey about the array'. Indeed, adults show patterns of relative difficulty similar to those of children (Presson, 1982). Presson and Somerville (1985) have therefore argued that perspective-taking tasks cannot be used to demonstrate the individual's internal representation or knowledge of space; but rather tap the developing symbolic skills of the child, as applied to the abstraction involved in reading a picture.

Performance of children in experiments on the coordination of perspectives has been shown to be determined by the kinds of stimuli presented; by the complexity of the relations among the presented stimuli; and by the types of response required (Houssiadas and Brown, 1980; Kurdeck, 1978). The accumulated evidence indicates that perspective relations can be handled successfully by much younger children than Piaget suggested—and that, equally, one can devise tasks in which adults respond 'egocentrically'.

Topological to Euclidean space: Piaget's claim examined

As we have seen, Piaget and Inhelder (1956) described young children as possessing only topological concepts of space, that is, concepts that allow the encoding of locations as next to one another, but do not entail a full reference system. Only in later childhood is the individual said to acquire a Euclidean system, metric in nature, and based on a full reference system.

The Piagetian claim has been subjected to empirical and conceptual challenges. Landau, Spelke, and Gleitman (1984) conducted a series of eight experiments to demonstrate spatial knowledge in a 2-year-old congenitally blind child. Once she had travelled along specific paths between landmark objects in a novel layout, she was able to make spatial inferences, by finding new routes between those objects. She could also access her spatial knowledge to perform successfully on a simple map-reading task. Blindfolded control subjects—young children and undergraduates—gave comparable results.

On the basis of these results, Landau et al. challenge Piaget's characterization of spatial knowledge in the pre-school years. They claim that their congenitally blind subject (and indeed, the blindfolded 2- and 3-year-old controls) demonstrated a Euclidean frame of reference:

The use of spatial knowledge depends on a logical inference in which the geometrical properties of the system (i.e. its primitives, axioms and postulates) serve as the major premises, the spatial properties of the familiar paths serve as the minor premises, and the conclusions from these premises are the spatial properties of the new path.

Newcombe (1982) argues that in the experiments by Landau *et al.*, the child's behaviour does not seem to demonstrate a precise knowledge of angular displacement, and suggests that the experiments were procedurally flawed. We shall discuss other evidence on the young child's capacity to follow routes in more detail in a later chapter.

Few other experimenters have claimed full Euclidean knowledge for the very young child, though some have expressed dissent from Piaget's position. One such is Martin (1976a,b), a mathematician, who has delivered himself of a forceful critique of Piaget's own understanding of the concepts of topological and Euclidean space; and has discussed Piaget's data in some detail, before presenting his own, conflicting, results. He concludes that the evidence presented to show that topological representation precedes Euclidean is 'hazy'. Many of the later studies, attempting to confirm Piaget's hypotheses, have used close replications of his methods (e.g. Laurendeau and Pinard, 1970); but when one uses a different range of tests, as Martin (1976b) does, the results do not support the theory that topological concepts develop prior to Euclidean and projective concepts in the child's representational space. When children were asked to match to sample from an array, 4-year-olds actually chose matches which preserved Euclidean properties in preference to those which were topologically equivalent to the sample.

Kato (1984) used a similar matching procedure, in both visual and haptic modalities; and, although the proportion of topological responses decreased with age in haptic matching, it did not in the visual similarity matching condition. In fact, even among the youngest children in the sample, the 4-year-olds, topological choices did not predominate. Kato concludes that by this age children can recognize shapes on the basis of Euclidean features.

Active movement and the development of spatial abilities

Many of the studies reviewed so far have involved a static infant: most spatial problem-solving in real life involves the individual in activity. What is the relation between movement, exploration, and the development of spatial thought? How does early crawling experience, for instance, affect the infant's spatial orientation abilities? One does not need to espouse either an orthodox Piagetian or Gibsonian position to acknowledge the probable centrality of activity to the development of spatial abilities.

In the last section, we saw that the second half of the infant's first year has been identified by some researchers (e.g. Acredolo, 1978) as the period when the transition to allocentric coding begins to take place. Acredolo links this with the beginnings of locomotor independence. McComas and Field (1984) provided an empirical test of this link: they hypothesized that early experiences following the onset of self-mobility would lead to a greater tendency for infants to respond objectively rather than egocentrically on the standard Acredolo spatial orientation task. But they found that there was no significant difference in performance between their inexperienced (two weeks' crawling experience) and their experienced (eight weeks' crawling) groups; and therefore the experimenters urged caution in accepting claims for the importance of mobility in spatial concept development.

However, Berthenthal, Campos, and Barret (1984) tested the same hypothesis with a very similar test procedure and found significant effects of locomotor experience upon the rate of allocentric responding in the Acredolo task. Short of explaining the differences away by reference to cross-cultural differences between New Zealand and American babies, or, as McComas and Field hint of the Berthenthal et al. methodology, to certain procedural irregularities, we must rest the case as non-proven, and ask what mechanism would link mobility to a changed reference system for spatial locations.

Acredolo, Adams, and Goodwyn (1984) suggest that movement leads to enhanced attention to changes in visual perspective, as the infant tracked its target. But, as McComas and Field (1984) point out, the pre-locomotory infant already has considerable experience in coordination of the experiences that result from head, hand, and body movement. Indeed, in the first weeks of crawling, the very act of engaging in this novel form of movement may demand such concentration that attention is actually diverted away from the surrounding world for a while. Once locomotion is more competently achieved, the infant is more likely to begin to notice a growing number of anomalies (Bremner, 1978); and the egocentric strategy—only partially adequate during the latter phase of relative immobility—has to be replaced by the allocentric.

Recent discussions of the relationship between movement and spatial abilities (e.g. Bremner and Bryant, 1985) have begun to examine the relationship in greater detail than hitherto was generally the case: earlier experiments in which the infant was passively moved by the experimenter in mid-session have received critical scrutiny, as have statements about a crucial change occurring as crawling starts.

Consider once again the pre-crawling infant. As Bremner and Bryant remind us, once the infant is able to sit up, unaided, the control of head movements precedes control over trunk rotation: hence, 'we may need to distinguish between position relative to the body, position relative to the head, and position in the external world'. During the period when the infant has little trunk rotation, the relation between body and world remains relatively fixed, and the body-centred system is confounded with any stable external system of reference, whilst the head-related system is dissociated from both as head movement takes place.

Hence, active head movements—say from about 6 months old when stable sitting is achieved—will enable the infant to deal with changes in the relation between environmental positions and the head in a sophisticated manner; but, because manual responses are coordinated with the body system, dissociation of place and response will come only when the infant had full control over body movement.

And, in turn, consider that the act of crawling: it is likely to give practice in the kind of transformations of the world that are associated with forward movement rather than those associated with left–right linear displacement.

Developmental psychology, in its greater awareness of the need for ecological validity of its studies has come to realize that in everyday life, the infant's own self-induced changes of viewpoint are of much more consequence to the development of spatial cognition than are their reflections upon the disappearance and reappearance of objects, which has for so long been the typical test situation.

Motion continues to be of importance in the development of spatial understanding when full competence in mobility has been achieved, as we shall see when we consider, in the next chapter, the child's development of a cognitive map of the everyday spaces that surround him or her—from familiar rooms and buildings to street, neighbourhood, and city. There have been many experiments at this level that have examined the role of activity through the environment for the construction of these broader spatial representations (see a summary by Cohen, 1982).

Indirect evidence for the importance of activity in developing spatial representations comes from the demonstration of the relationship between activity range and environmental knowledge (e.g. Hart, 1979); and of that between mode of travel and type of knowledge (e.g. Maurer and Baxter, 1972). More-direct studies include Heth and Cornell's (1980) comparison of way-finding in a maze by newly-walking 1-year-olds, and 3-year-olds (though as yet we lack published experiments that compare infants who walk and those of the same age who do not, in such an orientation task). In one of a series of experiments, Cohen and Cohen (1982) compared children walking through an environment with and without interaction with landmark objects, and found that the children developed a more accurate map when their activity was given a theme that functionally links landmarks.

In summary, children—like adults—gain much of their environmental information from their interaction with their surroundings; and the nature of the setting, how the environment is encountered, the goals and purposefulness of the activity, and the social and emotional importance of events encountered, have all been demonstrated to affect the uptake of information, as we shall see in the next chapter.

Figure 4.1 Underestimated competence? As soon as mobility permits, the infant explores novel spaces with avidity—provided a secure base (the parent) is available—and a huge amount of environmental learning occurs through such exploration, although the value of earlier passive experience may be less easy to assess.

On searching for objects in space

Developmental psychologists have been tracking infants tracking objects in space since well before there was a (formally-designated) developmental psychology: for such behaviour gives us information on a wide range of topics: including object preferences (e.g. Darwin, 1877; Valentine, 1914); attention and habituation (e.g. Cohen, 1973); mnemonic strategies (e.g. DeLoache and Brown, 1983); concepts of object permanence (e.g. Piaget, 1929); and problem-solving strategies and general planning (e.g. Wellman, Fabricius, and Sophian, 1985). Reading through this literature in historical sequence, one is struck by the ever-increasing tendency within research on early cognitive development to recognize the positive competencies of the young child, and not just cognitive deficits that contrast with later capacities (see Sophian, 1985).

One such area of competency is the spatial awareness that is revealed in the object searching of even quite young infants. Piaget is responsible, as we have seen above, for focusing research attention upon the errors in the infant's searching (and in particular upon the perseveration that characterizes the $A\overline{B}$ error at his Stage IV). Let us (with Horobin and Acredolo, 1986) instead stress the factors that might underlie the individual's eventual success in locating objects.

Infants can, from birth, *track* objects visually; and Acredolo (1983) suggested that such visual tracking of spatial locations may also be a useful strategy during the transition from egocentric to allocentric coding. Her studies indicate a relationship between tracking and improved spatial search; and (in Horobin and Acredolo, 1986) between increasing visual attentiveness (the infant 'keeping an eye' on an object as it is hidden) and improved manual search. (Visual attentiveness is, in its turn, related to the distinctiveness of the objects sought.) Keeping an eye upon the object as one moves through space oneself has become a main strategy since the beginning of the crawling period. Working with 7–10-month-old infants, Horobin and Acredolo observed a behaviour 'amazingly reminiscent of the "pointing behaviour" in dogs: quite often the body, as well as the eyes, was oriented toward the hiding site in a very steadfast fashion'. Indeed, on pilot trials, when the experimenters tried to distract the infant by clapping and calling, they were often unable to draw its attention away from a hiding place. Such attentiveness is much more characteristic of those infants in the sample who had longest experience of sitting unaided and of crawling: indicating support for the hypothesis that developments in spatial representation are related to motor development milestones (see further discussion of this point in both the preceding and following sections).

Keeping an eye on a moving (and to-be-hidden) object provides a strategy that comes to replace the perseverative strategy (look where the object was last found) characteristic of the earliest months; but may well not completely replace it, as Sophian and Sage's (1985) comparison of 9- and 16-month-olds' strategies indicate. (Indeed, as adults, do we not occasionally catch ourselves acting like the perseverating infant, when we are frustrated in our search round the house for a missing object? Logic gives way to superstitious behaviour!) In the Sophian and Sage studies, infants *did* show significantly more errors to the previous hiding place than to a control location (in other words, a clear indication of perseveration); and yet they also showed significant selectivity when choosing between prior and current location information. This latter, as the researchers point out, does not accord with the Piagetian explanation for perseverative errors—that infants cannot differentiate the object from their own actions. Rather, it would seem that the infants' errors are occasioned by lapses of memory or attention—or the incomplete development of such a strategy—rather than 'profound misunderstandings about the nature of objects and space'.

Spatial monitoring—updating one's representation of the positions of objects that have moved, and maintaining the stable representation of non-moving objects—draws upon perception, memory, and logical inference (Sophian, 1986). This last becomes particularly important when direct perceptual monitoring is not possible—where an object's position after movement has to be inferred because that movement has been occluded, or because the object is within a container. (Many of the Piagetian tests involved such invisible displacement of the object inside a container.) Improvements in the performance of, say, $2\frac{1}{2}$-year-olds compared with 5-year-olds, solving these Piaget transposition tasks, can be demonstrated to result from improvements in attentional strategies that enable them to monitor more than one object at a time; and allocating attention to key features of the situation.

The *reasons* for attending to particular features also affects the way the child monitors space: for example, Gauvain and Rogoff (1986) gave one half of their 6–9-year-olds an instruction to study the layout of rooms as they explored a new play-house; and the other half the instruction to attend to the route travelled. The resultant differences in the information about the play-house were clearly related to the instructional set.

In searching for an object, the child (as indeed an adult) may well ease the burden upon memory by using a mnemonic strategy. There exists a large body of literature on the use of such strategies among school-aged children and adults (see the review by Brown, Bransford, Ferrara, and Campione, 1983); but it is only recently that we have had studies demonstrating the precursors of mnemonic regulation of searching in the very young child (DeLoache, Cassidy, and Brown, 1985). When, for example, the child's (highly motivating) task is to remember and then—after a delay—find an attractive toy, observers have noted the child engaging in a range of potentially mnemonic behaviours. Some have been as simple as the 'pointing', or 'keeping an eye on the object' we have already noted; some strategies have been more symbolic: one 4-year-old child 'looked at the baited cup, and nodded her head yes, looked at the unbaited cups and shook her head no, then looked at the correct cup nodding affirmatively' (Wellman, Rutter, and Flavell, 1975).

Children as young as 20 months have been shown to engage in rudimentary versions of these strategies: De Loache, Cassidy, and Brown (1985) report some children verbalizing about the toy and its hiding place, others looking fixedly at the hiding place, or pointing, or approaching and hovering. When young children are more uncertain about the task (for example, when it takes place in an unfamiliar laboratory rather than at home), the incidence of these strategies markedly increases. There is no claim that children of this age are *consciously* adopting these strategies with the aim of better performance, but these strategies are, none the less, demonstrably successful in increasing the child's ability to find objects.

When children learn spatial information then, as Rogoff and Waddell (1982) have shown, they also develop skills in making strategic use of the *contextual organization* of the array of locations. The role of context has, until recently, been under-emphasized in research on memory development (Rogoff, 1982), but the power of a spatial schema as an organizing framework for memory, instead of the individual simply learning a serial list, has been acknowledged as an effective mnemonic strategy since the time of the Greek Theatre of Memory (Yates, 1966). If the objects to be remembered already have a spatial arrangement one with the other (and do not artificially have to be associated with mnemonic locations, as in the Greek method), then the method should considerably improve performance. Rogoff has argued, however, that pre-schooler children use contextual organization to facilitate remembering a layout in a tacit and unreflective way; and only later in the early school years do they come to use contextual organization deliberately, and to select tasks for which this strategy is appropriate.

Where the task of spatial searching for missing or hidden objects becomes more complex, the individual has in turn to employ more complex strategies: whether to search at random, or systematically retrace one's earlier actions (say if one has dropped an object whilst tracking through an area), or search previously successful locations (say if one is searching for a missing pet animal). Solution of search problems involves one applying to one's spatial knowledge (and perhaps knowledge of target behaviour) a particular searching strategy or combination of strategies. Wellman, Somerville, and Haake (1979) showed that children as young as 2 years of age were capable of sustained logical searches (where the physical demands of the task were not great, and distractors were few); and performance improved with age.

Both type of task and age of child will determine whether the individual adopts a *spatial-associative search strategy*—based on knowledge of locations strongly associated with the object or event; a *general search strategy*—a procedure for exhaustively covering the space, and monitoring which locations have been checked and which are still to check; or a *logical search strategy*— procedures that select from a potential general search just those locations that suit the immediate task. The first and last strategies might sound similar on first description—both involving subsets of the whole—but the associative search requires little more than a listing of places associated with the object, together with their relative or absolute positions and the rudiments of a travel plan. The logical search requires much more specific memory of events, order and sequences, and the ability to use logical inferences to prioritize the search, and to eliminate some possible locations.

The increasing use, with age, of the more efficient logical search procedures can be related to increases in the child's abilities in both memory and logical deduction (Wellman, Somerville, and Haake, 1979); but, it should again be stressed, later-developing strategies do not supersede earlier ones; nor are younger children entirely dependent on the less sophisticated strategies. Indeed, recent studies have used hiding-and-spatial-searching tasks to demonstrate impressive sensitivity to temporal order information in children of 3 years and younger, and to show that infants in their second year can use knowledge of the rules governing the sequence of events to make inferences about a particular unseen event or location (Somerville and Haake, 1985).

With increasing age, too, comes a greater development of complex heuristics which have regard to the effort/payoff relationship involved in searching. When, for example, Cornell and Heth's (1986) 6- and 8-year-olds had to hide and search for marbles scattered somewhere between many possible locations, these children's strategies were reminiscent of the foraging strategies reported among bird and animal species where there was a premium upon optimizing search (Kamil and Sargent, 1981). Cornell and Heth report behaviours indicating that the children were sensitive to the spatial distribution of likely hiding places, and adopted strategies that both maximized the chance of finding objects *and* minimized the search effort.

These 6-, 7- and 8-year-olds are showing the fruition of a planning process for searching that, as we have seen, has its origins much earlier: studies of children in their second and third years has been strongly suggestive of early planning abilities—and serve to emphasize the emerging picture of the young infant as 'an especially logical, deliberate, intelligent searcher' (Wellman *et al.*, 1985, p. 147); a conclusion about early competence that has implications well beyond the field of object location.

Keeping track of one's own position in space

In Part I, we reviewed work with adults—as highly skilled navigators through space—that bore upon the question of how the individual continually updates his or her position in space during travel. We must now turn to see the beginnings of this skill in young children; and to see how it links with various other themes already developed—on emerging reference systems, on the coordination of perspectives, on movement through space as a factor in spatial learning, and on the location of objects in space and searching skills.

By the time the young child has enough self-mobility to make keeping track of his or her position in space an important issue, he or she will, as we have seen, already have gained a foundation of expectations about the relative locations of objects, and their collective relation to self. Active movement through a small space accessible from a single viewpoint with continuous information from the environment can utilize a strategy of keeping continuously oriented to a number of significant objects in space. Where the setting is not accessible from a single viewpoint then the task of keeping track of one's position becomes more complex. Pick and Lockman (1981) suggest that the child *could* do it by updating an egocentric response after movement, but only with considerable computation where the movement through space was complex. Alternatively, and apparently more efficiently, the child could develop and operate upon an allocentric representation—with current position related to the whole. Hazen, Lockman and Pick (1978) walked 3- and 6-year-old children through an interconnecting suite of rooms; and showed that, whilst the younger children were as competent as the older in being able to reverse their routes, they appeared unable to infer where they were on the route relative to parts of the route 'through the wall'. Pick and Lockman (1981) interpreted this as showing that, by the age of three, children can update egocentric responses, but do not yet possess a general allocentric reference system within which their own position can be continuously updated.

Rieser and Heiman (1982) have examined spatial orientation in still younger ambulatory children; and, in particular, the emergence of this self-reference system to solve spatial problems. Acredolo (1978) had already shown that qualitative changes occur in the use of the body for spatial orientation during the second year of life (her procedure in this experiment left no landmarks for the infant to search by). Thus, Rieser and Heiman selected 18-month-olds as the age-group for their two experiments. The first was designed to examine the young child's ability to remain spatially oriented by keeping track of the direction and distance of his or her movements past a target location—one of eight identical windows in an otherwise featureless round enclosure. The children did not search with precision, yet it was clear that they related their movement back to the target by their previous movement away from it. In the second experiment, the procedure within the test chamber was altered, to test the child's ability to choose the most efficient route (not necessarily by reversing the initial movement away from the target). The 18-month-olds—and some 14 month old children—could perform such spatial tasks.

To summarize: during the first year of life, infants do not show an ability to relate their own movements to knowledge of spatial layout and their own position within it. During the second year, young children begin to relate their own movements to their knowledge of target locations. Initially, their search is imprecise—probably as a result of imprecise self-monitoring of movement, and of a general distractability. Strategies for self (and object) location improve with age—older children tested in the Rieser and Heiman task turn much more precisely, for instance. By 3 years of age, route reversibility is easily achieved; and the child is—as we shall see in the next chapter—beginning to develop a more complex cognitive mapping of a whole area.

Can different modality effects be demonstrated in spatial understanding and memory in children?

In Part III Three, we discuss the especial problems faced by the blind in learning and handling spatial tasks, and consider the ways in which education and enriched experience can ameliorate their situation. Within the context of the present chapter, studies of spatial cognition by the blind child will be considered briefly in as much as these studies may indicate the modality-specific nature of spatial learning.

As we have already indicated the Piagetian position is that the individual develops spatial concepts and memories by abstracting from his or her actual actions in space: visual imagery being largely irrelevant. Against this, cognitive psychologists have argued that spatial memory may either depend upon verbal strategies, or upon visual imagery: Huttenlocher and Presson (1979) for example have argued that individuals (children and adults alike) visually image spatial layouts, and mentally track positions on such an image.

Millar (1985) conducted a study with three age-groups of blind and sighted children, in order to test hypotheses arising from these three views on the importance of imagery in memory for spatial position. She argued that the hypotheses that spatial inputs are coded *verbally* would not predict differences between blind and sighted children; but that one should expect verbal strategies to become more efficient with age. If visual representations were important in facilitating spatial recall by sighted children, then one would predict differences in recall strategy between blind and sighted children. A significant interaction between sighted status and recall type was indeed found by Millar, indicating that the blind children relied upon haptic (or tactile) memory, which decays with time or is interfered with by subsequent movements, in other words they did not rely upon verbal coding and rehearsal. The sighted children used visual representations which facilitated performance on the experimental tasks requiring backward recall. Millar's findings indicated that the modality of representation affects efficiency and processing in spatial recall; and that visual imagery has a special role in sighted children's spatial recall. Older children were, as expected, more efficient in recall, but age differences did not relate to sighted status.

Amount of vision and performance on spatial tasks have been found to be closely related (Birns, 1986); but the blind are equal to or better than the sighted on simple tactile discrimination tasks. It seems that the problem lies in the transition from these early stages of spatial cognition to later, more complex ones. Rieser, Guth, and Hill (1982) have demonstrated that perceptual capacity emerges in blind toddlers, but then fails to mature and subsequently deteriorates in later childhood due to lack of visual input. Simpkins and Siegal (1979), for example, have shown that, whereas blind and sighted children have similar performances in topological space, the blind have more difficulty in translating to projective space.

Research on the importance of age at onset of blindness as a factor in the child's spatial skill development is, at the moment, somewhat equivocal on how long a period of useful sight is necessary for normal development, although there is agreement that having had vision is generally helpful to the acquisition of spatial concepts. The mediating factor may be visual imagery, although Jurmaa (1973) has found that this benefit may decay if the onset of blindness is before the child is 6 years of age. However, in a recent study which paid careful attention to the child's past history of sight, Birns (1986) found that age at onset of blindness was not a predictive factor in the child's mastery of spatial concepts because congenitally and adventiously blind subjects showed the same range of performance on Piagetian tests of projective space. It has been confidently stated by some developmental psychologists (e.g. Bower, 1977) that congenital blindness in itself puts a ceiling on the acquisition of spatial concepts: the Birns study, among others, indicates that such children *can* achieve mastery of projective space. Equally, the Birns study shows that among both congenitally and adventiously blind children, there are many who *fail* to make this transition to projective space.

To summarize: at the moment, we have not sufficiently unequivocal evidence on the factors central to the development of spatial concepts in the blind to allow us to draw firm conclusions about, for instance, the role of visual imagery in guiding spatial performance in individuals whether blind or sighted. However, the field has advanced considerably since the days when, typically, the experimenter would try to equate the performance of blind children and of sighted children under blindfolds: clearly the first group would have operated using long-developed personal strategies, whereas the second would be in the process of rapidly developing novel strategies to cope with their newly imposed sensory restriction. More-sensitive studies with both blind and sighted children are now provoking thoughts about the basic processes involved in spatial concepts and, particularly, their role in mobility through space, as described in Chapter 11.

Children's use of spatial relationship terms as an indicator of the development of spatial concepts.

Research with young blind children has often suggested that they may be delayed in the correct use and application of spatial terms such as 'right' and 'left' [the Birns (1986), study referred to above is but the latest in a line of such studies]; and we can link this with the general approach to children's understanding of spatial concepts via the study of their use of spatial relationship terms exemplified by Clark (1973), who has claimed that a child's acquisition of spatial terms will directly reflect his or her understanding of perceived space. Thus, perceptual difficulty; will map directly on to linguistic difficulty; and, following on his own classification of spatial dimensions by degree of difficulty, Clark predicts that terms relating to the vertical dimension should appear first, followed by front–back terms, and then left–right terms. Cox and Richardson (1985) have provided a direct test of the Clark hypotheses, with children from 3 to 10 years and a group of adults. Subjects had to communicate to another person of the same age the position of an object within an array—a three-dimensional plastic grid, within which the reference object was a coloured ball placed in the central position. A trial consisted of the experimenter placing the target ball in one of the other holes in the grid and the subject attempting to describe the relationship between the balls so that the friend behind the screen could correctly position the ball on his or her grid.

More correct spatial terms were used for the vertical dimension than for the two other dimensions from age three: although there was a change in the terms used for the vertical dimension. 'At the top', 'up', 'at the bottom', 'down', and 'under' are the terms used most frequently by children; few children used the terms 'above' and 'below' which predominated among the adults.

There is, contrary to Clark's hypotheses, a cross-over on the other two dimensions: 3–6-year-olds showed better performance on the horizontal-frontal dimension ('front', 'back' predominating) than they did on the horizontal-lateral dimension ('left', 'right'); whereas from 7 years of age appropriate terms for the horizontal-lateral dimension increased, and those for the horizontal-frontal dimension became more varied. The youngest children used non-specific terms ('here', 'there'), especially in the two horizontal dimensions; general environmental cues ('towards the window', 'towards the ceiling') were most frequently found among 5- and 6-year-olds; and after that age spatial cues predominated.

Cox and Richardson (1985) attribute the dramatic increase in the correct use of 'left' and 'right' at age seven to concerted educational pressure to use these labels exerted at about this time (although they in fact offer no evidence that such pressure actually peaks at this age, or that the concepts are gained then as a result of explicit teaching).

Such experiments—whilst providing valuable data chronicling the emergence and use of the various spatial terms as the child develops—do not in the end really address Clark's central contention: that usage directly reflects compre-hension. They are more concerned with the communicative act that is central to the experiment. Waller (1986) has shown that , during this period, the child comes to develop listener-specific skills in the use of spatial terms. Earlier stud-ies (e.g. Shatz and Gelman, 1973) had already shown 4-year-olds to be capable of shifting to a simplified style of speech when addressing 2-year-olds. Weller's experiments demonstrate that it is not until 7 years of age that children are able to gauge the effect of terms 'left' and 'right' upon a specific listener. Similarly, when children were asked to describe routes around the school, 5-years-olds tend to adjust their speech by the heuristic-based method of responding purely to their listener's age, but by the age of eight, they are more likely to use the more analytic method of responding to the listener's known or presumed ability.

Children also bring to their use of relational terms expectations derived from their everyday experience: thus, for example, Keil and Carroll (1980) found that 5-7-year-olds made fewer errors in using the word 'tall' when it was applied to objects that are often described as tall (mountains, for example), than to objects not usually described as tall (in their experiment, objects such as blankets). Relational and dimensional terms may thus be used differently with different objects in a systematic and sophisticated way. Confirmatory evidence for this also comes from Smith, Cooney, and McCord's (1986) study of 3-5-year-olds' use of 'high' and 'low'. They too found that the categorical use of relational terms involves 'a rich and intricate knowledge system', and that it takes children a considerable time to acquire and organize the relevant information about the world. (To add further complexity, both poles of a dimension may not be used by the child from the same date: thus Smith et al. found that children's understanding of 'low' lagged behind their understanding of 'high').

The relationship between spatial cognition and the development of other cognitive skills

We concentrate in this book on spatial competence and its development during childhood; but clearly this development is in parallel with—and probably in interaction with—a whole range of other cognitive skills and understanding as they develop through childhood. Few of the studies listed in the book put spatial cognition into its boarder context, by considering the other competencies manifested by the children under study, and how they may interelate with spatial skills.

One exception is a review by Harris (1985), who brings together two areas which might initially seem very disparate: the development of search during infancy, and the infant's perception of number. He argues that knowledge of how to search for an object, and the ability to perceive number, have a reciprocal influence upon one another. Searching may often involve noting and recalling how many objects are missing. Equally, the concept of number—of there being several possible instances of the same category of object—centrally involves the concept of object displacement: distinguishing between the same object encountered in two different places, and encountering two similar but distinct objects in two different locations.

Two objects side by side pose little problem of assessment by the infant: the problem arises when the encounters are successive—how then to tell how many objects exist? Would the safest strategy be to assume that each encounter is with a separate object unless plausible connecting movements can be put forward?

We have discussed earlier in the book how the youngest infants are poor at predicting future positions of a moving object; but that, by about 6 months, infants begin to use local landmarks for such predictions (e.g. Acredolo, 1978). A year later, the young child is showing evidence of a grasp of the mutually exclusive nature of earlier and later positions. Inaccurate performance at 18 months Harris suggests, is attributable to the infant's not being sure how many objects he or she is dealing with—for, by this stage, the infant has both an expectation of lawful relationships, and the use of number skills. Although very young infants are capable of discriminating between arrays containing one, two, or three items, the concepts of subtraction and addition—which are essentially transformations of an array by the displacement or replacement of an item—only become available to the child at the period when he or she is able to work with the displacement of objects in space.

Finally, as Harris observes, confidence about number is of itself likely to add an extra insistence to searching: knowledge of the number of objects hidden will be checked against a tally of those recovered, and used to determine whether the search need continue.

These examples from one domain indicate that we can expect to find an interrelationship between spatial cognition and cognition in general; and that, as West, Morris, and Nichol's (1985) review shows, spatial knowledge can affect performance on a broad spectrum of cognitive tasks; which, in turn, may have implications for later academic performance.

Spatial cognition and imagery—including the use of imagery in thought and problem solving—should be considered together: Kosslyn (1973) has been a major advocate of the spatial properties of imagery. He has presented considerable experimental evidence to suggest that mental images containing spatial content preserve relative metric distances between places, objects, or features. Scanning time, when subjects were asked to summon up and then examine images, was found to be linearly related to 'distances' within the image.

Imagery has been shown to facilitate the learning of both verbal and pictorial material; to play a major role in the recall process; and to have a role in solving problems by inference [for a large range of supportive studies, see the review by West, Morris, and Nichol (1985)]. Adults and children tend to recall spatial locations of objects even when this is irrelevant to the task: indeed, it is often easier than remembering details of the objects themselves (Hazen and

Volk-Hudson, 1984). In fact, Hasher and Zacks (1978) have concluded that spatial information is encoded automatically, and is present at a very young age, although it may not be until middle childhood that spatial context is used as a conscious mnemonic.

In their review, West, Morris, and Nichol (1985) argue that, although there is an extensive literature on the relationships between spatial ability, mental imagery, and *higher level* mathematical and scientific skills (e.g. Bishop, 1980), the contribution of spatial cognition to the child's acquisition of basic academic skills has not received sufficient attention. The kind of relationship they suggest is that between spatial sequencing and successful reading, and spatial order deficits and problems with reading.

To a certain extent, one must still speculate about the interrelationship between spatial skills and cognitive processing: the role of imagery and schemas in learning, memory, and recall is still in active debate; but, to the extent that such imagery is involved, it is likely to be spatially organized, and to rely upon the individual's knowledge of spatial relationships in the world it represents.

It can also be argued that young children may be disadvantaged, both in education and in testing, when their spatial skills are not employed in a task: we know that, for example, spatially organized imagery may be more accessible to young children than abstract propositional representations (Kosslyn, 1975). We should then, both in our research with young children and in their teaching, make more use of graphic presentation of material, and use concrete as well as abstract examples. Other techniques recommended by West, Morris, and Nichol (1985) include:

> Presentation techniques in which all items are arrayed before the child simultaneously; encouragement and training to use visual imagery; emphasis on the strategic use of spatial cues and spatial organization strategies; tests in which stimuli are embedded in real world scenes.   (p. 33)

Will training in one area—say spatial skills—have any effect upon another, such as mathematical preformance? Later chapters consider the implications of the whole range of research reviewed here for environmental education, including children's use of spatial information sources such as maps: we close this chapter by speculating, with West, Morris, and Nichol, that the study of the way spatial cognition develops may relate to many other, as yet untested, cognitive skills.

CHAPTER 5

The child in geographical space

We have seen in earlier chapters how a general consensus is emerging within environmental psychology on the nature of the skills of orientation and navigation; and the reader will not be surprised to learn that developmental psychology has also been concerned with the emergence of these skills, as well as offering a major contribution to reseach on close-body space, as we saw in the last chapter. Yet there has been little cross-referencing between the adult and the child work—each publishing in its own journals, and thereby missing opportunities for cross-influence.

In discussing adult, skilled use of geographical space, we have discussed the rapid microgenesis of cognitive maps when newcomers learn a novel area; here, we have to consider the slower ontogenesis of cognitive mapping skills, and to see whether these grow out of the immediate space skills whose development has been considered in the last chapter. In earlier chapters, we have discussed basic processes of uptake of special information: here, we ask how early these skills are evidenced, and what are their precursors (is there a spatial equivalent of pre-language?)

We will therefore describe the range of theoretical positions adopted in developmental studies, and contrast these with those described in environmental psychology—we will then consider the emerging links with computational and with comparative approaches before moving to specific aspects: route learning; the use of landmarks; and the role of spatial inferences in developing survey knowledge.

The development of the field

Throughout the early history of developmental psychology, there have been isolated studies on the spatial knowledge of children, often atheoretical. Working in America, Lord (1941), for example, cited few previous studies, and was not aware of Piaget's work (at that time, largely only available in French). She was much concerned to test children's ability to point to the cardinal points, to point in the direction of distant and nearby cities, and to local environmental features; and to maintain orientation during travel. This last was perhaps the most ambitious (and saddest) of the Lord experiments: children were driven on two mile trips round Ann Arbor at 20 miles per hour, with elaborate means of recording their route-learning performance at the ready. Unfortunately, '50 per cent of the subjects were lost so far as fixed directions were concerned before they ever reached the first stop.' (Lord, 1941, p. 500).

In one of the earliest post-Piagetian discussions to bring everyday spatial cognition before an audience of developmental psychologists, Pick (1972) saw the 'voyage of discovery' just starting. He listed many of the topics that have become central to the field: how children think about familiar and novel spaces, how children orient themselves in space, how they remember where events happen in space, and how they structure and represent space.

Pick, in this position piece, clearly felt that the Piagetian concept of perceptual spaces—sensorimotor space, postural space, and visual space—would provide a useful basis, *if extended*, for the consideration of the child's understanding of the geographical scale environment. One would, however, have to take more direct account of how children learn different scale parcels of space via a variety of means of access: Pick talked of automotive, locomotive, and aviomotive spaces, arguing that our theory-building should follow the actual experiences of the child—especially as increasing maturity is associated with wider geographical experience.

Pick's own experiments at the time were simple but pioneering; for example, questioning young children in their own homes about what they might see through walls were they transparent, or identifying from the outside of the house which window belonged to which room.

Moore (1986) has recently recalled how limited the studies of children's environmental awareness had been 20 years ago: reviewing the child development literature as a young designer hoping to find useful research, he had found the search 'almost fruitless':

> Most of the research did not reach beyond five-year-olds; nearly all came from work conducted with special problem groups under isolated conditions, in laboratories, clinics or psychologists' offices. Hardly any related to ordinary children in settings of everyday life.   (Moore, 1986, p. xii)

We shall see, in Chapter 11 on children's needs, how Moore himself has helped to correct the balance.

Pick dissociates his 'frame of reference' approach to cognitive maps from a possible S–R strategy for linking landmarks and appropriate actions; and his approach has prevailed. [Pick himself had been raised in the behaviourist tradition, and indeed he harks back to Maier's (1936) study on reasoning in children—which compares young children's maze running unfavourably with those of adult rats].

Whereas we have, for convenience, treated the child operating in geographical-scale space in a separate chapter from more localized space, Pick's early article lays stress on considering all scales of space together. Thus, he finds evidence for some kind of 'cognitive map' in the earliest weeks by examining studies on how the infant is able to get its thumb into its mouth (originally almost random contacts, to the point where the infant is able to get thumb to mouth from any point in space). He moves on to studies with other children on cognitive maps of familiar rooms, and on the learning of novel environments via a map, admitting that these scattered studies had not, as yet, enabled him to do more than hypothesize that one developmental trend in the use of frames of reference goes from object-relevant to more abstract, and another goes from molecular to molar.

Seven years later (Pick, Yonas, and Rieser, 1976), there was much more evidence to cite on the role of spatial reference systems in perceptual development. ['Frame of reference ... is not a tight explanatory concept ... it is defined here as a locus or set of loci with respect to which spatial position is defined' (Pick et al., 1976, pp. 115–116]. By 1979, Acredolo's work had begun to chart the importance of landmarks in encoding spatial relations; Braine's studies had indicated how the up–down orientation of objects was determined (e.g. Braine, 1979); and Pick et al. were able to review numerous papers on frames of reference for left–right discrimination. By 1979 there was, however, only a limited research literature to call upon when considering what reference systems children might use to orient themselves when moving about their environment. Lockman, Hazen, and Pick had, in 1976, shown how 6-year-olds could make much more competent spatial inferences than could 3-year-olds, about the layout of a suite of rooms through which they had been led, and could better represent this configurational knowledge in building a model of this suite. Pick et al. (1976) suggest in their review that older children seem to orient themselves in the environment to increasingly remote geographical frames of reference, although they do not cite any published studies to support the observation. One curious omission from the Pick et al. review is reference to what many have subsequently seen as a seminal paper: Siegal and White (1975).

These theorists proposed a developmental model somewhat in contrast with the post-Piagetian analyses then current. In the Siegal and White model, the first stage in the acquisition of spatial knowledge involves landmark information; with, next, recognizable paths or routes being established between landmarks. Initially, spatial knowledge of the routes is topological; later, it acquires metric (though not necessarily *accurate*) properties.

Clustering of these landmark-and-paths sets follows: initially, there is a higher level of coordination within each set, but only looser, topological relations between these places.

Finally, an overall coordinated frame of reference develops, linking all the clusters: this survey knowledge has the kind of Euclidean properties previously only found within clusters.

Siegal and White's model of spatial representations is thus not only developmental but hierarchical: the local environmental descriptions (places and paths); route instructions between places; all within a configurational knowledge of the whole area.

In 1980, the American Social Science Research Council sponsored a conference at the University of Minnesota to encourage the investigation of basic cognitive processes as they operate in natural settings: spatial orientation's time had arrived. The conference, and the resultant book (Pick and Acredolo, 1983), brought together geographers, psychologists, linguists, and computer scientists, and indicated an increased concern for theory of spatial orientation, although it still seemed to us at the time (Spencer and Darvizeh, 1981) that many theorists were underestimating the abilities of young children, often for the kinds of methodological reasons discussed below. Valsiner (1987) still believes that there is a considerable way to go: 'Contemporary developmental psychology is largely atheoretical in its mainstream', and, he suggests, higher priority is set upon the collection and analysis of empirical data than upon its integration into coherent theory. Although the discipline has acknowledged the need for explicit study of children within their natural settings (e.g. Bronfenbrenner, 1979), we still have need to develop adequate ways of systematically conceptualizing child–environment interdependence, ways that will change psychology away from its traditional individualistic emphasis.

The next section of this chapter reviews the current position, to assess whether Valsiner's strictures apply; and shows how developmental psychology is now consciously reaching out to other, related, disciplines in order to examine the questions that theory should address.

Current theoretical positions, and the linking of developmental psychology with computational and comparative approaches

Directly facing the issue of theory development are several major research groups; and, interestingly, the interdisciplinary nature of the 'environmental psychology' enterprise has been brought to bear upon developmental issues by one of these groups.

Golledge—a geographer with strong interests in AI research—has published with educationalists and psychologists a conceptual model of way-finding (Golledge et al., 1985). They explicitly link their work to cognitive psychology's research on the representation of knowledge structures, which are assumed to be the basis for interpreting objects, actions, and events. (See our earlier discussion in Chapter 2). However, 'most of the knowledge domains which have been investigated using computational process models involve well-defined and abstract systems having minimal correspondence to an external physical reality'. In contrast, 'spatial cognition ... has become an increasingly important area of study since it represents a major type of human knowledge with considerable practical significance' (p. 126).

They lay down four prerequisites for a computational model of the development of spatial cognition, prerequisites that derive from major issues in the empirical literature on spatial cognition and its development.

1   Concerning knowledge acquisition: both environmental learning theories and developmental theories assume that knowledge of the environment is a function of accumulated and organized perceptual experiences representing interactions between the organism and the environment. Thus, from a series of episodes, a more generalized and context-independent knowledge structure emerges that is capable of sustaining a wide range of spatial behaviours.

2   Landmark, route and configurational knowledge represent a mixture of declarative and procedural structures. Declarative representations permit efficient and organized storage, and allows the individual to derive relationships between places, whose relationship had not been explicitly realized before. The individual's knowledge of particular routes which implies specifying goals, recognizing landmarks, and performing appropriate actions at choice points, is best described as procedural.

3   A model of learning by experience must have the ability to reproduce the 'flaws' that one finds in individuals' knowledge structures (what Golledge graphically describes as the 'holes, folds, tears and cracks' in portions of the cognitive map).

4   Behavioural errors follow in real life from inaccuracies in the spatial representation.

The Golledge *et al.* model explicitly addresses all four issues. First, it incorporates episodic knowledge, stored in long-term memory (LTM), as the basis of most route-finding knowledge. Second, route knowledge is represented as procedural in form (as links between episodes in LTM); and other aspects of knowledge are represented declaratively, with plots as frames. Third, incompleteness of knowledge is the model by varying the salience of different environmental objects: as yet, genuine errors of perception have not been incorporated. Fourth, the model will eventually simulate human errors in performance.

Testing of the model procedes via both computational and real world empirical tests: the latter so far published consist only of the detailed case study of route acquisition by an 11-year-old boy. The resulting empirical data are strongly supportive of the detailed hypothesis derived from the conceptual model: more information is coded near choice points—with most where there are many alternative actions possible; choice points serve to segment the route in LTM, and repeated exposure to link these segments into a route. Errors occur most frequently where choice points are complex; and, finally, the generalization process leads to a hierarchical representation of route elements in LTM.

The Golledge *et al.* model would seem to have great potential for developmental psychology: it is clear and it ties in with what we know of the acquisition and storage of spatial and route information, and its propositions are testable both conceptually and empirically. 'Potential' because, as yet, truly developmental empirical studies have not been published, in which the route-learning of younger, less accomplished children are studied, against a range of routes varying in complexity.

Just as, in the Golledge *et al.* model described above, developmental psychology is currently strengthening its position by using the intellectual techniques of AI to examine the task of the child, so also are some writers making explicit links with other methodologically rigorous approaches. Heth and Cornell (1985), for example, have pointed out the wealth of comparative work already available on the efficient use of space by animals.

Very few developmental psychologists writing about the child's searching strategies (see the previous chapter) or movement through geographical-scale space (the concern of the present chapter) even make mention of the large literature that exists on search strategies in animals; and few seem aware of the relevant anthropological literature.

Heth and Cornell acknowledge at the outset that search procedures and ways of utilizing spatial knowledge are likely to differ between species: we should recognize, they say, that natural selection would favour searchers who are efficient *regardless* of how their behaviour is mediated. Indeed, reviewing the literature, they discuss many cases of efficient use of space in species that might not be able to anticipate the outcomes of search.

Their review has three parts. The first gives examples of search as a component of foraging by animals—and each is evaluated relative to the organism's niche. In the second part, they describe in some detail ethological studies of optional foraging: essentially, an economic analysis of search and travel strategies with relation to the distribution of resources across the animal's area. In their final selection, Heth and Cornell describe anthropological studies in order to suggest analogies between animal and (adult) human solutions to the requirements of search, before finally extending the analogies to describe the strategies employed by children in locating resources. Their emphasis upon the comparitive is welcome not just for the new light shone on a particular set of children's behaviour, but because—as with the AI approach discussed earlier—it forces the field to ask central questions such as: What is the most direct way to represent the bearing of an unseen landmark? How can such interpretations be translated into symbolic form for retention or communication? Is search better performed by reference to general or particular memories? What algorithms could be used to group individual locations? What are the effects upon search strategies of finding (and of not finding) a resource? How is the spatial distribution of resources related to the individual's strategies for space use? Can we set a balance between the benefits of locating a resource and the costs incurred in searching? And—turning now to specifically human questions—what mnemonic strategies can be employed to aid successful navigation, and location of resources? What is the relation between immediate experience, personal strategies, culturally trained strategies, and external stores of information in the navigational process?

To take the last first, the implication is *not* that we should expect in the young child anything as elaborate or as integrated as the geographical information system used by modern-day hunter-gatherers that Heth and Cornell describe. Nor should we expect that the child is likely to work through space as efficiently or as systematically as a cacheing and seed-eating bird or squirrel. Rather, the message from such a comparative review is that, in developmental psychology, we have not asked the whole range of process and strategy questions that are being asked (and very well answered) elsewhere. Secondly, the approach of such ethological and anthropological research should be to reinforce the trend towards greater ecological validity in developmental psychology—a greater awareness of where, when, and why the child is seeking and using spatial knowledge in everyday life.

Developmental psychology, and indeed much of the environmental psychology dealing with adults' use of the geographical scale space, has tended to ignore the individual differences approach: where differences between individuals have occurred in empirical data, they tend to be attributed either to differences in cognitive stage or in amount of experience, rather than to longer-standing personality characteristics. Indeed, early review papers within environmental psychology (e.g. Canter, 1977) found only weak relationships between various environmental–behaviour measures and scores on conventional personality instruments.

More recently, environment-specific inventories have been developed to measure, for example, individual differences in environmental sensitivity. Thus, McKechnie (1977a) developed a multi-dimensional measure of environmental dispositions—the Environmental Response Inventory (ERI), whose rules discriminate between a range of behaviours that include design preferences, recreation and leisure preferences, and locational preferences.

A body of research, using ERI, has shown that people have predispositions to differing types of environments and to environmentally-defined behaviours. How such predispositions evolve is little documented, and Bunting and Cousins's (1985) study is one of the first to examine the beliefs, attitudes, and values that children acquire about their world.

McKechnie's ERI has well-tested psychometric properties; it was thus a logical step for Bunting and Cousins to construct and validate a children's equivalent—CERI. What little literature exists on child personality studies indicates that personality dimensions can be measured in young school-age children: consequently it was to this age-group that the new scale was tailored. Items were constructed to tap eight dimensions, derived from ERI, which are:

Pastoralism: a positive responsiveness to natural environments.
Urbanism: a broad attraction to the human made environment.
Environmental Adaptation: a belief in the right of humans to use technology to adapt and dominate nature.
Stimulus Seeking: an affinity for increased activation via adventurous interactions with environment.
Environmental Trust: a sense of confidence when dealing with all kinds of environment.
Antiquarianism: emotional responsiveness to the historical past and to traditional environments.
Need for Privacy: a positive appreciation of solitude.
Mechanical Orientation: an attraction to mechanical structures and the enjoyment of manual activity.

The psychometric properties of CERI are reported to be as good as those of the adult version; and preliminary findings indicate that the scale has face validity when related to children's environmental activities.

Bunting and Cousins's initiative should be taken up by others concerned with the development of environmental cognitions and behaviours—both in the specific use of their research instrument and, more generally, to inject more of an individual differences orientation into the field. CERI's variety of scales indicates the range of relevant ways of construing individual differences—from preferences to sensitivities to environmental competencies—and sets an agenda for the study of their development.

Differences, if not innate, may well originate very early in the individual's life. Work by Cassidy (1986) has shown that the quality of attachment to the mother is predictive of the infant's ability to negotiate the environment: subskills within this competence included those needed to move around a play-area without stumbling, to cross distances successfully, and to position oneself comfortably with relation to toys and activities. There are suggestions here that environmental competence can arise most effectively when the mother provides—literally and metaphorically—a secure base whence to explore the environment: a suggestion made also by Ainsworth and Bell (1974).

From now on in this chapter, we concentrate on specific aspects of the child's understanding and use of geographical scale space. We ask what is involved when the child learns a new route and how landmarks are encoded, and we discuss the nature of spatial inferences made from separate pieces of information.

In the next chapter we consider the resultant cognitive map, comparing the *concept* as it has been used in developmental and in environmental psychology, and we also consider the spatial problems of its *assessment* in children.

We then return to reconsider the various sources of information contributing to the cognitive map, and to discuss the role of familiarity, experience and range, town versus village, type of activity undertaken, and the use of inferences in, for example, the estimation of distances.

Finally, we consider the implications of research on children's environmental cognition for the planning for children's needs. How do young children learn novel routes? This seemingly simple question provides us with a useful opening, in that it has implications for both process and competence.

The learning of novel routes

Route-learning involves acquiring information about the temporal and spatial relationships between environmental features (Allen, 1982); and a distinction is made by many authors between the fundamental skill of route-learning, and the acquisition of survey-type knowledge dependent upon the individual's ability to use inference to link into a spatial arrangement that goes beyond direct experience.

We have already seen that there was some interest in the topic of route-learning nearly half a century ago, and that, however laudable was the direct experimental method—working out in the real geographical scale environment—the theoretical framework employed was found to be faulty. Children manifestly (within Western cultures at least) did not use the cardinal points as a reference system into which to fit new information about routes through the everyday environment (Lord, 1941).

As we have also discussed, over the past 15 years developmental psychologists and environmentalists have stressed the competencies of the young child, rather than emphasizing the incompetencies: this is as true of the child's abilities with respect to the environment as it is in other areas (e.g. Liben, 1982; Spencer and Darvizeh, 1981). In one of our own series of experiments (e.g. Darvizeh and Spencer, 1983), we set out to test this competence in young children's novel-route learning, and to ask how does the child extend out from the home area? What features of a new area or a new route would aid its learning and its use?

Evans (1980) had discussed two competing models of route- and area-learning. One position, starting with Lynch (1960) has argued that people initially build up area knowledge from a set of route descriptions and the linkages between districts they provide. Only later, when they are more familiar with an area, do they rely upon its landmarks for orientation (and, we would add, for novel route planning). Siegal and White (1975), however, had proposed that environmental learning is landmark based, with a path structure developing later between the original landmarks. They argue that, with further experience (and also, perhaps, the development of higher order cognitive skills) these multiple routes are organized into configurations. Such coordinated representations enable the individual to navigate through the environment in a more flexible fashion. Since the proposal of Siegal and White's model, there have been several studies that have given it general support, and show the very early importance of landmarks to the child. But, as Cousins *et al.* (1983) have pointed out, research is needed to assess children's way-finding competence in the same environment in which their cognitive-mapping competence is given formal assessment: most researchers have opted for the convenience of the small-scale, or the simulated, environment. In the Cousins *et al.* study, children of 7, 10, and 13 years of age were asked to 'create and walk three novel and efficient routes', and then to perform a number of ranking and recognition tasks with relation to these routes. However, in their experiment, the routes were 'novel' only in the sense that they were routes across the school grounds that the child did not routinely take during school-day activities: virtually all the children performed them in error-free fashion straightaway. 'Landmarks' too were indicated by picking out photographs from an array.

Travels with a 3-year-old

We felt that the Cousins *et al.* approach could be improved upon by working with younger children, earlier in their development of environmental competence, and on full-scale tasks that were truly novel. We therefore devised a situation in which to examine the learning and recall of completely novel longer-scale routes by pre-school children. We also wished to study the extent to which an adult can facilitate the process by mentioning on the 'training trip' the presence of a number of usable landmarks. Studies such as chosen by Acredolo, Pick and Olsen (1975) have demonstrated that, in a limited environment such as a school corridor, the presence of distinguishable landmarks considerably aided recognition.

A witness of our study would have seen a 3-year-child walking a complex, suburban route with the be-chadored figure of Zhra Darvizeh: who, as an obvious foreigner, would have difficulty in retracing a route through the child's city without the child's taking control of the trip. (In fact, all 20 of the children knew the experimenter very well from her work in their nursery school, but were happy to engage in a reversal of their usual fate of being towed helpless through the city streets by an adult!)

The experimenter took each child separately on a novel route, selected to take about 15 minutes at a 3-year-old's walking speed. She explained that they were going to play a game in which she would take the child on a walk; and that, a few days later, she would ask the child to lead her on the walk as if she were a stranger.

In one condition ('unaided') the first trip was carried out with child and adult engaged in casual conversation; in the second condition ('aided') an equivalent route was walked with the experimenter making explicit reference to a standard set of eight landmarks which, on the evidence of pilot studies with other children, would be useful in retracing the route. These were located at choice points on the route, and included, for example, a solitary tree, a bright poster, and a green door in a garden wall. The experimenter pointed each object out as if for its own sake, rather than making its landmark value explicit: a poster for the circus coming to town, rather than a circus poster marking where the route turned right. Comparison of the children's ability to retrace the full route (this time as leader) showed striking evidence of the aided condition's effectiveness in planting landmarks in the child's internal representation of the route. *All* retracing trips in the aided condition were successful, given the criterion of reaching the end point by the same succession of roads, paths, crossings, etc., and given some allowance for the kind of distractions any journey with a 3-year-old is subject to. *No* directional corrections were required of the experimenter.

In contrast, only six of the 20 unaided trips were retraced to criterion, with the other 14 trips needing the experimenter's intervention, as the children took wrong turns and became confused. (Children were their own controls, in a counter-balanced design in which half the children walked route A unaided and route B aided, and the other half were unaided on B and aided on A.)

Indication of the importance of landmarks in learning and then retracing a route is provided by analysis of the tape recordings made on the trips. Clearly, the potential landmarks existed on a route, regardless of whether the trip past them was aided or unaided; yet we found that in the protocols from the retracing trip, children in the aided condition mentioned 51% of the stressed landmarks when explaining the route to the experimenter, as compared with 32% of these landmarks being mentioned by children when in the unaided condition (who, by definition, had had to notice the landmarks for themselves).

Young children, when learning and retracing a route, do make use of landmarks from the first: the experimental procedure in our experiment has only served to accentuate a process that is going on all the time.

Analyses of the child's verbal account of these and other trips indicate an extensive use of a whole range of other potential landmarks: a postbox a lifting garage-door, writing on the pavement, particular cars, leaves, an empty can, etc. Young children may well include ephemeral as well as permanent features noted on a route. Take the following exchange:

HELEN (4 years, 2 months): 'We cross the road here, by the tree.'
EXPERIMENTER: 'How do you know?'
HELEN: 'We saw that step, and there was an ambulance [here last time].'

Figure 5.1. Cues used in way-finding: 1. Three- and four-year-olds remembered this junction as 'the place with the trees': an adult giving route directions would probably make reference to the signpost.

Note in this example, the coexistence of items past and present: for Helen, the fact that this place was where the ambulance had been parked makes it as usable a landmark for her as the tree or the step. Although ephemeral items do not predominate over permanent in the accounts we have studied, we are convinced from walking the routes with the children that such items do represent an important element in the initial cognitive map and, indeed, if they are sufficiently striking, they may persist as the child consolidates his or her knowledge of the area. [Adults almost certainly also use some ephemeral and remembered landmarks, but tend to exclude them from accounts they give as directions to another individual, as if realizing their private quality: see also Allen (1982) on the differences between the landmarks adults and children use.]

Figure 5.2. Cues used in way-finding: 2. Children frequently use, in route descriptions—and potentially in route memory—landmarks which are personal or ephemeral.

A final point about the landmarks that occur in young children's accounts of novel routes is that: although many of the landmarks lay close to choice points, and served to trigger an appropriate choice, some items included in the accounts could not have served such a function, and might appear to the adult observer as being mere 'local colour', adding nothing to successful route performance. Such a view, we believe, may understate the importance to a traveller of having the route confirmed by such items. One suburban street may be relatively similar to another, and thus such strictly redundant items may increase the child's confidence that an earlier, landmark-guided decision was right.

Can we conclude from Darvizeh and Spencer (1983) and other similar studies that landmarks precede routes as the initial pegs upon which an area description is built, to return to the theoretical debate between Lynch and Siegal? Impressions from walking routes with children would incline one towards accepting the primacy of landmarks as pegs for routes. However, if an experimenter were to work solely in the laboratory a different conclusion might be reached (and this, we suggest, might be the source of some of the published disagreements): for if one were to ask a child to construct a map of a newly learned route then, as we found in the same experiments, many such representations will be primarily structured around routes, with roadside details added in later.

We used a set of two- and three-dimensional mapping symbols for 3-year-olds to construct maps of the novel routes that they had just learned: below is an abbreviated account of the construction of one of the best maps:

> Mathew (3:4) has been provided with the symbol for the building which was the starting point by the experimenter. He adds a road, adjoining the building; then puts symbols for a tree and a building touching the end of the road. At right angles to the first road, he places a second road, with another building ('This is the Museum') mid-way along; and a further building and a tree towards its end. A further road is then added at the end of the second road, again at right angles; and this road connects successively a gate (by which a shorter side road is added, with cars parked beside it, and ending with a lamp post), a tree, a building, a tree, and, finally, the church which marked the end of this particular route.

Mathew, in this example, used roads and landmarks together, to unfold his map as he remembered it. However, one could equally have chosen as an example other children whose (ultimately very similar) map was begun by fitting together the entire road structure before 'labelling' it with landmark symbols.

Strong individual differences were also noted by Hazen (1982). She worked with 2- and 3-year-olds, and found that she could classify children consistently into active and passive explorers of novel spaces. (Hazen observed her subjects in a museum room and then in the laboratory). Active explorers developed a better spatial knowledge of each setting, although all the 3-year-olds were able to reverse routes and infer alternatives quite easily. She concluded that it was the individual's characteristic mode of explanation that mattered more than the total amount of exploration. Such a conclusion is in line with the results of Poag, Cohen, and Weatherford (1983), who showed that children of 6 years, when directing their own movement through space, could give better estimates of distances if an adult had directed their viewing than if they had walked directing their own viewing.

Cornell and Hay (1984) have further demonstrated the importance of active exploration in route-learning: 5- and 8-year-old children viewed a route either by a slide presentation, a videotape or by walking the route with a guide. Each child viewed the route only once, and then had to retrace it in the same medium— from start to finish, or in reverse. They found very little difference in overall performance between slide and videotape conditions, but significantly fewer errors were made by the walking-condition children, especially when asked to indicate their way back to the start.

How children actively explore and learn a route or a large-scale space is clearly related to their goal: information related to the immediate goal of an action is remembered more effectively than information that is not directly goal related. To demonstrate this, Gauvain and Rogoff (1986) gave children the opportunity to explore a novel area, with one group of the children given an expectation that route knowledge would be important to recall, and the other group focused upon survey layout information. Those children given instructions to study the layout remembered more layout relevant information, whereas the route-focused children recalled much less information on, for example, the location of places off the route.

From route knowledge to survey and layout knowledge: the role of spatial inferences

It is easy to accept the suggestion that a child's overall knowledge of an area develops after a number of routes in that area have been learned by the processes discussed earlier, with the implication that these routes provide the skeleton, the frame of reference for the overall area representation. We now need to consider the rather more difficult question of how the child constructs this representation from separate pieces of information, and how the process of spatial inferences works. A skilled, sighted adult needs a considerable effort of imagination to understand the child's development of a spatial inference system. Although some inferencing abilities occur in early childhood, research indicates that spatial inferences emerging later in childhood require some effortful processing (Anooshian and Siegal, 1985). As adults, we rapidly and easily make decisions about a novel route through a familiar area, or point directions and give approximate distances. We are, as adults, drawing upon knowledge arguably stored as a configurational or survey map: we can therefore gain some limited insight into the pre-configurational child's understanding by considering the research, described in Part I, on how adults learn a new area: but the analogy is not perfect, in that the adult brings to a new area expectations about (say) usual city layout, and, more fundamentally, processing routes, which encourage him or her to establish a frame of reference almost from the outset.

Rieser (1983) offers a convenient way of describing the nature of spatial inferences, in terms of three dimensions:

1 Functional purpose served by the inference: inferences which help observers orient to places out of view, and inferences for extracting the spatial layout of places within an area.

2 Frames of reference: mediation by a self-reference system or by an environmental reference system.
3 Psychological process underlying the inference: inferences involving relatively deliberate, computational processes or relatively automatic perceptual
   processes.

The first two of these dimensions have been fully discussed already, but the
final dimension perhaps deserves amplification. By 'deliberate, computational',
Rieser indicates those occasions when the individual solves spatial problems by
cognitively linking existing pieces of information: a newcomer may, for example, draw or actively imagine known routes, and then attempt to work them
together. There may be a range of alternative explicit strategies that the individual can use to manipulate mental images, or compute estimates of distance
and direction. These cognitive processes contrast with Rieser's category of 'relatively automatic perceptual processes', used when, for instance, one is aware
what lies on the other side of a wall one cannot hear or see through.

> We do not know why observers behave as if they perceive novel spatial relationships
> in some situations whereas they need to figure them out in others, although our
> introspections are that the perceptual processes operate mostly in relatively small
> locales and in very familiar locales.   (Rieser, 1983)

The development of spatial inference processes in the maintenance of orientation
(Rieser's first dimension) has already been discussed, in the preceding chapters,
where we considered the infant's earliest movements through local space, and
saw how early, if imperfectly, children used self-related directions (e.g. 'left of
self') or even some environmental cues in their orientation. In the first years
of life, they do not perform efficiently, because they tend to fail to update
self-related directions as they move through space, or, having used an external
landmark, fail to realize when movement makes its use as a marker no longer
appropriate.

   Independent locomotion puts a premium on developing efficient inference
strategies and it provides a constant stream of experience whence to abstract
inferencing rules, with, in particular, visual experience probably playing a key
role. Evidence of its importance comes from comparisons between the strategies
and performance of late-blinded with early-blinded adults. Rieser, Guth and
Hill (1982) demonstrated that early-blinded adults (i.e. congenitally blind, or
with total sight loss before the age of three) did not automatically up-date their
orientations in a locale by relating their physical movements to their knowledge
of a spatial layout, in contrast to late-blinded adults, who made inferences as
sighted adults did on the same task. Early-blinded individuals have to use more
deliberate and conscious strategies, in the way we can presume the young child
must when executing a complex spatial movement that is performed relatively
effortlessly by the older child.

Many of the studies of children's spatial inference processes—investigating Rieser's two remaining dimensions (frames of reference, and psychological processes)—have used laboratory or miniaturized situations, in order to obtain close control over the stimuli involved; some of these have indeed imposed tasks so hard that many adults have found them difficult. In a much-cited early study, (Hardwick, McIntyre, and Pick, 1976) children and adults were asked to imagine themselves standing at various places within a large, familiar room, and to aim a sighting tube at various target objects within the room, as if they had indeed been standing at the places. Six- and seven-year-olds either responded 'egocentrically'—e.g. they ignored the instructions to imagine themselves elsewhere—or else, realizing that such a response was inappropriate, responded 'chaotically', unable to find an appropriate strategy. Eleven-year-olds, and some of the adults, generally pointed the sighting tube in the general direction of the objects but only some of the adults were able to respond with accuracy on all occasions. Rieser, Doxey, McCarrell, and Brooks (1982) designed an ingenious task to examine the spatial inferences of children in the first two years of life: infants were held up, so that they could view a one-choice maze, and then allowed down to crawl towards their parent along this maze. In order to navigate the maze, the infant would need to realize the identity of 'aerial' and 'ground' mazes; recall the layout from the aerial view; and to apply this knowledge to the ground-based task. Only the 2-year-olds were able to perform significantly above chance in the maze, after receiving their aerial view of it.

Cohen and Weatherford (1981) have demonstrated that active learning of an area results in more-accurate knowledge than does passive viewing: in their experiments, school-age children viewed a model town from its periphery, or were able to walk through it, and then had to make a series of judgements about the town.

Whether the environment is a model or full-scale, locomotion provides a continually transforming series of perspective views—potentially overloading memory and, one could surmise, necessitating the inference of invariant spatial relations within the area.

Anooshian and Siegal (1985) argue that, as the individual's range extends, there is an increase in the range over which spatial inferences are made: 'It makes sense that infants make inferences in a small reaching space, older preschoolers make inferences in a configuration of small rooms, and only 12 year olds make inferences in a large neighbourhood area' (p. 56). As the reader will guess from the position we have earlier advocated, we feel that Anooshian and Siegal somewhat underestimate the potential competence of pre-schoolers; but their general point is evident: the larger the area, the greater the processing demands. For inferences requiring greater effort, one should expect, following Hasher and Zacks (1979), a later emergence.

Now, if the mental effort required to construct a configuration in working memory varies with the size of the space being represented, and competence in such representation is clearly age-related, then it seems worth checking to see whether there is equivalent development in other inferences that the child might make.

Anooshian and Siegal (1985) argue—convincingly—that the study of (non-spatial) cognition and cognitive development is more mature than the study of cognitive mapping; but that spatial representation and inference can be seen as paradigmatic of non-spatial thought. They quote Huttenlocher's (1968) demonstration that syllogisms are solved by constructing a spatial image consistent with the premise information; and Johnson-Laird's (1982) expansion of the concept of mental models and their role in problem-solving. Evidence is now beginning to accumulate that there is a clear relationship between the development of cognitive-mapping skill and success in general problem solving (e.g. Haake and Somerville, 1985). The stronger claim is that spatial inferences are basic to the development of memory strategies: Anooshian and Siegal suggest that the first mental models constructed by children are representations of the temporal sequences of landmarks. Such linear orders provide an organizational tool for remembering events and objects, as well as places (as has been recognized since ancient times in the mnemonic technique, the Method of Loci, where objects to be remembered are associated with, for example, an imagined trip through a theatre (Yates, 1966).

Most innovative of Anooshian and Siegal's (1985) propositions about cognitive and procedural mapping is that, as with non-spatial thought, we ought to acknowledge the role of the emotions in the individual's spatial thought. Having stressed that cognitive and procedural mapping reflects constructive aspects of memory, they remind us that, since the work of Bartlett (1932) it has been recognized that when remembering, we construct details to fit our overall attitude or feeling about the remembered event.

So far, the available evidence, especially as it concerns the development of the child's cognitive map, is suggestive rather than conclusive on the importance of the emotions. One can cite Presson and Ihrig's (1982) infants, who coded event-locations with reference to their emotional centre—their mother; Darvizeh and Spencer's (1983) Iranian pre-schoolers, who included valued landmarks in their route maps, regardless of whether they marked a choice point or not; and Beck and Wood's (1976) adolescents, whose developing maps of newly visited cities centred round areas of interest, excitement, and even danger. It seems entirely reasonable to expect that the learning of routes and of areas should be considerably affected by the emotional experiences of the individual; and Anooshian and Siegal's proposition is worthy of further investigation.

CHAPTER 6

Investigating the child's cognitive map

The reader will recall that in Part I we saw how studies of the cognitive map had started with a descriptive phase, moved into a period of self-doubt about methodology and have now acquired new impetus by realizing the key role of some form of cognitive representation of the known environment as the basis for the individual's action plans. Or, put more dramatically, environmental psychology's crisis of confidence over cognitive maps was resolved (or were the tricky methodological points merely shelved?) when it met and found common cause with the self-confident world of cognitive psychology and AI.

Developmental psychology's consideration of children's cognitive maps has not drawn as fully as it might from these other literatures, and few developmentalists have as yet made the role of such maps in action-planning central to their study, although such a role is frequently mentioned (e.g. Hardwick, McIntyre, and Pick, 1976). Developmental psychologists, however, have made many constructive and innovative suggestions about the greater practical problems involved in 'stalking the elusive cognitive map' of young children, and especially of those who could not use drawing or description to express their environmental knowledge and its pattern of organization.

Writing in 1982, Siegal felt that 'cognitive mapping of large scale environments has become an industry' within developmental psychology; but argued that this 'recent flood of both empirical and theoretical writing about cognitive maps and mapping is much more than the reinvention of the wheel': because developmental psychology had proceeded well beyond the early studies discussed in the previous chapter.

Many of the earlier studies within developmental psychology were firmly rooted in the laboratory [e.g. Piaget, Inhelder, and Szeminska's (1960) sand-box modelling, or Kosslyn, Pick, and Fariello's (1974) distance judgements with and without barriers on a layout]. From such experiments we can, of course, learn much of value about the development of cognitive processes involved in spatial representation: the Piaget *et al.* studies for instance indicated the importance to 4–7-year-olds of the serial order of landmark information: because each portion of a route would be constructed serially, with the various subsections only loosely related. Errors in estimation of distances reflect functional distances, rather than actual visual distance: the influence of motoric representations when recalling a route. Seven–nine-year-olds exhibited the capacity to group objects in terms of a fixed reference system of landmarks; but it was not until after nine that an overall, abstract coordinated system was used. We should, however, be cautious in interpreting this kind of developmental data, as our discussion of the value of various methodologies below will indicate. [And, indeed, several subsequent model studies of children's spatial representation have shown little evidence of age difference (e.g. Blaut and Stea, 1971; Siegal and Schadler, 1977).]

The main objection to relying exclusively on laboratory-based studies of cognitive representation and its development is not, however, methodological: but is that such studies divert our attention away from what children at the different ages and supposed stages, are needing to achieve, using their cognitive representations, in their everyday lives:

> Looking at children in the rooms of an experimental laboratory and in the room of a school, researchers have most frequently interpreted age changes in learning, memory, cognitive mapping and the like as reflecting mechanisms of cognitive growth and quasi-embryological structural development. But our everyday knowledge ... is that children travel from place to place   (Siegal, 1982, p. 84).

Therefore, argues, Siegal, one could profitably focus on the *functional* needs of the child in travelling and exploiting the world—and in collaborating with other people. Many have previously argued that the *structural* development of competence must be adaptive but, as Siegal says 'such arguments have been pretty vague about adaptation for *what*'. Good naturalistic studies of how children function in the world are fewer than one might expect, given the number of calls from influential theoreticians from Dewey (1902) to Bronfenbrenner (1979) for an ecologically valid developmental psychology. One can call up few systematic developmental studies to stand alongside those of the ecological psychologists (e.g. Barker, 1978), and those planners and environmental psychologists who have studied the child's world of play (e.g. Hart, 1979; Moore, 1986). Such studies, bordering on being an anthropology of childhood, are yet sufficiently aware of the psychological processes to be useful to our present concerns. Barker and colleagues (e.g. Barker and Wright, 1955) have documented the changing and extending settings of childhood in a midwestern American small town and its counterpart in the Yorkshire Dales. Secondary sources, commenting on this work, have tended to concentrate upon its demonstration of a powerful situational determinism: that, in order to predict behaviour in a particular setting, one is better off with knowledge about the physical and social-rule character-istics of the setting than one is with, say, personality or demographic data on the individuals entering and occupying the setting. The ecological psycholo-gists have also, we argue, offered the cognitive developmental psychologists the challenge, to describe *simultaneously* how the child develops both a spatial–geographical knowledge *and* an awareness of a social expectancies of each set-ting: because undoubtedly the child is learning aspects of both simultaneously. As scientists, we may for purposes of analysis, choose to describe a behaviour setting in preponderantly physical or social terms: one's everyday experience of settings is of interacting socio-physical systems.

Hart (1979) studied the increasing range of children's experience of their local world, as their area of adult-tolerated play and other activities widened in a New England town: and from this account, we can see vividly how knowledge is acquired, not just in the course of, but also in the service of desired, and important activities. (Strong male–female differences in the nature of their cognitive maps can be traced back to differences between boys and girls in their allowed—and indeed non-allowed but undertaken—activities, which in their turn reflect the culture's gender-stereotyping in action.)

'Perhaps because of their pre-occupations with the learning of free-floating, placeless, decontextualized cues and symbols', developmental psychologists tend to ignore the work of the ecological psychologists and their successors, argues Siegal (1982, p. 87). Yet cognitive maps are not isolated and contextless entities: they are formed during purposive activity in the everyday world of the child, and, in as much as they encode the location of resources, valued friends, mem-ories, and aspirations as well as factual information about geographical layout and routes, they should perhaps better be described as cognitive/affective maps (as we have argued earlier: see Chapter 1). Environments are seldom experi-enced as neutral: Barker and Wright (1955), for example, describe how Roy Eddy, a 6-year-old in the small town of Midwest, was ignored in some settings, welcomed in others, restricted and coerced in some settings, and given great social approval in others.

Thinking of 'cognitive maps', or 'spatial representations' in this way, has clear implications for the way in which we attempt to investigate them: many techniques, to be discussed below, stress factual knowledge, to the exclusion of the personal importance and functional salience of the information to the child. Questioning the child about cardinal points, or asking for distance estimates, does not leave much opportunity for the child to tell the experimenter about how such information fits into his or her everyday life.

Let us, before considering the methodologies currently in use, reiterate the caveat issued in Part I: the metaphor of a map in the head is so persuasive that we are tempted to believe that it is no metaphor, but rather that our questioning of the child is the search for the dimensions of a real 'thing'. We must remind ourselves of this danger—whilst at the same time recalling why the map is a convenient metaphor. The map is an expression of relationships, and particular structures are derived from it by the user. And, as Downs (1981) reminds us, cartographic maps are themselves models, just as internal representations are models: 'the latter is readily acknowledged in the spatial representation literature; the former is forgotten' (p. 151). A further similarity: cartographers create maps for specific purposes (rather than there being a single possible map of the world); all that we know of how individuals address their stored knowledge of the environment would suggest that the individual engages in what Downs usefully distinguishes as *mapping* in order to solve a particular problem:

> A mapping permits the person to generate a spatial model that is useful in the given context. It can be useful because the resultant map already contains the necessary solutions (the map as repository) or because the solutions can be discovered within the map patterns (the map as creative tool for creating hypotheses). (Downs, 1981, p. 162)

Assessment methods for working with children

We have, in Part I, already reviewed some of the conceptual problems associated with the externalization of cognitive representations (see also Evans, 1980). We shall not, therefore, reiterate points that also apply to working with children. Many of the earlier methodological points are also equally valid here; and we will raise them as appropriate in the following brief review of some of the current techniques.

Reliance on the graphic and expressive powers of an adult subject, to generate some form of representation of a representation, is, as we have noted, incautious of the experimenter: to do so when investigating the young child's cognitive maps is more obviously unwise. As (1976) Neisser argued:

> Cognitive maps are defined by information pick-up and action, not by verbal description. Travel is one thing, travelogue another. A child can find his way long before he can give an adequate account of where he has been or how he got there.

An experimental comparison of techniques

Reliance upon inappropriate techniques has, we have argued elsewhere (Spencer and Darvizeh, 1981a,b) been at the root of the underestimation of children's environment knowledge and skills. One can demonstrate fairly easily how each technique has not only its domain of appropriateness, but also how each elicits a different sub-set of the total store of spatial knowledge. Consider the elicitation of knowledge that, say a 3- or 4-year-old might have of a route recently travelled: Spencer and Darvizeh (1981b) compared the kind of information that the experimenter would glean if relying upon the child's recall via either verbal description, drawing, modelling in two dimensions, or modelling in three dimensions. We found that—not suprisingly—the verbal accounts of young children were limited in scope and did not contain many of the landmarks they would actually use when following the route, although we were later to discover cross-cultural differences because Iranian children of the same age used fewer directional indicators and more descriptions of scenes and places *en route* than did British children, perhaps reflecting each *adult* culture's preferred way for describing routes [see Darvizeh and Spencer (1983) for a further disscussion]. All children, by the age of three, clearly understood the conventions of giving a route description: accounts, although fragmentary, typically included initial orientations, often reference to a major road, and many indicated an identifying feature at the end-point of the route. Yet a researcher, relying on such an account of a familiar route would receive a very impoverished subset of the child's total knowledge of the route.

Were the researcher to switch to sketch maps as a means of investigating the young child's representation, as the majority of experimenters have done, the product would be found to be even less satisfactory. Evans (1980), reviewing adult studies, warned of the selectivity of information that the sketch map techniques elicits. This is a point easily ignored when one's adult subjects turn in detailed maps, but most obvious when dealing with the most random-appearing efforts of a 3-year-old (who may indeed complain about his or her own inability to get down all that they know in graphic form).

All but one of the children in the Spencer and Darvizeh (1981b) study drew *something* on the paper provided, with apparent sense of purpose, when asked to draw, say, the way from nursery school home; but most products consisted of a wandering line, with, in a minority of cases, a recognizable sterotyped building as its end-point. Butterworth (1977), in discussing children's drawings in general, has argued that the drawn product should not be analysed without regard for the child's *intentions* in drawing. We therefore encouraged children to talk us through the drawing as they produced it; and analysis of these tape-recorded protocols makes clear that the child possesses much more social and geographic knowledge then is evident from the drawing.

Graphic and expressive limitations clearly limit the usefulness of these two techniques with the younger child, but modelling the environment may well circumvent these limitations, and has been used by a number of experimenters. In our study we have compared the result of the two- and three-dimensional modelling of routes with verbal and graphic techniques. Children were either given standard pictorial elements in the form of felt cut-outs of cars, houses, larger public buildings, trees, roads; or as two-and-three-dimensional simple models of these elements.

After familiarizing the child with the range of available elements, the experimenter requested the child to make a picture (or a model) of the journey between the nursery school and a named end-point. The child was given, as the first element, the nursery school symbol (or model, according to condition).

Some children needed neutral prompting ('What comes next?'); but for all children, both techniques were accessible, appeared enjoyable, and in most cases resulted in a map-like product, which the child was happy to assert was 'the way to X'. Thirty per cent of the 3- and 4-year-olds showed some tendency to play with the elements rather than restrict their use to mapping (amassing parallel collections of road symbols, for example); but in the majority of cases, a rudimentary map resulted, which preserved many of the terms of the route and included landmarks actually used by the child when walking the route.

Children were willing to persist longer with the three-dimensional modelling kit than they had been with the two dimensional one. The number and variety of elements included in the 'map' was higher, the degree of complexity was greater, and the tendency toward a 'perseverated pattern' (as we saw in some of the two-dimensional exercises) was minimal. In other words, few children laid the elements side by side in their categories, rather than connected up as in a map. In part, the presence of model cars in the kit may have facilitated the connectedness of the road-layout that we observed in this condition.

Judgement of the accuracy of 'maps' produced by the four techniques is to some extent, subjective. Yet one can conclude that, for *all* the 3- and 4-year-olds we studied, at least one technique, and generally more, evinced mapping activities and a map-like product. Second, if the techniques are ordered with decreasing reliance upon expressive skills and increasing realism in the provided elements, the amount of information recalled by the child, and its degree of realism increases.

Thus, the modal 3-year-old child, who could only draw a wobbly line between two blobs, and whose verbal description was fragmentary and disjointed, would be able to connect the two-dimensional felt elements with the clear intention of linking start and finish, including corners, landmarks, and other features seen on the way; and, if given the three-dimensional model kit, would generate a passable road layout, with good alignment of pavements, buildings and junctions, for even a complex route, taking some 15 minutes to walk.

The most complete three-dimensional maps used between 35 and 45 symbols; in comparison, the protocols of the child's description of the route as it was actually walked (as opposed to description from memory) extend to 90 sentences of (prompted) monologue about choice-points, landmarks, traffic, people, wind, noise, etc. Many landmarks were mentioned that never found their way on to even the best maps.

Could an experimenter capture such information by moving from recall to recognition tasks? One technique for investigating the child's knowledge of routes and the use of landmarks that approaches the descriptions *en route* in the sheer amount of information it elicits is to use photographs of a route. (Spencer and Darvizeh, 1981b). This technique affords the child nearly as many prompts as does the actual route, but offers an investigative advantage over the actual walked-over route, in that one can test memory for sequences. Walking a partly remembered route, the child may be able to rely quite heavily on the *sequence* of landmarks: knowing the initial direction, the child sets off, and the appearance of a landmark prompts the next decision, and so on, but a shuffled pack of photographs does not permit this strategy.

In photographing the route, care must obviously be taken not to include cross-referencing landmarks between shots in the sequence: otherwise, a child could rely on the internal logic of the pictures to reassemble the journey.

We walked a novel, 10-minute route with all the 3- and 4-year-olds; then photographed 10 points on the route, from child height, facing in the direction taken on the outward route. Most of the photographs were taken at a node—a choice point where several paths joined.

Each child was presented with the photographs, in a shuffled order; and, as a first task, was asked to re-order them as seen on the route. In the second task, the experimenter took the child through the photographs (in their correct sequence), asking for each photograph 'What did we see here?' and , in addition, for each node 'Which way did we go here?', indicating the possible alternative routes.

All the children found recognition of the correct choice considerably easier than the reassembling of the route-sequence: and the large majority of children were able to recall all choices correctly—which we found a striking result for a once-travelled, relatively complex novel route.

These are the same aged children whose scribbled drawings and fragmented accounts might well lead an experimenter to believe 3- and 4-year-olds spatially incompetent: travel is one thing, travelogue another—but, with a modicum of ingenuity we can offer children a much better chance of revealing their true level of competence.

The range of techniques currently used

Reading the numerous studies now published on the child's cognitive representation of space, one will find a variety of techiques of elicitation used. There will often be two or three techniques, used to cross-reference and to take advantage of the particular subsets of spatial knowledge that a technique is best targeted upon. Thus, for example, Cousins, Siegal, and Maxwell (1983), in studying the development of cognitive mapping in later childhood (their subjects ranged between 7 and 13 years of age), used photo recognition tasks to assess landmark and route knowledge (being careful to include decoy photographs); a swinging arrow-pointer, to assess configuration bearing estimates; and, to assess distance estimates, a strange home-made light-box. Subjects' actual routes through the experimental area were also assessed. Cousins *et al.* tested children's knowledge of a comparatively limited area, but Doherty and Pellegrino (1985) have also shown the usefulness of multiple photographs to investigate their subjects' knowledge of an extensive area of city suburbs (their study confirming that in later childhood, the extensive knowledge demonstrated by younger children becomes more systematically locked into an overall representation of the area).

Further comparative studies are needed of the types of information elicited by different media, such as that conducted by Matthews (1984a–c). Investigating the child's route from home to school, and children's knowledge of the area around their home, he asked his subjects to respond using either recall mapping, or the interpretation of large-scale plans or of a vertical aerial photograph. The choice of technique was shown to have a considerable bearing upon children's imagery: the latter two, structured, techniques prompt much richer and broader recall than did the first, unstructured, technique. Aerial photographs have been used with success by researchers since Blaut and Stea (1971) to prompt children's thoughts about the interconnectedness of geographical features: and by 3 and 4 years of age, children are well able to handle the iconic, rotated form of information provided by such photographs (see Chapter 8). Spencer, Harrison, and Darvizeh (1980) suggested that toy play may give a useful training for moving between ground-level and aerial views of an object such as a toy car). Young children seldom link such a photograph to an actual, familiar locale. Such linkage comes in the period studied by Matthews (his subjects were aged between 6 and 11 years of age and, incidentally, numbered 501 in total—surely one of the largest cognitive mapping studies ever published).

Many experimenters have used the child's estimates of distance and of bearing as an entré into the cognitive representation of space, either as an abstract exercise [e.g. the sighting-tube experiments of Hardwick, McIntyre, and Pick (1976)] or in the rather more motivating context of a game in which, for example, the child has to find a short-cut between two points (e.g. Yamamoto and Tatsuno, 1984).

Anooshian and Young (1981) used cross-referencing pointing from landmark to landmark to assess the 7–14-year-old children's knowledge of their home neighbourhood; and Conning and Byrne (1984) showed that pointing techniques were useful with children as young as three and four. Conning asked her subjects to point the direction, as the crow flies, of the target by imagining that everything between them and the target had fallen down so that they could see it, or that they were Superman or Wonderwoman, who could walk through walls ('The more anxious children took a very popular glove puppet with them on the walks'). Using such careful and sensitive techniques, she was able to demonstrate that some children, aged between 3 and $4\frac{1}{2}$ can show consistent Euclidean knowledge, especially around the home; and that some of these are also able to develop an accurate spatial representation of a novel setting (in her case, a garden).

Since Piaget's use of table-top models of the environment, several experimenters have used miniaturizations of the environment to examine the child's spatial understanding: either providing a layout or, nowadays more often, asking the child to construct a model layout (Weatherford, 1982). The subject is cast in the role of the observer, able to a have a whole view of the configuration (e.g. Huttenlocher and Presson, 1973; Lepecq, 1984), as compared with the successive views the child normally has of an area [unless, as in Spencer and Easterbrook (1985) the children live in tower-blocks overlooking their city].

Modelling techniques have—as we argued above—the advantage that they do not impose the same expressive constraints upon young children as do mapping and drawing. Children do, however, still have to deal with scale-reduction (which may sometimes be a problem for young children). When, for example one compares how children perform in such a miniaturized situation and in a full-scale mock-up of a familiar space (e.g. re-arranging familiar furniture) it is clear that there is some information-loss from full-scale to model (Liben Moore, and Golbeck, 1982). And when Golbeck, Rand, and Soundy (1986) asked 4-year-olds to create a small-scale model of their usual pre-school classroom whilst they were inside the room itself, they found that children benefited from an adult's guidance; adult guidance here consisting of the adult asking the child to point to the real item in the classroom before placing the model version of the item in the model layout.

In a thoughtful review of the whole modelling literature, Weatherford (1982) has noted how few studies using models have then gone on to compare the child's performance at this scale with their capacity to handle full-scale geographical space. It could well be that the processing demands for either manipulating or representing space at model scale are different from these at full-scale; although Weatherford remains encouraged at the extent to which the vaious findings of model studies have been supported by the large scale studies.

Hart (1981) has, however, warned that modelling is, in itself, a learned skill and that children's success on small-scale modelling tasks improves with experience with models in general. Similarly, the child, asked to draw objects or layouts as she or he knows them, will reflect drawing experience and the learning of techniques as well as spatial knowledge in the resultant product. As Chen and Cook (1984) point out, the young child who attempts to draw a picture of a three dimensional scene must decide the appropriate level of abstraction for drawing the objects; select the aspects of the scene to be included; and then solve the problem of representing three dimensions on a two-dimensional piece of paper. It is possible to demonstrate developmental trends in the strategies the child adopts to cope with these problems (Freeman, Lloyd and Sinha, 1980) Willats (1977) has described the child's progress towards the use of depth cues in representing three-dimensional space as 'slow and painful'; and his empirical work indicates a succession of stages. The child starts from an initial inability (objects are drawn in isolation) through literal top-to-bottom and side-to-side representations; thence to a symbolic stage, with occasional incorporations of objects as known rather than seen (table tops are rectangular, even when seen from the side), and the early, rather uncomprehending use of perspective, until, finally, some of us manage adequate perspective applied to the reality around—

and many of us never do! Clearly, the transition between these later stages, at least, is affected by the child's artistic experience in school and home; and researchers, relying on graphic techniques, should beware of assuming that differences in graphic representations necessarily signal differences in cognitive representations. Indeed, one can demonstrate that consistent individual style exists in the drawings of children as young as 5 years old (Hartley, Somerville, von Cziesch Jensen, and Eliefja, 1982).

The reader interested in following up these and other graphic-representational issues, as they apply generally, will find an extensive literature on styles and strategies (e.g. Beagles-Roos and Greenfield, 1979; Freeman 1980; Gardener, 1980), the child's recognition and use of particular aspects—e.g. vertical and horizontal—in drawings (e.g. Perner, Kohlmann, and Wimmer, 1984) and naive versus learned techniques of making and recognizing pictures (e.g. Jahoda, Deregowski, Ampene, and Williams, 1977; Walk and Pick, 1978). In one such study Hochberg and Brooks (1962) were so committed to discovering how far pictorial recognition was an unlearned ability that they reared one of their own children until the age of 19 months with 'extremely restricted exposure to pictures' and 'no exposure to picture plus naming experiences'. The unfortunate infant, returned to the normal world, was able to identify successfully simple and complex line-drawings and photographs of familiar objects. It is not recorded what his opinion was of the experiment—or of his parents.

Methodologies for studying cognitive representation abound; within developmental psychology, few workers have linked their approach to the questions of function that Siegal (1982) would have us address, or have framed them in ways that those in AI would find immediately applicable in providing a description in system terms. What we need, following on from the descriptive level studies discussed in the present chapter, are more studies of the child's spatial representations as he or she solves the practical, navigational problems that the real world presents, studies of the kind reported by Golledge et al. (1985), discussed in the previous chapter—which consider the child-as-environmental-problem-solver with a program to model, and hence to conceptually tease out the processes basic to the storage and retrieval of spatial information. Too many of the methodologies reported above make the tacit assumption that there is a *single* entity, the cognitive map, to which all practical problems are addressed, rather than, as Siegal (1982) has so persuasively argued, a range of possible representations, which can be called upon according to the demands of the task.

CHAPTER 7

The role of direct experience of the environment in the development of cognitive representations

So far, we have discussed the structural properties of the child's cognitive map, its development and its measurement, and the uses to which the individual puts these cognitive representations. We conclude these three linked chapters where we might have begun, by considering the sources of information that the child calls upon in developing this representation of the environment.

Research has asked questions about how environmental characteristics themselves influence spatial representation. How does growing up in a village, as compared with a big city, shape not only one's environmental knowledge, but the nature of the representation itself? What is the general effect of familiarity with different kinds of setting? How does one's pattern of activity—active versus passive travel, extensive or local home range—affect the cognitive representations? How do children infer spatial relationships? How do they integrate landmarks and directional indicators into the developing image? A further question might be : how is directly observed and media-presented information linked? We consider in Chapter 8 how one *indirect* source of information about the environment—the cartographic map—can be used by children (and there we will demonstrate the surprising competence of even young children in using this source). Then, in Chapter 9, on the child's image of distant places, we again consider how media information, geographical education, and personal experience all combine. But first, let us consider the role of direct experience in building up the cognitive map of the local environment.

116

Characteristics of the area as a determinant of spatial cognition

This section of the chapter really should not be needed: and yet it is with a shock of recognition that one realizes that is necessary when one reviews practically all the developmental psychology research discussed so far in the light of a recent observation by Golbeck (1985). She argues that neither the developmental psychology tradition (examining the emergence of spatial representation) nor the geographical–architectural one (studying representation as basic to behaviour-in-the-environment) have systematically examined the proposition that characteristics of the environment influence the representation. Cognitive developmental psychologists, in the main, have been concerned with the general characteristics of spatial representation, but not the specific characteristics of the spatial referent. Golbeck sees the other tradition (including the work of environmental psychologists)—in its concern with particular types of settings (schools, hospitals, etc.)—as not considering 'the general features cutting across these places' (p. 226).

Can we, then, identify a taxonomy of such general features of the environment as they are relevant to spatial cognition? Golbeck offers such a scheme. (It is curious to reflect how the first attempt to do this—Kevin Lynch's *The Image of the City* (1960)—has so often described as 'seminal', and has yet had so few direct offspring!)

Golbeck's taxonomy categorizes the characteristics of the *physical* environment into first, *structural features*—themselves subdivided into the degree of differentiation by the presence of landmarks; the proximity of containing features, such as walls, pathways, and other potential boundaries to perceived space; and the presence of barriers to travelled space. The second category—*organizational features*—includes clustering, orientation and saliency. For each offered sub-category, it is possible to demonstrate how such features of the physical environment can be powerful influences upon the learning and representation of the environment. Much of the research evidence has already been presented in the present book in one context or another, or will be detailed in the later sections of this chapter e.g. Acredolo's (1981) direct test of the role of landmarks in locating a lost object, and Cohen and Weatherford's (1981) manipulation of barriers in distance estimation tasks. What is original about Golbeck's taxonomy is that it attempts to bring all these features together as joint and potentially interactive factors determining the nature of the spatial representation. Social and ecological factors are explicitly excluded from this taxonomy, even though our field will eventually have to undertake the daunting task of including them for, as the ecological psychologists so convincingly demonstrated, it is the standing demands of the *socio*-physical environment that shape the individual's daily behaviour (Barker, 1978). Also excluded are aesthetic and affective factors—which is another ironic reflection on the pioneer boldness of Lynch, whose concept of an area's *legibility* not only encompassed most of the features in the Golbeck taxonomy, but also was predictive of the area's aesthetic appeal. We have, in the nearly 30 years since Lynch wrote, carefully researched most of the structural and organizational features of the image, whilst remaining largely uninvolved with discussions about what it is about places that makes them aesthetically and socially satisfying.

Do rural and urban children differ in their spatial representations? Barbichon (1975) thought so: when rural children in his study made sketch drawings, they stressed houses and people, whilst urban children presented almost only commercial buildings.

Dupré and O'Neil-Gilbert (1985) also asked children to map their home area, and again found a rural–urban difference: villages had boundaries, a clear shape, and were relatively consistently drawn by all children from the same area. Town children varied considerably in the area represented, each one building outward from their home to include more distant elements; with no clear-cut boundaries being obvious (or, probably, available to them).

From studies such as these, we can tentatively conclude that there is a relationship between the nature of the space to be represented, and the organization of the cognitive representation of that space—with experience and familiarity an important intervening variable. Clearly, this is a field where more research is needed, to develop Golbeck's taxonomy of places.

Familiarity: the child's range of experience as a factor in the development of spatial representation

If it is trivially true that the child's spatial knowledge largely reflects those areas he or she has experienced, so we argue that it is also importantly true in the sense that travel and range of experience may be crucial to the very process of forming spatial representations. We have already noted that the growth of cognitive mapping in children reflects directly the range and variety of experiences that their travel allows them and we would now like to go further and propose that this relates to the strategies the child has for travel in, and further learning of, new environments. [Just as one can demonstrate that, with adults, the cognitive strategies of much-travelled individuals differ significantly from those of little-travelled (Murray and Spencer, 1979).] Hence, when stressing the role of experience in shaping cognitive representations, we are proposing that there are qualitative and strategic changes—and not just a quantitative growth in information—as the baby's limited range broadens into the infant's local (often house-bound) range, and next into the young child's close-neighbourhood range. Many have described this increase in experience (e.g. Acredolo, 1982; Hart, 1979; Piaget, Inhelder, and Szeminska, 1960), but we need more research about its impact on the skill of environmental cognizing. We, ourselves, have been struck by the strength of cognitive images among early-exploring infants [e.g. Spencer and Easterbrook's (1985) streetwise children, free to explore large areas of a major pedestrianized housing project from their earliest mobility], and feel that systematic, comparative studies would be worthwhile. An early study by Acredolo, Pick, and Olsen (1975) showed how familiarity with an environment interacts with the complexity and differentiation of that environment (aspects of the Golbeck and Lynch taxonomies discussed in the previous section) as determinants of the child's memory for a spatial location. In the same way, we argue that the *product* of a lifetime's spatial experience (namely the level of competence in environmental cognition) will interact with the characteristics of a specific environment (its structural, organization, social and affective features) to determine what particular image the individual develops of a setting. Individual and developmental stage differences in competence are not, in our opinion, sufficiently central to otherwise very useful accounts such as the Golledge *et al.* (1985) AI–developmental model of children's acquisition of spatial knowledge, discussed in Chapter 5. They acknowledge that younger children, who have less local neighbourhood knowledge, 'fail to show much differentiation as a function of accumulated episodic experience' (p. 149): we would press this further, and argue that not only is knowledge accumulating with greater experience, but as a consequence so is the child's capacity to construct and operate with a complex frame of reference for handling a mass of environmental information. Once this is developed as a result of extensive experience within one setting, this extended competence is available for use in

Figure 7.1 Range of environmental knowledge. During middle childhood, the home range extends considerably with a corresponding growth and differentiation of environmental knowledge. Some elements—like the local sweet shop—are likely to occur in every child's mapping of the neighbourhood; other elements are more idiosyncratically included.

Figure 7.2   By adolescence the image may be city-wide. Increasing independence, spending money, and range of interests all mean that by early to mid adolescence the individual may have developed a complex, detailed, and highly idiosyncratic city image.

the more efficient construing of other environments. By adolescence, as Wood's (1973) peripatetic experiment demonstrated, most individuals have the capacity for the rapid and efficient structuring of information about newly visited cities: strong individual differences exist—whence did they come? Working with blind adolescents as they learned a new area (Spencer and Travis, 1985), we were struck by strong individual preferences in style of exploration, and of integration of new information into the developing frame of reference. Interestingly, writers on the spatial competence of the blind do place considerable emphasis upon the cognitive–structural importance of environmental experience: and as we indicate in Chapter 10, there is much evidence to suggest that individuals who were later-blinded have greater capacity to integrate novel environmental information within a spatial frame of reference than do congenitally blind or very early blinded individuals (e.g. Warren, 1984).

Much of the literature on the effects of familiarity on environmental knowledge treats familiarity as an independent variable, but then tends only to ask how knowledge increases as a function of increased familiarity (Acredolo, 1982). It is also possible to turn the question around, and to ask what factors determine the extent of the child's familiarity with the environment: first must be amount of exposure, although, as Acredolo points out, this factor is often confounded with other variables, such as the emotional salience of the early settings. Second is the type of exposure: active versus passive travel; for example, Lee (1963) compared the cognitive and emotional differences between children who walked to school and those whose bus journey to school might leave them (he argued) feeling isolated from the security of home. Acredolo has suggested that individual observer characteristics above and beyond the age and developmental stage of the child should also be considered as factors; and she instanced Kozlowski and Bryant's (1977) study, where subjects who judged themselves 'to have a good sense of direction' were objectively better at learning a novel environment than those who believed themselves to have a poor sense. Thorndyke and Stasz (1980) have shown how acquisition of novel information (in their experiment, from maps) can be related to the subject's scores on a test of visualization. We clearly need more such work on these basic individual differences and how they interact with familiarity and experience variables in the development of spatial cognition.

There already exists a series of such carefully controlled demonstrations of the effects of specific activity and travel patterns on the acquisition of spatial information [see Cohen (1982) and Herman and Roth (1984) for full reviews]. Some experimenters have worked with a small scale environment: Kosslyn, Pick, and Fariello (1974), for example, had their subjects walk through and learn the location of targets within a simple 17-foot-square layout with barriers which were either transparent or opaque. Pre-schoolers were more influenced by functional (i.e. travel) distances between objects than were adults, although all individuals tended to overestimate distances between places separated by opaque barriers [Newcombe (1982) has, however, suggested that this may be an artefact of memory, rather than a result of travel distance]. Herman and Roth (1984) have shown how young children in particular are aided in their knowledge acquisition when travelling through a novel setting if there is some kind of mnemonic linkage of the objects and places visited: their children either heard a story linking the model man, barn, horse, forest, and so on, as they walked through a layout within a room, or simply walked between their locations with no story.

There have also been larger-scale investigations: Cohen, Baldwin, and Sherman (1978) substituted the real mountains and buildings of a boys' camp area for the developmental psychologist's usual small-scale visual barriers in their study of distance estimation, and showed that distortions occurred not only when direct sight-lines were obscured, but also when the sheer effort of movement from place to place entered into consideration.

A great variety of subsequent experimental conditions have now been published—comparing, for example, walked versus not-walked paths (Cohen and Weatherford, 1981); viewing only versus viewing and walking (Herman and Siegal, 1978); children's self-directed versus adult-directed movement (Hazen, 1982; Poag, Cohen, and Weatherford, 1983); and free exploration versus walking a prescribed path (Herman, 1980). Cohen (1982) reminds us that in much of this research, the activity studied has been the travel between locations, ignoring the activities performed at each location visited, which may provide a crucial mnemonic framework for the pattern of travel. [Echoes, too, of the plea to consider the functions of the child's everyday travel through their environment from Siegal (1982), which we discussed in Chapter 6.]

Inference as a source of spatial knowledge

Travel offers the opportunity to integrate disparate items of spatial information, and to develop the framework for such an integration. Stress on the importance of travel and experience, above, should not obscure the crucial role of going beyond the information given in both the integration and structuring of spatial knowledge, and the read-out from this knowledge to perform novel tasks. It is the nature of the geographical scale (and therefore the weakness of conducting research with single-overview models or layouts) that, ordinarily, real environments cannot be perceived from one location but require observations over a period of time to build up an image.

We do know from early table top experiments that children as young as 3 years old (and probably younger) are good at making spatial inferences: Mohr, Kuczaj, and Pick (1975) trained children to move their hidden hand from an origin point to three different target positions, and then tested their ability to move directly between these three positions. Hazen, Lockman, and Pick, (1978) found that similar-aged children failed to make similar spatial inferences when the task involved moving through a set of rooms—although Hazen (1982) later attributed this failure to the expressive demands made upon the Hazen *et al.* (1978) children, rather than to any cognitive inability.

Herman, Shiraki, and Miller (1985), however, found that 3–5-year-old children seemed to lack the symbolic capacity to make adequate spatial inferences: their subjects were tested in a large, familiar setting consisting of the whole of their nursery school, and were asked to estimate the bearing of particular target places, by pointing to them from sighting locations. This involved the child imagining they could 'see through the walls'. Five-year-olds were more accurate than 3-year-olds in pointing to places within the school that were not connected by a straight-line walking path—which the authors believe to reflect a greater information processing capacity. (Differences in experience with the locality— which is probably the alternative explanation that has already sprung to the reader's mind—can be ruled out here: Herman *et al.*'s study pair-matched 3- and 5-year-olds for the length of time they had been attending this school.) However, 5-year-olds will generally have also had wider experience of *other* complex locations—arguably leading to more efficient strategies for spatial inferences: such differences in experience were not investigated by Herman *et al.* They do, however, speculate that the more accurate estimates given by boys might reflect their greater freedom to explore around the home base.

Accuracy was not great, however, at either age: using the most liberal criterion, of being within $30°$ of target, 3-year-olds were only 48% accurate, and 5-year-olds 62% accurate. But should we take pointing and angle-estimation as a crucial test? None of the children in the study had any problem in taking the experimenters directly to the target locations. Maybe we should investigate the capacity to make spatial inferences via tasks closer to the child's everyday life: searching for lost objects for example. Anooshian, Pascal, and McCreath (1984) used just such a situation, to show that only those children who represented routes in their cognitive maps were likely to make the logical inference that a missing object might be found somewhere between the last place that it was used and the first place it was discovered missing. To reinforce the point made earlier, Anooshian *et al.* concluded that 'generalized experiences may determine how a space is represented more so than the amount of past experience with the particular space' (p. 1827).

Landmarks and their role

Landmarks occur in both popular and scientific accounts of route-finding and spatial knowledge: they are used explicitly in the directions we give others, and so it seems natural for us to assume that they play a key role in the structuring of space for the individual. We have already discussed the empirical evidence in favour of this position: the present section is concerned with the way in which they are actually used.

We have evidence that infants as young as 9 months old are able to use a landmark-centred reference scheme: in Presson and Ihrig's (1982) study, the child's mother was, in effect, just such a spatial landmark. Seated in yet another variant of the laboratory settings we reviewed in Chapter 4 on the location of objects (where young infants have objects flashed out of windows at them), 9-month-olds either had their mothers move with them during rotation trials, or the mother remained in a constant position within the laboratory whilst Presson (or Ihrig?) moved the infant to the next viewing point. The latter condition offered the possibility of coding spatial events as one moved around— and the infants availed themselves of it and responded more accurately than when the mother was not so available. Now, the position of the mother may not in everyday life be a reliable landmark, but may be sufficiently stable to be of use for object location over short periods. In other words, even the young infant may respond non-egocentrically, establishing a local and transitory frame of reference based on a salient landmark. Acredolo and Evans (1980) have indeed shown the value of such landmarks to children as young as 6 months old when they search the environment.

People are supplanted as landmarks by other recognizable visual configurations: typically, buildings, trees, signs, or (as we have noted earlier) more idiosyncrative and personal ones, such as a place–event tie ('this is where I saw the ambulance'). A number of researchers have examined the child's selection and use of landmarks in naturalistic contexts (e.g. Allen, Kirasic, Siegal, and Herman, 1979) and have shown that children and adults extract different features from a set of slides of a journey for their preferred landmarks. Cohen and Schuepfer (1980) used a slide-sequence to teach a journey through a series of halls; their subjects then undertook the simulated 'journey' again without the landmarks being present. Younger children in this study were much more influenced by the presence, position and sequence of landmarks than were older children and adults: they made significantly more errors when the landmarks were removed, recalled fewer landmarks that were not crucial to the route, and needed considerably more time to realize if a sequence of routes was altered by the experimenters.

The Cohen and Schuepfer study shows us that younger children in fact rely heavily upon landmarks, and have not got a readily integrated set of route-sequences on which to fall back. The older children's greater integration of routes and of spatial knowledge generally came out clearly when asked to draw a sketch of the route 'travelled'; the adults showed a still further move towards a survey knowledge of the area.

In map drawing of real, familiar environments, landmarks play an important role for the young children; for instance, Biel (1982) has stressed the not surprising fact that the child's home occupies a key position in the 6-year-old's representations. And if, for example, one asks a child of such an age to imagine him- or herself at various known points at or near home, and to then decide which of two other landmarks that the child has mentioned is the nearer, then one finds the child's representation of the location of these landmarks to be internally consistent, and to coincide with their actual locations. Biel cites this as evidence for 6-year-olds being able to use projective and Euclidean concepts when dealing with a known area.

How did they do it? Biel, splendidly, actually bothers to ask them (how few developmental psychologists seem to take the time!). Most children replied that they had imagined themselves walking to the landmarks; a few said that they 'just knew'. One recalls Poag et al.'s (1983) opinion, cited earlier, that from a number of theoretical perspectives, active movement through the environment has been assumed to be an almost essential condition for the construction of spatial representations of larger-scale environments. And Cohen and Cohen (1982) have also demonstrated that, in active exploration of an area, spatial representations containing functionally useful landmarks are better integrated than those containing landmarks of no functional value.

Young children may be heavily dependent upon landmarks for learning and using their environment and they also may well include such landmarks in their drawings and descriptions of routes through their area. But it would seem from Waller's (1986) investigations that younger children may be less aware than older ones of the value of landmarks in explaining a route to a stranger; although we have found some cross-cultural differences—for example, Iranian nursery-school children intersperse their descriptions with non-functional landmarks more often than did British children (Spencer and Darvizeh, 1983). Younger children are less adept, too, in recognizing possible ambiguities in directions received: e.g. Flavell, Green, and Flavell (1985)—though, as these authors re-mind us, such cognitive monitoring skills were also lacking in some of their college-aged subjects! And even when the young children initially understood and could later recall that the directions they had received were ambiguous, they tended to ignore this fact when following routes. Flavell et al.'s subjects were responding to instructions on where to drive a toy car along a road map drawn on paper. We can imagine how much more difficult the translation of instructions into actions would be for the young child travelling through an environment where all the possible routes were not open to simultaneous inspection as they are in a map.

Information received from maps, and the child's ability to use maps in forming travel plans, has recently become the focus of research, which we review in the next chapter.

From distance and direction estimates to a functional approach to the child's spatial representation

We have seen, in Part I, that many adults have problems with angle and distance estimation, but that none the less some investigators of cognitive representations of space have believed such estimates to be useful: they avoid, for example, problems for the subject with graphic expression.

Several developmental psychologists have seen this advantage too, and have felt that comparative distance and direction questions fitted easily into discourse with children. Simple tasks, for instance, might include having the child recon- struct a real-world area by placing markers at appropriate distances apart on a featureless model-base (e.g. Anooshian and Wilson, 1977; Siegal and Schadler, 1977), or in an empty test room (Cohen, Weatherford, Lomenick, and Koeller, 1979). Subjects might be asked to estimate the time taken for walking par- ticular segments of a route (Herman, Norton and Roth, 1983). Children may confuse duration estimates with distance cues, although there is clearly an age effect here (Acredolo and Schmid, 1981; Herman, Roth, and Norton, 1984).

Many writers having started with the assumption that such estimates were a good way of examining the child's cognitive map, have now conceded that many factors contribute to distortions and errors in distance estimates, and the field has subsequently turned around to focus on the effects of such (erstwhile) error variables.

Thus, Cohen and Cohen (1982) established that the type of activity engaged in as the child walks a novel route may affect their estimates of distance, and Herman, Roth, and Norton (1984) examined the effect of *speed* of travel on such estimates. The nature of the terrain covered may also be a major biasing factor: segmented journeys (e.g. through the different rooms of a school) are likely to be judged longer than unsegmented journeys of the same distance—for example directly across the playground (Kahl, Herman, and Klein, 1984). Sim- ilarly, what Herman, Norton, and Roth (1983) call 'clutter'—the number of objects encountered on a route—has a tendency to increase distance estimates. None of these findings will come as much surprise to those who remember the data of classical experimental psychology on factors biasing estimates. Some- what novel distorting factors, peculiar to spatial perception, have been suggested including a 'route angularity factor'.

Sadalla and Magel (1980) had found, with young adult subjects, that a path containing seven turns was estimated to be significantly longer than one of the same length that contained only two turns. Herman, Norton, and Klein (1986) have, however, been unable to replicate this finding with samples of 8-, 10- and 12-year-olds and suggest that, in the original experiments with adults, numbers of objects encountered might have been a confounding factor.

What can we draw from this literature, focussed as it has now apparently become on the *distortions* in the uptake and recall of distance information, that is of value for our more general interest in the child's environmental represen- tations? First it serves to link considerations of the *processes* of environmental learning, and the *sources* of information about the environment (the subject of the next chapter) to the way the information is represented, the concern of the previous chapter. Thus, for example, Anooshian and Nelson (1985) showed that young children were less accurate in giving direction estimates requiring spatial inferences along an unfamiliar route than along a familiar one. (Their subjects had lived within the test neighbourhood for at least six months before the experiment.) Younger children—but not 12- and 13-year-olds—were also less accurate for direction estimates requiring the mental reversal of the direction of travel along a known route. Familiarity—one of the topics to be considered in the next chapter, also emerged as an important individual difference: the richer had been the child's prior exploration of the neighbourhood, the greater was directional accuracy on Anooshian and Nelson's tests.

The second point of value to us in the various distance and direction estimate studies is that they can, when intelligently handled, corroborate or qualify other techniques' findings. Thus, for example, the triangulation methodology [e.g. Hardwick, McIntyre, and Pick's (1976) sighting tube] allows one to derive an overall spatial configuration from the separate direction estimates; Allen, Kiriasic, Siegal, and Herman's (1979) methodology, ranking the child's interlandmark distances, can then use multidimensional scaling to derive a best-fit spatial configuration; as can the various other combinational techniques for considering direction and distance estimates [as discussed above: see also Siegal's (1981) 'projective concordance' technique].

Siegal (1981) has argued that all these techniques are valuable in that they can provide a map-like representation of the subject's knowledge of the directional and distance relations between places in the large-scale environment; and Anooshian and Kromer (1986) were initially similarly enthusiastic: 'the final products are comparable and can be evaluated similarly (e.g. in terms of directional or distance accuracy)', although the tasks presented to subjects are quite different in each case.

Two issues should give us reason to worry: first, there had been no multimethodology studies, cross-checking that mappings derived from a child's distance estimates in fact matched those derived from his or her direction estimates. Second, in view of the earlier studies on the *processes* underlying making such estimates (subject as they seem to be to essentially irrelevant factors like the amount of clutter encountered on a route), is the stress of Siegal and others on accuracy not surprising? Curtis, Siegal, and Furlong (1981), for example, show how readily one can assess 'accuracy' of cognitive spatial representations by comparing the similarity ('congruence') between the experimentally derived configuration and the actual configuration of places within the world represented. Yet in other writings, Siegal has urged a functional view of cognitive representations (1982). If, for example, young children give distance estimates that vary according to which way they are facing, or according to whether or not the route is filled with interesting places [shades of the hotly disputed 'Brennan's law' (Lee, 1962) of shoppers estimating distances towards the interesting centre of town versus distances out to the suburbs], then are we really talking of *accuracy* as being the main focus of interest? Are we content to see all the child's (or indeed adult's) separate judgements and estimates adding up to a *single* map-like configuration? We can—as we have seen when discussing the sketch map technique—force subjects to produce an integrated spatial representation of their knowledge of space, and then forget to question whether this has any direct relationship to the subject's own *cognitive* representation of the environment. Equally, our statistical ingenuity in combining estimates into a configuration has blinded us to the need to ask under what circumstances the child makes use of such estimates. Knowing that a target place lies ahead of one, rather than behind, may well suffice for many navigational tasks where routes are well defined in the world: what need then for the child to make a precise estimate of direction? Similarly, the child may in practice only need approximate and relative distance estimates in order to be able to make efficient choices between destinations to be visited. (And, indeed, such choices may be more swayed by the features of interest anticipated on the route than in the simple estimate of time and effort that might be expended.)

So, back to the first point: in practice, when one compared them, configurational maps constructed from *distance* estimates differ from those constructed from *direction* estimates: Anooshian and Kromer (1986) compared children's 'knowledge' of their school campus using a variety of techniques, and concluded that measures derived from direction estimates were actually *independent* of those derived from distance estimates. Distance estimates were found to be most inaccurate for long distances; and inaccurate direction estimates most often occurred when the child had to point to a *close* landmark, especially if a wall obscured the sight-line.

Anooshian and Siegal (1985) have argued that children construct different procedural maps for the purpose of representing direction versus distance information; and we would concur with their conclusion, that 'a complete understanding of procedural mapping will require research' [and techniques] in which the diversity of demands associated with acquiring and retrieving spatial information for very different purposes is examined' (Anooshian and Kromer, 1986). In such an enterprise, distance- and direction-estimate techniques, intelligently employed, have their place, alongside a functional analysis. As this chapter has shown, we are not lacking techniques for studying the child's environmental cognition.

CHAPTER 8

Maps and their use: symbolic sources of information about the environment

Introduction

In this chapter we will describe the purpose of maps and the research which has been carried out into both children's and adults' ability to understand maps. It would be satisfying to present a description of the development of map skills across the age range, but unfortunately the relevant research only provides a fragmentary picture of such development. Despite the importance of maps there has been surprisingly little research into the way they are used, and what published research is available has been conducted in a number of different disciplines including cartography, geography, psychology, and education. The different aims, and methodologies, of these disciplines has led to very diverse, and sometimes contradictory results.

Cartographers have been primarily interested in the design of maps, geographers in the applied uses of maps, and educationalists in the way to teach map work in school. Psychologists have carried out a few experiments involving maps but these have, more often than not, been designed to examine specific aspects of cognitive functioning, such as visual memory or mental rotation, and have rarely been directed at the problems of map-using *per se*. To complicate any description of the development of map abilities, researchers in one discipline have too often uncritically accepted the findings from other areas of research. For example, virtually all the educational studies of children's performance with maps accept a traditional Piagetian framework without taking into consideration the more recent developmental research in psychology which has produced results that are often at variance with Piaget's original conclusions. Similarly, cartographers have tried to explain adults' map performance in terms of models of cognitive processing that have long been superseded in the psychological literature (see Blades and Spencer, 1986b). Therefore, when describing the map related research we will emphasize the various approaches that have been taken and point out how these have influenced both the design of different studies and the sort of results obtained.

Maps and map skills

Cartographic maps are a particular way of representing the world using specific conventions and symbols. In doing so they reflect the spatial relationships that are present in the environment. These relationships may be portrayed in direct scale to the spatial relationships in the world. For instance, the distances on a large-scale Ordnance Survey map will have the same proportional relationship to the actual distances in the environment that it represents. At the risk of simplification, this can be called an example of a Euclidean map because a measurement is always directly proportional to the same measurement in the world. On the other hand, many maps employ projective geometries; for example, various projections can be used to portray the globe as a two-dimensional representation (see Downs, 1981).

Maps can be used in a number of different ways and these can be broadly summarized under three main headings. First, map-reading, which is the use of the information provided by a map directly. Someone who wants to know the capital city of a country can search a map of that country until he or she finds the appropriate symbol that represents the capital, and then read the corresponding name. Secondly, map-interpretation, which involves going beyond the immediate information provided by the map to draw particular conclusions. For example, to estimate the comparative proportion of agricultural land to urban areas. Thirdly, maps can be used for navigation. A car driver can use a road map to plan a route to a novel destination. These and similar distinctions have often been made in the cartographic literature (e.g. Board, 1978; Keates, 1982). Such distinctions are not mutually exclusive because most map tasks require a combination of abilities—the car driver has to be able to 'read' the map in order to find the destination before planning the route—but none the less it is likely that the different uses of maps require different skills. Map-reading requires an understanding of map conventions and symbols; map interpretation may need the ability to identify patterns and to group information; and using a map for navigation involves relating the map to the environment it represents.

Unfortunately, little is known about how people use maps in different circumstances. There is, however, some evidence to suggest that even adults may not have fully mastered the basic skills necessary for map-reading and interpretation. Giannangelo and Frazee (1977) tested teachers' ability to perform straightforward map tasks such as locating a place on a map using the key, or estimating distances on a road map. Although the teachers were selected for the test because they were responsible for educating elementary school children about maps, and therefore should have had some map proficiency, the majority failed to achieve half marks on the test. There is also evidence that adults are not very good at using maps in practical circumstances; for example, adults have been shown to be poor at using maps to navigate, and in fact most people travelling in unfamiliar areas prefer to rely on road signs or to ask for directions and tend to avoid using maps at all (see Blades and Spencer, 1986a). This lack of competence and confidence with maps suggests that even for adults the ability to understand a map cannot be taken for granted.

Adults' poor performance suggests that understanding a map is not an easy task. Map understanding probably involves complex mental abilities, but as yet there have not been any analyses of the cognitive processes required for successful map-using. Therefore, when adults prove incapable of carrying out map tasks it is not usually possible to say exactly why they have such difficulty using a map.

Research with adults and children

Most of the map-related psychological experiments with adults have concentrated on testing subjects' memory for maps. Tversky (1981) analysed the distortions that occur when adults try to recall well-known maps or specifically learnt artificial ones. She found two common distortions were due to subjects incorrectly aligning or rotating the remembered map. For example, North and South America were often thought of as vertically aligned with each other, and when subjects were given a test item including San Francisco Bay (which runs northwest–southeast) they tended to remember this feature orientated directly north–south.

Stevens and Coupe (1978) asked subjects to memorize simple maps. These maps, in a rectangular frame, consisted of a single line that divided the map into two areas and within each of these areas there were specifically marked places. Subjects were tested with questions such as 'Is place x to the east of place y?'. Stevens and Coupe found that if the area containing x was predominantly to the east of the area containing y, subjects often inferred that x was east of y even when this was not in fact the case. Stevens and Coupe suggested that people do not usually recall the exact location of individual places but instead they infer the comparative position of two places from the spatial relationship of the areas containing them.

The only experiment that has examined children's memory for maps tested children with maps that were very similar to the ones used by Stevens and Coupe. Acredolo and Boulter (1984) showed 7- and 9-year-olds simple rectangular maps divided into two areas and then asked them to judge the comparative location of two places, one in each of the different areas. Children of these ages, like adults in the study by Stevens and Coupe, tended to be influenced by the relative location of the areas containing the places, rather than the exact relationship of the two places. In other words children usually treated all places in an area that was mainly to the left of the map as left of all places in an area to the right of the map irrespective of the actual locations of those places. Acredolo and Boulter interpreted their findings in the context of Piaget's theory of spatial development and we refer to this interpretation in the following section.

Some psychological experiments have examined the strategies used by adults to memorize novel maps. Thorndyke and Stasz (1980) asked subjects to study a map for 2 minutes and then draw it from memory; this procedure was repeated six times. During each of the study periods subjects were asked to 'think aloud' to explain how they were trying to learn the map; the resulting series of verbal protocols was analysed by Thorndyke and Stasz who were able to distinguish several specific strategies. For example, a subject might have tried to learn just one area of the map on each trial, or alternatively may have attempted to memorize all the states' names on one trial, then all the names of the towns on the next trial, and so on. This indicated that a single map task could be attempted in more than one way. We are unaware of any similar research with children, though clearly such an approach might be an effective way to analyse how children memorize maps and would allow comparisons between their strategies and those used by adults.

A few studies have used computer models to simulate the processes involved in planning a route on a map. Hayes-Roth and Hayes Roth (1979) gave a subject a map of a town and a list of errands (to go to the bookstore, grocery shop, cinema, etc.) and asked him or her to plan a route to include these visits. At the same time the subject was asked to give a verbal description of how the task was attempted. Hayes-Roth and Hayes-Roth analysed this description and designed a computer simulation of the strategies indicated by the subject. In another study, Streeter and Vitello (1986) asked car drivers to plan a number of journeys on a map and compared the way their subjects did this with several computer-based models. Such research is a useful approach to the analysis of how people select routes on navigational maps. At present there has been no research at all into how children might use a map to plan a route, or whether children will use the same or different strategies from adults.

The results from the psychological research with adults described above are necessarily fragmentary and we still know little about the abilities required to use a map successfully. This is a particular problem when we turn to a consideration of children's performance with maps, because without knowing the skills involved in understanding a map it is difficult to say what abilities children need to learn or how these abilities develop in the child.

The cartographic research has traditionally been concerned with aspects of map design; for instance, to discover the most appropriate symbols, typeface or colour coding, etc., for use on particular maps.) More recently cartographers have also started to look at the strategies adults use in specialized map-reading tasks [for a review of this work see Blades and Spencer (1986b)].

One or two cartographic studies have considered the legibility of maps designed for children. Gerber (1982) examined the most appropriate typeface to use on maps in school atlases. Children were shown four maps, each with a different typeface. The maps consisted of a large number of city names and the size of the typeface for each name corresponded to the population of the city. Children aged 9–15 years were asked questions such as 'Which is the nearest place with under 100,000 people to Rome?'. From the children's performance Gerber was able to draw conclusions about the legibility of the type and recommend the particular typefaces that were most easily recognized by children. Miller (1974) gave 9–11-year-olds four maps each of which represented the same area but was printed in different combinations of colours. He tested children's ability to identify places and road names on the maps and was able to make a number of suggestions about the use of colour on maps designed for children.

The influence of Piaget

The majority of textbooks and papers concerned with the development of children's map knowledge have discussed this in the context of Piaget's theory of spatial development. However, it should be noted that most textbooks have been written by cartographers (e.g. Robinson and Petchenik, 1976) or by geographers (e.g. Boardman, 1983) who have rarely taken into account the more recent psychological research that has been critical of Piagetian methodology and has often produced results that differ from Piaget's original findings (see earlier chapters). Furthermore, Piaget himself said nothing directly about children's map abilities and therefore to make Piaget's theory relevant for map studies many authors have drawn inferences from his research. But most of these inferences have not been tested empirically and may not be justified.

We have already described Piaget's theory in Chapter 4, and return to it in Chapter 9. In this section we concentrate on the way that it has been interpreted with regard to children's understanding of maps. Piaget suggested that children progress through three stages of spatial awareness; the topological, projective, and Euclidean stages (Piaget, Inhelder, and Szeminska, 1960). In the topological stage, up to the age of about 7 years, children can only consider the relationship between two places in space in qualitative terms. For example, some places are 'near' to each other or 'distant' from each other. If young children do view the world in this manner it has been argued that they will have difficulty with a map because a map is based on projective and Euclidean transformations and therefore will not correspond with a young child's understanding of the world.

As has been noted in Chapter 4 there is no longer agreement that children's spatial development progresses through three distinct stages. In particular, mathematicians have been critical of Piaget's use of terms such as topological (e.g. Kapadia, 1974) and studies of these concepts in children have not always confirmed the order of stages proposed by Piaget (Geeslin and Shar, 1979; Martin, 1976a,b).

Piaget also considered that young children were spatially egocentric, that is they cannot appreciate any view of the world other than their own. This conclusion stemmed from Piaget and Inhelder's (1956) experiment with a model of three mountains in which children had to describe the model from the viewpoint of a person looking at the same model but from a different position from that of the child. Children before the age of 7 years tended to ignore the fact that the other person was looking at the model from a different angle and often described their own view of the model rather than the view of the other person. Piaget took this as evidence that young children have an egocentric view of space and that they cannot appreciate any perspective that they have not personally experienced. This conclusion has led to the suggestion that young children will have difficulty with a map, because a map is drawn from an artificial viewpoint 'above' the world. This is a perspective that the child can never have experienced and will be quite different from the child's own view of the world.

It is no longer thought that children are as spatially egocentric as Piaget suggested (see Chapter 4) and in general the idea of egocentrism as a specific age-related stage of development has not been supported by the experimental evidence (see Presson and Somerville, 1985).

After about 7 or 8 years of age, children are considered to be in the projective stage of development and can appreciate some, but not all, spatial relationships. In the literature related to map research the most frequently quoted Piagetian task is Piaget and Inhelder's (1956) model-village task. Children were shown a model village and asked to reproduce it by making their own model or by drawing it, at the same or a smaller scale than the original. The model included features such as a church, houses, trees, etc., and some children before the age of 7 years could reproduce small groups of these features (e.g. the child might accurately place the tree in front of the house to the left of the church) but only after the age of 7 years could they copy the arrangement of all the features. At this stage the children placed the features in the correct spatial relationship to each other but did not usually reproduce the distances between the features accurately. From about 9 or 10 years of age, at the start of the Euclidean stage of development, children were able to draw the model preserving the exact distances between the features, and by 11 or 12 years they could make an accurate small-scale plan of the given model.

Given the interpretation that has been placed on the Piagetian experiments referred to above, it has often been thought that children before the age of

7 years, being limited to the topological stage of development and being spatially egocentric, are too young to start any map work. In many schools, 7 or 8 years is still the age at which children first start to learn about maps, and they are not expected to understand aspects of maps involving Euclidean concepts (such as scale or grid references) until they reach the appropriate developmental stages.

The influence of Piaget's research has been far reaching and has had three important consequences. First, as noted above, on the age at which maps are introduced into the school curriculum. It is only very recently that teachers have attempted to use maps with children aged under 7 years, often with suprising success, and some of this educational work will be discussed below. Secondly, there has been virtually no educational research with children younger than 7 yearsd, simply because such children have not been expected to understand maps at all. Thirdly, the research with older children has often been interpreted within a Piagetian framework even when this has been inappropriate. For example, in the experiment by Acredolo and Boulter (1984) described earlier they found that children remembered the relative position of two places in different areas of a map by reference to the relative location of those areas. Acredolo and Boulter interpreted this finding in Piagetian terms, by suggesting that the children in their experiment were particularly sensitive to the topological properties of the maps and that 'the topological notions of enclosure, belongingness and similarity may have been operating to distort the preoperational children's memory for distance and direction' (1984, p. 422). But Stevens and Coupe (1978) had already found that the same distortions occurred in adult's memory for similar maps. If Acredolo and Boulter's interpretation of the children's performance is correct then the same explanation is implied for adults' performance as well, but this is tantamount to saying that adults are also limited to a topological understanding of space. Rather than relying on Piagetian terminology the results from such experiments might be better described by reference to particular cognitive processes affecting both children's and adults' memory and perception of maps.

Map-teaching

A number of geography books have described ways to teach children about maps (e.g. Catling, 1981) and these books usually suggest that map work can be broken down into different components, such as symbols, grid references, scales, contours, etc. However, there is little agreement about the order in which these components should be taught. Nor is there any agreement about the ages at which children can first be introduced to the different aspects of map work.

There has been surprisingly little assessment of the different methods that have been advocated for map-teaching, and only a few experiments have compared children's performance before and after specific training. Ellis (1974) compared three groups of 8–9-year-old children, two groups received different teaching about land use patterns from aerial photographs and maps, and the third served as a control. Ellis found no difference between the teaching methods, but the children in both experimental groups performed better than the control group in a post test. Carswell (1971) gave 9–12-year-olds a course in reading and interpreting topographic maps. All the children improved, but unfortunately Carswell did not describe the course and did not include a control group. There is clearly a need for teachers' suggestions about map work to be more rigorously assessed in formal experiments, otherwise the effectiveness of different teaching methods can only be judged from the subjective reports of individual teachers' classroom practice.

The problem of selecting the most appropriate methods of map teaching is particularly relevant to the issue of how children should first start to learn about maps. In a survey of the literature we found more than a dozen different approaches advocated for beginning map work with young children (see Blades and Spencer, 1986a). These included looking at models from above, using aerial photographs, drawing maps of the classroom, building models and toy layouts, and making plan views of objects. These methods are not necessarily exclusive and they may all contribute to a young child's understanding of a map, but only two of the suggested approaches have been tested experimentally. Muir and Blaut (1969) used aerial photographs to teach a group of 5- and 6-year-olds about maps and compared these children to another group who were taught without the use of such photographs. The children in the 'photograph' group performed much better than the other children in later map tests. In another study, Atkins (1981) taught 4- and 5-year-olds about maps, globes, and compass directions (though unfortunately Atkins does not describe exactly what instruction the children received). These children were compared with a control group who did not receive the instruction. The former performed better than the control group, both immediately after instruction and again a year later. These two experiments indicate that some approaches are effective, but without more assessment (and without direct comparisons between different methods) it is not yet clear which are the most useful ways to introduce maps.

Both the studies by Muir and Blaut (1969) and by Atkins (1981) included children who were much younger than the age traditionally associated with the start of map work, and there are also reports from teachers of successful classroom work with equally young children (Blades and Spencer, 1986a). These reports imply that children may be able to learn about maps well before they reach the projective stage of spatial development at the age of 7 or 8 years.

Educational research

Most of the experimental educational research tends to be normative because the majority of studies have examined a single, or at the most two, age groups differing only by a year or two, and the results from such studies are usually ex-

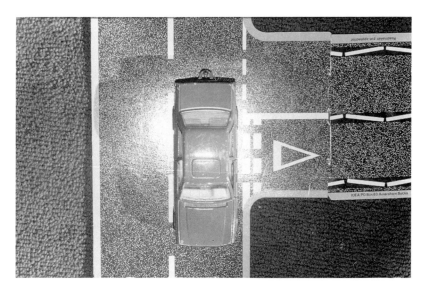

Figure 8.1   Can young children understand plan views? From earliest play with objects, the child receives practice in translating between viewpoints: the aerial views of a toy car anticipate the plan representation that would be found in a drawing of the car from above.

pressed in terms of the proportion of children at a given age who can perform a specific task. [For reviews of the research with young children, see Catling, (1979) and for older children, see Boardman (1983).] Much of the educational research is subject to two serious limitations. First, experiments related to the same aspect of map work have often used very different materials and methods to test children's ability. This point can be illustrated by reference to the experiments concerned with the concept of scale. Gerber (1981) tested 6–8-year-olds' understanding of scale by showing the children a metre rule and then asking them to estimate the length and breadth of their classroom and also longer distances of over 100 metres. Nearly half the children could do this with some accuracy over the shorter distances, but were very poor at judging long distances. Gerber suggested that this result indicated that such children 'will have little chance of understanding anything about scale' (1981, p. 130) and that they will therefore not be able to estimate distances on a photograph or a map. It is tempting to wonder how well adults would have judged distances with only a metre rule for reference, but, in any case, the process of estimating a distance in the real world and using a scale on a map is so different that any conclusions about map ability from such a test may not be valid.

Towler and Nelson (1968) assessed the concept of scale using a model of a toy farm on a board. Children (aged 6–12 years) were given a small board, one quarter of the size of the area of the model, and a set of symbol shapes representing the farm buildings. Each shape was provided in five different sizes and the children's task was to select, and place on the small board, the appropriate one-quarter scale symbols to represent the buildings of the model. Only the oldest children could select all the correct symbols and Towler and Nelson concluded that children do not develop a concept of scale before the ages of 10 or 11 years. However, this general conclusion ignores the children's varying ability to select particular shapes. Children at all ages were proficient with some symbol shapes (e.g. circles and ovals), but with other shapes (e.g. rectangles) most children had great difficulty selecting the correct quarter size symbol. In other words, the children's performance was not only influenced by their ability, but also by the materials used in the experiment. Most other published studies of children's ability with scales have not included a description of the experimental materials used to test the children. Therefore, it is not easy to make comparisons across different studies, and the lack of any consistent methodology makes it difficult to draw general conclusions about the development of children's understanding of scale. For the same reason it is not possible to make any conclusions about children's understanding of other map concepts. With a few exceptions [e.g. Gerber's (1984) study of children's use of symbols] most educational experiments are not fully reported and different studies have used various methodologies and test materials.

A second limitation to the educational research is the emphasis on group performance (usually expressed as the mean scores of specific age groups) with the consequence that little is reported about how individual children attempted the tasks or about the difficulties encountered by the unsuccessful children. Without an analysis of the children's performances it is not possible to describe the strategies that they attempt to use to solve particular map tasks, and without some indication of the children's strategies little can be said about how the children learn and develop procedures to use maps and carry out map tasks.

Psychological research

In the following sections we will describe some of the more psychologically based studies related to maps. These can be grouped around specific topics; the understanding of aerial photographs, the use of coordinates, and young children's ability to use simple maps. We discuss these topics with reference to both the educational research and to Piaget's theory of spatial development. Finally, we mention briefly the recent research that has considered the relationship between maps and written text.

Aerial photographs

Aerial photographs have often been recommended as an important aid to map teaching (Glendinning and Pearson, 1983; Muir and Blaut, 1969), and in particular they have been advocated as a useful way to introduce maps to young children, because aerial photographs have been considered a transitional step between the real world and a conventional map (Riffle, 1969). Interpreting an aerial photograph requires some but not all the processes that have been assumed to be involved in reading a topographic map. An aerial photograph involves reduction in scale, a degree of abstraction (for example, in a vertical aerial photograph houses are 'represented' by roofs rather than their three-dimensional shape), and they also require some understanding of the world as portrayed from above. On the other hand, aerial photographs do not include conventional symbols or labelling as does a map.

If children can benefit from working with aerial photographs the question is at what age? Piaget argued that children are spatially egocentric before the age of 7 years (see Chapter 4). This might imply that such young children will not understand aerial photographs because they portray a perspective of the landscape outside the direct experience of young children. None the less, a number of experiments have demonstrated that young children do in fact have some understanding of aerial photographs.

Blaut, McCleary, and Blaut (1970) examined 6-year-olds in the United States with oblique colour photographs of a view of the countryside, and a vertical black-and-white photograph of a suburban area. The children were asked to name and point to any individual features that they could identify on the photograph. Virtually all the children recognized the photographs as views of the landscape and on average could identify at least six features (such as roads, houses, trees, etc.) on both types of aerial photographs. Blaut *et al.* also carried out a similar study with Puerto Rican children using a vertical black and white photograph of their own school and its neighbourhood. These children performed similarly to the North American children. Blaut *et al.* pointed out that even such young children could have had some experience of aerial views of the world from television and magazine pictures, but they also mention a further successful replication of the experiment with peasant children in St Vincent, West Indies, who had had no experience of television and only limited access to any pictorial publications. Stea and Blaut (1973) conducted further experiments with Puerto Rican children across the age-range of 5 to 11 years. The youngest of these children could usually identify between two and five features on the aerial photographs.

In a more recent experiment with British children, Spencer, Harrison, and Darvizeh (1980) tested 3–5-year-old children with six vertical aerial photographs and with perceptual maps. The latter were oblique perspective cartographic views of particular cities with selected landmark buildings and features designed for use by tourists. The children, who saw all the photographs at the same time, were allowed unlimited time to look at the photographs and were encouraged to talk about them. Each child identified a large number of different features (between 6 and 25) and there was a close correlation between the children's performance with the photographs and with the maps. The number of features mentioned by the children is larger than the scores of older children in previous studies and is probably due to the different procedure and less structured approach that was taken in this experiment. Children commented on geographical areas such as the differences between town and country areas on the same and across different photographs, and were particularly good at recognizing roads, houses, trees, rivers, roundabouts, railways, parks, and cars. Fewer children referred to features such as hills or fields. In describing the photographs the children often applied contextual cues; for example, having identified a road they would then pick out cars on the road and roundabouts at the junctions. In other words, having recognized one feature they could identify other features related to it. Dale (1971) noticed a similar strategy being used by older children, aged 7–11 years, with aerial photographs and maps of their own village. Children would first locate a familiar place and then follow routes through the village identifying other features, though of course, the children in this study had the advantage of knowing the area depicted on the photographs and maps.

The studies with aerial photographs have demonstrated that children as young as 3 years of age can decode features in aerial perspective, and their success with such photographs has prompted the suggestion that learning about aerial photographs can contribute to learning about maps. Surprisingly, there have been no studies of untrained children's ability to understand maps rather than photographs. We thought that if young children performed so well with aerial photographs they might also have some appreciation of maps. Of course, maps differ from aerial views in a number of respects. In particular, maps simplify the environment that is represented, and usually include conventional symbols and labelling. To test children's understanding of maps and their ability to cope with symbols we carried out an experiment with 4–6-year-olds who were asked to name features on a specially designed map (Blades and Spencer 1987b).

The map used in the experiment is illustrated in Figure 8.2. The original was 46 cm × 48 cm and drawn in colour. Although imaginary, the map was intended to represent a possible urban environment, with roads (grey) lined by small and large houses (red). There were two roundabouts at road junctions. To the south-west two roads crossed by bridges over a river (blue) and to the east there was a road bridge over a railway line (black). In the north-east a large irregular area was coloured green to represent a park or playing field. The map also included symbols for particular buildings; two 'churches' (shown as black crosses), two 'schools' (shown in 'playgrounds') and in the south-east corner, three black oblongs to represent a 'station' next to the railway lines. The names of these buildings are in inverted commas to emphasize that without a specific map key there is no objective description of these black symbols and we were particularly interested to find out if and how young children would identify them.

A total of 108 children between the ages of 4 and 6 years took part in the experiment. Half the children were asked to name the symbols as each one was pointed out to them on the map. Altogether there were 10 symbols (road, river, park, roundabouts, bridge, school, church, railway, station, and house). Some leeway was allowed in how the children named these; for example, 'stream' and 'water' were accepted for river, but not "pond", 'sea' or 'lake'. The other half of the children were given the names of each feature and were asked to point to an example of the symbol representing that feature on the map.

By the age of 6 years nearly all the children could identify the majority of the symbols on the map, but even the 4-year-olds could recognize at least half of the symbols. Very few children failed to recognize anything at all on the map or describe it simply in terms of lines, shapes, or colours. It was easier for the children to find examples of named features than to have to suggest names for the symbols on the map. Not all the symbols were of equal difficulty; roads, river, and park were easily identified by nearly all the children, but the symbols for station, church, and school were harder to identify, though by the age of 6 children either recognized them, or were able to suggest quite appropriate definitions (such as 'hospital' or 'factory').

The results from this experiment and the findings from the research into children's ability to understand aerial photographs indicate that young children can appreciate a view of the world from above even when, as in the case with a map, the view is one that is conventionalized and includes symbols.

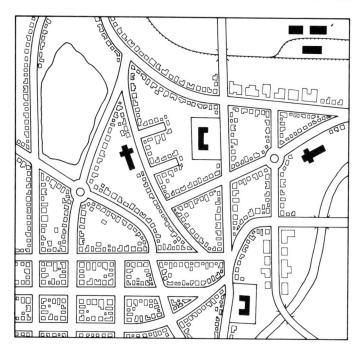

Figure 8.2   Children were shown this map and asked to say what they thought the symbols represented.

Coordinates

Many maps include coordinate reference systems in the form of vertical and horizontal grid lines which may be labelled or numbered so that particular points or areas on the map can be specified by a grid reference. Educational texts (e.g. Mays, 1985) usually suggest that children can start to understand simple grids labelled with letters by about 8 years of age and can cope with grids labelled with numbers after about 10 years. This assumption has been influenced by Piaget's research into children's understanding of spatial coordinates.

Piaget, Inhelder, and Szeminska (1960) studied children's ability to locate a point in space. They showed children two identical rectangular pieces of paper, on one of which a single point was marked, and the children (who were given measuring equipment) were asked to duplicate the position of the point on the second piece of paper. Piaget *et al.* found that children could only do this successfully after about 8 years of age, and in a replication of this experiment Carlson (1976) found that children could not locate a point accurately until the age of 10 years. However, in both these experiments the children were not provided with a coordinate system, but rather they had to calculate the coordinates of the given point for themselves.

In an experiment that did provide a partial coordinate system, Towler (1970) gave children a card showing a number of dots and asked the children to draw the dot pattern on a second card. Some of the cards included vertical and horizontal reference lines to form a simple grid. Towler found that children below the age of 8 or 9 years did not use the reference lines when trying to copy the pattern of the dots.

In contrast to the results from the above studies, Somerville and Bryant (1985) found that 4–6-year-olds could use given coordinates in simple tasks. For example, children were shown an opaque square board that was placed over two rods; one rod protruded from the left or right side of the board (to provide a horizontal coordinate) and one from the top or bottom of the board (to provide a vertical coordinate). The children had to extrapolate from the visible portions of the rods and indicate where they thought the rods crossed under the board by selecting one of four given points marked on the top of the board. Somerville and Bryant discovered that some children as young as 4.5 years could do this successfully, and that most 6.5-year-olds could perform correctly in a number of variations of the task. Somerville and Bryant's conclusion that children can understand coordinates from the age of 4 years is in marked contrast to Piaget's finding that they could only do so after 8 years of age.

Although Somerville and Bryant's findings are suggestive of greater ability in young children than expected, it is not clear how equally young children would perform in tests involving the use of grid references and coordinate systems in map-like tasks. Therefore we carried out a series of experiments to find out if young children could utilize a grid reference.

Using a grid reference involves two steps. First the grid reference must be read correctly and the reference points on the axes of the map frame have to be found. The second step involves constructing vertical and horizontal lines (parallel to the map coordinates) from the reference points until the lines intersect at the required location. Somerville and Bryant's (1985) experiment indicated that young children can carry out the second step effectively. To find out if children could perform both steps we tested 4–6-year-olds using a board that incorporated 16 sunken squares in a 4 × 4 layout. Each square contained a different picture hidden by a close-fitting cardboard cover. Vertical and horizontal coordinate lines were drawn across the board and intersected over the centre of each covered picture. The vertical coordinates were numbered 1, 2, 3, 4, and the horizontal coordinates were lettered a, b, c, d. The children were given a grid reference card (such as '2a' or '3c') and a copy of the correct hidden picture was fixed to the back of the card. The children's task was to find the appropriate square on the board for a given grid reference. When they had selected a square on the board they could remove its cover and then turn over the grid reference card to see if the pictures matched. The majority of the 6-year-olds were very competent at this task, but only a few of the younger children could do it successfully.

We considered that the younger children's comparatively poor performance might be due to the fact that they could not carry out both steps involved in using a grid reference, or alternatively these children may simply have been confused by the labelling of the coordinates because few of the children were proficient with the alphabet or with numbers. Therefore we repeated the experiment with another group of similarly aged children, but labelled each grid coordinate with a different colour. The grid reference in this case was a card with two colours on it (one for the horizontal coordinate and one for the vertical coordinate). Half the 4-year-olds and the majority of the 5- and 6-year-olds were successful in this task, which indicated that they could use a grid reference and that their poorer performance in the previous experiment was probably because the coordinates were labelled with symbols that were unfamiliar to them. In a further study, other young children demonstrated the ability to carry out the reverse procedure—they were shown one of the pictures on the board and had to select the grid reference appropriate to that picture.

The children's success in these experiments and the studies by Somerville and Bryant (1985) suggest that even 4-year-olds are capable of using coordinates and combining information from two dimensions. However, as pointed out above, Piaget *et al.* (1960) argued from their experiments that children could only start to use coordinates after the age of 8 years. This discrepancy may be a consequence of the different tasks used to test young children's ability—Piaget *et al* did not provide a coordinate grid for the children, who had to construct their own grid with measuring and drawing equipment. It may be that children find it particularly difficult to reach a solution to a task that involves generating a coordinate grid on an unmarked piece of paper and this may account for the comparatively late age at which they can do so. None the less it is clear, from the more recent experiments, that when a grid is provided even young children have little difficulty in using a coordinate reference. Further research is necessary to discover the extent of children's abilities in this area, but the immediate implication of the results described above is that children's competence in this aspect of map work has been very much underestimated.

Map-using

One of the most frequent uses of a map is for navigation, that is, to find a place in an unfamiliar environment. As pointed out earlier in this chapter, there has been virtually no research into how adults navigate with a map and similarly there have been few studies of children's map-using. The experiments which have been carried out have been concerned with children aged 3–8 years. Because of the practical difficulties of testing young children in the real world, the usual format for these experiments has been to give children maps of rooms or large-scale layouts that they can walk through and to ask the children either to use the map to find a specific place in the layout or to follow a route.

In general, these studies have provided children with two-dimensional representations, in the form of maps or plans, of the three-dimensional layouts used in the experiments. Nearly all the children used as subjects in the various studies would traditionally be considered to be in the topological stage of spatial development. In order to understand even a simple plan, children have to recognize that it is a representation of a layout from above, and appreciate any symbols or conventions used. This might be thought to be beyond the capabilities of many of the children tested in these studies, but as we describe below, even very young children have a surprising ability to use maps in various experimental situations.

Bluestein and Acredolo (1979) showed 3–5-year-old children a map of a small rectangular room which included a table, chairs, and four identical green boxes to serve as hiding places for a small toy. The boxes were placed at the mid-point of each wall. In one corner of the room there was a door and in each of the other three corners there was a different salient object (for example, a red box). Children were shown, on the map, the box that contained the hidden toy and then they were asked to find the correct box in the actual room. The children saw the map either inside or outside the room and either correctly orientated with the room or rotated 180° relative to it. When the children saw the map in the room and correctly orientated, half the 3-year-olds, three-quarters of the 4-year-olds and all the 5-year-olds could find the toy successfully, but only the 5-year-olds could also use the map correctly when it was rotated. This result indicates that children as young as 3 years can use a map in certain conditions.

Bluestein and Acredolo analysed the mistakes made by the children in terms of 'egocentric' errors. This was when a child, in the condition with the 180° rotated maps wrongly selected the box directly opposite the correct box. In other words, the children may have assumed that the rotated map was correctly aligned with the room. This was a prevalent error, especially when the children were shown the map in the room.

Presson (1982) suggested that children might try to use rotated maps in at least two ways—they could look at the given map and the mentally rotate it until the map corresponded to the room, or they could use a strategy that related the correct hiding place to one or more 'landmarks' in the room (for example, in Bluestein and Acredolo's experiment the correct box might be the one between the red box and the door). Presson carried out a study similar to Bluestein and Acredolo's, but with 6- and 8-year-old children. Presson used a small room that included four hiding places, one in each corner, and just a single landmark (for example, a chair placed against one wall, midway between two of the hiding places). Children were shown maps rotated 90° and 180° relative to the room that indicated which hiding place contained a toy.

Presson examined the children's errors and suggested that the majority of the errors reflected a tendency to select a hiding place on the basis of whether it was near or far from the landmark. For instance, if the chair was placed as a landmark between two of the boxes, one of which contained the hidden toy, children who did not go to the correct box often went to the second box near the chair, rather than the other boxes in the room. In other words the children appeared to identify the hiding place by reference to the landmark, rather than by attempting to mentally rotate the map. This is an important result and indicates how children might try to use a map, but it is not without some ambiguity, because Presson also found that the children performed better with maps that were rotated $90°$ than with maps rotated $180°$. This latter finding could be accounted for if some of the children had attempted to mentally rotate the map and were more likely to make errors with maps requiring a greater degree of rotation.

In order to clarify Presson's (1982) conclusion and also to find out if children younger than 6 years of age also identified places from maps by reference to landmarks, we carried out an experiment using a layout of paths and hiding places as illustrated in Figure 8.3. The layout consisted of five paths, one of the paths led to the centre of a 'crossroads' and at the end of each path of the crossroads there was a box in which a toy could be hidden. A large, red, plastic bucket was placed to the north-east of the layout so that it could be used as a landmark. Children, who were aged 3–6 years were given several different maps

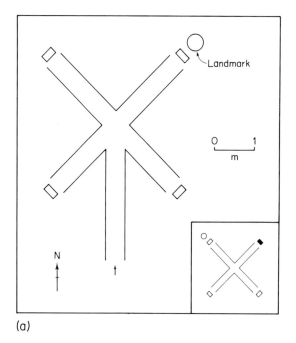

(a)

Figure 8.3(a) Plan of layout and map used to find out if children could use the map to find a hidden toy (indicated by the shaded box on the map).

(b)

Figure 8.3(b)   One of the layouts used for testing young children's ability with maps.

(each attached to a clipboard) showing the crossroads, a red circle to represent the landmark, and the box that contained the toy was shaded. The maps were given to the children rotated 90° or 180° relative to the layout. The children's performance was not affected by the degree of rotation, but they were much more likely to find the toy when it was hidden in the north-east box, adjacent to the landmark, than when it was in the other boxes. They were also more likely to find the toy in the south-west box, directly opposite the landmark, than in the north-west and south-east boxes, which were equally distant from the landmark and which may have been difficult for the children to differentiate.

The results from all these experiments indicate that very young children can use a map to find a particular place and that when they do so they refer to the landmarks that are available in the layouts and on the maps. This may reflect a general preference to rely on landmarks in the environment because the ability of 3- and 4-year-old children to use landmarks effectively has been demonstrated in laboratory experiments (e.g. Acredolo, Pick, and Olson, 1975) and in studies of children's way-finding in real environments (e.g. Darvizeh and Spencer, 1984).

In the 'crossroads' experiment we found that when trying to use the 180° rotated maps a few children made what Bluestein and Acredolo (1979) described as an 'egocentric' error. This labelling of such errors reflects the Piagetian idea that young children are spatially egocentric. However, it might be better to explain such errors as a result of the children making a false assumption that the given maps were correctly orientated with the areas that they represented. This is an error that is not limited to young children. In a study of 'you-are-here' maps (which are maps placed on the walls of public buildings and shopping precincts to show visitors where they are) Levine, Marchon, and Hanley (1984) found that adults nearly always assumed that such maps were correctly aligned with the environment so that a place shown higher on the map was directly ahead in the environment. Consequently, when the map was not aligned most people failed to take this into consideration and nearly always moved away from the map in the wrong direction from the destination that they wanted. Undoubtedly, incorrect assumptions about the orientation of a map can be made by people of all ages, and is not necessarily an error that is specific to a particular stage of spatial development.

One additional result from our experiments (Blades and Spencer, 1986a) is worth noting. In a study with preschool children we found that it was possible to teach 4-year-olds how to orientate simple maps. The children were shown how to align an incorrectly orientated map so that it corresponded to a layout before they attempted to use the map to find a place in the layout. The majority of the children who were trained learnt to do this quickly and could apply the same strategy effectively in different situations. This result suggests that it is feasible to start map work and teach aspects of map-using even to pre-school children.

In the experiments described above, children had to find a particular place. In all these studies small areas were used and in every case the children could see the whole of the experimental environment from a single viewpoint. However, maps are usually used when a route has to be planned through an environment that is not completely visible, therefore we designed a test to find out if young children could use a map to navigate through an environment that which they could not see from a single vantage point (Blades and Spencer, 1987a).

A 25-metre-long maze was drawn on the floor of a school playground (see Figure 8.4). This consisted of three T-junctions, and large screens were placed on the positions shown in Figure 8.4; these limited the children's view across the maze. Wooden boxes placed across the paths served as 'roadblocks' and

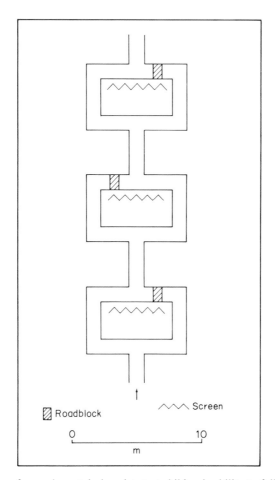

Figure 8.4   Plan of maze layout designed to test children's ability to follow a route with a map.

the screens hid their position so that the children could not see them before making a route choice at each of the T-junctions. The children were given a map (scale 1 : 100) of the maze showing the position of the roadblocks. The map was attached to a clipboard, which they carried as they walked through the maze. The children's task was to get through the maze without 'crashing' into any of the roadblocks.

Sixty children in five age-groups between 3 and 6 years of age had six trials each in the maze, and for each trial the positions of the roadblocks were changed. The children in the youngest age-group did not perform better than if they had been guessing which way to turn at each junction, but the majority of the children in all the other age groups were able to use the maps effectively to find the correct route through the maze.

A few children were generally successful, but made errors in particular trials. Some children were observed pointing along the route with their finger on the map as they walked through the maze, and there were occasions when they failed to update their position on the map. For example, a child approaching the third T-junction in the maze might be seen pointing at the second T-junction on the map, and this sometimes resulted in an incorrect turn at the third junction. All three junctions in the maze were identical and this may have sometimes confused the children. To see if this was a problem we repeated the same experiment with a further 60 children of the same age, but placed distinctive landmarks at each junction (these were different brightly coloured objects). These landmarks were marked on the map with appropriate colours. In this condition the overall performance of the children improved, which suggested that the children were able to take advantage of the presence of the landmarks to help them find their way through the maze. The maze experiment demonstrated that from the age of 4 years children could use a simple map to follow a route, and their improved performance when the landmarks were present suggests that the children were sensitive to any additional information provided by the map. In the maze study, the landmarks that were placed at each junction were unique, because each landmark in the maze (and therefore also on the map) was different. Such uniqueness is not typical of conventional maps because most maps, although they may have different symbols for each type of landmark (e.g. traffic lights, church, school buildings, etc.) will include several examples of the same symbol. In a further experiment we examined young children's ability to use maps that had more than one instance of the same landmark symbol (Blades and Spencer, 1987c). The layout used for this experiment is illustrated in Figure 8.5. It was an octagonal layout of paths, 7 metres across, and at each of the eight vertices there was a cardboard box. The boxes were open at the top so that a child could see inside a box when standing close to it, but could only see into one box at a time. On the inside base of each box there was a large painted circle which served as a landmark, and some of the boxes contained circles of the same colour. In the example illustrated in Figure 8.5 the

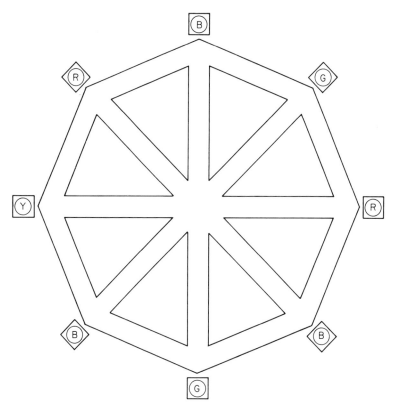

Figure 8.5   Plan of the layout with coloured landmarks designed to examine how young children used the landmarks to find their way through the layout.

landmarks were, clockwise from south—green, black, yellow, red, black, green, red, and black. Maps (scale 1 : 50) of the whole layout were drawn and these included appropriately coloured circles to represent the landmarks in the layout. One particular path to the centre of the octagon was marked on the map. The children were asked to carry the map and walk round the outer path of the layout (clockwise from the southernmost part of the layout) until they reached the path marked on the map and then to turn down that path to the centre of the layout. The maps were never given to the children correctly orientated with the layout.

Sometimes the correct path was marked by a unique landmark (e.g. the yellow circle in Figure 8.5). Sometimes by one of two similar landmarks (e.g. one of the two red landmarks) or by one of three similar landmarks (e.g. one of the three black landmarks). Children carried out a series of tests with different maps and layouts. The experiment was designed to identify the different possible strategies that the children might use. For example, if the correct path was indicated by the single unique landmark on the map (the yellow), children only had to find this landmark in the layout to know that they were at the correct path. If the correct path was marked by the second red landmark, children had to differentiate between the two red landmarks. One way to do this was to consider the preceding landmark (e.g. to think of the correct red as the red after the green). If the correct path was marked by the third black landmark, it was not sufficient to consider only the preceding landmark because two of the black landmarks were preceded by red landmarks. One way to distinguish the correct black landmark was to take into account at least two of the preceding landmarks (e.g. the black after the red after the green). Depending on the pattern of the landmarks in the layout, there were eight possible strategies that the children could use to find the correct path. All the strategies could be identified by the pattern of the children's performance, by considering the sort of errors they made, and by observing their behaviour in the layout.

The 48 children who took part in the experiment were divided into three age-groups (4.5, 6 and 7.5 years old). None of the children had any difficulty with the maps that showed the correct path marked by a unique landmark. But when the maps included more than one landmark of the same colour, the younger children tended to choose the first path in the layout marked by that colour and ignored the fact that the maps included more than one landmark of that colour. However, by the age of 7 years the majority of the children realized the need to consider more than just a single landmark and most of these children attempted a variety of strategies to find the correct path. They did not always apply the most effective strategy for a particular map, but these children did realize the need to take into account the order of the landmarks in the layout rather than attend only to the colour of the landmark at the end of the correct path. In other words, they were aware of the need to consider two or three elements of information from the map at the same time. This is perhaps surprising given the age of the children and the fact that none of them had had any previous experience of map work. Although further experiments are needed to discover the extent of their ability, it is clear that 7-year-olds (and some individual younger children) can apply reasoned strategies to difficult maps.

Recently, Ottosson (1987) tested 5–12-year-old children's ability to use standard Scandinavian maps in realistic situations; the children would be told where they were on the map and shown a particular destination on the map. To reach the destination they had to work out which way they were facing at the start, plan an appropriate route on the map, and then follow the route until they reached the exact destination. Ottosson interviewed the children as they did this and kept detailed notes of their performance, including any errors that they made. Ottosson's study is important for a number of reasons: many of the children were able to follow all or part of the routes without help; by observing the children so closely Ottosson was able to describe the ways children attempted to use the maps; and he also noted that they often had common problems (e.g. sometimes the children did not take into account that the map was not necessarily orientated with the environment and this led to specific errors). We cannot summarize all of Ottosson's (1987) experiment here, but his results provide a good example of the detailed and important findings that can come from naturalistic studies in practical situations.

In this section we have described a number of studies demonstrating that very young children can use simple maps to find places and follow routes, and that it is often possible, by manipulating the experimental maps and layouts, to analyse how the children use the maps. In summary, untrained children from the age of 3 or 4 years have an appreciation of a two-dimensional representation of a given area. This is considerably earlier than might be expected from the interpretations of Piaget's theory of spatial development, which imply that such young children are too limited in their understanding of spatial relationships. As yet there have been no other studies of map using with children older than 8 years of age (and for that matter there has been no research at all into how adolescents and adults use a map to navigate), therefore little can be said at present about how the ability to navigate with a map develops across the age-range.

Maps as a learning aid

So far we have discussed experiments related to map-reading, map-interpretation, and map-using, but there is also a further important aspect of map work which we describe briefly in this section. This is the effect of maps as a learning aid when presented with text. Although maps are often used as illustrations in much published material, ranging from newspapers to school textbooks, it is only recently that there has been any investigation into the usefulness of such maps.

There is some evidence from research with adults that maps can aid the learning of geography texts. For example, Gilmartin (1982) tested university students' ability to recall a passage about the physical geography of a fictional continent. Some of the subjects simply studied the passage, but others were given the same passage accompanied by maps of the continent. Gilmartin found that the subjects who had the benefit of the maps remembered more of the geographical information from the passage (both immediately after and also a week after studying it) than did subjects who were not shown the maps. Mastropieri and Scruggs (1983) examined 12–15-year-old students' memory for information from a text about a fictional island. One group of students received a map showing the location of features referred to in the text, and this group recalled more information from the text in a later test.

Kulhavy, Lee, and Caterino (1985) have suggested that maps may be an effective memory aid because written text and map information may be separately coded in memory. In other words, textual material is remembered in a linguistic mode whereas a map is remembered as a spatial representation. If this is the case, it implies that at the time of recall the subject is able to draw on both the linguistic and spatial representations, which increases the probability of remembering information from each. Kulhavy *et al.* called this the conjoint retention hypothesis and they tested its feasibility in an experiment with 10- and 11-year-old children. All the children heard a passage giving a history of a fictitious town and the passage included information about the location of particular historical events. Half the children had a map of the town and the other half had a written geographical description of the town. The children with the map recalled more information from the history passage than did the children with the geographical description. This would support the conjoint retention hypothesis put forward by Kulhavy *et al.*, because information from a spoken narrative and map (being encoded linguistically and spatially) was better remembered than the same information from the spoken and written narratives (both being encoded linguistically).

The experiments described in this section demonstrate that maps, when used to illustrate texts, can be a beneficial aid for learning novel information. Further research is needed to find out if maps are similarly beneficial for all ages, including children younger than those already tested in these experiments.

Conclusions

In this chapter we have attempted to survey some of the research related to map-teaching, map-learning, and map-using. As we pointed out at the beginning of this chapter, the research has been conducted in a number of different disciplines and with a diversity of methodologies. Direct comparisons across disciplines or even between individual experiments is often difficult, but we hope that future studies will be more sensitive to the research being carried out in related fields.

Rather than trying to summarize this chapter it may be easier to emphasize two points. First, how little we know about map abilities; if future research is to be effective we need cognitive analyses of exactly what is involved in all the map-related tasks—for example, what does it mean to recognize a symbol on a map? How can people interpret contour lines as three-dimensional shapes? How do we compare and combine information from maps at different scales? How do we relate map-based information with our personal experience of the real environment? And so on.

Secondly, how little we know about children's abilities. Perhaps the most important aspect of many recent experiments has been to demonstrate that children, and especially young children, are often underestimated. In other words, children may have some appreciation of maps several years earlier than expected; but beyond this we know very little about the development of any map abilities, or the ages at which particular map skills can be taught. Again, these are issues that would benefit from more investigation.

CHAPTER 9

The child's image of distant places: media, maps, and formal geography expand the area known

Maps offer an additional source of information about those areas that one is experiencing directly: they also provide one way in which individuals can, imaginatively, link their known world to a larger world, and gain some knowledge of the world that is beyond the range of direct experience. Other sources of information predominate in the child's development of images of distant places: the media, intentional teaching, and the unwitting social transmission of stereotypes about peoples and places, all of which concern us in the present chapter.

Developmental psychology made an early contribution to this area when Piaget (1928, 1929) discussed the child's developing concepts of his or her own area, town, region, and country; we review this briefly below. We argue that this tradition has tended to pay too little attention to the child's sources of information about the world, and concentrated all its efforts on conceptual development. Social psychology, in contrast, has been able to encompass both these aspects in its discussions of social cognition and its development: in its consideration of, for example, the role of the media in the development and reduction of prejudice, it has been able to link sources of information and the cognitive (and emotional) aspects of understanding the relation between own and other groups. There has been a modest amount of social psychological research on intercultural contact (e.g. Collett, 1971) and on the psychology of tourism and travel (e.g. Pearce, 1982)—very little of it explicitly linking these experiences with children's conceptual development but which, by modest extension, could be relevant reading for the developmental psychologist interested in the area.

156

Related research by behavioural geographers has been principally concerned with the image rather than its origins: Gould and White's (1986) 'mental maps' were in fact the preference spaces that guide, for example, the individual's choices about places to holiday in, move to for work, and so on. Little consideration is given by geographers to how these develop in the individual; and yet, for these accounts to become useful to developmental psychology, we would urge behavioural geographers studying such place images to consider process alongside pattern [see Spencer and Blades (1986) on the convergence of behavioural geography and those aspects of psychology concerned with the individual in the environment].

Of all the related literatures, that of education (and, in particular, geographical and environmental education) has been most explicitly concerned with the child's developing awareness of the world around and those areas that are beyond direct experience. The implications of developmental psychology's research for geographical and environmental education considered in Part III on the applications of research. In this chapter, we are concerned to learn, from what research and practice exists in the field of education about local and distant places, the importance for our basic understanding of the child's cognitive development.

We turn, therefore, first to the conceptual groundwork laid by Piaget in some of his earlier writings.

Concepts of country, and accounts of the natural world

In his 1928 study of judgement and reasoning of the child, Piaget includes a discussion of children's concepts of country. It appears as an illustration of the main argument about the child's developing understanding of relationships, and runs thus. If children under 9 years of age were asked if they were Swiss, very often they would deny it, saying that they were Genevan, or Vaudois, or give other cantonal labels as appropriate. Piaget reports that 'Up to the age of 9, three quarters of the children denied the possibility of being both Swiss and Genevan (or Vaudois, etc.)'.

In many cases, it was not that the child lacked the information that their canton was within Switzerland, but rather, Piaget argues, that they had difficulty in schematizing the information. The difficulty lies in the relation of part to whole: being 'in' something does not necessarily entail being part of it.

In the Piagetian account, there are three broad stages in the development of the idea of country, of which we have just been describing the middle, transitional, one. Initially, country 'is simply a unit along with the towns and districts', presumed by the child to be of similar size: Geneva, Switzerland, France are all alongside each other. Next, comes the stage already described, in which the child knows that the district is within the country, and yet it is talked of as if it were a piece of land enclosed in a foreign country. At the third stage, the child gains a correct idea of the relationship: 'one can be Genevan and Swiss at the same time'.

Given this view of the child's limited understanding of own and immediately neighbouring places, it is not surprising that the Piagetian account does not extend to the child's conceptualization of more distant places. Nor is there more than a passing mention of how education might affect the process, and the child's use of other sources of information about places. Early childhood is seen as necessarily a place where egocentricity limits the child's capacity to comprehend relationships in the surounding world.

Piaget also asked children, 'Where do countries come from?' According to Froh (age 7 years) building contractors make countries as the need for them arises. Similarly, in Piaget's (1929) study of children's conceptions of the natural world, children at this stage may have *artificial* views of the origin of sun and moon, sky, rivers, mountains, the sea, etc. The children see as these as products of human creation, rather than attributing creative activity to things themselves. The child makes no distinction between astronomy and metereology: the sun and moon are of the same order as the clouds, lightning, and the wind.

For the youngest children in the study (2–6-year-olds) the sky seems to be situated somewhere near the height of roofs or the mountains; it is blue, solid, and *constructed*—whether by God or by man. Similarly, the clouds may be the product of man's fires; lakes, and rivers must have been dug; and even water— some children guess—could have had a human origin: Roy, aged 6 years, suggests that 'there were a lot of men who spat a lot'. (He probably had other thoughts too, writes Piaget, but was too polite to express them). And Rob (aged 7) was also concerned with the size of the labour force needed to build the world: 'It takes a lot of men to make mountains: there must have been at least four'.

Such artificialism, charming as it may seem, could also be seen as a reasonable position for the child to adopt, Piaget argues:

> Lakes and rivers are bordered by quays, their beds are cleaned by dredgers, drain-pipes may be seen running into them from the banks, etc. Thence to conclude that nature depends on human activity may easily be but a short step. (1929, p. 352)

However, we still have to explain why children seem to prefer to adopt an artificialist account, ignoring the manifestly wild qualities of much of nature.

There exist some later replications and extensions of Piaget's work on the concepts of city, region, and country: Jahoda (1963), for example, found Glaswegian children of 6–11 years to be progressively less confused about the relationship between Glasgow, Scotland, and Britain, although some 12% of the oldest children were as puzzled as were the majority of 6-year-olds. And Piché (1981) conducted clinical interviews with 5–8-year-olds on their expanding understanding of the world, from most local to most distant places. Five year olds may be happy to describe a building, a district, a city, and a country all as the same kinds of *place* because one could go there.

Those children that Piché described as being in transition to the concrete operations stage were in receipt of enough information from parents and others to realize that hierarchies might exist between them, for example, home, street, town, and country. And during the concrete period, geographical information given to the child comes to be organized so that he or she can produce some passable maps. Such information may not have much salience for the child unless given by travel or special interests (for example, natural-history programmes on television). Lee (1963) once suggested that, for many children, *all* places beyond the immediate home range belong to the 'elsewhere' schema.

Whether it is personally salient or not, children manifestly encounter much information about the wider world via the media, and the next section of this chapter asks how far children's use of media is related to the development of stereotypes about distant places and peoples.

Children's use of the media: the examples of stereotypes, prejudice against other people and other nations—and the ambiguous role of media-supplied information

Pundits not infrequently cite ignorance as the root of prejudice, and suggest that greater information, via the media, would help to reduce such feelings against other people and places. Inconveniently for them, the research evidence does not point to the media—even the well-intentioned educational media—as unambiguously helpful in this cause, as we shall see. Indeed, another group of pundits are equally sure that we can trace back to the media the origins of many of the stereotypes that abound in society.

In this section of the chapter, we will briefly note a number of studies that have examined the role of the media in establishing and in changing stereotypes—and we draw in examples from related areas of prejudice.

Thus, for example, we can indicate an extensive literature on sex-role stereotypes and the media (see a major review by Butler and Paisley, 1980), which offers evidence that much of the media output presents strongly stereotyped versions of sex roles. But do children learn from this output? Durkin (1984) notes that few studies go beyond the initial presumption that children do notice, and are then influenced actually to investigate the effects. His study explored young children's perception and comprehension of stereotyped sex roles in television, examining it against the broader social context of the child's life. Four- to nine-year-old children watched clips of typical television programs, and demonstrated considerable awareness of the sex-role expectancies. They recognized standard scripts and were able to use these to explain the motivations of the stereotyped characters portrayed in the extracts.

In the case of sex-role stereotypes, the media lead and support prejudices that the child is also in receipt of from everyday life; in other areas, the media are the major or sole source of information. An example of this comes from Johnson, Middleton, and Tajfel's (1970) study of children's knowledge of and preferences for other nations; they investigated the readership of various types of children's commic, and found that those children who read war-stories comics 'shared a pattern of national preferences more congruent with the alliances of World War Two' than children who did not read these comics. And, an important general point, amount of knowledge that a child had about a foreign country was not predictive of how the child would feel about that country. Thus, for example, middle class children had, on average, a knowledge of foreign countries approximately two years ahead of the working class children—yet the national preferences of working- and middle-class children were very similar. Tajfel had for long argued that children are capable of absorbing, both from the media and from social discourse, attitudes and prejudices about other nations and other groups well before they have any factual information about them (e.g. Tajfel and Jahoda, 1966). The young child is at an early, but important, stage in the development of a social identity—related to the in-and-out groups as specified by the surrounding culture; and the acquisition and interpretation of factual information about own group and other groups will be related to this frame of reference. In other words, information will be selectively sought, received, and remembered, in ways that are supportive of pre-existing (pre-judged) categories (Tajfel, 1981).

If the media play a part in supporting and developing stereotyped positions, then what role can they play in changing them? Educational television, for example, is frequently targeted upon changing stereotypes. Let us return to the previously cited example—that of sex-role stereotypes, and, in particular, the strongly expressed views of the 'appropriate' or 'likely' employment roles of the sexes. Educational television has the potential to challenge such traditional sex roles. Durkin and Hutchins (1984) have examined its likely impact by studying the effectiveness of a series of explicitly counter-stereotyping careers broadcasts aimed at young teenagers. Compared with traditional sex role broadcasts, and an implicit counter-stereotyping program, the explicit programs were expected to have greatest positive effect; in fact, Durkin and Hutchins found evidence of *opposition* to the programme's message, and a further entrenchment of traditional sex-role stereotypes.

Just as the portrayal of women in 'traditional male roles' may have unintended effects, so also may educational media misfire when the target is children's knowledge of and feelings for other countries, as we found in one of our own experiments (Stillwell and Spencer, 1974). We argued in this study that one of the principal sources of information for children early in the development of attitudes toward other nations is the formal and informal curriculum of the school; and we sought to use the children's intake of information via wallcharts and classroom displays—a frequently used technique in primary schools.

Prior to the displays going up, we interviewed each 9-year-old in the study, asking about knowledge of and feelings towards four target countries: India, Germany, the USA and the USSR ('Russia'). The displays consisted of wallcharts with everyday street scenes, transport, local dress, and the country's position on a world map. These were pinned up for a week, with no supporting teaching or discussion because we did not want teachers to influence the child's perceptions during the experiment.

All children showed a significant increase in information about all four countries in the second, post-display interviews. But what relation was there between knowledge and preference? Our British subjects had, on initial interview, been strongly pro-American, and anti-German, with India and Russia being just on the positive side of neutral. The effect of increasing information was not uniform: America remained popular, Germany moved to a strong positive, Russia remained relatively neutral, and India moved to a negative preference.

Germany's initial negative position supports Johnson, Middleton and Tajfel's (1970) observation about the influence of war comics (two of the more extreme comments from the present sample's initial interviews were: 'all the men wear uniforms', and 'no cars, only jeeps'.) Many children initially stressed the differences between Britain and Germany, saying that towns, clothes and skin colour were 'different from here'. (Jahoda, in 1963, had found evidence to suggest that 9-year-olds were repelled by the strangeness of foreigners). America, on the other hand, was awarded strong initial preferences: it was, in consequence, believed to be 'like us, only better': 'The sun shines there, and the people are always out', and 'the houses are like ours, but bigger'. Jaspars, Van der Geer, Tajfel, and Johnson (1963) found that children preferred the countries that they saw as near to their own in cognitive space.

Initially, Russia and India had been largely unknown quantities: neither clearly like us, nor yet very dissimilar was the theme of initial comments.

What then must have happened when the children saw what the countries and their people were actually like?

Children who had previously maximised the differences between Germany and Britain saw pictures of very similar towns and people—and shift preferences according to the positive. America is confirmed as 'bigger and better', and Russia is also confirmed, as mildly different from Britain.

The pictures of India, however, portrayed scenes where the differences from Britain were noted by all—and the 'not like us' feeling and negative evaluation followed. Thus, we cannot conclude that education and the media, in providing more and more accurate information will necessarily increase understanding and thus acceptance: children may test this against earlier stereotypes, as in the Durkin and Hutchins study, or use the information to assess similarity of a country to the valued own country; and thence preference.

Figure 9.1 Images of other peoples. Examine the sources of information readily available to the child about distant peoples and places, and then consider the nature of the stereotyopes that children hold.

Popular media and the development of images of distant places

Popular media as well as educational media contribute to the child's image of distant places: David Attenborough's "The Living Planet" for example, reached over 10 million viewers on its first showing in Britain (Burgess and Unwin, 1984). Twelve of its programs were devoted to the world's major ecosystems, with the thirteenth program focusing on man's effect on the world; and Attenborough's specified aim was to give pleasure, and be scientifically responsible:

> If you make a natural history film truthfully, without too much pretention on the one hand or simplification on the other, then a child of six and a professor of science can get pleasure from the same program. A child of six may have never seen a snake in his life. If he sees one on film crawling over a log, that in itself is an amazement and a fascination. But it may be a snake that no hereptologist has seen alive before, so it can give him just as much of a thrill.
> (Attenborough, in Burgess and Unwin, 1984, p. 104)

Popular media may, indeed, be such a dominant source of images that formal education is swamped: Birns (1967) quotes a survey of American children's images of Africa. Twelve-year-olds' images included, as predominant words: Wild animals, jungles, witch doctors, and 'Daktari' (a popular television big game adventure). Even 17-year-olds, who had followed a school course on Africa still gave witch doctors, drums, wild animals, and 'Daktari' as their predominant associations. Children's images of the third world had undergone considerable changes by the 1980s, with 'poverty', 'malnutrition', 'unequal distribution of wealth' and 'low life expectancy' replacing the 'witch doctor' and 'mud-hut' image (Hibberd, 1983): again, one may argue that this must be the effect of a powerful media presented image, the children in Hibberd's study having had no formal teaching on Third-World issues.

News items, if sufficiently dramatic, clearly capture children's imagination, shape their games and may provide a strong basis for stereotypes. Webley and Cutts (1985) were able to talk to schoolboys in Britain and Argentina immediately after the countries had been at war. Children completed maps of their own countries, picked pictures to represent the Falklands/Malvinas, and discussed the origins of war. There emerged clear national differences: the Argentinian children stressed territorial rights, the British the issue of principle. Clearly children as young as 7 years had efficiently learned the rhetoric predominating in their own country at the time of the war.

One specific—and intentional—source of images of distant places (as well as interpreter of the more local scene) that the child is certain to encounter during the middle years is the teacher of geography. It is only relatively recently that this profession has become self-aware, suddenly conscious of geographical texts' power to impart value-laden images of other places, and now recoils from texts with titles such as 'How the Empire works for us'. In a scholarly review, Glacken (1967) traces the development of environmental thought in European geographical writing. He shows that in many instances, depictions of national characters are described as if they are environmentally determined; ideal climates produce ideal civilizations (populations who are enlightened, industrious, and clever), whereas other parts of the world are described as if they were predestined to be barbarous, stupid, and unclean. Elliott (1979) suggests that, until the mid twentieth century, 'this type of geographic writing was the rule rather than the exception'. He has described the evaluation of peoples and places by eminent and influential regional geographers—Ellen Churchill Semple, Hendrick van Loon, Ellsworth Huntingdon—as well as their precursors in general world literature—including Henry Buckle (fl. 1850), Georg Hegal (1820), Johann von Herder (1800); Montesquieu (1740); and the Hadid Al-Alam (a Persian geographical treatise on the regions of the world, published in AD 982). For each, Elliott draws up a world map, dividing the globe into five categories, from 'regions of highest praise' to 'regions of highest condemnation', with the latter tending to be those most distant—geographically, racially, and religiously.

Such texts both reflected and shaped the culture that surrounded the child, as well as being direct teaching texts. Even today, when the compilers of regional geographies are much more aware of the argument about value-laden writing, it is still possible to convey, perhaps more subtly, strong and potentially evaluative images, as has been shown by Wright's (1979) study of the visual images contained in current textbooks on Africa. Photographs, he argues, create strong and lasting impressions for pupils; and therefore an author's or editor's choice of a balance between 'traditional' and 'modern' images of Africa may have more than a side-influence upon the child's perceptions of the continent and its peoples. For example, few of the texts he reviewed contained pictures of industrial activities, while farming (often using traditional methods) was well represented. Tourist brochures, not surprisingly, promote a similarly selective image of potential destinations, as we argued in Chapter 2 (Dilley, 1986).

Figure 9.2   Images of distant places. The travel-agent's filter allows through a very selective view of the world.

Clearly, at some stages in history, individuals *have* tried to use literature as propoganda: Eirik the Red naming the large, inhospitable island 'Greenland' in the hope of attracting settlers is a tenth-century example. In Eirik's Saga, it is recorded that 'he named it Greenland, for he said that people would be much more tempted to go there if it had an attractive name' (Magnusson and Palsson, 1965, p. 78). William Gilpin's exploitation of the concept of the Great Plains Region is a nineteenth-century American example. Lewis (1966) has shown how, in a series of articles, pamphlets and books, Gilpin played down the desert character of the region, and emphasized the rich pastoral potential ('the wonderful buffalo-grass . . . winter pasture for millions of aboriginal cattle'). As a consequence, his writings proved a powerful motivating image for settlers for decades during the last century.

Our concern is that unwitting propoganda contained in present-day teaching material should not produce a similarly distorted image of the world. Publishers and teachers might find it instructive to evaluate the messages and images that children gain from texts, over and above the factual material therein. And publishers, teachers, and psychologists concerned with the child's developing understanding of the world could not fail to gain from reading Wood's (1987) celebration of the new breed of imaginative atlases now being produced.

Children, Wood argues, spend hours with reference material of their own choosing: with the television guide, with the sports scores in the paper, with books of world records, with enthusiasts' guides to types of locomotive or species of bird. Traditional school atlases, he suggests, are much less likely to capture the same attention as are this new generation of works. Using all the good graphics that are now becoming commonplace in general publishing for children, these new atlases tell a story, by interpreting world events for them. Wood describes how children read and re-read *The War Atlas* (Kidron and Smith, 1983) in stunned amazement. 'Afterwards kids are propelled to action, to ask, "What can we do?" *Gaia: An Atlas of Planet Management* (Myers, 1985) provides one answer. Kids *read* this and begin to think constructively about their role in our collective futures.'

The media, maps, and direct experience as sources of geographical knowledge that the child needs to articulate

Asked which direction home lies from school, the child will most probably resort to personally acquired route knowledge rather than any formally provided source of information. But ask the child to indicate the direction of the capital city, and immediate, local knowledge of orientation will have to be articulated with knowledge derived from a formal map. Such articulation characterizes a number of spatial tasks: learning on foot the layout of a new town, whilst having accessible for consultation a town plan for example. (We can offer a small empirical demonstration of the effect on cognitive structure this can have. Students coming to our university are all given a campus plan with a clear north orientation; after two years in residence, we found that over 80% of them drew a sketch map of the campus with the same orientation.)

Thorndyke and Hayes-Roth (1982) have investigated how information derived from maps and from navigational experience in large-scale space may differ: they focused primarily on *adults'* spatial judgements, but we can assume that something of the same kind applies to children, in that their analysis relates to the distinction between procedural descriptions and survey knowledge, discussed in many of the previous chapters.

They argue that when an individual scans a map, he or she acquires an image of the map isomorphic with the original map, and giving survey knowledge. Calling up the image of the map, in order to answer spatial questions, the individual operates on the canonical, vertical, 'view' of the original map, and is thus enabled to give relatively undistorted judgements about distances, angles, groupings, etc.

Procedural knowledge, acquired during direct exploration of an environment, will be recalled from the canonical, *horizontal* position: and to compute spatial judgments, the individual uses the same procedures used during navigation. Thus, claim Thorndyke and Hayes-Roth, people combine mental stimulation of travel through the environment and informal algebra to make such judgements.

Their subjects either learned a novel environment from direct navigation or from a map. With extensive exposure, neither source of information allows a superior performance on judgement tasks; but with only moderate exposure allowed, map-learners give better judgements than navigators on relative locations, and straight-line distances; but were poorer on orienting themselves with respect to unseen objects, and estimating route distances. Map-learning, in other words, gives a rapid bird's-eye view of the environment, encoding survey knowledge efficiently. Navigationally acquired knowledge may require some further computation in order to solve some spatial questions but extensive navigation can be shown to lead to qualitative changes in knowledge. 'People with extensive navigation experience can in some sense "look through' opaque obstacles in the environment to their destination without reference to the connecting route' (Thorndyke and Hayes-Roth, p. 586).

At this point, their performance equals that of those with map-knowledge.

The individual may acquire information about distant places from sources other than formal maps. The media, as already noted, may exert a powerful influence upon the individual's image: and, as Fryman and Wallace (1985) have shown, high media attention to certain areas (e.g. world trouble-spots) may lead to considerable distortions in the map image. Subjects in their study, asked to report the relative size of countries, exaggerate those that have been in the news.

We need more information about the interaction between such media-borne images, formal map information, and directly gained knowledge of the world; how children's expanding exposure to all sources of information with increasing age leads to a more complex overall image. Brown and Broadway (1981) have documented how the process continues into adolescence; and, in particular, they discuss the leap in regional knowledge that comes after the (American) adolescent starts to drive a car; those adolescents who were denied access to this form of travel were found to have much less accurate maps of their region.

Beck and Wood (1976a,b), too, have contributed a study of adolescents' expanding horizons—and their integration of media-generated, map-learned, and personally experienced information. To understand their design, you must imagine a coach tour of Europe with a group of American adolescents visiting for the first time in their lives, a series of historical cities; before the trip and each day during the tour, the data on the adolescents' images are collected by Denis Wood, with such zeal that eventually the tour-managers suspect the young graduate-student experimenter's motives, and throw him off the coach. For a full account of the vicissitudes that may befall the cognitive-map researcher it is worth seeking out Wood (1973).

Beck and Wood found that initial images of the city as anticipated from abroad were derived from media and from the tour-leader's discussions of the proposed trip: putting these into map form really indicated how these 'images' were little more than listings of the main tourist features of the city to be visited. From the first hours in the city itself, the initial image undergoes rapid transformation—a much stronger spatial organization is evident; with, not surprisingly, the routes initially travelled forming a structure, with their hotel as the centre point of the image. [A similar observation is made by Canter (1977), who conducted a small-scale study of tourist impressions of a single city—London—over the first few days of a visit.]

These findings have a parallel in the way young children begin to organize their representation of their *own* city: Nelson (1981) argues that children's knowledge of the city is first organized in scripts describing their actions in space and time; from these scripts, children are later able to derive more abstract, categorical knowledge. And Axia and Nicolini (1986), in their study of Venetian children's knowledge of home—and distant—parts of Venice, found that 5- and 6-year-olds represented *only* the less-familiar areas of town by scripts that describe their own actions in them. Core areas are more generally, less self-referentially, represented, and information contributing to these images will come from media, maps, and others' accounts.

To conclude: we have seen how, through a combination of sources of information, the child comes to form images of distant places that will in turn affect his or her feelings, and, perhaps in later life, behaviour such as the choice of residence, workplace and tourist destination. Throughout this chapter, we may have implied that through increasing knowledge, the child's incomplete knowledge, misperceptions, and stereotypes will gradually give way to an accurate and unbiased view of the world in adulthood. Would that this were true!

Part III

Applications of Environmental Cognition Research

CHAPTER 10

The child with special needs and the physical environment

Throughout the main section of this book we have been concerned with the interaction between the child and his or her surrounding environment. We have documented the achievement of the young child in coming to have a full working knowledge of that environment and the necessity of this for full interaction with it.

However, for some of the children this interaction may be hampered, the knowledge of the environment an even greater achievement, and their independent mobility within it an even more demanding skill. For some their perceptual development may be altered by handicap—blindness being probably the most serious—and for others, some form of physical or mental handicap may mean fewer and less-active interactions with their surroundings.

There can be no doubt that for some children their environmental needs will be considerably different, and it is the effect of different handicaps and how they alter an individuals' needs with regard to their environment that is the focus of this Chapter. We aim to indicate some of these issues by concentrating principally upon the consequences of visual impairment for the child's spatial skills and environmental needs. We also discuss the educational responses—including mobility training—that have been designed to deal with these. However, since there is already a well-established practical literature concerned with mobility techniques, environmental familiarization, and teaching practices, we largely concentrate on the more theoretical issues, such as the understanding about space that the young children are capable of, whether or not they are capable of spatial images, and so on, to draw from this to considerations of how the present mobility teaching deals with these and how it may be altered to deal with them better.

When we consider the interaction of the blind child with the environment we find that there is a theoretically well-grounded literature but, as we illustrate later, most of the published papers dealing with other handicapped populations have little discussion of the perceptual problems faced by these children in their environment. Having said this, though, there is more available on their environmental needs within the literatures of psychology, education, and the design professions.

There is a clear need for good research on the environmental comprehension of particular groups of handicapped children: what are the cognitive consequences, for example, of the physically handicapped child's reduced opportunities for exploratory play? Does mental handicap have implications for environmental information processing, which in turn would have implications for, to take a specific example, road safety education for these children?

In the second, and shorter, section of this chapter we will illustrate some of the existing research on the needs of children with other forms of handicap by taking mental handicap as our example. The balance of research, however, as already indicated, is concerned with our main topic—visual handicap.

SECTION 1: THE VISUALLY HANDICAPPED CHILD IN THE ENVIRONMENT

As we have already said, within this first section of the chapter, we concentrate on research with the blind and their mobility in space—in the context of our earlier discussions on the basic processes of spatial cognition—after which we consider the implications of this research for practice and mobility, illustrating this with examples of novel training methods with young blind children.

You must be mobile

Obviously, effective movement and activity within space is essential to our understanding of the environment and to the development of our knowledge about the space around us. For the sighted child the development of this skill plays a major role as a marker of development—whether it be the infant who takes his or her first steps, or the school child who is allowed to go to town unguided for the first time—and because of this it indicates the importance attached to the ability to move safely, purposefully, and independently through the environment (Welsh and Blasch, 1980). Without this skill even the most basic of tasks, such as getting from the bedroom to the toilet, are impossible. The immobile child will become the immobile adult, and will be dependent and reliant on others throughout life—something that will not only lead to problems later in life but may also lead to psychosocial (Wilson, 1967) as well as adjustment problems (Bauman and Yoder, 1966; Graham, 1965).

Unlike the 'normal' sighted child blind children will tend to be immobile. Lacking the stimulation of vision there is little motivation to be mobile, to look for things in space, and to explore the world around them; and why should they be motivated when all too often parents will carry them, bring things to them and (understandably) help them as much as possible?

Blind children frequently lack the motivation to move in space, and this is made worse by the fact that all too often when they do move they bump into objects, fall over obstacles, and frequently hurt themselves. For most of the children this then becomes an upsetting consequence of movement in space and so the motivation to move is added to by a fear of moving. This lack of movement and activity within open space will often result in many young visually handicapped children exhibiting *blindisms*—rocking, flapping, etc., and when outside will be found standing on the spot, twirling and flapping their hands. Therefore, when young blind children come into school a great deal of time has to be spent encouraging movement, getting them to locate noises as quickly as possible, following the teacher as he or she walks in the gym, running while holding the teacher's hands etc.—anything that will get them to move through the space around them. When blind children are pre-school age, their parents are encouraged to take them walking, to let them play outside as much as possible, and so on. Often it is found that getting the children to walk while pushing

Figure 10.1   Social and spatial isolation. A fear of the world around them means that many visually impaired children become isolated within space and spend most of their 'free activity' standing still or turning on the spot. The result of this is both social and spatial isolation.

a large toy in front of them will encourage movement within space (because the toy will hit the object first), and as we will discuss later, we have actually found that with young school-age children between 7 and 8 years the use of a long cane (well before the normal age of use) is beneficial to children reluctant to move through space around them.

What does the travel task require?

The fact that such importance is attached to mobility, and that it serves as an important marker for development, indicates that it is not an easy skill to acquire. It is a 'complexly determined ability' (Warren and Kocon, 1974), which is performed in a continuously changing environment and which necessitates that a whole number of sub-skills be acquired before proficiency can be reached. Individuals not only need to be able to move efficiently within space, thus necessitating the acquisition of skills such as posture, gait, and good balance, but also need to understand the world in which they are moving and to use this understanding to build up a cognitive representation that will serve to guide travel in that space when necessary.

Foulke (1982) has provided a number of criteria which he feels ought to be incorporated within a definition of mobility. These include 'the ability to travel safely, comfortably, gracefully, and independently', as well as the criteria of purposeful travel. For this purposeful, goal-oriented, travel it is essential that the travellers know where they are at present, where their goals are, and can deduce from this information how to move to them from their present positions. This necessitates that motor, perceptual, and representational skills are attained by the traveller. It also requires that when individuals are in unfamiliar areas they have some general expectations about the structure of the environment in general. It is necessary to have concepts such as 'blocks'—the fact that there is a considerable predictability about the arrangements of objects on streets and the intersections of streets. This regularity or 'environmental grammar' (Kay, 1974) constrains travel to some extent, but also assisits the blind traveller by providing comparatively clear and predictable paths in these directions. Other things, such as objects that could be obstacles, also conform to regular patterns. Rows of fences or lampposts are found on one side of the road rather than the other, cars are parked in characteristic patterns and so on. All these regularities can actually help the blind individual when travelling in space but can only do so if that person is familiar enough with the physical environment to know these facts.

Therefore, it is essential that time is spent building up these general environmental concepts from when the child is very young. Children should be taken for walks, the environmental grammar should be made known to them explicitly—for example, by letting them feel where the lampposts are, by having it explained to them that there is usually some fencing then a gate in front of someone's house, that cars park on one side of the pavement and the houses are on the other. They need to have these things shown to them otherwise blind children will not find them out while being walked along by a sighted adult.

In addition to this general knowledge however, it is essential that blind children (or adults) are able to conceptualize where they are in space and how their activities within the space alter this relationship, in order that they can be truly mobile. It is this conceptualization of space, how it is altered by visual handicap, and how teaching techniques can be employed to compensate for this, that we concentrate on throughout the rest of the chapter.

An analysis of the task

Over the past decade researchers have shown an increased interest in the travel skills and spatial abilities of the sighted, but few have attempted to provide an analysis of the task as faced by the blind individual. There are several exceptions to this, for instance Dodds, Howarth and Carter (1982), Rieser, Lockman, and Pick (1980) and Strelow (1985). Foulke (1982), attempts to provide an analysis of the task faced by the blind pedestrian and provides us with a flowchart of the processes involved in mobility (see Figure 10.2).

We can see from the first four steps in this that, initially, the child must be oriented in space, and if he or she is not then the information necessary to allow orientation must be acquired. Steps 5 and 6 indicate that performance is guided, in part, by information obtained from the memorial representation of the space in which the task is performed, while steps 7 to 14 indicate, that it is also partly guided by observing the space in which the task is performed, while the task is still in progress. Obviously, as we have already mentioned, if you have some idea of the environmental regularity within that space then this is going to lessen the information-processing load for you.

This information supplements spatial knowledge and functions as feedback, which is added to the already formed spatial representation. Although not explicitly stated in the flowchart, it can be inferred from it that the relative contribution of the information obtained while the task is in progress depends on the amount of previous experience in that space. If an individual has had relatively little experience within the area then the perceptual information gained about that environment while walking through it, is very important.

It will guide travel through the area, in the absence of a cognitive representation of the area, as well as providing the essential information necessary for the formation of this representation. This in turn will help to guide travel at a later encounter and supplement the role of perception. Foulke (1982) produced this model as an analysis of the task faced by the blind traveller, but theories such as those reviewed in Parts I and II of this book, concerned with human navigation and way-finding by the sighted, would appear to be very similar in their analysis of the task faced by the sighted traveller (Gärling, Böök, and Lindberg, 1984a,b). Nevertheless, because Foulke's formulation is one of the

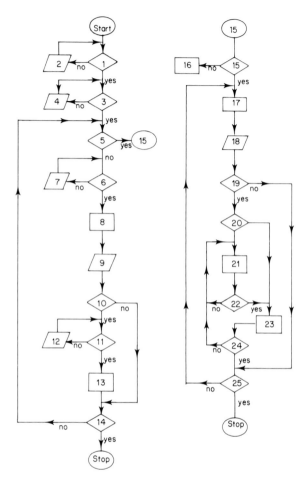

Figure 10.2   A flow diagram to illustrate the processes involved in mobility by the visually handicapped traveller. 1. Is goal position known? 2. ACQUIRE INFORMA-TION; 3. Is starting position known? 4. ACQUIRE INFORMATION; 5. Is memorial representation of sector of environment containing starting position and goal position sufficient to afford knowledge of one or more routes to goal? 6. Is memorial representation of environment containing starting position and goal position sufficient to permit choice of direction? 7. ACQUIRE INFORMATION; 8. ADVANCE IN CHOSEN DIRECTION TO NEXT POSITION; 9. ACQUIRE FEEDBACK DATA; 10. Do feedback data indicate error? 11. Do error data specify required correction? 12. AC-QUIRE DIRECTIONAL INFORMATION; 13. MAKE CORRECTION; 14. Does present position equal goal position? 15. Is there one and only one route to goal?; 16. DISCARD ALL BUT BEST ROUTE; 17. ADVANCE TO NEXT ROUTE POSI-TON; 18. ACQUIRE FEEDBACK DATA; 19. Do feedback data indicate error? 20. Do error data specify correction? 21. ADVANCE AT RANDOM UNTIL INTER-PRETABLE FEEDBACK INFORMATION IS ACQUIRED; 22. Is correction spec-ified? 23. MAKE CORRECTION; 24. Is route regained? 25. Does present position equal goal position?

ew that actually deals with the task as faced by the blind, it will be the one followed in this chapter.

All accounts of human way-finding agree on the role of perception, not only in the guiding of locomotion, but also in the building up of a cognitive representation of space. Using such representations, travellers need to know where they are, where in relation to their current position their destination is, and then to move to it, using their perceptions of the environment and its landmarks to update their position within their cognitive representation, and determine their future courses of action. It should be noted that the destination is not always directly perceptable for the sighted traveller from the starting point, but in situations such as these, the individual can use spatial knowledge (derived from these representations) to infer direction and route from present position. Such travel actions will then feed back into the representation of space that has already been formed (Gärling *et al.*, 1984a,b).

How do we perceive the altering environment as we move through it?

For the sighted individual travelling through both familiar and unfamiliar terrain, the most obvious and abundant source of perceptual information is the visual system. Indeed, it has been suggested that 'the perception of obstacles beyond arms reach' is 'inextricably linked to the visual system' and that 'no other sensory modality seems to offer the same possibilities for the localization of objects and theories of space perception' (Strelow and Brabyn, 1982). Foulke 1982) also describes the visual system as 'the spatial system par excellence ... providing a large field of view, and selectivity of regard better adapted to space perception than any other sensory system available to the individual' (p. 61)—it provides the capacity to know where things are and what they are (Howard, 1973), and provides the individual with anticipation for their movement ahead. Such suggestions emphasize the need for vision as a means of locomotor guidance, yet other researchers have gone still further and have assumed that vision is essential for any kind of spatial understanding.

Such an argument was put forward by von Senden (1932, 1960) and his followers (e.g. Hartlage, 1969; Hebb, 1949), who thought that all real knowledge of space, was gained through vision alone. They argued that a concept of space could only be achieved through the use of vision, and that the internal representation, as well as the external perception, of space was essentially visual in character (Attneave and Benson, 1969; Huttenlocher and Presson, 1979; Schlaegel, 1953). To this extent, theories of human navigation and wayfinding, as reviewed in earlier chapters, are based largely upon the use of vision and stress the fact that the visual system is the primary source of information about space (Haber, 1978; Llewellyn, 1971).

Perhaps one of the most influential of these theories about space perception and visually guided motion, among researchers concerned with the spatial abilities of the blind, is that of Gibson (1958, 1979), which has been discussed earlier in the book. To recap, the key tenets of Gibson's theory of visually guided mobility are first, that object motion results in characteristic, within-field changes; secondly, that in the absence of such local, within-field changes the objects in the visual field are assumed to be stationary; and thirdly, that body movement produces changes throughout the whole visual field as well as perspective changes, and that these provide the higher order invariants that are the basis of locomotor control.

But what about the visually handicapped traveller?

Gibson (1958, 1979) has provided us with an analysis of the travel task primarily in terms of visual processes, but in doing this he, like the others we have already mentioned, has assumed that movement through space is essentially a complex visual task and has denied—implicitly rather than explicitly—the ability of the blind to move competently and safely through space.

However, anyone who has met or worked with blind individuals will have noticed that they are capable of moving through space, and do so very efficiently, even in the absence of all vision. We are therefore faced with an obvious paradox, since travel skill in the absence of vision must indicate that it is not, of necessity, a visually based skill (Strelow, 1985).

To achieve independent movement through space in the absence of all vision must mean that the blind are able to replace the missing visual information with alternative sensory perceptions. It is obvious given our clearly defined sensory system that 'each perceptual system, is, by evolutionary design, better suited to some tasks than others' (Foulke, 1982), but differentiation does not mean isolation, and it would seem only plausible that when the sensory components of one system are so severely impaired that they have little or no remaining function, that some of the missing information may be acquired by sensory substitution, or by resorting to a perceptual alternative.

Such is the case with the visually handicapped traveller. Vision is held to be the primary 'spatial' sense and the sighted traveller relies almost exclusively upon this sensory system to provide information about the environment being travelled through.

However, blindness can arise from damage to any of the sensory components of the visual system—the eye, the optic tract, the visual cortex, or any other areas of the brain associated with visual perception—with the result that the visual system has little or no remaining function. Therefore, in the case of the visually handicapped traveller, this system either serves as a very limited source of perceptual information, or has degenerated to an extent that it is rendered totally useless. As a result the visually handicapped must resort to alternative sensory systems as sources of perceptual information about the environment through which they are travelling.

Alternative perceptual systems used by the blind traveller

Through the utilization of many types of nonvisual information, and a reliance upon senses that the sighted have little recourse to use, the blind are able to achieve considerable proficiency of mobility. These alternative senses, used for locomotor guidance and thereby mobility, are the auditory system, the haptic–proprioceptive system, the tactile–kinaesthetic system, and, to a lesser extent, the olfactory sensory system. We discuss each of these in turn.

The auditory sense

The traveller, unaccustomed to using this sensory system, might find a few problems when using it to guide travel and provide information about the space around. There would seem to be several problems associated with the use of the auditory system as a source of perceptual information about the world (Foulke, 1982). First, as a provider of information about the world ahead, its field is large and nonspecific; sounds can reach the ears from all directions, many of the things present in the auditory field are not the sources of the sound, and many are only the sources part of the time. Therefore, although it would seem that the individual could use the auditory field to anticipate locations, in practice it offers a less certain and definite picture than would vision.

Secondly, the auditory system has little or no selectivity of regard. Although auditory observers can, by turning their heads, favour the reception of some sounds over others (Wallach, 1940), on the whole, auditory selectivity falls far short of visual selectivity (Howard, 1973).

Thirdly, auditory observers are less successful than visual observers in excluding from attention intruding stimuli, and there is, therefore, a greater chance of interference when using the auditory system, than there is when using the visual system (Green, 1978).

The fact is, though, that for the blind traveller audition remains the main channel for providing distal information (Wanet and Veraart, 1985). The auditory system may show poor selectivity, but as a guide for movement, travel, and the perception of objects, walls, and buildings, all of which are important for the successful travel of the individual, and may or may not be beyond arm's reach, then the auditory system is superior to any of the alternatives available to the blind. It can provide information about the surroundings without the need for direct contact, and unlike the other major senses available to the blind traveller, it is useful both indoors and out, actively and passively.

The passive use of this sense requires that the individual simply takes note of the available sound information. Through this passive use the individual learns to appreciate depth by the distance through space to a sound-emitting source. This can be fostered within the classroom by having a music box by the milk trolley, in the gym by getting the children to walk to a noise, and simply by just drawing the children's attention to noises as they are walking, standing, or whatever. It can enable the individual to comprehend the characteristics of the environment indoors (e.g. whether the room is full or empty) and outdoors (e.g the type of environment they are travelling through—for instance, the sound of heavy traffic may identify a buisness area). Thus, audition becomes useful in helping the children build up some idea of the general environmental grammar. Often children on mobility lessons will be taken to different streets, and asked to identify whether it is a busy or quiet street. Similarly, on the same walk they may also be asked to identify busy and quiet shops and so on.

It often aids individuals in maintaining their orientation in the environment if, while walking down a busy street, they can use sound tracking of the flow of traffic to guide their travel and to make sure that they maintain a path in the right direction. If they then cross the road they can use this to ensure that they are still travelling in the same direction.This is a ploy often used by mobility teachers, who will draw their students attention to this information by asking them to face in the right direction after having crossed the road. They will then explain the use of this auditory information to their students if they were not aware of this already.

Once travelling the correct route, and in the right direction, sound can be useful in ensuring individuals free and safe movement along that route. It helps them to determine whether it is safe to cross the road, just how far away the edge of the road is, how near to the wall they are, and so on. However, audition is not just of general use. It can also be of help when travelling along a route, by aiding the individual in the identification of landmarks, obstacles, decision points, etc., all of which are then incorporated into their specific spatial representation of an area. For instance, the record shop at the end of the main street, or the large clock at the end of a corridor, may be very useful travel cues for the blind traveller. Hollyfield and Foulke (1983), for instance, found that their visually handicapped subjects located places that they could not have located without hearing. They reported that whilst travelling a designated route, they established the locations of houses by inductive reasoning from fragmentary evidence such as 'the sound of a slamming door, the noise made by an air conditioner and so on' (p. 208).

Discrimination of these sounds is also important. The ability to discriminate and differentiate between similar sounds may enable travellers to determine their location more accurately. For instance, by deciding that the sound they are hearing is the sound of the fan in the chemists shop, rather than the air conditioner in the restaurant next door, they could avoid the confusion of finding no tables and chairs in their expected places, or of asking a waiter for cough mixture. In a similar way, blind individuals can make use of sound shadow to determine landmarks and locations. A sound shadow is created when an object comes between the traveller and the sound source and muffles it—for instance, walking under a bus shelter muffles the sound of passing traffic making it easy for the blind traveller to know where he or she is.

The use of reflected sound is also important to the traveller. This may, for example, enable the individual to maintain a course parallel to walls, allow the detection of alleyways and recesses, allow the detection of corners (by the noted absence of reflected sound) and enable the individual to turn them without physical contact, as well as enhance the capacity to detect obstacles.

The use of sound to detect obstacles is labelled obstacle perception and involves the passive use of the auditory system. This should be differentiated from the related phenomena—echo detection—which involves detecting the presence or absence of a surface or object, outside one's path, by utilizing reflected sound in an active way.

It was initially felt that this phenomena was due to the compression of air on the face (see Burklen, 1924; Diderot, 1916), but a series of experiments, which became known as the Cornell experiments, discovered that this ability was linked to hearing (Supa, Cotzin, and Dallenbach, 1944), the basis of it being changes in pitch within the higher frequencies (Cotzin and Dallenbach, 1950). It was also discovered that this phenomenon was not unique to the blind, and that sighted individuals (Supa *et al.*, 1944), as well as less-efficient blind individuals, could be taught this skill both indoors and out (Ammons, Worchel, and Dallenbach, 1953; Worchel and Mauney, 1950).

Despite evidence to the contrary, it would appear that the blind do not talk of this skill as an auditory one, but instead describe it as an all-over-body feeling, and often claim to feel some facial pressure (Worchel, Mauney, and Andrew, 1950). Jurmaa (1965) has suggested that this facial pressure could be the result of a rise in tension in the head muscles, due to the fact that it is the area most likely to be injured first. Therefore, the person detecting a wall by referred sound experiences tenseness due to a rise in tension in the face muscles. Hill (1975), however, probably describes this skill best by a combination of both these ideas when she says that object perception is 'neither touch nor echo, nor movement, but a synergistic blending of all these awarenesses'. Although, traditionally, these studies tested the ability of individuals to detect a large masonite wall ahead of them, it was decided that there were in fact other things within the environment that could serve as hazards to the visually handicapped individual; so later researchers (Rice, 1967; Rice and Feinstein, 1965) tested the ability of subjects to detect obstacles in their way—a task bearing much more resemblance to the true life task involved in mobility. These tasks, contrary to those used previously, revealed that individuals tended to make mistakes in their judgements, especially if they had to detect thin shapes such as a door left ajar, a pole, or thin shelves. Indeed, Strelow and Brabyn (1982), in an extension of such experiments designed to be as near to the real-life problem as possible, found that although subjects could maintain a useful level of control in remaining parallel to a wall, over half the tasks with pole targets resulted in collisions with the poles.

Echo detection, on the other hand, involves the individual in detecting obstacles and surfaces by emitting sounds, such as finger clicking, heel clicking, and whistling, and all of these noises are then reflected by the obstacles and surfaces. In this sense, echo detection involves the active use of the auditory system, since the individual has actively to make a noise, which through its reflection then serves as a source of information.

Kellogg (1962) looked at the size, distance, and material of objects that could be perceived aurally. Allowing subjects to make any noise they wanted to help detect the objects, he found that they revealed a discrimination ability at 30 cm and that they could distinguish metals from all other materials except for glass, which was confused with metal and wood. He also found that it was possible to make very fine discriminations, like distinguishing between velvet and denim.

Similarly, Myers and Jones (1958) found that generating artificial noise enabled good detection of objects and increased the chances of perception. Obviously, this serves as a far superior means of obstacle detection, and many children will, of their own accord, learn to slap their feet down, click their fingers, or (if they are really discrete) make a small coughing noise. However, one problem with this is that making these noises serves to draw attention to the individual concerned, and merely highlights the fact that the blind are not 'normal'. On the other hand, the use of the touch technique, as it is employed in cane use, exploits this skill, and because the cane is an accepted aid for the blind, it does not draw undue attention to the blind traveller.

Thus, to summarize: the potential importance of the auditory system to the blind individual, as a source of information about the environment, both general and specific, is paramount and should not be underestimated. Despite the previously discussed problems of field size, lack of specificity, and so on, it is central to orientation and localization for the blind, as well as the detection of obstacles—all without the need for direct contact.

The increased reliance upon this sensory system by the blind does not, however, necessarily bear out the traditional idea that the blind compensate for a visual loss by an increase in acoustic abilities—indeed there are a number of experiments indicating that this is not so. In experiments designed to look at sound descrimination abilities (Hare, Hamill and Crandell, 1970; Stankov and Spilsbury, 1978), there would appear to be little difference between the blind and the sighted. Similarly, whilst there has been little work on auditory localization skills, the experiments that have been done seem to suggest that there is little difference in the ability of the blind and the sighted to judge whether or not two sounds have come from the same or different places. When they have to establish the absolute position of the sound source, the blind are inferior to the sighted (Speigelman, 1976) and sight actually seems to help (Jones, 1975). Even though auditory observers can make judgements concerning distance (Fisher and Friedman, 1968), direction (Simpson, 1972), and state of motion of sound sources (Mills, 1972), it would appear that these judgements are not as accurate as those of visual observers (Howard, 1973). To draw the conclusion from this that the blind do compensate for visual loss through increased auditory ability therefore seems somewhat tenuous. Indeed, throughout their early pre-school and school years the young blind child has to be constantly reminded about the use of this sense and encouraged to use it whenever possible. A great deal of teaching effort has to go into the development of this skill, both in the class room setting and in the gym setting.

The haptic and proprioceptive senses

Another system available to the blind traveller is the haptic–proprioceptive system which incorporates the haptic and tactile senses, as well the proprioceptive. To distinguish between the haptic and tactile senses: the former is active, in the sense that it is the sensation of actively touching something, while the latter is passive, in the sense that the individual is touched by something. Haptic perception provides us with information about where we are, where objects are in relation to us, and what they are, all by direct contact with the surfaces of these places and objects.

There are several problems associated with the use of this sense as a provider of information about the world through which the individual is travelling, just as there is with audition. This 'haptic–proprioceptive system', like the visual system, does have a good selectivity of regard, in fact to an extent, as Foulke (1982) has pointed out, exceeds that of the visual sense, but there are several fundamental ways in which the system differs from the visual system.

First, it provides less information about the composition of space beyond arm's reach, since many visually observable (and auditorily detectable) things are not accessible by touch because: the scale is wrong and they are too small to be noticed by touch or too large to be experienced as a whole through the use of touch; they cannot be reached; they are too fragile/flimsy; or too dangerous to touch (Foulke, 1982; Foulke and Berla, 1978). Secondly, little can be observed at any one time and without direct contact. Therefore, everything has to be examined serially and there is little perceptual anticipation possible. Whereas the information obtained by the visual system is parallel and allocentric in nature, the information obtained by the haptic sense is both serial and egocentric.

Nevertheless, having said this, the haptic sense is far from redundant as a means of obtaining perceptual information about the world. Certainly, as with audition, a haptic awareness has to be fostered early within the life of the visually handicapped child. They should be made aware of the different sensations caused by touching different objects, of walking over different surfaces—sand, mud, gravel, etc.—with varying gradients, and of moving their whole body through different mediums. Swimming is known to be a useful therapeutic tool, and we have found it useful in our mobility work to take children to small, warm baths in which they can be relaxed, and through relaxing become aware of the different sensations within their body. As we have said, many objects are too large to feel by hand and we have met parents who have rolled their children over cars, across floors, pushed them up walls, all so that they gain some awareness, through touch, of the size and textures of objects and places. By making the children aware of these sensations, we also make them aware of the presence of objects outside their own body, and which have an effect upon their body. This is especially important for young congenitally blind children who will all too often be unaware of the world around them, and who need to be made aware of the existence of a world beyond themselves. If they are not made aware of this then these children will often become very introverted, indulging in a fantasy world of their own, talking to themselves, and often exhibiting mannerisms such as rocking, eye poking, and so on.

In relation to travel through space, one major use of the haptic sense comes from the fact that the walker is always in contact with the road, and thereby gathers information about its texture, changes in gradient, and so on. These item of information not only contribute to the spatial representations that we build up, but also serve as useful references and landmarks for future travel in the area, and provide a degree of anticipation for the traveller.

Through haptic perception we are also able to obtain information about posture. For instance, if the road slopes then our postures alter, the pressure on our feet is different, and so on. This awareness of our posture, and sensitivity to the position of our body joints, is known as proprioception, and it is this sense that, in conjunction with the haptic and tactile senses, provides the traveller with information about the shapes and sizes of objects and obstacles, surface characteristics and states of motion of things, as well as their positions in space (Foulke, 1982; Welsh and Blasch, 1980). These cues are also integrated into our spatial representations of the environment, along with information about landmarks, decision points, and so on.

Foulke (1982) summed up the differences between these three senses when he said that although the visual sense provides answers to the questions of what and where,

> audition is worse at where, and cannot—except by associative learning—answer what, while the haptic–proprioceptive system answers what and where, but does have a limited field. To this extent in the absence of vision it [the haptic sense] is the best perceptual system for information about space.

Such a conclusion seems somewhat unjust. Certainly, the auditory system sometimes requires supplementary information from the haptic system to answer 'what'—as in the case of objects and obstacles, which emit no sound—but in many situations, particularly situations in which the individual is trying to gain information about things ahead, the auditory system seems to be of more use to the blind traveller than the haptic sense.

The auditory system allows the individual to follow walls without touching, o identify corners without the need for direct contact, and, through associative learning, it allows the individual to discover where places are without the need to bump into them—it allows the anticipation of objects beyond arm's reach. The haptic system, however, whilst it may have finer discriminatory powers, can only really be useful through direct contact with surfaces, and therefore its use is limited. We would like to contend, along with Wanet and Veraart (1985), that despite Foulke's arguments, audition remains the major channel of information for the blind traveller.

It would be fundamentally wrong for us to assume, though, that the blind are intrinsically different to the sighted, because we rely so heavily on sight while they have to rely on other sense systems (Millar, 1981a,b). All of us will have found record shops in new towns by following the direction of the noise, or detected fish and chip shops by the smell, and all of us know only too well the strain we feel in our calves, especially when we have walked up a steep hill. The problem is that because our visual sense is so powerful and efficient, we tend not to take as much notice of these other senses. As Hill (1975) says vision often serves to dull a person's sight to a totally integrated knowing ... people must not let their eyes blind them to the world. They need to elevate their level of conciousness to bring them closer to the world'. Only when it is dark and we have no sight to rely on do we find ourselves using these senses more, and operate in a way equivalent to the blind—yet not as effectively.

So far, then, we have seen that vision is not essential for guiding movement through space. Locomotor guidance can be achieved through the use of alternative senses, and the blind individual is able to move through the environment with relative safety, and without fear of danger, through the utilization of these 'different' sensory systems. However, 'mobility' in its fullest sense, requires that the individual can achieve 'purposeful and efficient' travel (Foulke, 1982), and to do this requires that the perceptual information obtained throughout a journey be incorporated into a cognitive representation of the space, from which action-plans become possible. It is this integration of information into a cognitive representation by the blind individual, and teaching techniques designed to enhance this process, that we now consider.

The role of perception in the formation of cognitive representations of space

To recap: we have already discussed the primary role of perceptual information as a guide to movement, and have shown that despite the suggestion that vision is essential for guiding movement through space (Gibson, 1958), the blind are capable of achieving mobility through the use of alternative senses. However, perceptual information is not simply used as a guide for safe, locomotor movement. The perceptual information that we obtain as we move through the world must be built up into a cognitive representation of that space—a cognitive map—consisting, possibly, of a symbol-like structure within long-term

memory, in which the symbols represent landmarks, places, and the relationships between them in a two dimensional form (Gärling, Böök, and Lindberg,
1984a,b; Rosencrantz and Suslick, 1976).

As Foulke (1982) pointed out in his analysis of the task—travellers need to
know where they are, where in relation to their current position their destination is, and then need to be able to move to it, using their perceptions of the
environment and its landmarks, to up-date their position within their cognitive
representation, and determine their future courses of action.

The process of knowing where we are, where our goal is, and how we are
going to move between them, requires that we not only build up a cognitive
representation of the area but also that we formulate a travel plan (Gärling,
Böök, and Lindberg, 1984a,b). This can be described as an action plan guiding
travel, which is based on the cognitive representation of the environment that
has accumulated through exposure to that environment—in Foulke's analysis
this corresponds to steps 5, 6, and 15.

Thus there is a reciprocal relationship between space perception, the formation of a cognitive representation of that space, and the travel plan. If, as in
the case of new areas, our cognitive representation has not been acquired then
the travel plan is 'the most important condition for acquisition' (Gärling, Böök,
and Lindberg, 1984a, p. 22). Through it we acquire information about the route
travelled as well as perceptual information about the layout of the environment
through which we are travelling. Even if the cognitive map has been acquired
already, then the inferences necessary to make the travel plan become incorporated into the cognitive representation, very often constituting new knowledge
about the environment.

As we travel a route, new information is obtained through our perceptions
of the environment which is added to the representation to refine it, as well as
enabling us to monitor and check our progress, within our cognitive representation. It enables us to up-date our positions within our cognitive map, and to
make decisions about our future travel plan.

Therefore, the perceptual information that individuals obtain as they travel
through space is of fundamental importance—both to the formation of a cognitive representation of the area, and the travel plan. If this information differs
between individuals then it is likely that the cognitive representation of that
space as well as the travel plan will also differ. Given this, it seems likely that
the spatial representations of the blind will differ from those of the sighted
traveller.

Their reliance on different sensory systems, and the differences in the information that they obtain, as well as the means by which they obtain it, means
that their spatial representations are likely to be very different from those of
their sighted peers travelling in the same area. However, in order to be able to
form any kind of mental representation the blind individual must be capable of
mental imagery; so one question that we do have to consider is whether or not

the blind are actually capable of mental imagery.

Are the blind capable of mental imagery?

Paivio (1971) suggested that humans probably use two different strategies for thinking and remembering—linguistic and iconic imagery—yet throughout the years researchers have stressed the idea that mental imagery is specifically linked to vision. Many researchers have suggested that without the availability of sight any form of visual imagery is impossible since, as Paivio has argued 'it is the dominant mode of contact with objects and events, for most people' (Paivio and Okovita, 1971, p. 506).

Kosslyn (1980) referred to visual images as 'quasi pictorial' experiences and there has been a general tendency by researchers to use visual terms both to instruct subjects in imagery experiments and to describe, metaphorically, how subjects in those experiments respond (Kerr, 1983). Obviously, if this is true then it would seem impossible for the blind to form any sort of mental image, including a mental image of space and the environment (Hartlage, 1976). Such a conclusion would concur with von Senden's hypothesis about the spatial abilities of the blind, and his assumption that 'the congenitally blind patient lacks everything that would entitle one to speak of a tactile awareness of space' (1932, p. 279). This theory of total deficiency is the most extreme view taken by anyone who has ever worked with, or observed congenitally blind people. In its extreme form it is difficult to accept and therefore has few supporters today because it is obvious that many congenitally blind individuals are actually quite spatially competent.

If, as von Senden (1932) suggested, the blind were incapable of building up a spatial image, then it seems likely that they would have to resort, instead, to the alternative method suggested by Paivio (1971) for enabling individuals to remember and think—the linguistic method. If the blind remember space this way then any activity within space would be remembered through a set of verbal instructions. Easton and Bentzen (1987) investigated this idea, using a selective interference paradigm, and found that whilst a linguistic, semantic interference task did not effect recall of a verbally presented route, a similar linguistic, spatial task did—for both the blind and sighted subjects—thus suggesting that the blind had transformed the verbal route description into a spatial image.

This idea that the blind are capable of imagery, and specifically spatial imagery, is not new. Recent evidence has suggested that performance on imagery tasks depends on image processing, whose characteristics are spatial rather than visual–pictorial (Kerr and Neisser, 1983; Neisser and Kerr, 1973). From this it would appear that the blind are capable of coding and processing spatial information.

Evidence for this can be found in the dream reports of congenitally blind subjects (Kerr, Foulkes, and Schmidt, 1982). Indeed, one young congenitally blind girl actually reported a dream to us, saying 'I couldn't see it during the day of course because I can't see, but during the night when I am asleep I can see', thus indicating her awareness that what she experiences during the day when she says 'see' is somehow different to the things she 'sees' when she is asleep. Also, Kerr (1983) found that congenitally blind individuals could preserve and process mental representations of spatial information, in patterns similar to those of the sighted, and Zimler and Keenan (1983) found that performance on verbal spatial tasks was similar for the blind and the sighted. They found that in a paired-associate task the blind, like the sighted, remembered more highly visual imagery pairs than any others, and that they performed as well as the sighted on free-recall tasks, and that when dealing with images of concealed objects, the blind like the sighted, showed superior recall of pictorial over concealed objects.

All of these verbal tasks indicate that image tasks are not uniquely dependent upon visual processing.

Kerr (1983) has said that the blind are incapable of a specifically 'visual' imagery due to their lack of vision (Kerr, 1983), but even non-tangible properties of vision, such as colour, can be acquired by the blind (Zimler and Keenan, 1983), and as Marmor (1978) found, the knowledge of colour relations by the blind is the same as that by the sighted—a result that Zimler and Keenan (1983) ascribe to learning through verbal instruction.

We have asked congenitally blind children, as well as children with light perception, and some who were partially sighted, between the ages of 5 and 11 years to draw a number of familiar (square, circle, triangle) and unfamiliar shapes in order to measure the children's drawing ability before they have drawn maps. As an aside we asked them to comment on the unfamiliar shapes and asked them to tell us what the shapes reminded them of. It was interesting that virtually all the children classified the shapes in the same way.

Figure 10.3(a) was classified as a house by most of the children, Figure 10.3(b) as a bridge and Figure 10.3(c) either as a bird or a person. This illustrates, then, that not only are the children capable of some sort of imagery that allows them to match shapes with objects they know and have an image of, but also illustrates that these images are universal, whether the children can see nothing and never have or whether they actually possess a good amount of useful vision.

All these tasks reported so far were verbal in nature, but several tasks using rotatable displays have also shown that vision is not essential for the build-up of a spatial image. Rotation tasks, such as those used by Marmor and Zaback (1976) and Carpenter and Eisenberg (1978), indicate that congenitally blind subjects show a linear relationship between a rotated figure and a standard comparison figure. A fact that those researchers leads to the conclusion that the imagery processing underlying performance on a mental rotation task need not be visually mediated.

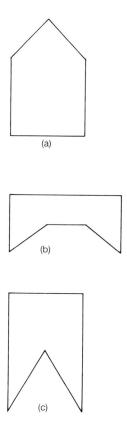

Figure 10.3   Three unfamiliar shapes given to the children—along with three familiar shapes—which they had to feel, draw and describe. Each of these was classified in the same way by nearly all the children.

Whereas it appears from this evidence that the loss of vision does not neces sarily mean a loss of spatial imagery, it may be that the quality of the imagery of the blind individual, is somehow different, due to their reliance upon alternative sensory systems, and thereby different sensory information.

This comparative approach is discussed by Hazen (1982) in relation to spatial orientation in sighted individuals. She begins by looking at the seemingly complex and very different means of navigation that exist in the inhabitants of the Caroline Islands, the Eskimos of the Canadian Arctic, and the Touareg Nomads of the Sahara, who all keep track of their whereabouts by discriminating, interpreting and organizing very subtle distinctions in what seem, to outsiders, to be completely undifferentiated environments. They all use very subtle and very different cues and yet they do have one thing in common and that is the fact that the navigators must have a cognitive representation of the environment and must, therefore, be able to tell where they are in respect to that environment. Whether or not we see the basis for these differences as due to cultural materialism, adaptation to ecological conditions, or whatever, Hazen suggests that they all arose because such cultures inhabit relatively undifferentiated environments and have adapted to cope with this fact. Taking this further it appears that 'any two groups who differ consistently in the sorts of spatial experiences that they encounter may well be expected to develop very different strategies and forms of cognitive representation as a result of their adaptation to their particular environmental challenges'.

This is essentially the case with the visually handicapped travellers. They too keep track of their whereabouts by 'descriminating, interpreting and organizing very subtle distinctions in what seem to be completely undifferentiated environments to outsiders'. Operating in an environment with no clear visual feedback they are able to use other senses to distinguish differences in their surroundings, which sighted individuals would find extremely difficult.If these differences do affect the spatial understanding and representations of the blind then we must ask in what ways these differences affect their representations of space.

How does the use of alternative perceptual systems affect spatial representation in the blind?

From what we have already said, it appears that contrary to von Senden's (1932, 1960) views, the blind are indeed capable of mental spatial imagery. Nevertheless, whilst few would argue with this statement today, there is still some debate over the extent to which the spatial representations of the blind are comparable to those of the sighted. Von Senden's theory, in its weaker form, states that the knowledge of the spatial relationships gleaned from auditory and tactual cues is inferior to that based on vision. The 'Inefficiency Theory', as this is called, is exemplified by Revesz (1950), who stated that 'what we deny is the assertion that it should be possible, by purely haptic perception, to get a homogenous idea of the form of objects which differ from well known, or less complicated spatial figures' (p. 124). Such a theory is supported by tasks such as Worchel's (1951) block identification and walking tasks.

A less extreme theory about the spatial abilities of the blind is the 'Difference Theory', supported by researchers such as Jurmaa (1973). He argued that the results from many of Worchel's experiments were due to a testing artefact, and said that all instances in which vision assisted performance on a spatial task involved optically familiar material. He argued that if the blind are asked to build up a spatial image of optically unfamiliar shapes (Jurmaa, 1965), then this disadvantage is lost (Jurmaa and Suonio, 1975), and the congenitally blind operate at a level equivalent to their sighted peers.

Jurmaa (1973) also postulated that the only reason for the superior performance of sighted children on spatial tasks was that the blind suffer from a developmental delay, as compared with the sighted, which is reduced as the blind child grows older. He hypothesized that, ultimately, the blind individual is capable of building up a cognitive representation that is not necessarily very different from the cognitive map developed with the use of vision. This idea finds support among some of the imagery literature cited earlier. Zimler and Keenan (1983) for instance, talk about the acquisition of non-tangible visual knowledge by the blind through verbal instruction, and say that where this occurs, a delay in cognitive development can be expected.

Therefore, in these situations you can expect to find adults performing at the same level, whether sighted or blind, but not children. Although this hypothesis only applies to non-tangible visual knowledge, and Zimler and Keenan (1983) ascribe the understanding of spatial relations to direct acquisition through touch, there seems to be no reason why we should not consider this delay as being applicable to directly learnt knowledge as well.

If we accept that blind children are delayed in reaching out into the world (Fraiberg, 1968), then we can assume that all direct experience beyond this first step is also going to be somewhat delayed, and conclude that blind children will also be at a developmental disadvantage compared to their sighted peers in areas of knowledge such as spatial knowledge, that are directly learnt.

Experimental support was given to Jurmaa's theory by the work of Gomulicki (1961). He found that although young sighted children perform better than their blind peers on finger and ambulatory mazes, by the age of 15 years, the two groups show equivalent ability on the two tasks. Similarly, McReynolds and Worchel (1954) found that when testing 15-year-old congenitally blind, partially sighted, or adventitiously blind individuals in a familiar setting, they showed no differences in the ability to point to places on campus, in their city, or in other cities.

The extent to which the cognitive representations of space posdsessed by the blind match those of the sighted is still a matter of some dispute. Most authors have supported the inefficiency theory advocated by Revesz (1950), leaving Jurmaa's theory with few supporters, but we point out in the rest of the chapter the extent to which the acceptance of the inefficiency theory has underestimated the spatial skills of the blind.

To build up a spatial representation we rely upon the senses that we have available to obtain information about the space around us and to process it so that it can be integrated into a spatial representation. How, then, and in what ways, do these different senses affect the spatial representations of the blind?

The quantity of information differs

The information available to the blind traveller through the auditory and haptic sensory systems differs in content and quantity from the information received through the visual system, and neither system is thought to be as good as vision for answering questions about the composition of space. As we mentioned before, the auditory system suffers from a lack of specificity, selectivity, and a reliance on associative learning to identify the source of stimulation, while for the haptic sense the problem is the need for direct contact, and therefore the necessity to experience space sequentially.

Not only is the quantity of information that the individual obtains through these alternative senses believed to be different, but the different means through which these systems gain information and process it, means that the encoding of this information is believed to be qualitatively different as well (Warren, 1970; Hartlage, 1976; Pick, 1974). It is these differences in the encoding of spatial information that are believed to be partly responsible for the supposed differences in the spatial representations of the visually handicapped, and it is these that we discuss next.

Each sensory modality is thought to have its own 'modality-specific' means of encoding perceptual information and data about the world (Hermelin and O'Connor, 1982: Millar, 1981b), linked to the ways in which information is obtained. This in turn is believed to alter the form of representation about the world that is possible by determining the frame of reference adopted for the perceptual information being encoded. The blind, who differ from their sighted peers in the extent to which they rely on the auditory and haptic sensory systems, are therefore believed to have a quantitatively as well as qualitatively different spatial representation of the world.

Modality-specific encoding differences

Numerous studies have been undertaken to examine the idea that each sensory system has its own, unique, means of encoding the perceptual information it has obtained. We discuss the auditory system first.

In contrast to the visual modality, which encourages a spatial encoding of perceptual information, it has been found that the auditory system encourages a temporal encoding of information (O'Connor and Hermelin, 1972). Given this, researchers have concluded that because the blind rely almost exclusively upon this system for perceptual information they are incapable of organizing auditory information spatially.

This was illustrated in an experiment by Battachi, Franza, and Pani (1981), who found that even if encouraged, the blind could not organize auditory information spatially, thus lending support to the idea that the blind are incapable of organizing perceptual information spatially.

It would also appear that while the visual system results in a parallel, allocentric, encoding of information, the other sense upon which the blind rely quite heavily for information about the world around them—the haptic sense—results in a sequential, egocentric, encoding of information. Blind individuals appear to use their bodies as a frame of reference for haptic stimulation (Rieser and Pick, 1976), and rely upon this rather than any visuo-spatial schema of an area (McKinney, 1964).

Therefore, it seems that the auditory system and the haptic system together result in a temporal, sequential, egocentric organization of stimuli for the blind. It is these differences in the encoding strategies of different perceptual systems that are believed to alter the way in which the blind build up their representations of space.

The organization of spatial knowledge and the effects of visual loss

We build up a representation of space by processing and integrating perceptual information available from space, and obtainable through our own movements within that space. Therefore, we rely very heavily upon the information obtained through our perceptual systems, and differences in the systems used result in differences in the information obtained, as well as in the ways in which it is encoded within our spatial representations. This representation can be built up using either an environmental or an egocentric reference system (Rieser, 1983). Using an egocentric reference system individuals relate the layout of space to themselves and to their own bodies, but with the environmental reference system individuals relate the position of each landmark, within the space, to every other landmark. Vision is the ideal perceptual system for enabling the individual to use these environmental reference systems (Rieser, Lockman, and Pick, 1980; Rieser, Guth, and Hill, 1986) and the inability to perceive these fundamental aspects of spatial understanding is, according to Rieser, Lockman, and Pick (1980) the source of differences between the blind and the sighted on spatial tasks.

To start with, very often we are able to see many spatial relationships directly, through vision. Secondly, when we move in space and have the advantage of vision, we can see the simultaneous transformations of the directions of objects from ourselves. Having had this experience, it is postulated (Rieser, Lockman, and Pick, 1980; Dodds, Howarth, and Carter, 1982) that when a view of the layout of space is not possible—perhaps because vision is occluded, it is dark, the individual has been blindfolded, or when the whole area is too large to allow all places to be observed at once—then it is possible for the sighted individual to extrapolate, from experience, the spatial relationships between places and areas, and thereby build up some visuo-spatial image of the area.

This idea has also been used to explain differences in spatial ability *within* the blind population. The adventitiously blind individual is believed to be spatially superior to the congenitally blind individual. It is often believed that individuals who have had some sight during early life—Rieser, Guth, and Hill (1982) suggest until the child is 8 years of age, others suggest until the child is 5 or 6 (Lowenfield, 1948; Schlaegel, 1953), while still others suggest that vision for only the first 3 years is sufficient (Fletcher, 1980; Warren, Anooshian, and

Bollinger, 1973)—have had enough visual experience to allow them to extract spatial relations, understand perspective changes, and so on, in a way comparable to the sighted, yet very different from those individuals blind since birth. In other words, adventitiously blinded individuals are believed to have a visuo-spatial imagery that allows the organization of spatial imagery in a two-dimensional rather than one-dimensional representation.

The knowledge of the spatial relationships between areas and landmarks, once attained, must then be organized. There are several ways of organizing this information (Rieser, Guth, and Hill, 1982), some of which promote more efficient spatial way-finding than others. Travellers, whether sighted or blind, may well memorize the routes travelled, listing the distances between places and the directions of turns taken from place to place. But with knowledge organized in this way, travellers are limited to this route and unable to make detours or short cuts. If the individual is operating through the use of an egocentric reference system then it seems likely that this would be the easiest way to organize a spatial representation. As Rosencrantz and Suslick (1976) point out, this would be a one-dimensional rather than a two-dimensional spatial representation. Although some individuals may realize the two-dimensional structure inherent within it, it is likely that most would not, and would, therefore, depend upon a string of self-referenced relationships organized in list form. If this is the case then inferring short-cuts and Euclidean distances, and angles between two places on the same route, but not directly linked on that route, would be very difficult for the individual concerned. In addition, the individual with this route based knowledge may find it difficult to spatially link several places when only a subset of the relationships has been learnt.

A more versatile way of organizing spatial knowledge would use a knowledge of the spatial pattern of the paths travelled. This would enable short-cuts and detours to be taken along that path but would only allow individuals to link places on any one route—they would find it difficult to infer the spatial relations between two different routes and the places along them. An even more flexible means of representing space corresponds to Siegal and White's (1975) survey map, in which numerous spatially patterned routes are integrated within a common frame of reference; this would allow individuals to figure novel paths from places previously learned on one route, to places learned along another route.

The visually handicapped individual relies upon systems which, it is believed, not only necessitate direct contact, and thereby a serial, self-referenced perception of places, but also encode information in a serial, egocentric manner, which is believed to be unchangeable. Therefore, it is believed that the blind individual who has never had the advantage of simultaneous and direct perception of spatial relations and perspective is limited to an egocentric-route-type representation of space. That person's idea of space, therefore, is not spatial in the true sense, but is a one dimensional, self-referenced, list of relationships (Rosencrantz and Suslick, 1976). This means that detours require a great deal of thought, estimating the direction and distance between two places not directly linked on a route will take longer and will be less accurate than by sighted individuals, and places on two different routes will be very difficult to link spatially.

The tasks employed to look at this issue range from simple finger-labelling tasks (Hermelin and O'Connor, 1971) to tasks involving shape identification (Pick, Klein, and Pick, 1966), discrete arm movements (Laabs, 1973; Martenuik, 1978; Millar, 1975, 1976), and large-scale spatial tasks (Dodds, Howarth, and Carter, 1982). It is the few small scale 'spatial relations' tasks (Warren, 1984), that we consider first.

Small-scale spatial relations tasks and the spatial understanding of the blind

The general conclusion derived from the small-scale spatial relations tasks is that whilst the sighted are capable of organizing their spatial representations not only spatially, but also allocentrically (Attneave and Benson, 1969; Goldsmith, Mohr, and Pick, 1977), the blind, due to the limitations of the perceptual systems that they can use, are only able to use self-referent, egocentric cues and to encode information non-spatially (Hermelin and O'Connor, 1975; Millar, 1979, 1981b). Furthermore, maze tasks have shown that if blind individuals have had some sight during their lives then they are more likely to encode spatial information spatially and allocentrically than if they have not had any visual experience (Berg and Worchel, 1956; Knotts and Miles, 1929; Merry and Merry, 1934).

These experiments, therefore, provide support for the ideas put forward previously in Part II, and from this one could conclude that the blind encode and process information in a way that results in an egocentric, one-dimensional representation of space. However, the extent to which these tasks bear any relevancy to, or show any indication of, spatial skills in the large-scale travel situation is somewhat dubious. No one has yet been able to show that performance on small-scale spatial-relations tasks, serves as any indication of large-scale spatial abilities or travel skills. Therefore we must turn to studies dealing with life-sized spaces, since these are more likely to tap such travel skills.

Large-scale spatial cognitions literature and the spatial understanding of the blind

The 'spatial cognitions' literature (Warren, 1984), deals with life-sized spaces and the knowledge an individual builds up about that space. It is not concerned with table top experiments nor with artificial settings, such as walking a straight line or a hypothetical triangle, but instead exposes individuals to a setting—

either set up by the experimenter or familiar to the individual—about which something has to be learnt, and then this knowledge is examined. Through these experiments it is thereby hoped that we gain a clearer insight into the spatial cognitions of the blind population.

We argued above that there were a number of assumptions about the way in which the blind build up representations of space and the ways in which this information is organized. With perceptual information encoded egocentrically and temporally, it has been suggested that the blind individual will form an egocentric, self-referenced, route-based representation of the space encountered. These differences in the organization of this information allow us to make several predictions about the spatial abilities of the blind; each is discussed in turn. One of the first predictions about the abilities of the visually handicapped in large-scale space is that, having travelled a route, making judgements about the direction and distance between two places not directly linked along that route will require more thought and, due to the necessary mental transformations, be less accurate.

Herman, Chatman, and Roth (1983), tested 12–24-year-olds in an unfamiliar route set up by the experimenters. They found that when asked to give pointer responses between places joined on that route, but not directly linked, the responses by the blind were less accurate than those of their sighted peers who were blindfolded. Fletcher (1980) used a number of blind and sighted children, aged between 7 and 18 years. They were shown a model or life-sized room, and were then asked a number of 'route' or 'map' type questions. Route questions were determined by whether or not 'the correct answer could be obtained directly from the route traversed on each trial', while map questions meant that 'the information required to answer the question had to be synthesized into a map' (Fletcher, 1980, 1981). She found that the sighted performed better as a group than the blind and that, in addition, the blind were better at route than at map questions, thus suggesting that they found the synthesis of this information into an organized and spatially structured whole very difficult. Similarly, Byrne and Salter (1983) found that the blind were far worse at estimating directions between places in a familiar setting.

Another prediction is that the blind individual will not be capable of spatially linking two areas that were not directly linked through personal experience. For instance, travelling from the bus-stop to the sweet-shop, and from the bus-stop to home, the visually handicapped individual may not be able to extrapolate the spatial relationship between the shop and home as effectively as the sighted individual.

Rieser, Guth, and Hill (1982, 1986) carried out several studies designed to examine just this. They set up a layout in which there were a number of different objects, and they familiarized their subjects with only a select number of the relationships—those between each of the objects and the starting position. After this their adult subjects—some of whom were sighted and blindfolded, and others of whom were totally congenitally blind or adventitiously blind—were asked to judge the spatial relationships between each object and every other object, a task that necessitated linking inferences from their previously limited knowledge. In other words, they had to be able to work out the spatial relationships between each object even though they had only experienced the object—starting position relationship. The subjects were asked to judge these relationships under two conditions—a locomotion and an imagination condition.

During the first of these the individuals were guided to each of the landmarks from which they had to make their judgements, whereas in the latter condition the subjects were asked to imagine standing at each location and then to make their judgements. The results of these two conditions revealed that with or without audition occluded, and even when the movement variable was controlled for, the blind were less able than the sighted.

Rieser, Guth, and Hill (1982, 1986), found that both the blind (early- and late-blind) and the sighted groups found the imagination task difficult—a result that was not surprising given that it required the participants to 'compute or otherwise transform the directions to the objects, they learned during the training phase'. However, what they did find surprising was that the early-blind—unlike the late-blind and sighted—found the locomotion task just as difficult and 'their responses were based on deliberate computational strategies similar to those used in the imagination task'—results that were supported by their poor response speeds and relatively high error scores. From verbal reports it appeared that these subjects tried to solve the problem by recalling the target object's direction from the start, the stations point from the start, their facing direction relative to the start, and then computing an answer based on these three pieces of information. Rieser, Guth, and Hill (1982, 1986) attribute this to the fact that visual experience plays an important role in the development of perceptual up-dating through the ability to perceive directly transformations in self-to-object directions and perspective.

Rosencrantz and Suslick (1976), provided a similar amount of information for their subjects, but verbally rather than through direct experience. They found that while on the whole, the sighted individuals could convert this one-dimensional route information into a two-dimensional representation, which enabled them to answer questions about spatial relations, the blind were largely unable to do this.

In a more realistic study, Dodds, Howarth, and Carter (1982) found that when 14-year-old boys were asked to make inferences between two learnt routes around two blocks, the later-blind were better than the early-blind, but both were worse than the sighted in making pointer responses between the two routes learnt seperately.

These studies suggest that, compared to sighted subjects, the blind find it more difficult to judge the spatial relationship of two places if they have not directly experienced that relationship. However, the studies described above have tested subjects in unfamiliar areas.

The third prediction that we discuss relates to the ability of the blind in known territories. If blind individuals' spatial representation is always egocentric and organized by routes they may be slower and less accurate than sighted peers, even when making spatial judgements in familiar areas.

Rieser, Lockman, and Pick (1980), looked at the ability of a number of blind and sighted subjects, aged between 24 and 60 years, to estimate both functional and Euclidean distances within a well-known area. Results showed that when judging Euclidean distances the sighted group performed best, then the adventitiously blind, and the congenitally blind group was the poorest.

In a similar experiment by Byrne and Salter (1983), a number of blind and sighted adolescents and adults had to make distance and direction estimates between pairs of well-known or well-used areas. Distance estimates were made by ratio scaling and bearings were estimated by the rotation of a circular disk. Byrne and Salter reported that while the blind did not differ from the sighted in the magnitude of their errors about distance, they were much worse than the sighted at estimating bearings, unless they were estimating the bearings from their home. This lends further support to the conclusion that 'blind subjects' orientation appears egocentric.

To sum up—throughout the last few sections we have found a great deal of evidence lending support to the idea that the blind encode spatial information using egocentric references. Relying upon the auditory and the haptic sensory systems, any information received by the blind individual is believed to be automatically encoded either temporally or egocentrically, rather than spatially and allocentrically.

So, it is believed that the resultant frames of reference, which are then used to organize the spatial information, themselves result in a spatial representation that is both egocentric and route based.

A second look at the evidence

The majority of researchers, over the years, have postulated that the blind will be severely impaired in their spatial skills—not just their understanding of space but also its cognitive representation. Without the use of the major (if not the only) spatial sense, the blind have to rely upon alternative sensory systems to provide spatial information. Since these differ so greatly from the visual sense, in the information that they can acquire, the means through which they acquire it, and the ways in which they encode it, it is believed that the spatial representations of the blind must therefore, by necessity, differ greatly from those of the sighted individual.

So far we have found a large body of evidence in support of these predictions, but caution is advised. When we look at the studies concerned with perceptual encoding strategies, there is evidence to suggest that the blind are not fundamentally different from the sighted in their encoding of auditory or haptic information. Although the emphasis has always been on the differences between the blind and the sighted, it may be wrong to assume that the blind are unique when responding egocentrically to perceptual information. As Millar (1981b) points out 'it is important for all animals to know where their limbs are in relation to their head and trunk, self referent systems are extremely important at all ages and we all use them when necessary'.

Evidence from various studies indicates that whereas the sighted, when they are able to see, encode auditory information spatially, and haptic information egocentrically, when they are blindfolded they, like the blind, respond temporally and egocentrically to the same stimuli (Attneave and Benson, 1969; Pick, Klein, and Pick, 1966). In fact, it would appear that these modality specific characteristics persist across all individuals, including those with handicaps other than sight.

Thus, in isolation from the visual system, the auditory system automatically encodes any incoming information temporally, and haptic information is encoded by the haptic system egocentrically—both within the blind and the sighted subject. However, if the individual has recourse to the visual system, then vision is such a powerful sensory system, that it overrides the natural encoding strategies of these senses and results in a spatial encoding of auditory information and an environmental encoding of haptic information.

Similarly, although the maze tasks, reported previously, seemed to provide support for the idea that the blind are poorer than the sighted, a number of other maze tasks have found no such evidence in support of this correlation (Berg and Worchel, 1956; Bottrill, 1968; Knotts and Miles, 1929). Gomuliki (1961), for instance, found that young blind children were poorer than sighted children on such maze tasks, but by 15 years of age this deficit had disappeared.

Just as it appears that the blind are not necessarily poorer at maze tasks than the sighted, and that they are not any different from the sighted in their encoding of perceptual information, so we can also find evidence that they are no different from the sighted in their large scale spatial abilities.

Although there is some evidence that the blind find it difficult to extrapolate the spatial relationship between two areas joined along a route, there is also other evidence to the contrary (Hollyfield and Foulke, 1983; McReynolds and Worchel, 1954). Similarly, there are a number of studies that indicate that the blind have few problems in linking two areas spatially, which have not been directly linked through their own experience (Herman,Herman, and Chatman, 1983; Landau, Spelke, and Gleitman, 1984). Landau et al. (1984), in one of the few studies to look at pre-school children, tested a 3-year-old congenitally blind girl in an experiment similar to that of Rieser, Guth, and Hill (1982, 1986), but which used fewer locations. They found that this young girl could, in fact, make the inferences asked of adults by Rieser et al. (1982, 1986).

These studies contradict those reported earlier that emphasize the spatial inefficiency of the blind. However, we do not need to look at these alone to find evidence against such ideas, for if we take a closer look at those studies reported earlier then we find that they in themselves are somewhat contentious. Most of the studies we have discussed were conducted using groups of blind subjects and groups of sighted subjects, and to this extent the data has been analysed in terms of the group, and ignored individual variations. For instance, we mentioned that the sighted, if blindfolded, show egocentric and temporal coding of information, like the blind. However, in most of these studies it is evident that even when sight is available, some sighted individuals use egocentric coding strategies for haptic stimulation.

Only Goldsmith *et al.* (1977) reported 100% geographical responses among the sighted subjects, but others such as Hermelin and O'Connor (1975, 1982) reported such figures as 60% of subjects using external cues. If it is possible for the sighted to respond egocentrically, when they have the benefit of sight and many years experience of using it, then it does not seem so unusual for the blind to respond egocentrically, especially when we consider that many have never had the benefit of sight, and are therefore unaware of any alternative method of coding. Even when individuals are aware of this alternative method of coding spatial information, it appears that they do not always use it.

Similarly, conclusions from these studies that the blind are only capable of showing egocentric coding strategies overstate the case, because some individuals do adopt environmental coding strategies. For instance, Hermelin and O'Connor (1971) indicate that some of the congenitally blind children made primarily location responses, and were operating spatially, and Millar (1971) comments that in many of her experiments 'some—if few—of the blind participating did not respond egocentrically'. Results such as these would seem to indicate that the blind do not always rely upon the egocentric coding of information and that at least some individuals are capable of using environmental reference systems for the encoding of spatial information. The anomalies that we find in the spatial encoding literature are also to be found in the large-scale 'spatial cognitions' literature. For instance, while Fletcher (1980) found that, on the whole, her sighted subjects were better as a group than the blind, a number of her blind subjects performed at a level equivalent to the sighted on map questions, thus showing that at least some of the blind were capable of making spatial inferences comparable to those of the sighted. Similarly, Rosencrantz and Suslick (1976) reported that some of their congenitally totally blind subjects were as capable as the sighted subjects. Also Dodds, Howarth, and Carter (1982) found that one congenitally blind boy showed spatial abilities comparable to those of the late-blind subjects, who also took part in their study.

In the light of this evidence, then, it would appear that the blind are not as spatially incapable as most researchers have implied. There are a number of contradictory studies as well as anomolies within the data of those studies stressing the spatial inefficiency of the blind.

We are now faced with the need for an explanation of these diverse results. With the tendency being to highlight the skills of the sighted, and the weaknesses of the blind, data showing that at least some of the blind are as spatially competent as the sighted have been largely ignored, or dismissed. It is this data that requires more emphasis. If some blind individuals can outperform other blind subjects in the same task it is important to identify the ways in which the spatially good differ from the spatially poor. The identification of such differences leads us to a better understanding of the problems faced by blind individuals and hence to better ways of overcoming those problems.

The work of Rosencrantz and Suslick (1976) typifies this approach. They provide some support for the proposition put forward by Jurmaa (1973), that the reason for spatial differences between the blind and the sighted, is due to different rates of development. However, because only a few of their subjects improved with age they concluded that this was evidence against Jurmaa's theory. But, this evidence is inconclusive in both directions, and Jurmaa could as easily argue that those very 'few' subjects are evidence against Revesz (1950) and support for him. Rates of development differ and experience may also have an effect, both of which we need to consider before we draw any conclusions in either direction. Similarly, in the pattern recognition tasks, Hunter (1964) concluded, from a task similar to that of Drever (1955), that the blind were less efficient than the sighted. Favouring Hunter's (1964) results over Drever's (1955), despite the fact that Hunter (1964) produced no data, means that sceptics have been able to support their ideas concerning the spatial inefficiency of the blind.

An explanation of contradictory results

One of the reasons for the conflicting results is the diversity of experimental techniques used to examine spatial abilities. These tasks range form the small scale maze tasks to the large-scale 'real-life' experiments dealing with locomotion in familiar and unfamiliar space, and the techniques used and responses required from subjects even when the experiments are ostensibly looking at the same question vary considerably. For instance, one of the major problems with the large-scale locomotion studies is that a large number of them are carried out in laboratory settings, which are completely unfamiliar to the subjects. Experimental settings in themselves can make individuals feel uneasy, whether sighted or blind, but the fact that the blind rarely explore novel areas alone (Dodds, Howarth, and Carter, 1982) means that they are much more likely to feel apprehensive about completely unfamiliar areas. So, if they are asked to familiarize themselves with unusual layouts by walking around them, without any idea of what to expect, it is likely that blind subjects are going to need more time than sighted subjects to feel at ease even before beginning to understand the spatial layout—especially if the subjects are children. In addition, walking itself is often a stressful activity for some blind individuals, even when they are in familiar areas, and this should also be taken into account.

The problem, though, is that more often than not, blind subjects are not given the extra familiarization necessary, but instead have to make judgements based on the same amount of familiarization with an area as sighted subjects (Fletcher, 1980; Reiser, Guth, and Hill, 1982, 1986). Bearing this in mind, it therefore seems possible that results such as those obtained by Reiser *et al.* (1982, 1986) may not be due to spatial skills at all, but may reflect differences in the confidence of blind and sighted subjects in the experimental setting. In other words, the results may reflect differences in the ability to cope with new areas and to absorb information about space whilst being apprehensive and nervous, they do not necessarily reflect differences in spatial abilities.

If this is the case it is not surprising, therefore, that we find individuals in the Herman, Herman, and Chatman (1983) study performing better than those in the Reiser *et al.* studies (1982, 1986). They were able to glean some idea (even if it was somewhat inaccurate in terms of distance and angle) of the test area before having to walk in it.

Working with, and observing, visually handicapped children between the ages of 5 and 11 years, in both natural and laboratory settings we have found that there are a large number of children who are very apprehensive in large unfamiliar areas. This apprehension stops them from observing and absorbing any information about the space. Consequently, their results on spatial tasks tend to be low. If, however, we give the same children similar tasks but get them to examine a map of the area beforehand, we find that their scores are much better, and their movement within the area is very much more confident. They themselves report that they now have some idea of the area and can therefore decide where to go without fear of crashing into obstacles.

Several researchers have found that a subject's performance in the same experiment may improve are tested in an environment in which he or she feels at ease (e.g. Acredolo, 1979). This may apply particularly to blind subjects and it is worth noting that the high levels of performance in experiments such as that of Landau, Spelke, and Gleitman (1984) may reflect the fact that the child subject involved was made to feel comfortable in the experimental environment by the presence of her mother. We have found that when 'playing' with children in their homes, results from model tasks and locomotor tasks are much higher than when similar tasks are carried out in school. This would seem to be due to the fact that many children, when at school, often express concern at the idea that they are being 'tested', and this added pressure and uneasiness stops them from concentrating on the task at hand.

A further problem with many of the large scale tasks, which involve walking, is *veering*. Many of these tasks only measure the ability of the individual to reach the goal landmark (Herman, Herman, and Chatman, 1983; Landau, Spelke, and Gleitman, 1984), and do not take into account the fact that whilst the individual may well have a clear idea of their destination point, and may even start off heading in the right direction, they may veer off at an angle. Therefore, when the individual fails to reach the end point, the researcher all too often concludes, that it is due to an error in distance or angle judgement and a lack of proper spatial knowledge (Herman, Herman, and Chatman, 1983). Landau, Spelke, and Gleitman's (1984) study, which contradicted that of Rieser, Guth, and Hill (1986), has been criticized for this very reason. Warren (1984) suggested that because the young girl in their experiment was not able to move in a straight line from landmark to landmark, that she was using perceptual information to up-date her position rather than having any real knowledge of the spatial layout. However, this is a somewhat dubious criticism. If the child was heading in the right direction but tended to veer off course, then correcting this veer through the use of perceptual information does not mean that she had no idea of where she was going. Indeed, contrary to this, it indicates that she had a good idea of her environment, and her position in relation to that environment and the landmarks to which she was heading, in order that she could correct her course efficiently.

Veering is a major problem for the visually handicapped individual who has no aid on which to rely, and we have found in a number of our studies that even if children have a very clear idea of a spatial layout, as indicated by their facing direction, they can easily become lost by veering off course. Once they have veered off course, it is often impossible for the children to find their way to the next landmark because they are not sure of the extent or direction in which they have veered. This does not mean that the children have no idea of the spatial layout, but rather that without efficient kinesthetic feedback, they have failed to realize the extent or direction of veer and, without vision, could be anywhere within the experimental area. Perhaps, then, we should begin to consider ways in which we can make individuals more aware of their veering and find ways to help them compensate for this problem.

From what we have said already it appears that part of the explanation for the differing experimental results is the use of different techniques, some of which place the blind at a greater disadvantage than the sighted, irrespective of spatial skills. It would be a mistake to assume that a single experiment reflects any true spatial skill or ability. The approach which we have adopted is the use of various techniques in various different settings. By doing this and working with the children over a number of years, we hope to get a clearer insight into their spatial abilities. Through the use of different designs we hope to be able to pinpoint differences between individuals as well difficulties that they have with different designs.

These differences may be related to the specific tasks used and reflect little to do with their spatial skill in general, or they may bear a fundamental relationship with the individual's spatial skill as a whole.

Perhaps another explanation of these as yet unanswered questions is experience. Maybe the results from these experiments should not be thought of as indicative of spatial abilities as much as experience. The sighted have more experience with space and they have more experience with the sorts of tasks that are required in spatial experiments than do the blind. It does not mean that the blind would be any less capable than the sighted if given the same amount of experience, but because they have had less they perform worse than the sighted in spatial tasks.

Research with the blind has to consider the differential experience of the blind and sighted take, for instance, the encoding tasks; from the studies we described earlier it appeared that in isolation from vision, the auditory system resulted in the temporal organization of sound while the haptic system resulted in an egocentric organization of stimuli for both the blind and the sighted. These encoding strategies appear to be inherent characteristics of these sensory systems and as such the blind do not differ from the sighted. A lifetime's exposure to these sensory specific methods of encoding information is bound to result in a lack of awareness of alternative strategies and thereby a failure to use them—especially in situations where there is no encouragement to do so.

This was the case with many of the experiments like the finger-labelling task of Hermelin and O'Connor (1982). Even in situations in which the blind are actively encouraged to use alternative strategies for the encoding of perceptual information they may not do so—not because they are incapable of doing so, but rather because they have not had the experience that would allow them to do so. If however, the blind are given experience of alternatives and are encouraged to use them, it may be that they could do so as efficiently as their sighted peers. Rieser, Guth, and Hill (1986) concluded that the sighted perform better in spatial tasks even when their sight is occluded because over the years of movement within space they have learnt about perspective changes and stable spatial relationships, and this general knowledge can then be used in situations in which they cannot rely on sight. However, for the blind, who have always relied on the auditory and haptic systems, and have managed quite well doing so, there is no reason to think of any alternative way of organizing spatial information other than the one imposed through these senses.

With a heavy reliance upon self-contact to obtain spatial information, the use of sensory systems whose inherent characteristics are to encode this information egocentrically and temporally, as well as a lack of awareness of the alternative ways of organizing spatial information, the spatial representation of the blind has a tendency to be one-dimensional and route based.

This in turn results in the inability to make a number of spatial inferences, as we discussed earlier and saw reflected in the large-scale spatial cognitions literature. We have found evidence in support of this idea with our own work using children who are partially sighted or congenitally totally blind. We have found that even when the experimental room is large and dark, and therefore any residual sight is of little use, that the partially sighted children are better at spatial tasks than the majority of the totally blind children. This suggests that even when an individual has a minimal amount of sight, the availability of this sense serves to draw attention to external reference systems, and thereby to a means of organizing spatial information, which is then used when the individual is deprived of what little sight he or she has. It may be that the benefit of sight may not be that it, of necessity, leads to an environmental coding system, but rather that it serves to draw attention to the possibility of using external reference cues (Millar, 1981b). As Millar has said

> during blindness information about the relations between you and objects external to you is at best intermittent, and more often than not unreliable.Because of this the idea that external relations can serve as useful references is lost to the blind child and so they choose to rely upon coding relative to their body, which has throughout their life provided constant and reliable feedback in many tasks.

Visual experience enhances attention to external cues and facilitates the internalization of spatial relations between external cues.

However, it is incorrect to assume that the blind are fundamentally incapable of these skills if they have not had the benefit of sight. We have seen clear evidence of this in a number of studies, where a few blind subjects have far excelled their peers even without this visual experience (Dodds, Howarth, and Carter, 1982; Fletcher, 1980; Rosencrantz and Suslick, 1986). It seems likely that for these individuals this experience has been supplemented in some way. They are aware of alternative coding strategies as well as the advantages of using environmental reference systems, and we are therefore faced with having to find ways in which this missing visual experience can be replaced for other individuals, so that we can ensure mobility teaching is made as efficient as possible. It is all very well ensuring that the blind have the necessary travel skills but without flexibility in their spatial thought they can never become truely efficient and independent travellers.

A key to the ways in which we can do this may well come from the individuals themselves. They have obviously developed superior spatial abilities and can organize perceptual information in a truly spatial way. Researchers should begin to look at why it is that these individuals use these alternative strategies more readily than others, and what has encouraged them to do so, in order that we can then try to educate other blind individuals to do the same. It may be important that this experience comes early in life for it to become an established part of spatial thought.

Jurmaa (1973) may well be right, and the problem faced by the blind individual is essentially a developmental one. As we have already mentioned, blind children are delayed in their development as compared with sighted children, and it seems that their spatial skills develop later than those of the sighted individuals. However, just as blind infants need their attention drawn to auditory stimuli for them to begin ear–hand coordination, so it may be that blind children, also, need to have their attention drawn to environmental reference systems and encoding strategies before their spatial skills can develop.

It is also likely that the amount of experience that individuals have in space, and therefore the amount of familiarity they have with these systems, will effect their rate of development and spatial skills.

So, without encouragement early in life then it may be that their spatial skills will not develop to their fullest potential. Several authors have suggested that there are different times in the lives of blind individuals when they are most receptive to spatial concepts. During these periods, it is suggested, they will develop better spatial skills if they are encouraged to move about and experience space than if they are not (Fletcher, 1980; Landau, Gleitman, and Spelke, 1981; Landau, Spelke, and Gleitman, 1984).

This may well explain why most of the studies we have reported, have shown the blind to have poorer spatial skills than the sighted. Most of these studies have looked at the spatial skills of adults and older adolescents. By the time of testing these individuals, they will have well established habitual spatial strategies which may be difficult to modify.

Implications for teaching

The area concerned with teaching travel skills to the blind individual is generally known as Orientation and Mobility (O & M) training. This area of teaching evolved out of the rehabilitation training given to wounded war veterans, and relies very largely upon common sense and good practice. The majority of the techniques employed have very little empirical backing, and have been extrapolated from the original teaching. The teaching techniques designed for young children have been adapted to accommodate ideas that teachers have had about the development and needs of the young blind child, but throughout the practical literature, there is a notable lack of reference to theoretical work within the area of psychology. In particular, there is little attention paid to the spatial understanding of the children, and to the psychology discussed in this chapter. In addition to this the teaching profession has a number of its own, untested theories about the spatial development of the blind child, the factors contributing to this skill, and how teaching should be designed to enhance this development. In the following sections we indicate, from our own work, the kind of procedures used.

Testing an old theory

One of the most widely held beliefs among those who write about orientation and mobility training, is that a well-developed *body-image* is the basis from which the young child learns to structure external space (see general discussion in Chapter 3). Body-image can be thought of as 'A knowledge of Body Parts, how these relate to each other, how the parts may be utilized individually and collectively for purposeful activity, and how the parts relate to the child's spatial environment' (Mills, 1970). The belief is that through the coordination of eye and hand comes the use of vision as the external verifier of the existence and identity of objects. As a child begins to reach out in space for objects, he or she lays the foundation of a concept concerning his or her own body and how it relates to the world around. This is built upon as children begin to move in space, and begin to see the changes that their own movements have on the relationship of their bodies to the space around them. Children learn that there are relatively stable landmarks on their own body that do not move relative to their own body, even though their body itself may move in space. Knowledge of that space then generalizes from the body, to more distant obstacles and events, and children learn that things can change position in relation to themselves. It is believed that this understanding forms the basis of their wider spatial understanding. Because the coordination of ear and hand occurs at a much later stage in development than does the coordination of eye and hand, it is believed that the blind child's concept of body-image will likewise be delayed, and that therefore teachers should spend the early years of teaching trying to ensure a well developed body-image. The idea behind this being that if this is not developed then spatial skills will also be poor.

However, in a recent study we found no such relationship between body-image and spatial skills. We tested the children's body-image as well as their performance on a number of spatial tasks in both familiar and unfamiliar areas and found there to be no relationship between the two. This, by necessity, must lead one to question the value of teaching body-image to young children. Perhaps mobility teachers ought to be looking towards alternative teaching methods for the improvement of large scale spatial skills in the young blind child rather than concentrating on close body skills.

Trying to encourage movement in space

We have said already that probably one of the most important factors in the build up of spatial knowledge is experience within space. This experience is important for both building up a representation of that particular area, as well as gaining some general awareness of the 'environmental grammar'. Indeed, we have conducted a questionnaire and interview study that revealed that, controlling for sight, the single most important predictor of spatial ability was the amount of experience the child had in space. We questionned parents about their attitudes to their child's handicap, the things which they encouraged them to do, the activities they encouraged, and so on, and we found that it was the children whose parents allowed them lots of free play outside, who made them help them in the house and who encouraged them to be independent that were the most spatially competent, and that this was irrespective of sight.

Obviously, the more experience that children have within space, the more familiar they will become with the layout of space and the relationships within it and how these alter as the child moves through space.

Therefore, it would seem that probably the best thing for teachers to do would be to encourage lots of movement by the children. This is not as easy as it sounds though, for teachers do indeed do this and spend lots of time getting the children moving in class. The problem lies in the children themselves, for many of them, especially the congenitally totally blind children, find moving in space very difficult and very stressful, and therefore when left alone will not move off the spot. Ironically, these are the children who need this movement most, but a fear of hurting themselves, of bumping into and falling over objects (as well as people!) and of getting lost within a large open space, results in a failure to move in space, and thereby a failure to learn anything about the features of the space around them. So how can we encourage these children to move in space when they are not under the guidance of an adult or another child?

We mentioned previously that one thing that does encourage young children to move in space is to give them a large toy that they can push in front of them,

Figure 10.4   From push-chair to long cane. For most visually impaired children, pushing toys such as this in front of them helps to encourage the needed projection within space and thereby increases spatial experience. It is only a small step from this to the long cane!

which will hit objects before they do. However, this is not a practical thing to use with older children, so we need to find some alternative to pushing a toy.

Obviously, the long cane serves this purpose. It is a well-known fact that one of the greatest ways to instil confidence into newly blinded adults, and indeed children, is to give them a long cane. It provides a multitiude of haptic and auditory cues that can aid travel, as well as functioning as an obstacle detecting aid, which will hit all objects before the person does. In addition to this, we had noticed that when children were given mobility training and canes, they would become very active and mobile—even when the cane was not in their hand. Therefore, it appears that the confidence by the aid extends far beyond the times when the individual is actually using it and spills over into all activities.

However, the established practice within Orientation and Mobility training is not to give a child a cane until about 11 years of age. With the need for certain motor skills to be achieved so that the individual adopts the right 'cane technique' it has been felt that the young child cannot possibly benefit from the use of the cane and may be liable to adopt faulty techniques. However, if the child is under supervision when beginning cane training, any faulty techniques can be modified. Even if it is not possible to modify poor technique the advantage to be gained by the child in terms of increased activity may far surpass any problems that might arise in the use of the cane.

For this reason we gave cane training to two congenitally totally blind boys aged 7 years. Before cane training, these boys were typically to be found at play-time, either standing in the playground turning in small circles or sitting down and indulging in many of the well known blind mannerisms, so often thought to be the result of a failure to externalize movement, such as arm flapping, rocking, etc. In physical education lessons they would remain immobile unless guided by teachers, and when moving between rooms at school had to be under constant supervision and given constant encouragement. After 4 months of training we found that their activity within free play had increased substantially, and they were even to be seen running across the playground on several occasions. In addition, they showed greater confidence in their movement around school, and although still fairly reliant upon teachers to verify their decisions, they demonstrated greater knowledge of their school environment.

Obviously for these children the introduction of the cane was profitable and productive and the confidence that it instilled spilled over into activities when the cane was not even present. This is not to say that the cane should be introduced to all young children. For some who are already active and mobile the cane may actually hamper movement rather than enhance it, but for some children who otherwise are largely immobile this may be a very important aid for encouraging essential movement within space.

However, having said this, cane training is not the only thing that is necessary if we are to encourage the children to move within space. We mentioned earlier that one of the biggest problems for blind children is the tendency to wander off at angles—or veer—and to get lost or bump into things within the space that they are exploring/moving in.

We have seen this in our own work. Very often children will have a good idea of the layout of the space around them, and know exactly where it is that they are going to. They will head off in the right direction, but after only a few steps will veer off course. Without knowing in which direction they have veered, or how far they have gone, the children become confused, disoriented, and all too often will begin to panic—this in turn prevents them from finding their way.

Sometimes if they do this in familiar territory and hit a landmark that they know, they will reorientate to the place they were initially meant to be going to, but if they do this in an unfamiliar area then they do not know the landmark that they have hit or how it relates to the layout of the space around them, and therefore its relationship to the place they were meant to be finding. Reorientation in these cases is therefore very difficult.

Another far-reaching effect of this veering problem, we feel, is that it destroys the children's confidence in their own abilities. If they are constantly wandering off course, and failing to find the places they think they are about to find then they will rarely accept that they are in fact going the right way. We have found this with a number of children who persistently veer. All too often they will ask whether or not they are going in the right direction or say things such as 'I know this isn't probably right but I think it's over there', 'is it over there—I doubt that it is?', and so on. They constantly look for reassurance on their own judgements, and find it very difficult to make decisions about where they are to go.

Obviously, then, one thing that is also necessary, if we are going to encourage free movement in space, is to try to reduce this veering and we have recently conducted the first in a series of studies designed to do just this. We worked with four congenitally totally blind children and two children with light perception, all aged between 5 and 8 years. There were three training sessions of 20 minutes for each child. We felt that for this training to be effective, it was necessary to have some form of automatic feedback for the children in order that they could then tell which way they were veering and correct it themselves as they walked. For this reason we decided to conduct this first study in a long, narrow corridor, with which the children were not familiar. The idea was that the sound reflected from the walls would alter as they got nearer to, or further from each wall, and that they should therefore be able to steer a relatively straight course down the centre of the corridor.

Therefore, the teacher stood at one end of the corridor opposite a child and called to them. The child then had to walk as straight as possible down the corridor and try to catch the teacher at the opposite end. It was hoped that doing this over a period of 3 weeks would actually reduce the child's veering in open spaces, and so before and after the training began we measured veering in an open space, as well as the veering of a control group.

We found that the control group did improve but that this improvement was not significant. However, the trained group also improved their veering and this was significant ($t = 2.481, p = 0.05$).

Encouraging an understanding of space

Obviously, these two studies have concentrated on encouraging the children to move in space, and as we said earlier, an important aspect of moving in space is having a well-developed cognitive representation of the space around them, which makes explicit the relationships that exist between areas. We mentioned that one explanation for the superiority of the sighted individuals on spatial tasks is that they are able, throughout their lives to see the overall relationships between objects within a space and that these general rules can then be used in a situation when either the area is too large to see all the relationships, or they are in a situation where they cannot see anyway. The blind do not have the ability to do this and to get some overall idea of the pattern of objects in space, and so somehow it is necessary to supplement this information for the blind. One way in which we could do this would be to give them a map of the area they are concerned with, since maps make explicit the relationships that exist within space.

There has been some debate as to whether or not the blind can actually use maps successfully. They are two dimensional rather than three dimensional and since it has been postulated that the blind cannot appreciate any view of the world other than that provided by their own experience, then it would seem sensible to postulate that they will not be able to use maps efficiently. For this reason we began our work with models. Essentially these convey the same information as maps but are three dimensional rather than two dimensional, and therefore should be easier for the blind to use as a representational medium.

Model work   Our work with models began with a very simple task. We had a number of pre-made objects, such as beds and wardrobes, and we asked the children to show us the layout of their dormitory using these. We found that whilst there were a number of differences between the ability of the children to use these models, these differences were not necessarily predicted by such things as sight or age. Overall we found that the children could represent their dormitories using these models very easily, and that also they seemed to be very accurate; so we then asked the children to construct a model of their school gym and compared it with the actual layout of the gym to see precisely how accurate the children were.

Previous to this model construction we also obtained pointing and facing measures from the children to each of the places within the gym and we were therefore able to compare the childrens' accuracy in pointing and facing with their accuracy of placing objects within the model. Since the door of the gym provided an easy reference point we took all the measurements from the door and also looked at their estimates to other places within the gym, from the door. We found that the children were much more accurate when placing the pieces in the model than they were at pointing and facing towards these places within the gym ($t = 4.877, p = 0.0003$ and $t = 3.523, p = 0.003$ respectively). Obviously then, it would appear that the children are far better at using the model to indicate their representation of the space than they are at pointing or facing towards the different places in the gym.

This appears to be something of a contradiction to the studies carried out with sighted children in which it has been found that children are not very accurate at using models as a representational medium, but we feel that this may be due to a problem inherent in asking the blind to point from a place. This is because to be able to point precisely from a place within space you have to know exactly where you are in relation to the object/place that you are pointing from and exactly in which direction you are facing, and to do this in an area where either there is no landmark to serve as a reference point, or the area is completely unfamiliar, or the experimenter is trying not to give too many clues, is an extremely difficult task, so it is very easy to be very unsure as to where it is that you are standing, etc. This is, however, avoided when using a model, for the space is completely under the control of the child and the whole space is within arm's reach.

This finding carries important implications for both the teacher of the blind and the researcher, since appears from this that probably the best way to assess the knowledge a child has of a space would be by using a model rather than using the traditional pointing and facing methods employed by both teachers and researchers.

Having said this, though, we would also like to point out that within our sample there were three children who were consistently very poor at using the model, and who were better at facing and pointing towards places. Therefore, it has to be said that (as is the case with all other teaching/assessment techniques) this is not necessarily the best technique for all children.

Carrying on from this, we felt that as the children could use models so well and could obviously represent areas very well with them, maybe they could be useful teaching tools. Therefore, having assessed the children's knowledge of the gym, we decided to work with some of them using the model of the gym in an attempt to try to improve their knowledge of the area. Therefore, we divided the children into those who had high error scores and those who had low error scores. The high group were further divided randomly into two, half of whom were trained with the model.

There were six children in the training group—three congenitally totally blind and three with light perception—and over a period of 3 weeks they each had three 20-minute training sessions with the model. In these sessions we would put things into the gym, discuss their relationships with each other and how you would get from one place to another, and also moved a small doll around the gym to illustrate this. After the 3 weeks' training we then retested the two low scoring groups. We found that whilst both groups had improved in their pointing and facing, the trained group had improved more—and significantly so ($t = 2.98, p = 0.024$).

Maps   Obviously, then, the children can use models well, but what about maps? We said at the beginning of this section that there has been some controversy over the extent to which the blind find maps useful, and so we began with the very basic question of whether or not the children could understand the principle that a map shows you where something is in space.

We again began by working in the child's dormitory, because of it's familiarity. We based the work on a game of hide and seek—we would hide an object in the room and then place a marker on the map to show where the object had been hidden. We then explained to the children that the mark on the map would show them where the object was hidden and asked them to go and find it. Obviously, if the children could find the object then they could understand the principle that the map shows you where things are in space. We found that all but the very youngest children found this task very easy, and found the object virtually every time. However, the youngest children found the concept that a mark on a map meant that there was something in space, very difficult. Having said this though, by the second time we used maps the children had a very clear idea of what it was a map was showing them.

Since then we have carried out a number of studies, replicating this in unfamiliar areas, familiarizing the children with unfamiliar areas and so on, but obviously, one of the most important questions is whether or not the use of maps confers a better spatial representation upon the blind child than could be obtained by simply walking within an area. We carried out a study to test this.

A room was set up as illustrated in Figure 10.5. There were 22 children altogether, six aged between 5 and 6 years, eight aged between 7 and 8 years, and eight aged between 9 and 10 years. Of these children eight were totally blind, eight had light perception, and six were partially sighted. Half of the children were shown a map of the area which they were allowed to free explore. As they did so they were told what each thing on the map represented and where they were standing. They were then asked to point to and face each of the landmarks shown on the map, and after this to go and find the different landmarks (in a random order). When they had found each of the landmarks they were then asked to come back to the starting place and to again point to and face each of them. The other, 'non-map', group were simply told that in the room there were a number of things and that it was their job to find them. They were told that they would not be given help unless absolutely necessary,

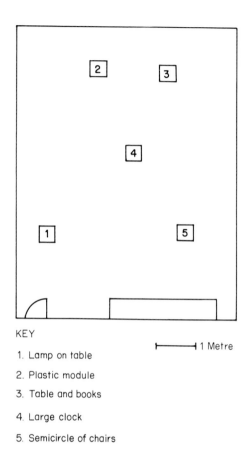

KEY

1. Lamp on table

2. Plastic module

3. Table and books

4. Large clock

5. Semicircle of chairs

Figure 10.5   A novel room was set up containing five landmarks. After being familiarized with its layout—either by a map or free exploration—the children were asked to point to each of the landmarks and their scores were compared to the actual angle.

but that because they were being watched there was no danger of them hurting themselves. They were then allowed to walk round the room until they had found each of the things mentioned, after which they came back and made pointing and facing responses.

This experiment was later repeated with a different layout (see Figure 10.6); this time the non-map group were given a map and the map group were allowed to free explore. This allowed us to compare each of the children across three different conditions—their accuracy in facing and pointing after free exploration, after reading a map, and after reading a map and then free exploring. We found that when all the data was taken as a whole, although the children seemed to

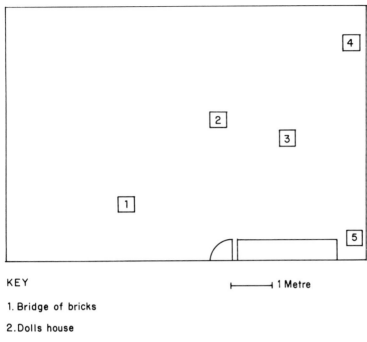

KEY   ├──────┤ 1 Metre

1. Bridge of bricks

2. Dolls house

3. Barrel

4. Teddies

5. Rocking horse

Figure 10.6

be more accurate when pointing and facing after using a map as compared with the free exploration, this was not significant. Nor was the difference significant when we compared the free exploration with map and exploration—despite the fact that here again the map and exploration had a lower mean than the free exploration. However, when we analysed the data in terms of age and sight, we did find some important effects. We found that when we looked at the groups in terms of sight the congenitally blind were significantly more accurate when using a map than when free exploring and that this accuracy improved when they were then allowed to explore the area afterwards. We found that the children with light perception were also better when using a map as compared to simply exploring an area (although this was not significant), but that they actually became worse when they were then allowed to free explore the area after having been given a map. The partially sighted children, however, were actually less accurate after using a map than after free exploring, and even worse when they were allowed to free explore after having looked at a map. A two-factor ANOVA revealed that there was a significant interaction here.

When we looked at the groups in terms of ages we then found that the youngest group, aged between 5 and 6 years, was significantly more accurate after using a map than after free exploration, and that they became even more accurate when they were then allowed to free explore. We found that for the 7–8 age-group exploring a map made little difference to their accuracy in pointing and facing, but that if they were then allowed to explore after looking at a map this did improve their accuracy (although again this did not reach significance). The 9–10 age-group, however, were actually less accurate after looking at a map than they were when they were allowed to free explore, and even poorer still when they were allowed to free explore after using a map. Again, a two-factor ANOVA revealed a significant interaction here.

Obviously, then, for some children the map is not a useful tool and we feel that this is likely to be due to some interference between already well established representational strategies and the strategies imposed upon the individual through map use.

SECTION 2: THE ENVIRONMENTAL NEEDS OF OTHER HANDICAPPED CHILDREN

In the remaining pages of this chapter, we raise a number of questions to do with other forms of handicap. As indicated in our introductory paragraphs, there is much less research available on the perception of the environment by those whose handicap is not a visual one; instead the bulk of the literature is to do with the physical–environmental needs of this very diverse group.

Much is in the form of design guidelines and evaluations of specially designed buildings, which we do not propose to review here; an example would be the British Department of Health and Social Security (DHSS) series of reports *Mental Health Buildings Evaluation* (1979–1980), which includes a number of special reports on residential accommodation for mentally handicapped children (see also Dalgleish and Matthews, 1981)

Some more-theoretical reviews exist, which often treat the environmental needs of handicapped children in with those of adults with similar handicaps (e.g. Haywood and Newbrough, 1981; Zimring, Carpman, and Michelson, 1987). For all age-groups there has been considerable stress in recent years on making the living environments of the handicapped as similar to those of the non-handicapped as possible, and integrating educational provision with the mainstream of education: instead of institutions and special schools there would be community care and integrated schools.

'Normalization' of housing was urged by Nirje (1970) who advocated making it possible for the handicapped to 'experience the normal rhythm of the day, the weeks, the seasons and the year, supporting the normal development of the life cycle'.

This now widely accepted, 'Normalization Principle' not only seeks to guarantee the rights of the mentally handicapped person, but has also been advocated as a method of active intervention for the amelioration of mental handicap. Normalization can be implemented in the programmes, the facilities, and the architecture for the handicapped; and of these, Gunzburg (1973) has argued that architecture might be the most basic and influential.

Although there have been several attempts to investigate the influence of the environment of the mentally handicapped, it is in practice very difficult to separate this variable from those relating to the social environment. Even in the case of studies where regime was held constant, and the environment systematically altered, the practical difficulties of a real time study become apparent: in the case of a study by Gunzburg and Gunzburg (1973) where the social and personal development of handicapped residents was rated before and 4 years after their ward was completely rebuilt, one finds that the staff conducting the ratings had changed and that only 16 of the original subjects remained. To overcome such problems, comparative studies such as that by Tyerman and Spencer (1980) adopt cross sectional comparisons between settings of different architectural design, matching as far as possible resident characteristics and management regime.

In our study, we found that a more normalized environment did produce, as predicted, an increase in participation and a reduction of stereotypy—the repetitive behaviour often shown by institutionalized individuals; but we felt, having done the study, that the full potential of normalization would only be realized when accompanied by self-help training programmes, keeping the use of staff help to the minimum practicable—just as we have argued in the previous section that over-protective parents run the risk of curtailing the exploratory play so necessary for the young child's conceptual development [see Gunzberg (1974) for a discussion of factors conducive to the social competence of mentally handicapped children].

The quality of residential settings for the mentally handicapped can be related not only to the institutional–community dimension of the home, but also specifically to its size and detailed design.

Staff–client groupings, and potentially their relationships, will be very different in homes with a few, large living rooms, from those with small rooms. Improvements in the individual's functioning, partly attributable to such factors, has been shown in several studies summarized by Felce, de Kock, and Repp (1986), who reasonably call for more research on the effects of residential design on the performance and attitudes of caring staff.

Architectural regime and social factors are likely, in practice, to be interactive: and isolating the effects of one category of factor upon the well-being of the handicapped individual is not a realistic proposition. Indeed, Richardson (1981) has urged us to adopt an ecological perspective to the living environments of the handicapped, in that ecology emphasizes the interaction between individuals and their environments. We will, none the less, expect to have to develop measures of particular aspects of the interaction: King, Raynes, and Tizard (1971) for example, have developed a Child Management Scale, to characterize the range of possible different management styles in children's homes; and Balla and Klein (1981) have sketched a taxonomy of institutions. With such tools it may then be possible to assess the extent of person–environment fit (Stucky and Newbrough, 1981), against which to assess the benefits of institutional versus community care (Heron and Myers, 1983). And, as Bayley (1973) has demonstrated in his study of handicapped people living in the community, it is often the case that an informal support system, consisting of relatives, friends, and neighbours, may be more important for the individual's well-being than formal social-work provision in the community setting.

And, we could surmize, such a supportive network might, in the final analysis, be a more important factor than any architectural or other environmental factor ever could be: in stressing the importance of physical environments here and elsewhere in the book, one must not lose sight of potentially even more important social features. Comparison of, for example, handicapped children's adjustment and well-being in schools clearly involves more than an assessment of the architectural design of each type of provision: a huge range of other factors are also there for comparison. Such a study might investigate pupils' self-images; teacher attitudes and motivations; parents' and the general public's stereotypes of handicap; pupils' attainments in formal and informal school activities; friendship patterns; ambitions and later careers; the list goes on.

There is now a huge volume of research on the needs of, and provision of services for the handicapped—some of it small scale, applied to particular local issues and destined only for working-paper publication; some larger scale and appearing in a range of professional and academic journals. As some indication of the amount of such work, the *Directory of Non-Medical Research Relating to Handicapped People* (Sandhu, Richardson, and Townsend, 1987) gives details of some 459 separate projects currently funded in Britain, many of which relate to children with handicap.

CHAPTER 11

Designing for the child's needs

Consider the domestic cat. Cohabiting with man, the cat is dependent and yet independent: the pattern of man's activities, including the shelter provided, determines much of the cat's life pattern, and yet the cat moves independently and privately through the gaps in this human pattern—using 'waste spaces', adapting places to alternative uses, and partaking of an alternative society almost under our noses, yet without our being more than superficially aware of its rituals.

We are, as adults, only marginally more aware of the children in our midst, especially by the time they gain sufficient independence to be 'off out'. Yet some of us plan for their needs, consciously shaping play areas, domestic rooms, hospital wards, school yards, leisure facilities, as if we had full knowledge of these needs. Children manifestly play: therefore we design a playground. Psychologists argue that imaginative play is important for development: and we, in consequence, design an *adventure* playground; and are rather insulted when it is largely ignored by the clientele, who, instead, stalk each other, have clubs, hold picnics, and happily 'do nothing' in the long grass of the 'space left over after planning' alongside the adventure playground. Equally, we know that city streets are dangerous, and are therefore rather worried to find that for many children, the street is a preferred area.

Can our researches into the child's developing awareness of the environment, at neighbourhood level, provide us with clues to the child's developing needs with respect to the neighbourhood? We could, for example, argue, along with Hill and Michelson (1981), that how children function in space reflects the development of cognitive processes: that young children simply do not have the capacity to understand and therefore to use the configurations of a neigh-

Figure 11.1   Consider the domestic cat. We need systematic natural histories of the child comparable to those we have for many mammals to give an account of the range of everyday behaviour, the fit between activities and behaviour settings, and the child's developing awareness of social and physical worlds.

bourhood. Much of Part II has debated the competence—performance issue: we will not weary the reader further with cautions about underestimating the child. Probably of greater significance are parental constraints upon activity, (e.g. Biel and Torell, 1977) and the child's own self-limitations, arising from physical capacity and from a desire not to stray too far from the familiar: for where parental constraints are relaxed at an early age, then even quite young children seem competent to understand and use fair-sized neighbourhoods (e.g. Hart, 1979; Spencer and Easterbrook, 1985). And by the age of 8 or 9 years, most urban children are aware of the kind of layout to expect in a town, reproducing typical groupings of elements in a model (Dijkink and Elbers, 1981): evidence for the emergence of a usable search-strategy wherewith to explore a novel environment. [Compare the equivalent set of expectations that Devlin (1976) has shown adults to bring with them when tackling a town they have recently moved to.]

Most of our experimental and investigatory procedures lay emphasis upon those aspects of environmental cognition that are to do with locational information: spatial relationships, distances, angles and elements such as routes, districts, and nodes. Yet, as we argued in Chapter 1, into this searching image of the neighbourhood also come important *affective* factors: areas of excitement, boring areas, places where one can expect to be private, and places which are good for a game. Hence, in asking how far environmental cognition research is a guide to children's needs, we are forced to acknowledge that most of the said research has been strictly that: cognitive, rather than cognitive and affective. Studies to be reviewed in the present chapter—on how, for example, children actually use the neighbourhood for a huge variety of play—should be a useful reminder of the incompleteness of the literature on the development of environmental cognition reviewed in Part II. The tradition of that literature has been to focus on the child's processing of information of where places are, without concerning itself with the child should wish to know.

The present chapter, therefore, briefly reviews what these 'traditional' cognition studies have to offer our present concern—demonstrating the circular relationship between knowledge and patterns of exploration; before moving on to consider the habitats of childhood. We shall ask about the child's needs and feelings for the natural environment, and shall discover that some of these remain intact even in the most unpromising of urban areas; studies of children's imaginative play show that, despite the worst attempts of over-planning or environmental neglect, children still manage to use the city as a resource in their social and personal development.

We shall ask whether through such studies of children's activities, and their representations of the social and physical resources available to them, we can discover what are the child's neighbourhood needs. These will clearly differ with the child's age and range; extending outwards from local spaces to street networks and associated places to the use of a larger proportion of the city or region. The city as perceived and used by teenagers represents a much more complex entity than the district of the young child; and here we have only the beginnings of an ethnography of adolescent life.

The design literature is potentially of use to developmental psychologists, in describing how the young use various important settings: the local shopping mall, the school, play spaces, the home, and leisure areas. Many worthwhile 'experiments' on individual's needs and perceptions have been conducted by designers and architects: their design briefs are really hypotheses stated about environmental influences upon behaviour, which are then operationalized when the building or project takes shape. Unfortunately, in most cases the 'experiment' sadly aborts, because the busy designer has no time to collect or analyse the behavioural data on how individuals actually use the new project, and to determine whether this differs from behaviour in other architecturally different but socially comparable projects. We can, however, cross-link this design literature with the classic observational work of the ecological psychologists, observing children's natural behaviour across the behaviour settings they encounter; and relate both to environmental psychology's more experimental literature on, for example, the effects of noise and other stresses on school performance, and the availability of resources for play on children's frustration and aggresssion within nurseries.

Finally, we can begin to abstract some more-general observations about the child's needs: for privacy, and for sociability, both of which relate to use of and control over spatial resources, and to what some researchers still persist in calling territoriality. We can also ask what are the influences of density and of stress upon the child's esperiences of environment? And, in considering the design implications of all the foregoing, we shall consider the success of those who have endeavoured to include children as planners of their own environments.

Neighbourhood knowledge and its relation to activities

We have already observed in Part II that children's knowledge of large-scale environments is likely to be affected by how they interact with that environment. However, as Biel and Torell (1982) have observed, studies seeking to relate such differences in experience to the extent and nature of their environmental knowledge are rare. We have, in Part II, already reviewed studies on, for example, distance judgement as a function of familiarity (e.g. Siegal and Schadler, 1977); but in general such studies use a fairly crude measure of familiarity—typically, the length of residence in an area (e.g. Anooshian and Young, 1981). Biel and Torell (1982) and Herman, Heins, and Cohen (1987) have taken the trouble to investigate the patterns of children's activity via diaries and by accounts of activity range. Their 6–10-year-old subjects confirmed Hart's (1979) observation that not only the extent of their activity range but also the way they explore—and hence learn about—the environment is strongly influenced by parental restrictions. A further important factor which Biel and Torell's study documents—again seldom taken into account in other studies—is the effect of friends and especially of older siblings. Yet another influence upon knowledge of neighbourhood was the extent to which children participated in organized activities.

There have been some other attempts to describe the personal geographies of the environmentally exploring young. Piché (1981) controlled children's exploration of what was, for them, a novel residential city area, and examined their uptake of information, and route planning and orientation, relating these to the amount of exposure to the area. Matthews (1984a–c) has taken naturally-occurring learning situations—the journey to school, and trips around the home area—and has argued that, although there is a clear relationship between age and experience, on the one hand, and the complexity of neighbourhood map drawn, on the other, the learning process is not a simple linear one. The journey to school requires, not surprisingly, that the child develop an awareness of sequential elements, whereas Matthews found that neighbourhood maps demonstrated a greater appreciation of spatial dimensions. Up to the age of 9 years, boys were able to recall slightly more information about their home area than girls; after this, girls recount more detail despite evidence that their activity field expands more slowly than does that of boys (see also Andrews, 1973; Matthews, 1984a–c).

The habitats of childhood

Planners and politicians, from the practical side, and psychologists and geographers, from the academic, need to give coordinated and explicit attention to the place needs of children, in distinction to those for adults. Why? What special needs can be discerned? Hill and Michelson (1981) have offered us a start; and their observations can be summarized thus:

1 Children and adults differ in behaviour patterns, with play and education having a major role for children.
2 Their land-uses and facilities differ; or, where shared, are often used for different purposes.
3 Daily ranging patterns differ, in ways that reflect adult's greater autonomy and access to resources.
4 Children face different (and possibly greater) threats from their environment.
5 Children are entirely outside the politico-economic decision-making process that determines land-use; adults have a greater chance of participating.
6 Children and adults differ in their interpretation of plans.

The existence, provision and geographical distribution of resources and opportunities relevant to children can clearly be argued to be a major influence on their patterns of behaviour (Hill, 1980) and, potentially, to their well-being. Yet we know very little about the distribution of such resources. The one attempt to map these, and to examine what effect access to these opportunities has on the activity pattern, has focused principally on the needs of older children and adolescents (Hill, 1980).

Hill and Michelson (1981) undertook to survey Toronto, plotting where children lived in the city against *child-relevant* features. Traditional land-use designation, as used by geographers and planners, gave way in their survey to a different scheme: 'a retail furrier and a real-estate office may be in the same category as an ice-cream store or a fast food outlet, but their relevance to children is hardly the same'. Going further, they argued that we need to know more: not just that, say, a swimming pool exists in locality, but also that it is accessible and available to the target age groups. The researchers cross-related the pattern of these resources to accounts of children's and teenagers' activities throughout the city (gathered by questionnaire); and were able to demonstrate relationships between, for example, distance and frequency of usage—thus the spacing of libraries seems to have an effect not only on which libraries teenagers go to, but on how often they go. Such factors will interact with other, socio-cultural factors already recognized as being related to patterns of resource use. Similar analyses are possible of the negative environmental features—immediate dangers, pollutants, noise levels—which may influence the child's well-being.

Using such data, we can hope to plan and manage the city's resources to provide a better habitat for children and teenagers; and, by being aware of the hazards, move towards persuading decision-makers to give high priority to their elimination. In the International Year of the Child, writers and planners from all over the world met to discuss 'the management of urban space in the interest of children' (Michelson and Michelson, 1980). Principally, their attention was to the formal provision of designated area—play areas, other leisure facilities, schools, and so on, which we will also discuss later in the present chapter. There was, however, also a welcome recognition of the unplanned, undesignated side of child-life; for instance Little (1980) contributed a 'social ecology of children's nothings'. He suggested that 'much of the pleasure that children get from living in cities is coded in personal symbolic terms that seldom get mentioned to anyone, let alone an experimenter or opinion pollster'; and sees much of children's activity as consisting of the pursuit of personal projects. Several other authors—from phenomenological geographers to urban planners (with regrettably few psychologists)—have provided powerful arguments for the importance to the child's existence (and potentially to the present and future well-being of the individual) of the unplanned environment, and it is to these we now turn.

Natural and man-made environments as settings for the private life of the child

The author most frequently cited on children's needs and the natural environment, Yi-Fu Tuan (e.g. Tuan, 1978), is best described as a phenomenological geographer, whose source material is a rich weave of literary quotations from East and West, extracts from autobiographies, and observations from anthropologists on the environment as experienced. In contrast, much of the work published on children in man-made environments cites more empirical studies (e.g. Hart, 1979; Moore, 1986: Moore and Young, 1978), which have considered the range of variables that may influence children's cognition, experience, and use of urban areas. Yet, whether the evidence is experiential or empirical, all writers are agreed that the physical environment is not a mere neutral backdrop for the child's social and personal development (as one might surmise from its virtual neglect in conventional texts on child development), but has the potential to be a major factor in well-being in childhood, and in consequent development into a fully realized adult.

Manifestly, children can be happy and can achieve successful development in a huge variety of habitats—and therefore the researcher seeking to investigate the needs of childhood must specify variables and *desiderata* at a level sufficiently abstract to admit their fulfilment by a whole range of concrete realizations. For example, we find researchers discussing the child's general need for privacy, and only then investigating how particular socio-physical environments under study permit its achievement. The conclusions to our brief review will therefore be at this abstract level, having reviewed illustrative evidence from a range of particular settings.

Our first question may seem almost mystical: do children, for their well-being, *need* access to and experience of the natural environment? Tuan (1978) warns one off romanticizing nature: 'We choose to forget that the infant mortality rate is much higher in New Guinea than in a modern metropolis'. Yet, he believes that human beings have 'an innate capacity to appreciate nature', which 'nonetheless can be rendered ineffectual' by, for example, being brought up in urban slums. (Tuan's evidence for this point is anecdotal, and does not seem to be borne out by empirical studies.)

Children in Hart's study (1979) reported that rivers and lakes were the places they valued most, and yet their experience of the local river was limited, and the lakes lay far away. More local streams and ponds were also valued, both in this study and in that by Moore (1986), as places where they could play and watch wildlife. Even small enclaves of the natural world in otherwise wholly man-made urban environments were highly prized by most of Moore's subjects. The most common children's social group found by Moore in his fieldwork (in three contrasted areas of England) was what he calls the 'best friends duet': sharing the world outdoors with a friend, an activity which had especial significance to his informants. He writes of the merging of 'pathway' and 'place' in the duets' use of the natural landscape. Many children made so many digressions from their intended goal that 'it became lost in a wealth of substituted activity'.

Both individual and group play were often found to be focused upon natural features of the environment: Moore describes as a typical example one girl's use of what, to an adult eye, might appear to be wasteland. For her, it was a private, wild-flower, play area: a place for buried treasure, picnics, sharing secrets— and an infinitely richer place to develop imaginatively than the designer-play equipment available to other children in his study.

'A term is needed that could stand for the special quality of children's relations with living environments and the particular knowledge and developmental support that can be acquired through playful interaction with natural materials and phenomena' (Moore, 1986, p. 9). Huizinga (1949) had suggested that our species is 'Homo Ludens'; to echo this, Moore suggests that the term we need is 'Terra ludens'—the basis upon which the child can 'acquire creative intelligence by interacting with the inherited world'. For, if Huizinga is right in labelling us a species characterized by often very elaborate play, then the setting facilitating such play must be an important and not an incidental design consideration.

But, we can still ask, pleasurable as such interactions may be, can we accept Moore's contention that they are *important* to the child's development? To

which comes the reply: the importance of play—both physical and fantasy—
has been extensively supported in contemporary developmental psychology [see,
for example, Smith (1982) for a review] and clearly, some kinds of environments
offer much more opportunity for either or both kinds of play.

Sensory qualities of natural, as well as man-made, environments may well
be important for stimulating the individual, both physically and imaginatively.
Certainly, such qualities occur repeatedly in the early chapters of autobiographies [see, for example, collections in Lukashok and Lynch (1956) and Ward
(1977)].

Similarly, it seems intuitively likely—and equally difficult to verify
empirically—that a sense of attachment to place or places (often with a stress
upon their physical qualities) is important to full human development: phenomenologists have written about this as sense of 'placeness' (Relph, 1976) or
'topophilia' (Tuan, 1978); and the planner Lynch (1960) has called it 'rootedness'. Places where one feels at one with the world may also have added reso-
nance for the individual when he or she realizes its continued existence through
time: it is not just that, say, rocks, woods, rivers, or fields have sensory qualities
that we, as investigators of the child's environmental awareness, may discover
as we get them to record their interactions with the world (e.g. R. Kaplan,
1985); but that, if we have the skill, we may elicit the child's response to a re-
alization that many natural features have a time-scale that is much longer than
that of human beings. As Lowenthal's (1985) extensive literary documentation
points out, awareness of such an historical dimension also adds considerably to
the individual's response to the man-made environment ('This house has been
in the family since the first Duke ...'; 'the village is recorded in the Domes-
day Survey'; 'Bronze Age farmers first cleared the forest from these moors').
Empirical evidence on the point is urgently needed: although Lowenthal argues
convincingly that the past is a topic of almost universal concern, little research
explicitly focuses upon how people in general see, value, or understand it.

Probably, of all the literature—impressionistic or empirical—on the importance of the natural environment to children's development and well-being, the
most eloquent is the testimony of Wood's studies with children in Puerto Rico
and in mainland USA (e.g. Wood, 1981, 1984/5, 1986). His sympathetic eye
caught kite-time in Barranquitas ('it started without warning. One day every-
body was flying kites. It lasted like that for almost four weeks and then began
to fade') and notes its importance in bringing the community together, as well
as engendering acute awareness of the wind and the outdoors. Air and the kite
itself are endowed with near-animistic properties during the years of middle
childhood.

Wood, in his 1986 paper, gives an eloquent account of 'doing nothing', which
Smith (1957) had defined as 'a state of being', and which Wood extends to be
'an unfolding of things to do, an unfolding of things that have no names like
mooning round a lamp-post or kicking stones into the drain across the street.'

Clearly, 'doing nothing' will involve man-made as well as natural objects, as in Wood's examples: our point in referring to it here is to stress the importance of the sensory environment in children's everyday activities. For, in 'doing nothing' the child is in active exploration of physical properties; for instance 'the curious kid sending the ball up the sidewalk to watch the jigs and jags in its return, and doing it again and again, now sending it up fast, now slow, now on this edge of the sidewalk, now on that'. Wood, like Moore, stresses the fluidity of activities of childhood and how such 'doing nothings' can turn into full-blown fantasy games, contests, or being sociable together.

The neighbourhood needs of the child

Can we now advance the argument and—acknowledging that the actual physical form of neighbourhood will differ considerably from instance to instance—assess the neighbourhood needs of the developing individual? Some authors have attempted this, sensibly confining their comments to a relatively narrow age band—for clearly, the needs of the youngest age-groups will differ from those of the middle years, and both will considerably differ from those of teenagers. (The specific needs of the different age-groups with relation to particular settings, such as home, school, play spaces, etc., will be discussed in subsequent sections of this chapter.)

Bryant's (1985) account of the sources of support available to 7- and 10-year-old children provides a useful starting point, in that her study emphasizes the multiplicity of such sources, and the need for us to consider both the social and physical neighbourhoods together.

How do children perceive their involvement with and support from family, friends, community, and the neighbourhood? And how do such perceptions relate to measures of well being in childhood? Bryant divides support into: others as resources (persons and pets); intrapersonal sources of support (e.g. hobbies, fantasies); and environmental resources (e.g. informal meeting places of the kind discussed earlier, and formally designated areas).

Her findings relate to her northern Californian study setting, but may well generalize. Social–emotional functioning of the child *was* found to be predicted by the child's perception of the general availability of psychological support; and, in particular, by his or her reports of a broad-based, informal network of social and environmental supports, with, not surprisingly, the range and extent of this network increasing significantly with age.

Bryant eschewed standard questionnaire and interview techniques in favour of 'the Neighbourhood Walk', a combination of structured and open-ended questions, whose novelty is that:

> each interview begins in the child's front yard, then progresses along a path of the child's choice, and returns to the child's home by which time the child is directly asked questions about his or her immediate neighbours.   (p. 19)

Figure 11.2   Designing safer environments. One frequently cited solution involves traffic and pedestrian separation, but busy streets remain popular areas of play.

Such a procedure was 'aimed at engaging the child in activity relevant to the interview, and eliciting meaningful cues regarding children's experiences in their home neighbourhoods'. Children then completed a battery of measures designed to assess their empathy, locus of control, acceptance of self, etc.

Need for privacy and the opportunity for autonomy, as well as direct support from others, emerge from the study as major factors predictive of well-being—privacy being a topic we return to below.

Other writers considering children's environmental needs have less theoretical, more practical orientations. Thus, for example, Verwer (1980) may be taken as an example of the considerable number of city planners who have written on the matter. In reaction to the 'extreme functionalism' of 1960s' planning, Dutch planners drew up guidelines for more humane residential areas, with special reference to children's needs. These guidelines indicate that children should feel safe to explore *throughout* their neighbourhood, and not have to be restricted to playgrounds, (the Dutch system of *Woonerven*, i.e. paved local-traffic only streets, has become world-famous in theory, but too-little emulated in practice). Areas should be congenial for children—i.e. planning should have due regard for prevailing year-round weather conditions; play areas should also be accessible (consider the plight of children in conventional high rise estates); they should be varied and lively (echoes of Lynch's concept of legibility, so conspicuously lacking in many habitats); play areas should be integrated into the plan as real meeting places; and so on. Such design guidelines were derived from the empirical literature on child development; and, as Verwer shows, in proposing design solutions Dutch planners are beginning to contribute their own empirical tests of these solutions. They have also shown how it is necessary to involve the residents in the management of their environment because as follow-up research on the implementation of other designer-concepts such as defensible space shows, *imposed* design solutions to social problems have much less chance of success than those arising from designer and residents working together (Wilson, 1978). [Defensible space, a concept developed by Newman (1972) refers to that space around dwellings that residents collectively hold as private areas against outsiders; and Newman suggested a range of physical features that facilitate it.]

Adolescents' perceptions of and use of their neighbourhoods

If the younger child spends much more time *beyond* the worlds of home, school, and the officially designated children's areas than most developmental psychologists had allowed, then this 'fourth environment' must be more significant still in the perceptions and lives of adolescents. Van Vliet (1983a) has reviewed the developmental significance of this home range of adolescents. A number of earlier studies had documented that the extension of home range with age, noted already with respect to childhood, accelerates into adolescence. Other studies have shown that the spatial extent of cognitive maps increases with social class (Orleans, 1973), probably mediated by differential access to travel, and by cultural preferences (Appleyard, 1970). And Maurer and Baxter (1972) have compared the city perceptions of adolescents from different ethnic groups. Just as we noted above that the local neighbourhood is an important source of social and personal support for the child, so the work of urban anthropologists, such as Gans (1968), and urban planners, such as Banerjee and Lynch (1977), indicates that the wider range of the adolescent may be crucial in development, by providing meeting places, and settings for social learning and social experimentation. Exposure to other adolescents and to adults outside the family context may provide role models, offer social skills and techniques, and develop the individual's self image as an adult and community member.

It takes us adults a moment to realize the 'alternative scripts' being worked through by adolescents in, say, fast-food cafes, bus-shelters, and street corners: scripts that are to do with self-display, assessing the roles of others and of oneself, establishing and maintaining solidarity with one's group. Marsh, Rosser, and Harré (1978) have, for example, described those away-from-match activities of football supporter groups whose society is finely regulated, hierarchical, and rule-governed—rather than being chaotic and anarchic, as imagined by many alarmed adults. Anthony (1985) describes the alternative functions of shopping malls: whereas adults primarily visit these to make purchases, many adolescents that she interviewed regularly spent up to 5 hours at a time 'people watching', surveying teenagers of the opposite sex, cruising round with friends, playing video games, and having occasional snacks. She suggested that 'One of the major attractions ... is the lack of organized activities, structures and schedules. For teenagers, the shopping mall may well serve as an antidote to the regimentation of school and home life' (p. 312). Such an ethnographic approach, one feels, comes to a much more insightful conclusion about the role of such areas for children and adolescents than the conventional attitude surveys conducted by geographers and market researchers—e.g. Smith, Shaw, and Huckle (1979)—who omit reference to the unofficial, but clearly vital, role of these shopping areas, and who concentrate purely on economic behaviour. Indeed, planners are now beginning to emphasize the potential of shopping malls to be social spaces for the *whole* community (Brown, Sijpkes, and Maclean, 1986) and the late twentieth century is beginning to acknowledge a need that the eighteenth- and nineteenth-century urban planners well recognized and provided for in the 'Winter Gardens' of resort and spa towns. Adolescents may be able to capitalize on the very existence of shopping areas for their social needs; the more inhibited adult generations may require the presence of activities or facilities that convey a 'public' quality, permitting them to use the space for social and recreational purposes.

'Hanging around' and 'doing nothing', which we noted as major activities of younger children, are also clearly important in the adolescent years. Wood

(1984/5) asked teenagers to define a neighbourhood, and the resulting collection of definitions, were they to be 'illustrated by Maurice Sendak, could comprise the text for a book called "Kids Hanging Around Make a Neighbourhood"' (p. 34).

Much of the above research is either American or European: and the reader may justifiably feel that a more international, comparative study of the spatial needs, perceptions, and behaviours of adolescents is needed. Just such a study exists, sponsored by UNESCO, and carried out in Mexico, Poland, Australia, and Argentina (Lynch, 1977). The research focused on adolescent use of space in low-income and low-resource areas of cities in these countries; and was intended to suggest public policies for neighbourhood improvement. In each area, cohorts of teenagers were interviewed, to assess their perceptions of the city—places they spent much time in, places that were important to them, places they liked or disliked or saw as dangerous, places they were not allowed to go to or perceived that they could not use. The research teams supplemented this data with naturalistic observations of the adolescents (although one gathers that the problems of coordinating international research were such that somewhat different techniques were used in the observation phase in each country). Home ranges and time-budgetting did differ between cultures, as one would have presumed, although the picture that emerges still shows communalities: in each of the cultures adolescent needs were sufficiently similar to differentiate their spatial requirements from those of both younger children and adults. And, wherever in the world they were studied, adolescents showed natural–pastoral values to dominate in their preferences for an ideal living environment (a univeral reaction against the twentieth century city?).

There were, however, very clear differences between the study sites in the way that the adolescents perceived their socio-physical setting, bringing out differences in the actual resources available to them, in each locality the prosperity of the community, its integration and its activities. And such differences in experience shaped their expressed preferences, leading Banerjee and Lynch (1977) to argue that one might, in making broad *international* comparisons of adolescent attitudes and perceptions, overlook striking differences within the same culture and region:

> Studies consisting of a regional patchwork of samples that compare micro-locations differing from each other in specific traits of environment, age or class may offer the most efficient way of instructing decisions and of building local research capacity.   (p. 114)

School as a behaviour setting

It was whilst studying the waking day of the 7-year-old Raymond Birch, at home, at play, and, for much of his day, in school in the small American town of Midwest, that Roger and Louise Barker, the founders of what we know today as ecological psychology 'shed the blinders of individual psychology, and it became clear that how a child behaves is not only determined by what he or she wants to do but by where he or she is' (Orzek, 1987; see also Barker and Wright, 1951). They realized that places were dynamic entities into which children and adults were incorporated and that, for instance, a school is not only a building with equipment but also a set of patterns of behaviour.

The achievement of the Barkers is to remind us as scientists (we already knew it as consumers) that the important thing about a behaviour setting is that it is the *immediate* environment of the behaviour: 'It is not the school; it's the school classroom as it's doing art, for example' (Orzek, 1987, p. 234).

Later ecological psychologists have continued to focus on the school. Gump and Adelberg (1978) have shown the consequences of community size for the quality of school life. Thus, in general, the larger the community, the more pupils there are in each of its schools. As school size increases, so the number of settings increases: there are more clubs, organizations, etc., and more roles within them. *But*, the empirical evidence indicates, the number of settings increases more slowly than the population of the school. Barker and Gump (1964) gave the example of an American small town high school with 117 pupils and 107 settings—a pupil to setting ratio of 1.09, and a city high school with 2287 pupils and 499 settings: a ratio of 4.88.

Pupil use of settings—involvement in the activities of the school, and, in particular, the extra-curriculur games, clubs, and activities—has been found to be less, the greater the density of pupils: i.e. the higher the ratio. Pupils report lower satisfaction in the bigger schools, feel less competent, and experience less sense of obligation to participate in activities (Grabe, 1976, 1981; Morgan and Alwin, 1980; Willems, 1967).

Academically marginal pupils in small schools were shown by Willems to report just as great a sense of obligation and involvement as their academically stronger peers; whereas in larger schools, the marginal students were significantly less involved than their peers. Barker (1978), also found similar positive effects of 'undermanning' in involving marginal individuals in other small behaviour settings such as churches and community organizations. Grabe (1976, 1981) has demonstrated the consequences of such lack of involvement with school activities on children's self-concept: this may in turn manifest itself in absenteeism or school drop-out, apathy, or membership of a deviant subculture within the school.

Educational psychologists have made a major contribution to the debate about the quality of life in schools, but only recently have writers such as Lee, Statuto and Kedar-Voivodas (1983) begun a systematic examination of children's perceptions of school life, and about how it could be made more relevant to their needs as they perceive them. Working with 7-, 9-, and 11-year-olds in the American public education system, Lee *et al.* found that the older children in the sample perceived less congruence between ideal and actual school life (in areas such as territoriality, privacy, and decision-making such as where one sits in class, what work is done when, and how class rules are evolved). This decrease in congruence with age is the result of children's ideals running ahead of their actual experience. Yet up to the age of 11 years at least, overall liking for school increases: for the school seems to communicate support and sympathy for the child's values, while at the same time, from the child's point of view, it limits the opportunities for the expression of social competence. What is now needed is a continuation study into the secondary school years, where one might predict that reported satisfaction scores might change when actual–ideal discrepancies widen beyond the individual's tolerance level.

Some natural experiments on the relationship between school setting and program, and satisfaction among adolescents have been conducted: Trickett, McConahay, Phillips, and Ginter (1985) have, for example, examined the impact of attending an alternative high school—which followed an ideology and organization different from the mainstream state schools: 'schools without walls', 'High Schools in the community', etc. Outcome variables studied included satisfaction, perceptions of influence on school policy, and reports of liking between teachers and pupils.

Perceptions of school, and the extent to which it can fulfil the child's or adolescent's needs, depend upon physical-organizational features as well as the social-organizational: witness studies on, for example, patterns of seating in the classroom (e.g. Kashti, Arieli, and Harel, 1984), and external stressors (Cohen, Evans, Krantz, and Stokols, 1980). Classroom seating can be seen as an expression of the teacher's definition of the situation: Kashti *et al.* see it as a part of the 'negotiation of classroom reality'. Thus, in one class studied, teacher and pupils agree on a social reality, expressed in seating patterns that differentiate and separate strong and weak pupils: 'the lessons are structured so that the strong pupils gain the most benefit and the "contract" includes a rule whereby the weaker pupils allow the teacher to teach the good ones'. In contrast, another teacher, struggling to impose her will and definitions of her role, constantly moves children round the seating plan, and uses distance between herself and the class as a whole.

Ahrentzen, Jue, Skorpanich and Evans (1984) have reviewed the range of stressors experienced at school, including noise: the school may be situated close to a major road, or, as in the case of Cohen, Evans, Krantz, and Stokol's (1980) study sites, lie in the flight path of an airport. In this extreme case, Cohen *et al.* found that compared with children in control schools, located in quiet areas of the same city, the noise-afflicted children were found to have higher blood pressure, and worse general health. They were also more likely to give up on a task, had developed no better attentional strategies to counter noise, and were more distractable: all indicating that prolonged exposure to noise affects basic cognitive processes (as earlier, laboratory-based studies had already indicated).

Many other topics concerning the child's life and well-being in school have received some empirical study: including the educational system, open-plan construction, availability of resources (and their effect upon sociality and competition), parental and community involvement in the school, etc. Gump, in three reviews (1978, 1980, 1987) lists some 200 studies, covering education settings from nursery school to university. In the 1980 review, he establishes a framework for integrating these separate observations: the educational setting as physical milieu, as human community, and as a collection of action structures or programmes, can be examined for the goodness of fit between the components. Indeed, in many establishments, what Gump calls the basic welding of physical and programme aspects is so clear that he questions the current practice of referring to 'the physical environment' and 'the social environment', and suggests that this represents a deficiency in conceptualization in social science.

Homes and 'homes'

We now attempt to summarize research on children's perception of their own and ideal homes, to elucidate some general propositions about the needs of the child and discuss how far institutions such as 'children's homes' and boarding schools can fulfil these needs (for a more comprehensive review, see Parke, 1978).

A multiplicity of methodologies has been used to study the concept of home, children's use of home, their spatial needs, adult and child's segregation or shared use of the household facilities: these include questionnaires, interviews, naturalistic observations and experimental interventions. Many studies have—rightly—concentrated upon the combination of social and physical features of the home: thus Caldwell, Huder, and Kaplan (1966) devised an inventory to assess the quality of stimulation received by the child from the earliest period onwards, under the following headings: parent's emotional and verbal responsibility; parental involvement with the child; variety of daily stimulation; availability of play materials; organization of the environment; and the use of restriction and punishment. Several studies have subsequently used the Caldwell *et al.* inventory to show relationships with child's later IQ level, language performance, etc. (see Parke, 1978). Negative features of the home may include high levels of ambient noise [related by Wachs (1976) to poorer cognitive development in the infant]; separation from outdoor play areas (e.g. Coleman, 1985); lack of privacy (e.g. Parke and Sarvin, 1979) although, as we shall see below, cultural expectations of privacy vary considerably: level of crowding [extensively reviewed in Wohlwill (1985)], and housing type (e.g. Marcus, 1974).

Parke concluded his 1978 review by calling for more direct attention to be given to children's understanding of the spatial–perceptual aspects of their home environments, as well as their changing understanding of the social organization of their home settings. In the decade since, there have been several such studies, which have gone beyond the early investigation by the architect, Thornberg

(1973), who used a modelling task that involved building a home for a family of dolls, to investigate children's conception of places to live in. Many of the developmental changes noted in this study reflect the development of representational competence, rather than children's changing concepts of home.

Many phenomenological accounts of the varied meanings attributed to 'home' (e.g. Norburg-Schulz, 1980) range so far away from the bricks-and-mortar level that one has the uneasy feeling that their interpretations owe as much to the writer's philosophical stance as to any empirical support. Yet phenomenology should surely seek to understand the everyday meanings found in society, using the child or adult as local expert: this would be possible using, for example, a sorting task. From this, the range of associations—happiness, belonging, responsibility, self-expression, and so on—generated by subjects could then be subjected to multidimensional scaling, and subsequently related to target homes—own home, ideal home, etc. Control over one's own activities and over access to particular areas emerges as an important dimension in this study, as in many others (e.g. Sebba and Churchman, 1983). These researchers interviewed children and their parents about their use of space within their house; and offer a description of home as a set of territories, each of which has a particular pattern of behaviour and attitudes. Some portions of the home are clearly effectively controlled by a single individual; some are shared by a sub-unit of the family; some are public areas, controlled by all; and some are described as mother's jurisdiction areas—kitchens especially were so described—used by all, but under mother's control. Those children who shared all areas, and had no conclusive use of part of the home, felt that *no* place in the home was available to them as primary territory [to use Altman's (1975) term]; and that (at least in the country of Sebba and Churchman's study—Israel) an area was only perceived as a territory—sole or shared—when it had a clear physical definition.

Many adults have seen apartment buildings as unsatisfactory environments in which to rear children [see van Vliet (1983b) for a summary of worldwide surveys, all indicating concern for children's well-being and development]. But, although parents may perceive them as likely to damage the child's physical and mental health, and to have an effect upon their social, emotional, and cognitive development, few studies have been conducted that specifically solicit the child-inhabitants' views. Nor are there sufficient longitudinal studies documenting the actual effects of living in apartments, although clearly parents feel that there is a major cause of concern.

Some children, from choice (generally parental choice) live away from the family home in boarding schools, and others, because of circumstances, live for long periods or permanently in institutions. There are relatively few empirical studies on the effects of leaving home to live at school (although the early chapters of British autobiographies frequently dwell on its apparently dire circumstances—in spite of which the individual grows up to become sufficiently famous to publish the story of his or her life). Fisher, Frazer, and

Murray (1986) have used retrospective interviews to study homesickness at boarding school (their retrospectors had yet to become famous, being only still in their first school year at the time); and have estimated that three quarters of the children (who were aged between 11 and 14 years) had experienced homesickness. This group also reported more illness and days off school than the remaining quarter of the sample (either or both directions of casuality seem plausible here). Age and sex differences were not found, nor was actual geographical distance from home predictive of the incidence of homesickness (once under school control, there is little prospect of escape, so distance may be immaterial).

Whereas some children are thus banished from home-type living, others find themselves in the care of a local authority or charity—most of whose efforts may well be directed towards creating a substitute for a biological-family home. 'Family groups' as an organizational ideal was first enunciated some 40 years ago (see Harris and Lipman, 1984) and has subsequently influenced architectural provision for children in care. Observational studies in such 'homes' by Harris and Lipman indicate a tension between this desire to create a family atmosphere, and the concerns of the responsible adult caretakers to supervize and control the children in their care. Use of spatial privileges as sanctions and rewards was noted; so too was the concern to keep male and female teenagers apart ('Homes' they may be, but 'brothers and sisters' they definitely were not).

Perceptions of play areas

The design and provision of settings for play has burgeoned in the design professions: landscape architects, city planners, architects, environmental psychologists, and others, have all contributed to this highly commendable activity; and design guidelines abound [see a summary in Cohen, Hill, Lane, McGinty, and Moore (1979)]. We do not intend even to attempt to summarize this literature here; but, rather, wish to remind the reader that, in the naturalistic studies of children's everyday lives, reported earlier in the chapter (e.g. Hart, 1979, Moore, 1986), formally designated play areas cropped up with surprising infrequency in the observations. And, indeed, the playground movement itself has published a number of studies that might indicate a moment of doubt, because from Hole's (1966) study onward it became evident that such designated areas supported a relatively small proportion of the child's available time for play. Traditional playgrounds (most often used by the younger children) and designer-adventure-playgrounds (used more by the middle age-groups) certainly fulfilled a function for most children: but they were only one among the many sites visited by children in the course of a day's play (Hayward, Rothenberg, and Beasley, 1974).

Renewed consultation of the child development literature by playground planners then followed (e.g. Cohen, Moore, and McGinty, 1980) leading to the

Figure 11.3   Places designed for play. Specifically designed play areas attract children for only a small fraction of their total time at play: imaginative play often seeks waste ground and the spaces 'in between'.

redesign of layouts and of play equipment. Brown and Burger (1984) have now subjected the whole gamut of designs, from traditional to 'contemporary' play equipment, to empirical investigation. They have concluded that, despite this attention to developmental theory, playgrounds with more contemporary designs, contrary to the expectations of their creators, did not necessarily promote greater amounts of 'educationally desirable social, language or motor behaviours'. Not that children played identically, regardless of playground type: the greater complexity and flexibility of layout in some of the playgrounds studied clearly elicited greater 'creative' play on the part of their users. And the availability of vehicles—tricycles, cars suited to the age group, etc.—clearly had a major effect upon the patterns of play and the length of usage. So too may the active, initiatory presence of adults facilitate the more imaginative side of play [see Smith and Dutton (1979) on the role of adults in seeding children's fantasy play].

Above all else, access to other children of approximately the same age may be a crucial factor influencing the quality of everyday life. Berg and Medrich (1980) in their interviews with children about four contrasted neighbourhoods as habitats for living and playing in, found all children concerned to interact with their peers. There were, however, significant differences between neighbourhoods in the extent to which the environment facilitated this end. In one of their studied areas, a low-density, hill neighbourhood, children reported a continuous preoccupation with the problem of planning a social life, in contrast to another, child-dense flat neighbourhood, where play was spontaneous, and groups had a continued existence. Play possibilities can be seen as shaped by the landscape and by the nature of the man-made environment. Only under some circumstances would formally designated play areas be important arenas for social contact for children. (Compare the use, by older children and teenagers of public indoor spaces, such as shopping malls and atria, as places for meeting and viewing peers, as discussed above).

Needs with relation to the environment: the implications for planning

We wrote, perhaps over-cynically, in the last section, of designers' earnest searching of the literature to establish guidelines for one aspect of the child's environment—play areas—and of children's tacit response to this well-intentioned effort. Now, we too embark on a brief survey of the literature reviewed in this chapter, to see what are its implications for habitat design. And, as a preliminary, we should raise an issue that has been implicit in many of the earlier discussions: that of the child's need for privacy.

Search the conventional child development literature, and it is unlikely that you will find the concept discussed, even though privacy has become one of the central concepts in environmental psychology's treatment of living environments and their relationship to human well-being. Altman (1975) brought together a large body of empirical evidence on the use of space, personal space, human territoriality, crowding, and various indicators of well-being, using privacy as a central, linking concept. Control and choice over one's level of social interaction is seen as the mediating variable in the achievement of an individual's optimum level of privacy (Laufer and Wolfe, 1977); and most theorists have been clear in stressing three dimensions of variation in the optimal level of privacy: cultural (see reviews in Altman and Chemers, 1984), situational (Argyle, Furnham, and Graham, 1981) and individual (Altman, 1975).

Wolfe (1978) has suggested that the developmental dimension should also be given serious consideration, arguing that we need to consider not just age of the individual, but life-cycle stage. Society's demands upon the individual change markedly between stages, as do the individual's roles, activities, available behaviour settings, and his or her experiences, needs, attitudes, and feelings. Superimposed upon this are the secular changes that happen to be occurring during the individual's lifetime, in other words, the cultural and economic changes in surrounding society.

We cannot, therefore, expect to be able to specify the needs and expectations of privacy within childhood without specifying many determining variables from historical periods [many writers have described how the concept of childhood has varied over the ages (e.g. Borstelmann, 1983; Ward, 1977)]; culture and sub-culture; economic circumstance; climate and local life-style; available resources and neighbourhood configuration.

With these caveats, we can then turn to the most extensive study of the meaning of privacy for children ever conducted: Wolfe and Laufer (1975) [see also Wolfe (1978) for a summary]. Nine hundred American children, aged between 5 and 17 years, were interviewed about the concept, about the occasions and places where they felt private, and about invasions of privacy that they had experienced. Altogether 36 separate coding categories were required to classify the nuances of 'privacy'—which can be grouped into autonomy and self-protection; socio-physical separation; social separateness; and information management. Clearly, privacy had a variety of meanings for individuals in their sample—not all individuals used every category group in either their definitions or their accounts; and some categories were much more characteristic of particular ages. To give one clear example, adolescents, not surprisingly, were the only ones who mentioned sexual activity as a reason for privacy. More subtly, the importance of privacy for information-control—for holding private conversations—changed with age.

Using signs of one's need for privacy increases with age—physical withdrawal, closing of doors, etc. and there are also clear increases in social sophistication in children's answers to 'How do [other family members] let you know when they want to be private?' Older children and adolescents use a wider range of settings in which to achieve privacy—with suburban and rural children having more outdoor places available to them than did urban individuals. Size of family and whether or not children shared rooms also emerged as important factors in the Wolfe and Laufer study.

Research on the consequences of privacy for self-esteem, coping, reactions to family and wider stress, cognitive and social development and a whole range of plausibly related variables is largely lacking: yet it is clear from the existing studies on children's perceptions, and experiences, that privacy, in its various guises, is valued by all individuals. Rather ethnocentric observations that some cultures place little value on privacy (a frequently adduced conclusion by American social scientists on brief visits to Hong Kong) have been answered vigorously by two Chinese-American social scientists (Loo and Ong, 1984): they argue that the fact that individuals can develop strategies for living under crowded conditions should not be taken as evidence for a low value being placed on privacy. They go on to argue that we must not assume that the concept of privacy means the isolation of the individual; but, rather, should be taken to include pairs' or larger social groups' control over social access to themselves.

Similarly unsophisticated reasoning characterized some of the earlier attempts to link crowding and density to health and other measures of well-being, studies which often make spectacular leaps from Calhoun's (1962) rodent crowding experiments to the problems of inner city living. Even otherwise careful laboratory experiments on the effects on children's play of increased social or physical density [see Aiello (1987) for a summary] have often failed to follow the social and emotional consequences of increased density through in their accounts. Few have noted, for example, the increased conflicts over resources that Smith and Connolly (1980) were able to document in their social ecology of nursery schools.

The most recent studies of density as it affects the quality of children's life, place this variable within the broad picture of the role of the residential environment in children's development. It has been a commonplace assumption that high density necessarily has adverse effects on the child: and it was certainly with such an assumption that a group of scholars was convened by the American Society for Research in Child Development in 1980 to assess the evidence on crowding and to suggest policies to planners for ameliorating its effects. Yet, the editors of the final report of this study group, Wohlwill and van Vliet (1985) concluded that 'research to date has simply not demonstrated unequivocally any direct, adverse effects of density on children, except under atypical and extreme conditions'. Research has, instead, indicated a whole range of more specific factors, attention to which by planners, policy makers and parents, would improve the quality of children's life. Many of these are the kind of points already made in this chapter and we need not do more than list some of them, as a reprise.

We have noted the need for children, as they gain independence to explore, to have *legible* neighbourhoods and cities, both for ease of comprehension and, referring back to the duality of Lynch's (1960) original use of the concept, for aesthetic enjoyment. Attention must be paid to the distribution of resources—both formal, such as playgrounds and swimming pools, and, probably more importantly, the informal spaces which children manifestly need. Children need ready, safe access to these; and planners can draw from the existing literature on children's everyday activities, *desiderata* for neighbourhoods to suit the changing and developing needs, in the same way as has long been done for adults (see e.g. Lee, 1968). Planners can learn from studies in settings as diverse as the wildflower-strewn waste plot and the smart shopping mall, of the needs of toddlers and parents, best friend duets, and teenagers wishing to 'hang out' and 'do nothing'.

A need for manifestations of the natural world may be more than aesthetic: studies of children's most valued places, reviewed earlier, stress time and again the centrality to children's lives of even small pockets of nature. This may be part of a 'rootedness' that some have claimed to be essential for the development of the self concept. A similar point, intuitively strong but difficult to test, can be made about the child's need for a setting that offers a sense of the individual's place in history, in a continuing time-span, manifested by people and places with evident links to the past.

Rootedness, sense of self, development of the child as an individual: clearly, all of these depend on a satisfactory social as well as physical setting. In this book, we are emphasizing the physical setting because, within developmental studies, it tends to be assumed rather than discussed. But in each of the specific settings discussed above (e.g. homes and schools) it is the total socio-physical setting that has to be considered by planners. We tend to split our worlds of expertise up, but the school as a totality should be the product of plans made by politicians, architects, educationalists, teachers, counsellors, and—not to be underestimated—school caretakers, as well as developing its culture in response to pupils and parents.

To close this chapter, we consider whether the planning process can move closer to these latter groups, the users of the designed environment, by including them more fully in the design process. Planners and architects have, in the main, been much more knowledgeable about the social science research findings about their potential user groups than has been popularly admitted. Would incorporating children into the planning process itself give them further insight?

A word of warning at the outset; environmental psychology, has already documented the problems the average adult-in-the-street has describing his or her needs to a planner, tending generally to ask for 'more of the known, but rather better painted'. It has then gone on to develop a range of techniques for facilitating the two way communication of ideas between planner and public (e.g Appleyard, 1977). Consideration of how far individuals can adequately formulate and express their needs will be particularly relevant when we are eliciting the views of children. In other words, it will take more than just bringing children and planners together, or even splendid schemes like Architects-in-Schools (e.g. Sutton, 1985), to fully realize the needs and desires of children.

One will need to have architects and planners taking as much trouble in providing materials for manipulation by children as was done by Noschis (1982), who, working at the Laboratory for Architectural Experimentation at Lausanne, has a large space in which children can build full-scale models of places they might wish to inhabit. Other simulation techniques can be used—e.g. drawings, photomontage, modelscopes (which can be driven through a model environment to give the impression of a trip through an as yet unbuilt area), and, technically the most powerful of all, computer-generated visualizations. But only the last comes close to giving an impression of what it would be like to be inside a space in the same way as full scale model building does. Both construction and computer simulation can be interactive. In other words, children can specify parameter changes, such as increased room height, changes in the articulation of rooms, so that sightlines are altered, etc., and experience the implications of their decision—albeit rather more quickly in the computer-generated than in the child-constructed case!

Stea (1985) has written of environmental modelling by children as both a research technique for planners and as a participatory planning tool, which frees the individual from reliance on verbal expression (although, in one's enthusiasm, one should not forget that individuals are also likely to differ in how well they can express themselves fully in this medium (see, for example, our discussion of the concept of graphicacy in the chapter on geographical education, Chapter 12). But as Nagy and Baird (1978) have shown, it is possible to use such planning techniques to elicit children's perceptions of not just single buildings but whole potential neighbourhoods.

We would wish to conclude this review of children's and adolescents' needs for living and playing space with the reflection that, while habitats might seem to be becoming less human in scale and more threatening to children, there can never have been a time when more serious, well-meaning, and effective attention has been given by planners and psychologists to the developing individual's needs.

CHAPTER 12

Geographical and environmental education

Rise Park is an Infant School on a rather bland, large, new estate near Nottingham; and Ladywood School caters for the whole nursery and primary age range in the South Yorkshire colliery village of Grimethorpe: neither setting, one might imagine, likely to inspire teachers and pupils to make geographical and environmental concepts a form of a whole range of educational projects. Yet in these, as in thousands of schools, teachers and their advisors have been realizing what the earlier part of this book has been arguing—that we have been underestimating the young child's environmental competence—and have overturned some of education's untested orthodoxies ('Children before the age of X cannot ...', 'Map work should not be started until ...') to produce some very exciting work. This work, it is clear to the visitor, is manifestly involving for the children themselves, and also serves to develop other skills and competencies in the child: children not only learn about their local and wider environments, but also develop basic graphicacy [Balchin and Coleman (1965) to be discussed below], literacy, numeracy, and articulacy via the description and discussion of geographical information.

   To illustrate this, imagine a visit to Rise Park School (a later trip will be taken to Grimethorpe, where we conducted some projects to evaluate the effectiveness of such education on the development of environmental concepts). The head of Rise Park School had been trained as an historical geographer, and her influence in letting things geographical spread through the school's teaching was very evident, although there had never been another geographer on the staff. She, like many teachers, keeps dossiers of some of the best work of pupils; and is particularly interested in the spontaneous ideas of her children. David, who is rising 7, had, for example, modelled in Lego the *interior* of Wollaston Hall (complete with the stuffed giraffe, which is rather bizarrely displayed there), and then, when his model was threatened with ultimate demolition (others needed to repossess the building blocks), he was able to map the ground plan of his model with considerable accuracy.

The school uses visits to such places as Wollaston Hall as stimuli for class projects which may last months: the head argues that visits should occur early in the term, to be built on in class, rather than being the usual year's-end 'ice-cream outings'. Trips to Sherwood Forest, Nottingham Castle, Wollaston, and a new folk museum were evident throughout the activities going on in school. Teachers tended to be working on a theme: for example, in the forest outings, one teacher had taken colours (and especially the varieties of green) as her theme; another had chosen to work with the children on round and triangular shapes. With these as initial items to hunt for, each sub-group had a focus for the visit, and was able to incorporate variations on their theme into a huge amount of subsequent work.

Other experiences also stemmed from the visits: being immersed (enarboured?) in the forest for a whole day led to discussions about the infrastructure of inhabited areas ('... thirsty: where are the taps?') Some were worried about finding their bus to return home; one group became genuinely lost, and their teacher allowed them to suggest strategies (a little track might debouch on to a forest ride—which might then lead to roads). In its efforts to find the way back, another group became aware of a gradation in forest types, and noticing clumps of flowers that they had seen before, realized they were on the right route.

Discussion back in the class brought back, as first memories, the playground visited at the end of the outing, the picnic food, the comfortableness of the coach. But with themes extracted from these memories, and supported by further physical prompts (bark, wood-boring insects, photographs of themselves with the centuries-old Major Oak) memories came flooding back. Forest paintings, notebooks, reading and writing exercises, and library checking all followed. One teacher suggested map-making, to recreate a trip to the Castle, and was surprised at the variety of memories this evoked. There the children had seen 'Grandma's room' recreated, with its coal-fire (surprisingly none of the children on the estate had ever seen coal burning before—despite their proximity to a major mining area); and constructed a similar display for the school—with clock, dollytub for washing the clothes, old family photographs borrowed from home (and shown off proprietorially to the visitor). Past and present lived more vividly in Rise Park, thanks to an approach to environmental and geographical education that is increasingly replacing old orthodoxies, and taking cognizance of children's real competencies.

Is your chapter really necessary?

If the Rise Park approach is becoming normative in primary education, then what need is there to detain the reader with further advocacy for a position already widely accepted within education? Consult such authoratative state- ments of geographical education philosophy as the recent UNESCO sourcebook (Graves, 1982), and one will find the traditional position still firmly stated, with- out any supporting empirical evidence. [As a hasty corrective, we would recom- mend the much more informed statement on geographical work with primary and middle schools by Mills (1981).] Read the call of the British Department of the Environment's Education Board (1979) for schools to allocate much greater priority to environmental education than they do at the moment. And even when a journal aimed at teachers *does* include useful examples of 'good practice' in the area, how seldom does the article provide any evaluation of the success of the teaching programme.

It would seem from all that we have discussed in the book that children are manifestly ready for, and are indeed using, 'geographical' concepts as early as 4 or 5 years of age: they do this—albeit with some eccentricity—at all levels: they have thoughts about the world's position in the universe; about distant places; local and immediate areas; and are able to use directly gained information about the environment to perform locational and orientational tasks. Yet, in an official survey of primary education in England (HM Inspectorate, 1978), it was found that there were substantial numbers of school classes where no use was made of even the standard tools of geographical education: maps, atlases, and globes. The use and making of maps and plans was given little attention even in relation to geographical aspects of children's work.

Catling (1979) has examined some of the beliefs held within education about young children's limited potential to use maps; and noted a long tradition, concluding with Prior (1959) and Satterley (1964), indicating that true under- standing of maps was not to be expected of primary school children.

Yet there *have* been earlier educationalists who took a very different view of the child: Lucy Sprague Mitchell's title, *Young Geographers: How They Explore the World and How They Map the World* (1934), indicates something of her approach to a geography curriculum for 'children from four through thirteen':

> To clarify my own thinking ... I made myself a sort of chart in which ... I entered the interests which children showed in their environment, the geographic relations which they had discovered, the kind of symbols they used in their play and art, in space relations, human geography and natural phenomena.   (p. 17)

Against these, she plotted the ways these interests could be developed in school, with particular attention to map work! And, in fact, her chart actually goes back before 4 years of age: she notes three stages from birth to 4 years of age for each of which she suggests some exploratory trips and proto-maps. Children themselves must be geographers, experimenters:

> They must hunt for sources, and study the relationships; they must explore the environment, they must analyze the culture of which they are a part, see what part of it is geographic, what part is historic, they must think, they must play. (p. 32)

And clearly this is just what her classes did, judging from the photographs illustrating the book: here we see 5-year-olds examine street furniture, 6-year-olds talk to the captain of a tug, 5-year-olds enact their impressions of the waterfront, 6-year-olds construct three-dimensional maps of Manhattan, and so on.

One can contrast this approach with that of teachers such as Marsden (1976), who bases his recommendations to fellow professionals on what one might call unreformed Piagetian concepts: the egocentricity of the young child leads *necessarily* to a domo-centric view of the world (Lucy Sprague Mitchell should have been told!). Hewes, writing in 1982, still takes from Piaget the basic premise of a systematic building of one level upon another, and suggests that his work be taken as the basis for the pre-school geography curriculum. The research of Donaldson (1978) and others is now beginning to have its effect on teachers' expectations of the child. Thus, for example, we find the Department of Education holding regional courses throughout Britain on geographical skills from age 4 onwards—and one resulting teacher's document citing Donaldson as 'suggesting very strongly that we have underestimated the astonishingly rational powers of young children, providing that their learning is done in a human, real life, meaningful situation' (Barnsley Education Committee Advisory Service, 1979).

Simultaneously, for the other end of the school-age-range, discussions were underway to re-examine the geography curriculum for 10–14-year-olds (Cooper and Masterton, 1980) and for 14–19-year-olds (Rawling, 1980). Both adopted the philosophy that one was trying to convey and develop skills and competence, rather than transmit specific sets of knowledge. In a traditional curriculum, students would, in effect, receive lectures on topics—say, for example, the causes and consequences of hurricanes; in an enquiry oriented curriculum, students will certainly attain knowledge of hurricane systems, but will gain this by, for example, handling original data, plotting information, researching effects via newspaper clippings, and discussing the priorities of rescue workers. (Project-based work is of course now commonplace in many areas of the school curriculum.)

Graphicacy: the fourth ace in the pack?

We wrote earlier of geographical education being central to the development of basic skills, and especially that of *graphicacy*—a term promulgated by Balchin and Coleman (1965) to describe the skill of communicating via plans, graphs, pictures, maps, etc:

> Graphicacy is concerned especially—but not wholly—with spatial relationships as in maps. It also uses spatial relationships, usually in two dimensions but sometimes three, to portray other kinds of relationships, such as time scales, rates of change, derivatives, abstractions, etc.

Graphicacy, unlike literacy, numeracy. and articulacy, 'does not begin to have much foundation in British schools until the age of seven or eight', but, argue Balchin and Coleman, there seems no reason why it should not begin from the very beginning: 'after all, the graphical talent is in fact more spontaneous than writing or numbers, and there is no need to leave it unchannelled'. Indeed, if one is not to miss the full complexity and sophistication of graphicacy, then, they recommend, one should teach the simple basic expressive techniques while the child is still very receptive.

Although graphicacy is basic to the expression and investigation of ideas in mathematics, design, and other areas in the school curriculum, it has been claimed by geographers as especially their concern (e.g. Boardman, 1983).

Maps, plans, and photographs are the spatial tools most widely used in schools for geography and environmental studies; and we have already devoted a chapter to the individual's developing skills in map interpretation. What is particularly encouraging about contemporary writing about geographical education, such as that by the Schools Council Geography Committee (1979), Coleman and Catling (1982), and Boardman (1983), is that much 'good practice' in developing graphicacy is being made available to teachers, with the encouragement to try techniques earlier on in school, when, on this evidence, children take to them enthusiastically; and to develop innovative map-use and map-interpretation work throughout school. Boardman (1983), for instance, sums up many dozens of practical applications in schools with a set of 100 graphicacy skills, and the ages at which they had been found to be appropriate. He is careful to say that this age frame is only broadly approximate, and invites an empirical approach by teachers. [We note with amusement that grid references are considered on his list as not appropriate until the 7–9 years age-group, having shown that 4-year-olds can use them with apparent full understanding and satisfaction (Blades and Spencer, 1986a).] One of the most exciting technical possibilities now becoming available to teachers is that of computer-produced visualizations of spatial and other geographical data, offering, for example, the possibility of transferring data on a two dimensional map into a three dimensional 'block diagram', whence the pupil can produce perspective views of the land surface from any point specified. A similar package could be used to produce images of, for example, commuters' journey patterns, or changing trade relations.

Map work is seen by its advocates as leading on to a whole range of other topics. Thus, Coleman and Catling (1982) demonstrate that one can use, for example, published land-utilization survey-maps not only to encourage map-reading skills, but also to open up discussions of land-use patterns—their relation to geology, climate, prevailing microclimates, social customs, settlement patterns, regional differences, and political—economic decision-making. This can lead to quantative work, discussion of trends over time, development of category systems and of other presentational techniques, and can be used, as Coleman and Catling's material demonstrates, from early in primary schools to sixth forms. Another, even more direct, method of stimulating children's understanding and analysis of the world is the use of aerial photographs. Pre-school children can read information from them, with evident pleasure, as we have discussed in Chapter 8.

In primary school, where aerial photographs are increasingly used (e.g. Glendinning and Pearson, 1983), it has been noted that children's ability to interpret them bore little relationship to teacher ratings of general school ability—many 'average' and 'below average' pupils find working with the photographs easy. Even satellite photographs—e.g. the Landsat images at a scale of 1 : 1,000,000—which are further removed from the child's everyday experience, can be used very successfully in primary school (e.g. Kirman, 1981).

How do maps and photographs compare for ease of use? Dale (1971) compared the accuracy with which children recognized images on a map as against an aerial photograph of the same area; and showed that the photographs led to fewer initial mistakes in interpretation. The main moral of the study would seem to be that one should use both together, each having their strengths: maps for clarity, photographs for immediacy.

If photographs, being closer to reality than maps, offer an improved means of learning about the world, then, asked Hart (1970), might direct perception from an aircraft be even better? In fact, experiments to evaluate short-term flying geography lessons for primary school children conducted by Hart and colleagues at Clark University, have failed to provide conclusive evidence on their merits, 'although Dr David Smith has given an entire semester geography course from the air, and has shown superior results compared with "ground controls"'.

Rather less expensive ways of enhancing children's experiences of the world are offered by Catling (1978), who has advocated using the cognitive maps of a class as source material for geography teaching. We have already spent much of Part II of this book considering these artefacts as a means of investigating the child's environmental cognition: here, what is being advocated is that children examine their own and their peers' cognitive maps to learn about what aspects of their experience are sufficiently salient to be included. Class discussions can then start as the maps are compared; and communalities of inclusion, group differences (e.g. children bussed in versus those living close to the school), and individual knowledge can be brought out. The teacher can suggest an analytic framework, and develop a whole range of activities around, for instance, the journey to school. What is not included can provide the next teaching/discussion focus—the things children pass on their journeys, but do not include: from this, the teacher can raise children's awareness of places, details, and patterns in the familiar neighbourhood. Causes can be suggested for the observed patterns; an historical dimension can be introduced (supported, perhaps, by old photographs of the area, which might explain, for example, the placing of a now-relict horse trough, or the extra storey on houses that had once been the workshops of weavers). At this point, 'geographical' and 'environmental' education merge, or rather show their continuity. Indeed, it seems somewhat curious to us, as outsiders, that there exist separate advocates of what should surely be a broad-based approach to increasing the individual's awareness and appreciation of the world.

Environmental evaluation and its allies

Who carries on from where the geographers leave off? This is the question posed by Goodey (1975), a geographer who has been active in linking environmental psychology and urban studies to his own original discipline. For him, geography should be experiential, and link up with issues more often dealt with in urban or environmental studies, on planning, environmental decision-making, participation, appreciation of the aesthetic and social qualities of townscapes and landscapes, evaluation of housing and other buildings from both a functional and aesthetic point of view, and social problems and the environment.

Most of these topics, under various banners—environmental education, urban studies, urban history, art in the environment—have produced a large literature in the period since Goodey was writing. There is now available a wealth of material for teachers' use, some accounts of good practice, and some few evaluations of how far this (intuitively worthwhile) movement has actually developed children's perceptions of and understanding of their neighbourhood and how it fits into the broader context. We will try to give a flavour of this initiative.

Burney (1975) reported a series of projects designed 'to develop children's environmental awareness and understanding, encouraging the acquisition of environmental skills and an interest in their environment which might lead to an active participation in the problems and decisions affecting it'. Much of the work at that date had been conducted in secondary schools, but the possibilities of work in primary schools were evident.

A similar action-orientation is evident in the 1979 (British) Department of the Environment report 'Environmental Education in Urban Areas', significantly subtitled 'the need to help people understand and improve their towns'. Environmental education, it concludes, 'should be centrally concerned with aiding people to participate more effectively in shaping their own environment'. Such education should be given a much higher priority in schools—especially at secondary level—than it was then receiving; and would benefit from input from the professional planning bodies.

> Finally, and more difficult to pin down, there was the development of a personal set of values, of moral attitudes to the environment. This was not something that should be imposed, but should arise naturally from a study of the environment. (p. 3.)

One obstacle the report identified was the lack of teaching material, especially at primary level. Even as they wrote, the situation was being rapidly rectified: the Town and Country Planning Association produced a lively monthly for teachers, the *Bulletin of Environmental Education*; City University, New York, coordinated projects, programs, and organizations working in the area in the *Childhood City Newsletter* (later renamed the *Childhood Environment Quarterly*); and local and national groups sprang up, generating similar material. One extremely effective network, under the heading of 'Art and the Built Environment', consisted of 36 local working parties of teachers, architects and planners, and children from 400 schools round Britain (250 architects round the country took part—roughly 1% of the profession). The avowed aim of the project was to challenge traditional art courses in schools, and to demonstrate that they can include descriptive-cum-critical studies of urban and rural environments; in practice, the materials offered in the resultant publication (Adams and Ward, 1982) would be useful well beyond art education.

Many other books now available have also arisen from the compilation of teacher's innovatory practices: Carson (1978), for example, has a collection that includes Goodey (1978) on trails through the city, and Collis (1978), on adapting environmental studies techniques for use in the first years of primary school.

The reader will probably be familiar with the idea of town trails, designed for visitors to an historic city. Goodey shows how these can be used in more ordinary areas—and then goes on to describe tree trails, road-safety trails, retail trails, and architectural trails. He is critical of much of the existing material: 'Too few trails seem to have taken advantage of published experience in the area ... many school-designed trails are scarcely distinguishable from amenity society guides to "twenty truly wonderful things in our town"'. Furthermore, he—and we—would argue that it is particularly important that projects are reported in the journals, and that teachers' experiments are evaluated in new contexts.

Published reports on the effects of environmental education on children's concepts, knowledge, and—taking up an earlier point—values, are few and far between, despite all the excellent teaching materials and courses now available.

Vhat measure of input can be offered for both classroom and real-world experiences? How much experience is necessary, how should it relate to formal eaching, how should teachers determine suitable ages and stages for introducing particular topics, concepts, and discussions? Many writers stress the importance of engaging the child's interest by centring the work round the local and personal experience: is this in fact really necessary, or could teaching materials, already professionally prepared for other areas, be just as stimulating to start discussion? Recall that, for instance, Glendinning and Pearson (1983), in their work with aerial photographs with primary school children, found that few of them could make the link between such photographs of their home area and their ground-level experiences. And, on the other hand, recall Spencer and Easterbrook's (1985) finding of a dramatic difference in the child's involvement according to whether we were discussing geography with them as done in school, or the same locational concepts as experienced as the 'streetwise' of Sheffield.

So, a paradox: never before has there been such enthusiasm for including environmental education in the curriculum; and yet there is a dearth of educational research evaluating its impact. Do children in such programs gain a greater environmental awareness, greater graphicacy, and better locational skills than comparable children not in such programs? (The reader may note that, in our questions, we are beginning to blur any distinctions between environmental and geographical education).

We argue that such evaluation is not only important but also entirely practicable for teachers and educational advisors to conduct themselves (who needs a psychologist?); and have published a series of illustrative evaluations (Spencer, Mitchell, and Wisdom, 1984) to make the point. These were carried out at the Ladywood School. This is a nursery and primary school (i.e. covering 3–11 years of age) in the coal-mining village of Grimethorpe: a school and community suited to our purpose for two equal and opposite reasons. First, teachers in the school had taken part in local education authority courses on the 'new' primary geography teaching, but had not embarked on any evaluation; second, the school's catchment area was almost entirely lacking in the kind of middle class parents whose influence might lay our study open to the charge that the children participating in them were unusually advantaged.

Our five projects were as follows: 3- and 4-year-olds learned about spatial relationships within a house; the same age-group investigated the three-dimensional structure of a house; and, in a third project, worked on a cognitive map of their route through the village to school. Project four was a more complex mapping exercise of the same daily journeys, this time with 7- and 8-year-olds; and project five was the classic 'mapping the classroom' exercise included—but seldom evaluated—in every textbook on beginning mapping. All these projects were chosen to be typical of the kind of exercise nursery and primary school teachers have been encouraged to undertake; and in each, the

simple, conventional procedures of an empirical study were outlined: befor
and after measures, control group, the development of category systems fc
evaluating children's concepts and achievements, etc.

Thus, for example, in the first project, it was possible to use as experimenta
and controls the morning and afternoon classes of the same nursery schoo
Both received pre- and post-tests, devised by us as formulations of the concep
the teachers hoped the children would acquire during the project: spatial term:
the names for places and furniture within the house, their usual relationship:
etc.

In the pre-test, the children were shown a doll's house, with all the four room
set out, and were asked to name all the items of furniture inside. The experi
menter's checklist also included a set of simple spatial terms—up, down, unde
behind, etc., which, if the child did not happen to include them spontaneously i
the account of the doll's house, the experimenter would find occasion to use i
the questions she asked. She then found a pretext for removing all the furnitur
from the house, and asked the child to put it back in the appropriate room. T
ensure that children were not just relying on a memory image of the previou
positions, the designation of the rooms was changed; e.g. the dolls had decide
to use a different room as their bathroom.

The teaching/discussion experience for the experimental group took plac
3 months after the pre-test. The children were told a story about a man wh
was moving house. Then, in small groups, the children were presented with th
empty doll's house, and 'Mr Smith', who was moving in, asked the childre
which of his furniture should go into each room. As each piece of furnitur
came out of the store box, the teachers and children discussed its placing an
function; and discussed why certain locations would be inappropriate. Finall
pairs of children were given 15 minutes to play with two dolls who were th
new inhabitants of the completed house. The post-test, for both groups, too
place two weeks after the teaching experience; and covered the same items a
the pre-test.

Analysis of results indicated the pre-test comparability of control and exper
imental groups; and showed very little change in the control group's knowledg
and concepts over the term between pre- and post-tests. In contrast, the experi
mental group's post-test performance was very significantly improved compare
with its pre-test. All trained children thus benefited considerably from the teach
ing program, with the slightly older children showing better performance tha
the younger at both pre- and post-test stages.

Qualitative differences were also noted as a result of training: whereas, a
pre-test, many children had simply arranged furniture in groups by commo
form (e.g. all chairs in a line, all kitchen tables and worktops together), th
trained groups had graduated to using the elements to represent a more usua
room layout. In this, one could argue, the brief training period had accelerate
the normal process: Downs and Stea (1977) have noted such a graduation fror

grouping to better spatial structure occurring unprompted between 3 and 6 years old. Some of the trained children also began to take a less egocentric view: whereas at pre-test stage no child had placed furniture in the doll's house with the back of the furniture at the (invisible) front of the rooms, by post-test stage many of the older trained children were doing this. Such planning of furniture in the direct line of vision would seem to be a major move forward in spatial awareness. Other such signs include tighter groupings of objects—e.g. kitchen chairs under the table, and stool under the dressing table.

Many books and chapters on geographical and environmental education conclude with a call for evaluation [e.g. Carson (1978) calls for the publication of checklists]: we hope to have demonstrated how possible as well as how desirable such evaluations can be. [We refer the reader to the original article for details of the other four projects in our study (Spencer, Mitchell, and Wisdom, 1984).] The recent generation of practical guides are now indeed tending to include evaluation packages.

We have in this chapter concentrated upon these two areas—geographical and environmental education. Many of the same points could be made about architectural education in schools (e.g. Catlin, 1981; Sutton, 1985) and about craft-design-technology (e.g. Williams and Jinks, 1985).

For several years, as we have indicated, there has been some elementary architectural teaching in both primary and secondary schools. Much of it has been based upon the teaching of observation and drawing. But Catlin has argued that this is misguided, because 'What children notice about a building is not that which makes it a good building'. Secondly, reliance on drawing may, because of children's expressive limitations, lead to frustration. In place of this approach, Catlin suggests that we start by stimulating 'a child's inborn interest in touching and feeling, looking and seeing, hearing, listening, speaking, smelling and building—for it is in true appreciation of these that the adult becomes aware of the most successful building' (pp. 346–349). (How easy to make the assertion, if one doesn't have to back it up with evidence.)

Craft-design-technology is developing in British secondary schools from the traditional handicraft subjects—and is relevant for our story because it is now identifying its role more explicitly in teaching spatial and graphic skills, identifying problems, proposing its solutions, realizing the design, and testing the project. Williams and Jinks (1986) have shown that the same principles can be used to great effect in the primary school curriculum. Indeed, in a sense, it has always been there—for a great proportion of the primary school day has been spent in 'making' and 'doing'; but the invitation is now to use this activity in more explicitly problem-solving ways, to link in with basic science education, and, we would argue, to develop children's analytic approach to the properties of the world about themselves.

In this chapter we have argued that graphicacy should be an explicit focus of the school's curriculum, and take its rightful place alongside the other basic expressive skills. Similarly, we feel that environmental awareness is as important to a child as is being made aware of the historical, literary, and scientific heritage. Furthermore, there is now available much good teaching material in geographical and environmental areas, as well as in art and design.

Conclusion

The development of spatial knowledge, from the neonate's awareness of self and the objects immediately around, through the young child's explorations of the home and its neighbourhood, to the adolescent's awareness of the parts of the world known from the media: this has been our principal theme. We started by reviewing the theoretical literature on environmental cognition, and we have just concluded the book by looking at three areas of applications: the importance of cognitive development studies for children with special needs; then for the environmental needs of children in general; and, finally, for geographical and environmental education.

Half a dozen different disciplines, including psychology, have contributed to our survey; with studies drawn from almost as many sub-disciplines of psychology (from artificial intelligence to social psychology). Not surprisingly, given this diversity of theoretical and methodological approaches, we have not been able to present the field as a completely coherent one; but, encouragingly, *despite* the diversity, a kind of consensus is emerging. Time and again, we have made the point that the environmental competence of the child is being reassessed by researchers from all traditions, with a general agreement that this competence has been underestimated in most earlier discussions.

Yet, as we suggested at the outset, in proclaiming the child's competence there is a danger in overstating it; clearly, there is much cognitive developement during infancy, childhood, and beyond, and we therefore devoted a considerable proportion of the book to an account of these developmental processes. There is now an appreciable literature to draw upon.

What of the future? Once the basic environmental cognition and developmental literatures have been more closely cross-referenced than they tend to be at the moment, we shall have a fairly systematic account of the *processes* involved and their development. This can be extended to consider its implications for, for example, the enrichment of experience and skills of the blind child; and for general environmental education; and to offer suggestions for the planner, designer and architect.

It strikes us as ironic that it is writers from these latter disciplines [for example, the planner, Moore (1986)] who, in doing their own field work on children's needs, are pointing to the lack of feeling and understanding about the child that has characterized much of the work published by developmental psychologists. Insights into what is important to the child, into what he or she values about places, into the fantasies, opportunities, and excitement afforded by the world around us: these are surely what we most need to add to psychology's account of the child's development of spatial awareness. Of course, we need to discuss object location, and route-following, and distance estimation, and geographical stereotypes: but cognition is, in real life, seldom divorced from affect. 'Cognitive maps' aren't just analogues of a spatial layout (or propositions about how to navigate from place one to place two): they also include the locations of favourite places (the toddler's den, the child's secret garden, the adolescent's parade ground); and places that are functional, or boring, or threatening. Lynch (1960) was right, in talking of the image of the city, to link the knowledge-function of such images to their aesthetic impact. (He too was a planner, not a psychologist.)

How can one convince one's hard-nosed colleagues that these are not just the epiphenomena of environmental cognition? Consider the added predictive power that knowing the individual's subjective meanings would add: people don't use space because they possess a good map of its layout—that is merely the facilitator (Herman, Miller and Shirak, 1987). And, if we accept the evidence of those empirical researchers who have argued the importance of aspects of the physical environment for the individual's well-being [Rachel Kaplan (1973, 1983) on the natural environment, for example, and van Vliet (1983b) on the man-made], then perhaps one can convince main-stream developmental psychologists to include physical as well as social milieu *routinely* in their accounts of factors affecting healthy development of the individual. This, then, is our first hope for future research: that environmental cognition should encompass affect, and that an account of the child's knowledge about, *and* feelings for, the environment should be a usual part of any developmental description.

A second direction in which we would hope to see research grow concerns the factors affecting the development of spatial and environmental skills. We have a richly researched literature on spatial skills from the traditional psychometric approach [extensive critical reviews of which have been given by McGee (1979) and Eliot (1987)]. This now needs both a developmental and educational dimension, so that to complement the psychometrist's analysis of the sub-factors of spatial skill, we have research to indicate how individual differences arise, and how a range of learning experiences can facilitate skill development. In the chapter on geographical education, we endorsed Balchin and Coleman's (1965) call for more emphasis to be placed on education for what they called 'graphicacy'; and discussed a range of techniques that might contribute to this and to general environmental awareness. At the level of basic spatial skill development, the wide availability and popularity of computer games represents a possible major and pervasive, but unwitting, training situation in aspects of spatial skills. As we write, some of the first carefully evaluative studies are being published (e.g. McClurg and Chaillé, 1987), to supplement the initial proselytizing claims of Papet (1980) and others for the value of computer-graphics experience for young children's cognitive development. Increasing children's competence in handling spatial relations via interactive computer systems may not be quite as fundamental to general development as at first claimed; but we would remind the reader of the research discussed earlier showing how far spatial understanding was tied in to a wide range of other competencies: early number skills being one example.

Lest the sceptical reader think at this point that most children's spatial skills and coordination will only be marginally improved by alien-zapping arcade games, we would point out that the level of complexity of such games has increased to the point of putting much more demand upon the child. Furthermore, there are even more ambitious programs now available that can simulate travel and exploration: we have used, for example, an orienteering program called 'The Forest', produced by the splendidly-named Cunning Running software house (Relf and Barrington Brown, 1986) which places very considerable demands upon the individual.

Activities that develop spatial skills and greater environmental awareness, and that demand formal evaluation from psychologists, range all the way from such computer games through actual orienteering in the real world [we have already referred in Chapter 8 to the pioneering work of Ottosson (1987) evaluating the cognitive demands of orienteering]; from environmentally aware teaching in schools, and a wider use of children-as-planners projects in local community developments, to the use of targeted spatial experience regimes for children with particular deficits. We think, as examples of this, of training that might be devised for dyslexic children—whose reading problems may well be associated with a whole spectrum of other temporal and spatial disorganizations (Brown, 1984). And one could also include 'Conductive Education' under this heading, as this at present experimental form of mass sensory stimulation and experience for severely handicapped children, originating in Hungary, aims to provide these individuals with greater control over their movements through space.

Indeed, this last could almost stand as a symbol for what we would advocate in general: making children active and positive explorers of the world around them, rather than passive and dependent travellers through the world. We need to evaluate what we, as parents, educators, and professionals are doing at present, so that our children will not be able to lament, with Garrison Keillor's fictional Son of Lake Wobegon:

> You have taught me the fear of becoming lost, which has killed the pleasure of curiosity and discovery. In strange cities, I memorize streets and always know exactly where I am. Amid scenes of great splendour, I review the route back to the hotel.   (Keillor, 1986, p. 254)

References and further reading

Acredolo, L. P. (1976). Frames of reference used by children for orientation in unfamiliar spaces. In G. Moore and R. Golledge (eds), *Environmental Knowing*. Dowden, Hutchinson & Ross, Stroudsburg, Pa.

Acredolo, L. P. (1978). Frames of reference used by children for orientation, *Developmental Psychology*, **14**, 224–234.

Acredolo, L. P. (1979). Laboratory versus home: the effect of the 9-month-old infant's choice of spatial reference system, *Developmental Psychology*, **15**, 666–667.

Acredolo, L. P. (1981). Small- and large-scale spatial concepts in infancy and childhood. In L. S. Liben, A. H. Patterson, and N. Newcombe (eds), *Spatial Representation and Behavior Across the Life Span*. Academic Press, New York.

Acredolo, L. P. (1982). The familiarity factor in spatial research. In R. Cohen (ed.), *New Directions for Child Development: Children's Conceptions of Spatial Relationships*, No. 15. Jossey-Bass, San Francisco.

Acredolo, L. P. (1983). Spatial orientation in infancy: role of body, landmarks and locomotion. Paper presented at the 19th Inter-American Congress of Psychology, Quito, Ecuador.

Acredolo, L. P., Adams, A., and Goodwyn, S. W. (1984). The role of self-produced movement and visual tracking in infant spatial orientation, *Journal of Experimental Child Psychology*, **38**, 312–327.

Acredolo, L. P., and Boulter, L. T. (1984). Effects of hierarchical organisation on children's judgements of distance and direction, *Journal of Experimental Child Psychology*, **37**, 409–425.

Acredolo, L. P., and Evans, D. (1980). Development changes in the effects of landmarks on infant spatial behavior, *Developmental Psychology*, **16**, 312–318.

Acredolo, L. P., Pick, H. L. and Olsen, M. G. (1975). Environmental differentiation and familiarity as determinants of children's memory for spatial location, *Developmental Psychology*, **11**, 495–501.

Acredolo, L. P., and Schmid, J. (1981). The understanding of relative speeds, distances and durations of movement, *Developmental Psychology*, **17**, 490–493.

Adams, E., and Ward, C. (1982). *Art and the Built Environment*. Longman, for the Schools Council, London.

Ahrentzen, S., Jue, G., Skorpanich, M. A., and Evans, G. W. (1984). School environments and stress. In G. W. Evans (ed.), *Environmental Stress*. Cambridge University Press, New York.

Aiello, J. R. (1987). Human spatial behavior. In D. Stokols and I. Altman (eds), *Handbook of Environmental Psychology*. John Wiley, New York.

Ainsworth, M., and Bell, S. (1974). Mother–infant interaction and the development of competence. In K. Connolly and J. Bruner (eds), *The Growth of Competence*. Academic Press, New York.

Ajzen, I., and Fishbein, M. (1980). *Understanding Attitudes and Predicting Social Behavior*. Prentice Hall, Englewood Cliffs, NJ.

Allen, G. L. (1981). A developmental perspective on the effects of 'subdividing' macrospatial experience, *Journal of Experimental Psychology, Human Learning and Memory*, 7, 120–132.

Allen, G. L. (1982). The organization of route knowledge. In R. Cohen (ed.), *New Directions for Child Development: Children's Conceptions of Spatial Relationships*, No. 15. Jossey-Bass, San Francisco.

Allen, G. L., Kirasic, K. C., Siegal, A. W., and Herman, J. F. (1979). Developmental issues in cognitive mapping: the selection and utilization of environmental landmarks, *Child Development*, **50**, 1070–1072.

Altman, I. (1975). *The Environment and Social Behavior*. Brooks-Cole, Monterey, Ca.

Altman, I., and Chemers, M. (1984). *Culture and Environment*. Cambridge University Press, Cambridge.

Altman, I., and Gauvain, M. (1981). A cross-cultural and dialectic analysis of homes. In L. S. Liben, A. H. Patterson, and N. Newcombe (eds), *Spatial Representation and Behavior Across the Life-span*. Academic Press, New York.

Ammons, C. H., Worchel, P., and Dallenbach, K. (1953). Facial vision: the perception of obstacles out of doors by blindfolded and blindfolded deafened subjects, *American Journal of Psychology*, **40**, 519–553.

Anastasi, A. (1958). *Differential Psychology*. Macmillan, New York.

Andrews, H. F. (1973). Home range and urban knowledge of school-age children, *Environment and Behavior*, **5**, 73–84.

Anooshian, L. J., Hartman, S. R., and Scharf, J. S. (1982). Determinants of young children's search strategies in a large-scale environment, *Developmental Psychology*, **18**, 608–616.

Anooshian, L. J., and Kromer, M. K. (1986). Children's spatial knowledge of their school campus, *Developmental Psychology*, **22**, 854–860.

Anooshian, L. J., and Nelson, S. K.(1985). Children's knowledge of directional relationships within their neighbourhood, Unpublished manuscript, cited in L. Anooshian and A. W. Siegal, (1985).

Anooshian, L. J., Pascal, V. U., and McCreath, H. (1984). Problem mapping before problem solving: young children's cognitive maps and search strategies in large-scale environments, *Child Development*, **55**, 1820–1834.

Anooshian, L. J., and Siegal, A. W. (1985). Children's knowledge of directional relationships within their neighbourhood, Unpublished manuscript, cited in L. Anooshian and A. W. Siegal, (1985).

Anooshian, L. J., and Wilson, K. L. (1977). Distance distortions in memory for spatial locations, *Child Development*, **48**, 1704–1707.

Anooshian, L. J., and Young, D. (1981). Developmental changes in cognitive maps of a familiar neighbourhood, *Child Development*, **52**, 341–348.

Antaki, C., Morris, P. E., and Flude, B. M. (1986). The effectiveness of the 'Tufty Club' in road safety education, *British Journal of Educational Psychology*, **56**, 363–365.

Antell, S. E. G., and Caron, A. J. (1985). Neonatal perception of spatial relationships, *Infant Behavior and Development*, **8**, 15–23.

Antell, S., and Keating, D. (1983). Perception of numerical invariance in neonates, *Child Development*, **54**, 695–702.

Anthony, K. H. (1985). The shopping mall: a teenage hangout, *Adolescence*, **20**, 307–312.

Appleyard, D. (1969). Why buildings are known: a predictive tool for architects and planners, *Environment and Behavior*, **1**, 131–156.

Appleyard, D. (1970). Styles and methods of structuring a city, *Environment and Behavior*, **2**, 100–118.

Appleyard, D. (1977). Understanding professional media. In I. Altman and J. Wohlwill (eds), *Human Behavior and Environment*, Vol. 2. Plenum, New York.

Argyle, M. (1973). *Social Interaction*. Methuen, London.

Argyle, M., Furnham, A., and Graham, J. A. (1981). *Social Situations*. Cambridge University Press, Cambridge.

Armstrong, A. (1979). *Planning and Environmental Education*. Centre for Environmental Studies, London.

Atkins, C. L. (1981). Introducing basic map and globe concepts to young children, *Journal of Geography*, **80**, 228–233.

Attneave, F., and Benson, B. (1969). Spatial coding of tactual stimulation, *Journal of Experimental Psychology*, **81**, 216–222.

Aust, A. M. Di F (1980). Kinesiology. In R. L. Welsh and B. B. Blasch (eds), *Foundations of Orientation and Mobility*. American Foundation for the Blind, New York.

Axia, G., and Nicolini, C. (1986). Children's representation of Venice. Paper presented at the Second European Congress of Developmental Psychology, Rome.

Baird, J. C. (1979). Studies of the cognitive representation of spatial relations, *Journal of Experimental Psychology*, **108**, 90–91.

Baker, R. (1981). *Human Navigation and the Sixth Sense*, Hodder & Stoughton, London.

Baker, R. (1987). Human navigation and magnetoreception, *Animal Behaviour*, **35**, 691–704.

Balchin, W. G. V., and Coleman, A. M. (1965). Graphicacy should be the fourth ace in the pack, *Times Educational Supplement*, 5th November.

Balla, D. A., and Klein, M. S. (1981). Labels for and taxonomies of environments for retarded persons. In H. C. Haywood and J. R. Newbrough (eds), *Living Environments for Developmentally Retarded Persons*, University Park Press, Baltimore.

Banerjee, T., and Lynch, K. (1977). On people and places: a comparative study of the spatial environments of adolescence, *Town Planning Review*, **48**, 105–115.

Barbichon, G. (1975). Espace villageois, espace urbain dans l'imagerie enfantine, *Revue Francaise de Sociologie*, **16**, 539–560.

Barker, R. G. (1978). *Habitats, Environments and Human Behavior*. Jossey-Bass, San Francisco.

Barker, R. G., and Wright, H. F. (1955). *Midwest and its Children*, Harper & Row, New York.

Barker, R. G., and Gump, P. V. (1964). *Big School, Small School*, Stanford University Press, Stanford, Ca.

Barker, R. G., and Wright, H. F. (1951). *One Boy's Day*. Harper, New York.

Barnsley Education Committee Advisory Service (1979). *Geography in the Education of Young Children* (2 vols). Barnsley Education Committee, Barnsley, South Yorkshire.

Bartlett, F. C. (1932). *Remembering*. Cambridge University Press, Cambridge.

Bartram, D. J. (1980). Comprehending spatial information: the relative efficiency of different methods of presenting information about bus routes, *Journal of Applied Psychology*, **65**, 103–110.

Battachi, M. W., Franza, A., and Pani, R. (1981). Memory processing of spatial order as transmitted by auditory information in the absence of visual cues, *Memory and Cognition*, **9**, 301–307.

Bauman, M. K., and Yoder, N. M. (1966). *Adjustment to Blindness Reviewed*, Charlces C. Thomas, Springfield, Il.

Bayley, M. (1973). *Mental Handicap and Community Care*. Routledge & Kegan Paul, London.

Beagles-Roos, J., and Greenfield, P. M. (1979). Development of structure and strategy in two-dimensional pictures, *Developmental Psychology*, **15**, 483–494.

Beck, R. J., and Wood, D. (1976a). Cognitive transformation of information from urban geographic fields to mental maps, *Environment and Behavior*, 8, 199–234.

Beck, R. J., and Wood, D. (1976b). Comparative developmental analysis of individual and aggregated cognitive maps of London. In G. T. Moore and R. G. Golledge (eds), *Environmental Knowing*. Dowden, Hutchinson & Ross, Stroudsburg, PA.

Bell, W., and Robinson, R. V. (1980). Cognitive maps of class and racial inequalities in England and the United States, *American Journal of Sociology*, **86**, 320–349.

Berg, J., and Worchel, P. (1956). Sensory contributions to human maze learning—a comparison of matched blind, deaf and normals, *Journal of Genetic Psychology*, **54**, 81–93.

Berg, M., and Medrich, E. A. (1980). Children in four neighbourhoods: the physical environment and its effect on play and play patterns, *Environment and Behavior*, **12**, 320–348.

Berland, J. C. (1982). *No Five Fingers are Alike: Cognitive Amplifiers in Social Context*. Harvard University Press, Cambridge, MA.

Berry, J. W. (1966). Temne and Eskimo perceptual skills, *International Journal of Psychology*, 1, 207–229.

Berry, J. W. (1971). Ecological and cultural factors in spatial perceptual development, *Canadian Journal of Behavioural Science*, **3**, 324–336.

Berthenthal, B. I., Campos, J. J., and Barret, K. C. (1984). Self-produced locomotion: an organizer of emotional, cognitive and social development in infancy. In R. Emde and R. Harmon (eds), *Continuities and Discontinuities in Development*. Plenum Press, New York.

Biel, A. (1979). Accuracy and stability in children's representation of the large-scale environment, *Goteborg Psychological Reports*, **9**, No. 2.

Biel, A. (1982). Children's spatial representation of their neighborhood: a step towards a general spatial competence, *Journal of Environmental Psychology*, **2**, 193–200.

Biel, A., and Torell, G. (1977). The mapped environment: cognitive aspects of children's drawings, *Goteborg Psychological Reports*, **7**, No. 7.

Biel, A., and Torell, G. (1982). Experience as a determinant of children's neighbourhood knowledge, *Goteborg Psychological Reports*, **12**, No. 9.

Birns, S. L. (1986). Age at onset of blindness and development of space concepts: from topological to projective space, *Journal of Visual Impairment and Blindness*, **80**, 577–582.

Bishop, A. J. (1980). Spatial abilities and mathematics education: a review, *Educational Studies in Mathematics*, **11**, 257–269.

Blades, M., and Spencer, C. (1986a). Map use in the environment and educating children to use maps, *Environmental Education and Information*, **5**, 187–204.

Blades, M., and Spencer, C. (1986b). The implications of psychological theory and methodology for cognitive cartography, *Cartographica*, **23**, 1–13.

Blades, M., and Spencer, C. (1987a). The use of maps by 4–6 year old children in a large-scale maze, *British Journal of Developmental Psychology*, **5**, 19–24.

Blades, M., and Spencer, C. (1987b). Young children's recognition of environmental features from aerial photographs and maps, *Environmental Education and Information*, **6**, 189–198.

Blades, M., and Spencer, C. (1987c). Young children's strategies when using maps with landmarks, *Journal of Environmental Psychology*, **7**, 201–218.

Blades, M., and Spencer, C. (1988). How do young children find their way through familiar and unfamiliar environments? *Environmental Education and Information*, **7**, 1–14.

Blaut, J. M., McCleary, G. S., and Blaut, A. S. (1970). Environmental mapping in young children, *Environment and Behavior*, **2**, 335–349.

Blaut, J. M., and Stea, D. (1971). Studies of geographic learning, *Annals of the Association of American Geographers*, **61**, 387–393.

Bluestein, N., and Acredolo, L. (1979). Developmental changes in map reading skills, *Child Development*, **50**, 691–697.

Board, C. (1978). Map reading tasks appropriate in experimental studies in cartographic communication. *The Canadian Cartographer*, **15**, 1–12.

Boardman, D. (1983). *Graphicacy and Geography Teaching*. Croom Helm, London.

Boden, M. (1987). *Artificial Intelligence and Natural Man: 2nd edn.*, MIT Press, London.

Böök, A., and Gärling, T. (1980a). Processing of information about location during locomotion: effects of a concurrent task and locomotion patterns, *Scandinavian Journal of Psychology*, **21**, 185–192.

Böök, A., and Gärling, T. (1980b). Processing of information about locomotion during locomotion: effects of amount of visual information about the locomotor pattern, *Perceptual and Motor Skills*, **51**, 231–238.

Böök, A., and Gärling, T. (1981a). Maintenance of orientation during locomotion, *Journal of Experimental Psychology: Human Perception and Performance*, **7**, 995–1006.

Böök, A., and Gärling, T. (1981b). Maintenance of environmental orientation during body rotation, *Perceptual and Motor Skills*, **52**, 583–589.

Borstelmann, L. J. (1983). Children before psychology: ideas about children from antiquity to the late 1800s. In P. H. Mussen (ed.) *Handbook of Child Psychology*, Vol. I. Wiley, New York.

Bottrill, J. H. (1968). Locomotor learning by blind and sighted, *Perception and Motor Skills*, **26**, 282.

Bower, T. G. R. (1975). Infant perception of the third dimension and object concept development. In L. B. Cohen and P. Salapatek (eds), *Infant Perception: From Sensation to Cognition*. Academic Press, New York.

Bower, T. G. R. (1977). Blind babies see with their ears. *New Scientist*, **73**, 255–257.

Braine, L. G. (1976). A new slant on orientation perception. Invited address, American Psychological Association Meeting, Washington, DC. Cited in H. L. Pick, A. Yonas and J. Rieser (1979) Spatial reference systems in perceptual development. In M. H. Bonstein and W. Kesson (eds), *Psychological Development from Infancy: Image to Intention*. Lawrence Erlbaum, Hillsdale, NJ.

Brantingham, P. J., and Brantingham, P. L. (eds) (1981). *Environmental Criminology*. Sage, London.

Bremner, J. G. (1978a). Spatial errors made by infants: inadequate spatial cues or evidence of egocentrism? *British Journal of Psychology*, **69**, 77–84.

Bremner, J. G. (1978b). Egocentric versus allocentric spatial coding in nine-month-old infants: factors influencing the choice of code, *Developmental Psychology*, **14**, 346–355.

Bremner, J. G., and Bryant, P. E. (1985). Active movement and development of spatial abilities in infancy. In H. M. Wellman (ed.), *Children's Searching: The Development of Search Skill and Spatial Representation*. Lawrence Erlbaum, Hillsdale, NJ.

Brewer, W. F., and Treyens, J. L. (1981). Role of schemata in memory for places, *Cognitive Psychology*, **13**, 207–230.

Brinkman, E. H. (1966). Programmed instruction as a technique for improving spatial visualization, *Journal of Applied Psychology*, **50**, 179–184.

Britton, R. A. (1979). The image of the Third World in tourism marketing, *Annals of Tourism Research*, **6**, 318–329.

Brody, H. (1981). *Maps and Dreams*. Norman & Hobhouse, London.

Brody, H. (1987). *Arctic Living: Hunters of the Canadian North*. Faber & Faber, London.

Bronfenbrenner, U. (1979). *The Ecology of Human Development*, Harvard University Press, Cambridge, Massachusetts.

Bronzaft, A. L., Dobrow, S. B., and O'Hanlon, T. J. (1976). Spatial orientation in a subway system, *Environment and Behaviour*, **8**, 575–594.

Brown, A. L. (1984). Dyslexia and spatial thinking, *Annals of Dyslexia*, **34**, 69–85.

Brown, M. A., and Broadway, M. J. (1981). The cognitive maps of adolescents: confusion about inter-town distances, *Professional Geography*, **33**, 315–325.

Brown, D., Sijpkes, P., and Maclean, M. (1986). The community role of public indoor space, *Journal of Architectural and Planning Research*, **3**, 161–172.

Brown, A. L., Bransford, J. D., Ferrara, R. A., and Campione, J. I. (1983). Learning, remembering and understanding. In J. H. Flavell and E. M. Marksman (eds), *Carmichael's Manual of Child Psychology*. John Wiley, New York.

Brown, J. G., and Burger, C. (1984). Playground designs and preschool children's behaviors, *Environment and Behavior*, **16**, 599–626.

Bruner, J. S. and Connolly, K. J. (eds) (1974). *The Growth of Competence*. Academic Press, London.

Bryant, B. K. (1985). The neighborhood walk: sources of support in middle childhood, *Monographs of the Society for Research in Child Development*, **50**, No. 3 (Serial No. 210).

Bryant, K. J. (1982). Personality correlates of sense of direction and geographic orientation, *Journal of Personality and Social Psychology*, **43**, 1318–1324.

Budd, B. E., Clance, P. R., and Simerly, D. E. (1985). Spatial configurations: Erikson reexamined, *Sex Roles*, **12**, 571–577.

Buffery, A. W. H., and Gray, J. H. (1972). Sex differences in the development of spatial and linguistic skills. In C. Ounstead and D. C. Taylor (eds), *Gender Differences: Their Ontogeny and Significance*. Churchill, London.

Bunting, T. E., and Cousins, L. R. (1985). Environmental dispositions among school-age children, *Environment and Behavior*, **17**, 725–768.

Burgess, J., and Unwin, D. (1984). Exploring the living planet with David Attenborough, *Journal of Geography in Higher Education*, **8**, 93–113.

Burney, J. (1975). The place of environmental education in the development of the school curriculum. Working Paper No. 12, Kingston Polytechnic School of Architecture, Architectural Psychology Research Unit, Kingston on Thames, Surrey.

Burklen, K. (1924). *Blinden Psychologie*. Johann Ambrosuis Barth, Leipzig, Germany.

Butler, M., and Paisley, W. (1980). *Women and the Mass Media: Sourcebook for Research and Action*. Human Sciences Press, New York.

Butterworth, G. (ed.) (1977). *The Child's Representation of the World*. Plenum Press, New York.

Byrne, R. W. (1979). Memory for urban geography, *Quarterly Journal of Experimental Psychology*, **31**, 147–154.

Byrne, R. W. (1982). Geographical knowledge and orientation. In A. W. Ellis (ed.), *Normality and Pathology in Cognitive Functions*. Academic Press, London.

Byrne, R. W., and Salter, E. (1983). Distances and directions in the cognitive maps of the blind, *Canadian Journal of Psychology*, **37**, 293–299.

Cadwallader, M. (1976). Cognitive distance in intraurban space. In G. T. Moore and R. G. Golledge (eds), *Environmental Knowing: Theories, Research and Methods*, Dowden, Hutchinson, & Ross, Stroudsburg, PA.

Cadwallader, M. (1979). Problems in cognitive distance and their implications for behavioral mapping, *Environment and Behavior*, **11**, 559–576.

Caldwell, B. M., Huder, J., and Kaplan, D. (1978). The inventory of home stimulation. Paper presented at the meeting of the American Psychological Association, September 1966. Cited in R. D. Parke (1978). Children's home environments. In I. Altman and J. F. Wohlwill (eds), *Children and the Environment*. Plenum Press, New York.

Calhoun, J. B. (1962). Population density and social pathology, *Scientific American*, **206**, 139–148.

Canter, D. (ed.) (1975). *Environmental Interaction*. Surrey University Press, Guildford.

Canter, D. (1977). *The Psychology of Place*. Architectural Press, London.

Canter, D. (1983a). The purposive evaluation of places: a facet approach, *Environment and Behavior*, **15**, 659–698.

Canter, D. (1983b). Putting situations in their places: foundation for a bridge between social and environmental psychology. In A. Furnham (ed.), *Social Behaviour in Context*. Allyn & Bacon, London.

Canter, D., and Canter, S. (eds) (1979). *Designing for Therapeutic Environments*. John Wiley, Chichester.

Carbonora-Moscati, V. (1986). Children's spatial achievement regarding the representation of the house. Paper presented at the Second European Conference on Developmental Psychology, Rome.

Carlson, G. R. (1976). Location of a point in Euclidean space by children in grades one through six, *Journal of Research in Science Teaching*, **13**, 331–336.

Carp, F. M., and Carp, A. (1982). Perceived environmental quality of neighbourhoods: development of assessment scales and their relation to age and gender, *Journal of Environmental Psychology*, **2**, 295–312.

Carpenter, P. A., and Eisenberg, P. (1978). Mental rotation and the frame of reference in blind and sighted individuals, *Perception and Psychophysics*, **23**, 117–124.

Carr, S., and Schissler, D. (1969). The city as a trip: perceptual selection and memory in the view from the road, *Environment and Behavior*, **1**, 7–35.

Carson, S. McB. (ed.) (1978). *Environmental Education: Principles and Practice*. Edward Arnold, London.

Carswell, R. J. B. (1971). Children's abilities in topographic map reading, *Cartographica Monographs* No. 2, 40–45.

Carter, P., Pazak, B., and Kail, R. (1983). Algorithms for processing spatial information, *Journal of Experimental Child Psychology*, **36**, 284–304.

Cassidy, J. (1986). The ability to negotiate the environment: an aspect of infant competence as related to quality of attachment, *Child Development*, **57**, 331–7.

Catlin, T. (1981). Look and learn: teaching architecture to children, *Architects' Journal*, 19 August.

Catling, S. (1978). Cognitive mapping exercises as a primary geographical experience, *Teaching Geography*, **4**, 120–123.

Catling, S. J. (1979). Maps and cognitive maps: the young child's perception, *Geography*, **64**, 288–296.

Catling, S. (1981). Using maps and aerial photographs. In D. Mills (ed.), *Geographical Work in Primary and Middle Schools*. Geographical Association, Sheffield.

Cavanaugh, J. C., and Perlmutter, M. (1982). Metamemory: a critical examination, *Child Development*, **53**, 11–28.

Chalermchai, H. (1980). Urban open space for children in the Bangkok metropolis, *Ekistics*, **47**, 121–123.

Chen, M. J., and Cook, M. (1984). Representational drawings of solid objects by young children, *Perception*, **13**, 377–385.

Clark, E. V. (1973). What's in a word? On the child's acquisition of semantics in his first language. In J. R. Hayes (ed.), *Cognition and the Development of Language*. John Wiley, New York.

Cohen, L. B. (1973). A two process model of infant visual attention, *Merrill-Palmer Quarterly*, **19**, 157–180.

Cohen, R. (1982). The role of activity in the construction of spatial representation. In R. Cohen (ed.), *New Directions for Child Development: Children's Conceptions of Spatial Relationships*, No. 15. Jossey-Bass, San Francisco.

Cohen, R. (ed.) (1985). *The Development of Spatial Abilities*. Lawrence Erlbaum, Hillsdale, NJ.

Cohen, R., Baldwin, L. M., and Sherman, R. L. (1978). Cognitive maps of a naturalistic setting, *Child Development*, **49**, 1216–1218.

Cohen, R., Goodnight, J. A., Poag, C. K., Cohen, S., Nichol, G. T., and Worley, P. (1986). Easing the transition to kindergarten: the affective and cognitive effects of different spatial familiarization experiences, *Environment and Behavior*, **18**, 330–345.

Cohen, R., and Schuepfer, T. (1980). The representation of landmarks and routes, *Child Development*, **51**, 1065–1071.

Cohen, R., and Weatherford, D. (1981). The effect of barriers on spatial representations, *Child Development*, **52**, 1087–1090.

Cohen, R., Weatherford, D. L., and Byrd, D. (1980). Distance estimates of children as a function of acquisition and response activities, *Journal of Experimental Child Psychology*, **30**, 464–472.

Cohen, R., Weatherford, D. L., Lomenick, T., and Koeller, K. (1979). Development of spatial representations: role of task demands and familiarity with the environment, *Child Development*, **50**, 1257–1260.

Cohen, S., and Cohen, R. (1982). Distance estimates of children as a function of type of activity in the environment, *Child Development*, **53**, 834–837.

Cohen, S., Evans, G. W., Krantz, D. S., and Stokols, D. (1980). Physiological, motivational and cognitive effects of aircraft noise on children: moving from the laboratory to the field, *American Psychologist*, **35**, 231–243.

Cohen, U., Hill, A., Lane, C. G., McGinty, T., and Moore, G. T. (1979). *Recommendations for Child Play Areas*. Centre for Architecture and Urban Planning Research, Milwaukee, WI.

Cohen, U., Moore, G. T., and McGinty, T. (1980). Environments for play and child care, *Architectural Psychology Newsletter*, **10**, 18–20.

Coleman, A. M. (1985). *Utopia on Trial: Vision and Reality in Planned Housing*. Hilary Shipman, London.

Coleman, A. M., and Catling, S. (1982). *Patterns on the Map: Land Utilization Sur-*

vey Maps as Resources for Teaching and Learning. The Geographical Association, Sheffield.

Collett, P. (1971). On training Englishmen in the non-verbal behaviour of Arabs: an experiment in intercultural communication, *International Journal of Psychology*, **6**, 209–215.

Collis, M. (1978). Educational patterns: the first years. In S. McB. Carson (ed.), *Environmental Education: Principles and Practice*. Edward Arnold, London.

Conning, A. M., and Byrne, R. W. (1984). Pointing to preschool children's spatial competence: a study in natural settings, *Journal of Environmental Psychology*, **4**, 165–175.

Cook, M. (1979). *Perceiving Others: The Psychology of Interpersonal Perception*. Methuen, London.

Cooper, J., and Masterson, T. H. (1980). *Geography from Years 10–14: A Curriculum Investigation*. Moray House College of Education, Edinburgh.

Cornell, E. H., and Hay, D. H. (1984). Children's acquisition of a route via different media, *Environment and Behavior*, **16**, 627–641.

Cornell, E. H., and Heth, C. D. (1983). Spatial cognition: gathering strategies used by preschool children, *Journal of Experimental Child Psychology*, **35**, 93–110.

Cornell, E. H., and Heth, C. D. (1986). The spatial organization of hiding and recovery of objects by children, *Child Development*, **57**, 603–615.

Cotzin, M., and Dallenbach, K. M. (1950). Facial vision: the role of pitch and loudness in the perception of obstacles by the blind, *American Journal of Psychology*, **63**, 485–515.

Couclelis, H. (1986). Artificial Intelligence in geography: conjectures on the shape of things to come, *Professional Geographer*, **38**, 1–11.

Cousins, J. H., Siegal, A. W., and Maxwell, S. E. (1983). Way finding and cognitive mapping in large-scale environments: a test of a developmental model, *Journal of Experimental Child Psychology*, **35**, 1–20.

Cox, M. V. (1977). Training perspective ability in young children. In G. Butterworth (ed.), *The Child's Representation of the World*. Plenum Press, New York.

Cox, M. V., and Richardson, J. R. (1985). How do children describe spatial relationships? *Journal of Child Language*, **12**, 611–620.

Craik, K. H. (1970). Environmental psychology. In K. H. Craik (ed.), *New Directions in Psychology*. Holt, Rinehart, & Winston, New York.

Cratty, B. J., and Sams, T. A. (1968). *The Body-Image of Blind Children*. American Foundation for the Blind, New York.

Cullen, G. (1971). *Townscape*. Architectural Press, London.

Curtis, L. E., Siegal, A. W., and Furlong, N. E. (1981). Developmental differences in cognitive mapping: configurational knowledge of a large-scale environments, *Journal of Experimental Child Psychology*, **31**, 456–469.

Dale, P. F. (1971). Children's reactions to maps and aerial photographs, *Area*, **3**, 170–177.

Dalgleish, M., and Matthews, R. (1981). Some effects of staffing levels and group size on the quality of day care for severely mentally handicapped adults, *British Journal of Mental Subnormality*, **27**, 30–35.

Darvizeh, Z., and Spencer, C. P. (1984). How do young children learn novel routes? The importance of landmarks in the child's retracing of routes through the large-scale environment, *Environmental Education and Information*, **3**, 97–105.

Darwin, C. (1877). A biographical sketch of an infant, *Mind*, **2**, 285–294.

Deering, M., and Collins, C. (1981). Real-time natural scene analysis for a blind prosthesis. *Proceedings of the 7th International Joint Conference on Artificial Intelligence*, Vancouver.

Dehn, N., and Schank, R. (1983). Artificial and human intelligence. In R. J. Sternberg (ed.), *Handbook of Intelligence*. Cambridge University Press, Cambridge.

Deloache, J. S. (1984). Oh where, oh where: memory-based searching by very young children. In C. Sophian (ed.), *Origins of Cognitive Skills*. Lawrence Erlbaum, Hillsdale, NJ.

Deloache, J. S. (1986). Memory in very young children: exploitation of cues to the location of a hidden object, *Cognitive Development*, **1**, 123–137.

Deloache, J. S., and Brown, A. L. (1983). Very young children's memory for the location of objects in a large-scale environment, *Child Development*, **54**, 888–897.

Deloache, J. S., and Brown, A. L. (1984). Where do I go next?: Intelligent searching by very young children, *Developmental Psychology*, **20**, 37–44.

Deloache, J. S., Cassidy, D. J., and Brown, A. L. (1985). Precursors of mnemonic strategies in very young children's memory, *Child Development*, **56**, 125–137.

Demick, J., Hoffman, A., and Wapner, S. (1985). Residential context and environmental change as determinants of urban experience, *Children's Environments Quarterly*, **2**, 44–54.

Department of the Environment, Education Board (1979). *Environmental Education in Urban Areas: The Need to Help People to Understand and Improve Their Towns*. Department of the Environment, London.

Department of Health and Social Security (1979–1980). *Mental Health Buildings Evaluation: A Series of Reports*. DHSS, London.

Devlin, A. (1976). The 'small town' cognitive map: adjusting to a new environment. In G. T. Moore and R. G. Golledge (eds), *Environmental Knowing*. Dowden, Hutchinson, & Ross, Stroudsburg, PA.

Dewey, J. (1902). *The Educational Situation*. Chicago University Press, Chicago.

Diderot, D. (1916). Letter on the blind. In *Early Philosophical Works*, pp. 68–141. The Open Court Publishing Co., Chicago and London.

Dijkink, G., and Elbers, G. (1981). The development of geographic representation in children: cognitive and affective aspects of model-building behaviour, *Tijdschrift voor Economische en sociale geografie*, **72**, 2–16.

Dilley, R. S. (1986). Tourist brochures and tourist images, *The Canadian Geographer*, **30**, 59–65.

Dodds, A. G., Howarth, C. I., and Carter, D. C. (1982). The mental maps of the blind: the role of previous visual experience, *Journal of Visual Impairment and blindness*, **January**, 5–12.

Doherty, S., and Pellegrino, J. W. (1985). Developmental changes in neighborhood scene recognition, *Children's Environments Quarterly*, **2**, 38–43.

Donaldson, M. (1978). *Children's Minds*. Fontana, Glasgow.

Downs, R. M. (1981). Maps and mappings as metaphors for spatial representation. In L. S. Liben, A. H. Patterson and N. Newcombe (eds), *Spatial Representation and Behavior Across the Life Span*. Academic Press, New York.

Downs, R. M. (1981). Maps and metaphors, *Professional Geographer*, **33**, 287–293.

Downs, R. M., and Siegal, A. W. (1981). On mapping researchers mapping children mapping space. In L. S. Liben, A. H. Patterson and N. Newcombe (eds), *Spatial Representation and Behavior Across the Life Span*. Academic Press, New York.

Downs, R. M., and Stea, D. (1977). *Maps in Minds*. Harper & Row, New York.

Drever, J. (1955). Early learning and the perception of space, *Americal Journal of Psychology*, **68**, 605–614.

Dryhurst, B., Spencer, C. P., and Baybutt, K. (1985), The evaluation of a training programme in orientation skills, *British Journal of Visual Impairment*, 3, 41–44.

Dueck, K. G. (1976). Imageability: implications for teaching geography, *Journal of Geography*, 75, 135–148.

Dupre, A., and O'Neil-Gilbert, M. (1985). Town and city children's macro-space cognitive representation: a comparative study, *Children's Environments Quarterly*, 2, 27–33.

Durkin, K. (1984). Children's accounts of sex-role stereotypes in television, *Communication Research*, 11, 341–362.

Durkin, K., and Hutchins, G. (1984). Challenging traditional sex role stereotypes in careers education broadcasts: the reactions of young secondary school pupils, *Journal of Educational Television*, 10, 25–33.

Easton, R. D., and Bentzen, B. L. (1987). Memory for verbally presented routes: a comparison of strategies used by blind and sighted people, *Journal of Visual Impairment and Blindness*, 81, 100–105.

Edney, J. J. (1974). Human territoriality, *Psychological Bulletin*, 81, 959–975.

Eiser, C. (1974). Recognition and inference in the coordination of perspectives, *British Journal of Educational Psychology*, 44, 309–312.

Eliot, J. (1987). *Models of Psychological Space: Psychometric, Developmental and Experimental Approaches*. Springer, Berlin.

Ellen, P., and Thinus-Blanc, C. (eds) (1986). *Cognitive Processes and Spatial Orientation in Animal and Man*. Martinus Nijhoff, Dordrecht.

Elliott, H. M. (1979). Mental maps and ethnocentrism: geographic characterizations in the past, *Journal of Geography*, 78, 250–265.

Elliott, R. J., and Lesk, M. E. (1982). Route finding in street maps by computers and people, *Proceedings of the National Conference of the American Association for Artificial Intelligence*, University of Pittsburgh, Pennsylvania, pp. 258–261.

Ellis, A. K. (1974). Concept and skill development in a primary geography unit utilizing alternate learning progressions, *Journal of Geography*, 73, 20–26.

Evans, G. W. (1980). Environmental cognition, *Psychological Bulletin*, 88, 259–287.

Evans, G. W. (ed.). (1984). *Environmental Stress*, Cambridge University Press, Cambridge.

Evans, G. W., Fellows, J., Zorn, M., and Doty, K. (1980). Cognitive mapping and architecture, *Journal of Applied Psychology*, 65, 474–478.

Evans, G. W., Marrero, D. G., and Butler, P. A. (1981). Environmental learning and cognitive mapping, *Environment and Behavior*, 13, 83–104.

Evans, G. W., and Pezdek, K. (1980). Cognitive mapping: knowledge of real world distance and location information, *Journal of Experimental Psychology, Human Learning and Memory*, 6, 13–24.

Evans, G. W., Skorpanich, M. A., Gärling, T., Bryant, K. J., and Bresolin, B. (1984). The effects of pathway configuration, landmarks, and stress on environmental cognition, *Journal of Environmental Psychology*, 4, 323–335.

Evans, G. W., Smith, C., and Pezdek, K. (1982). Cognitive maps and urban form, *Journal of the American Planning Association*, 48, 232–244.

Evans, G. W., and Wood, K. W. (1980). Assessment of environmental aesthetics in scenic highway corridors, *Environment and Behavior*, 12, 255–273.

Fabrigoule, C., and Maurel, D. (1982). Radio-tracking study of foxes' movements related to their home range: a cognitive map hypothesis, *Quarterly Journal of Experimental Psychology*, 34B, 195–208.

Felce, D., de Kock, U., and Repp, A. C. (1986). An eco-behavioral analysis of small community-based houses and traditional large hospitals for severely and profoundly mentally handicapped adults, *Applied Research in Mental Retardation*, **7**, 393–408.

Feldman, A., and Acredolo, L. P. (1979). The effect of active vs passive exploration on memory for spatial location in children, *Child Development*, **50**, 698–704.

Fishbein, H. D., Fehr, L. A., and Tieves, J. (1981). Children's and adults' organization of spatial relations, *Merrill-Palmer Quarterly*, **27**, 111–128.

Fisher, H. G., and Friedman, S. J. (1968). The role of the pinna in auditory localization, *Journal of Auditory Research*, **8**, 15–26.

Fisher, S., Murray, K. J., and Frazer, N. A. (1985). Homesickness, health and efficiency in first year students, *Journal of Environmental Psychology*, **5**, 181–195.

Fisher, S., Frazer, N., and Murray, K. (1986). Homesickness and health in boarding school children, *Journal of Environmental Psychology*, **6**, 35–47.

Flavell, J. H., Green, F. L., and Flavell, E. R. (1985). The road not taken: understanding the implications of initial uncertainty in evaluating spatial directions, *Developmental Psychology*, **21**, 207–216.

Fletcher, J. F. (1980). Spatial representation in the blind,1: development compared to sighted children, *Journal of Visual Impairment and Blindness*, **December**, 381–385.

Fletcher, J. F. (1981). Spatial representation in blind children, 3: the effects of individual differences, *Journal of Visual Impairment and Blindness*, **January**, 1–3.

Foley, J. E., and Cohen, R. A. J. (1984). Working mental representation of the environment, *Environment and Behavior*, **16**, 713–729.

Foulke, E. (1970). The perceptual basis for mobility, *American Foundation for the Blind Research Bulletin*, **28**, 1–8.

Foulke, E. (1982). Perception, cognition and mobility of blind pedestrians. In M. Potegal (ed.), *Spatial Abilities Developmental and Physiological Foundations*, Academic Press, New York.

Foulke, E., and Berla, E. (1978). Visual impairment and the development of perceptual ability. In R. D. Walk and H. L. Pick (eds.), *Perception and Experience*, pp. 213–240. Plenum Press, New York.

Fraiberg, S. (1968). Parallel and divergent patterns in blind and sighted infants, *Psychoanalytic Study of the Child*, **23**, 264–299.

Frake, C. O. (1985). Cognitive maps of time and tide among medieval seafarers, *Man: The Journal of The Royal Anthropological Institute*, **20**, 254–270.

Franck, K. A. (1984). Exorcising the ghost of physical determinism, *Environment and Behavior*, **16**, 411–435.

Freeman, N., Lloyd, S., and Sinha, C. (1980). Hide and seek is child's play, *New Scientist*, 30 October, 304–305.

Frisby, J. P. (1979). *Seeing: Illusion, Brain and Mind*, Oxford University Press, Oxford.

Frostig, M., and Horne, D. (1964). *The Frostig Program for Development of Visual Perception: Teacher's Guide*. Follet, Chicago.

Fryman, J. F., and Wallace, J. (1985). Distorted cognitive maps: college students' misperceptions of nation size, *Perceptual and Motor Skills*, **60**, 419–423.

Gale, N., Doherty, S., Pellegrino, J. W., and Golledge, R. G. (1985). Toward reassembling the image, *Children's Environments Quarterly*, **2**, 10–18.

Gans, H. J. (1968). *People and Places: Essays on Urban Problems and Solutions*. Basic Books, New York.

Garbarino, J. (1985). Habitats for children: an ecological perspective. In J. F. Wohlwill and W. van Vliet (eds), *Habitats for Children*. Lawrence Erlbaum, Hillsdale, NJ.

Gardener, H. (1980). *Artful Scribbles: The Significance of Children's Drawings*. Basic Books, New York.

Gärling, T., Böök, A., and Ergezen, N. (1982). Memory for the spatial layout of the everyday physical environment: differential rates of acquisition of different types of information, *Scandinavian Journal of Psychology*, **23**, 23–35.

Gärling, T., Böök, A., and Lindberg, E. (1984a). Cognitive mapping of large-scale environments: the interrelationship of action plans, acquisition and orientation, *Environment and Behavior*, **16**, 3–34.

Gärling, T., Böök, A., and Lindberg, E. (1984b). Adults' memory representations of the spatial properties of their everyday physical environment. In R. Cohen (ed.), *The Development of Spatial Cognition*. Lawrence Erlbaum, Hillsdale, NJ.

Gärling, T., Böök, A., Lindberg, E., and Nilsson, T. (1981). Memory for the spatial layout of the everyday physical environment: factors affecting rate of acquisition, *Journal of Environmental Psychology*, **1**, 263–277.

Gärling, T., Lindberg, E., and Mäntylä, T. (1983). Orientation in buildings: effects of familiarity, visual access, and orientation aids, *Journal of Applied Psychology*, **68**, 177–186.

Gärling, T., Säisä, J., Böök, A., and Lindberg, E. (1986). The spatio-temporal sequencing of everyday activities in the large-scale environment, *Journal of Environmental Psychology*, **6**, 261–280.

Gauvain, M. (ed.) (1985). Images of environments: a special issue in honor of Kevin Lynch, *Children's Environments Quarterly*, **2**, No. 3.

Gauvain, M., and Rogoff, B. (1983). The pragmatic nature of large-scale spatial knowledge. Paper presented at the XIX Intermountain Congress of Psychology, Quito, Ecuador.

Gauvain, M., and Rogoff, B. (1986). The influence of the goal on children's exploration and memory of large-scale space, *Developmental Psychology*, **22**, 72–77.

Geeslin, W. E., and Shar, A. O. (1979). An alternative model describing children's spatial preferences, *Journal of Research in Mathematics Education*, **10**, 57–68.

Gerber, R. (1981). Young children's understanding of the elements of maps, *Teaching Geography*, **6**, 128–133.

Gerber, R. (1982). An international study of children's perception and understanding of type used on atlas maps, *Cartographic Journal*, **19**, 115–121.

Gerber, R. (1984). The development of competence and performance in cartographic language by children at the concrete level of map-reasoning. In C. Board (ed.), *New Insights in Cartographic Communication*, *Cartographica Monograph*, **31**, 98–119.

Giannangelo, D. M., and Frazee, B. M. (1977). Map reading proficiency of elementary educators, *Journal of Geography*, **76**, 63–65.

Gibson, E. J. (ed.) (1987). Special issue: the ontogenesis of perception, *Journal of Experimental Psychology Human Perception and Performance*, **13** (4) (Whole issue) 515–620.

Gibson, J. J. (1958). Visually controlled locomotion and visual orientation in animals, *British Journal of Psychology*, **49**, 182–194.

Gibson, J. J. (1966). *The Senses Considered as Perceptual Systems*. Houghton Mifflin, Boston.

Gibson, J. J. (1979). *The Ecological Approach to Visual Perception*. Houghton Mifflin, Boston.

Gilmartin, P. P. (1981). The interface of cognitive and psychological research in cartography, *Cartographica*, **18**, 9–20.

Gilmartin, P. P. (1982). The instructional efficacy of maps in geographic text, *Journal of Geography*, **81**, 145–150.

Gilmartin, P. P. (1985). The design of journalistic maps: purposes, parameters and prospects, *Cartographica*, **22**, 1–18.

Gilmartin, P. P. (1986). Maps, mental imagery, and gender in the recall of geographical information, *The American Cartographer*, **13**, 335–344.

Glacken, C. (1967). *Traces on the Rhodian Shore*. University of California Press, Berkeley.

Glendinning, H., and Pearson, M. (1983). Using air photographs with young children: an experiment, *Teaching Geography*, **9**, 3–4.

Golbeck, S. (1983). Reconstructing a large-scale spatial arrangement: effects of environmental organization and operativity, *Developmental Psychology*, **19**, 644–653.

Golbeck, S. L. (1985). Spatial cognition as a function of environmental characteristics. In R. Cohen (ed.), *The Development of Spatial Cognition*. Lawrence Erlbaum, Hillsdale, NJ.

Golbeck, S., Rand, M., and Soundy, C. (1986). Constructing a model of a large scale space with the space in view: effects on preschoolers of guidance and cognitive restructuring, *Merrill-Palmer Quarterly*, **32**, 187–203.

Goldsmith, L. T., Mohr, D. M., and Pick, H. L. (1977). Cognitive maps in children and adults: inferences about spatial relations after rotation. Paper presented at the Eastern Psychological Association Meetings, Boston, April 1977.

Golledge, R. G. (1978). Learning about urban environments. In T. Carlstein, D. Parkes and N. Thrift (eds), *Timing Space and Spacing Time*. Edward Arnold, London.

Golledge, R. G. (1987). Environmental cognition. In D. Stokols and I. Altman (eds), *Handbook of Environmental Psychology*. John Wiley, New York.

Golledge, R. G., and Hubert, L. J. (1982). Some comments on non-Euclidean mental maps, *Environment and Planning A*, **14**, 107–118.

Golledge, R. G., and Rushton, G. (1984). A review of analytic behavioural research in geography. In D. T. Herbert and R. J. Johnson (eds), *Geography and the Urban Environment, Progress in Research and Applications*, Vol VI. John Wiley, Chichester.

Golledge, R. G., Smith, T. R., Pellegrino, J. W., Doherty, S., and Marshall, S. P. (1985). A conceptual model and empirical analysis of children's acquisition of spatial knowledge, *Journal of Environmental Psychology*, **5**, 125–152.

Golledge, R. G., and Spector, A. N. (1978). Comprehending the urban environment: theory and practice, *Geographical Analysis*, **10**, 403–426.

Gomulicki, B. R. (1961). *The Development of Perception and Learning in Blind Children*. The Psychological Laboratory of Cambridge University, London.

Goodey, B. (1975). Who carries on from where the geographers leave off? The visual urban environment. Paper presented at the 1975 Architectural Psychology Conference, 'Education for the Urban Environment', University of Sheffield, September 1975.

Goodey, B. (1978). *The City*. In S. McB. Carson (ed.), *Environmental Education: Principles and Practice*. Edward Arnold, London.

Goodey, B., and Gold, J. R. (1987). Environmental perception: the relationship with urban design, *Progress in Human Geography*, **10**, 520–528.

Goodnow, J. J., Wilkins, P., and Dawes, L. (1986). Acquiring cultural forms: cognitive aspects of socialization illustrated by children's drawings and judgments of drawings, *International Journal of Behavioral Development*, **9**, 485–505.

Gould, P. (1985). *The Geographer at Work*, Routledge & Kegan Paul, London.

Gould, P., and White, R. (1986). *Mental Maps*, (2nd Edition). Allen & Unwin, London.

Grabe, M. (1976). Big school, small school: impact of the high school environment, *Contemporary Educational Psychology*, **1**, 20–25.

Grabe, M. (1981). School size and the importance of school activities, *Adolescence*, **16**, 21–31.

Graham, E. (1982). Maps, metaphors and muddles, *The Professional Geographer*, **34**, 251–260.

Graham, N. D. (1965). Wanted: a readiness test for mobility training, *New Outlook for the Blind*, **59**, 157–162.

Graves, N. J. (ed.) (1982). *New UNESCO Source Book for Geography Teaching*. UNESCO Press, Paris, and Longman, London.

Green, D. M. (1978). Functional aspects of the auditory sense. In L. D. Harman (ed.), *Interrelations of the Communicative Senses*, Conference sponsored by National Science Foundation, Asilomar, California.

Guelke, L. (1979). Perception, meaning and cartographic design, *The Canadian Geographer*, **16**, 61–69.

Gump, P. V. (1978). School environments. In I. Altman and J. F. Wohlwill (eds), *Children and the Environment*. Plenum Press, New York.

Gump, P. V. (1980). The school as a social situation, *Annual Review of Psychology*, **31**, 553–582.

Gump, P. V. (1987). School and classroom environments. In D. Stokols and I. Altman (eds), *Handbook of Environmental Psychology*. John Wiley, New York.

Gump, P. V., and Adelberg, B. (1978). Urbanism from the perspective of ecological psychologists, *Environment and Behavior*, **10**, 171–191.

Gunzberg, H. C. (1973). The physical environment of the mentally handicapped, *British Journal of Mental Subnormality*, **19**, 91–99.

Gunzburg, H. C. (1974). *Social Competence and Mental Handicap: An Introduction to Social Education*. Balliere Tindall, London.

Gunzburg, H. C., and Gunzburg, A. L. (1973). *Mental Handicap and Physical Environment*. Balliere Tindall, London.

Haake, R. J., and Somerville, S. C. (1985). Development of logical search skills in infancy, *Developmental Psychology*, **21**, 176–186.

Haber, R. N. (1978). Visual perception, *Annual Review of Psychology*, **29**, 31–59.

Hagen, M. A., and Jones, R. K. (1978). Cultural effects on pictorial perception. In R. D. Walk and H. J. Pick (eds), *Perception and Experience*. Plenum Press, New York.

Haggett, P., Cliff, A. D., and Frey, A. (1977). *Locational Analysis in Human Geography*. John Wiley, New York.

Hall, E. T. (1966). *The Hidden Dimension*. Doubleday, New York.

Hapeman, L. (1967). Developmental concepts of blind children between ages 3 and 6 as they relate to orientation and mobility, *International Journal for the Education of the Blind*, **17**, 41–48.

Hardwick, D. A., McIntyre, C. W., and Pick, H. L. (1976). The content and manipulation of cognitive maps in children and adults, *Monographs of the Society for Research in Child Development*, 41, No. 3, (Serial No. 166).

Hare, B. A., Hammill, D. D., and Crandell, J. M. (1970). Auditory dessimination ability of visually limited children. *New Outlook for the Blind*, **64**, 287–292.

Harris, H., and Lipman, A. (1984). Social process, space usage: reflections on socialization in homes for children, *British Journal of Social Work*, **14**, 49–65.

Harris, L. J. (1977). Sex differences in spatial ability: possible environmental, genetic and neurological factors. In M. Kinsbourne (ed.), *Hemispheric Asymmetries of Function*. Cambridge University Press, Cambridge.

Harris, L. J. (1981). Sex related variations in spatial skill. In L. S. Liben, A. H. Patterson and N. Newcombe (eds), *Spatial Representation and Behavior Across the Life Span*. Academic Press, New York.

Harris, P. (1977). The child's representation of space. In G. Butterworth (ed.), *The Child's Representation of the World*. Plenum Press, London.

Harris, P. L. (1984). Landmarks and movement. In C. Sophian (ed.), *Origins of Cognitive Skills*. Lawrence Erlbaum, Hillsdale, NJ.

Harris, P. L. (1985). The Origins of Search and Number Skills. In H. M. Wellman (ed.),
    Children's Searching: The Development of Search Skills and Spatial Representation.
    Lawrence Erlbaum, Hillsdale, NJ.
Hart, R. A. (1970). Aerial geography: an experiment in elementary education, *Place
    Perception Research Reports*, No. 6. Clarke University, Worcester, MA.
Hart, R. A. (1979). *Children's Experience of Place: A Developmental Study.* Irvington
    Press, New York.
Hart, R. A. (1981). Children's spatial representation of the landscape: lessons and ques-
    tions from a field study. In L. S. Liben, A. H. Patterson and N. Newcombe (eds),
    Spatial Representation and Behavior Across the Life Span. Academic Press, New
    York.
Hart, R. A., and Moore, G. T. (1977). The development of spatial cognition: a review.
    In R. M. Downs and D. Stea (eds), *Image and Environment: Cognitive Mapping and
    Spatial Behaviour.* Aldine, Chicago.
Hartlage, L. C. (1969). Verbal tests of spatial conceptualization, *Journal of Experi-
    mental Psychology*, **80**, 180–182.
Hartlage, L. C. (1976). The development of spatial concepts in visually deprived chil-
    dren, *Perceptual and Motor Skills*, **42**, 255–258.
Hartley, J. L., Somerville, S. C., von Cziesch Jensen, D., and Eliefja, C. C. (1982).
    Abstraction of individual styles from the drawings of five-year-old children, *Child
    Development*, **53**, 1193–1214.
Hasher, L., and Zacks, R. T. (1978). Automatic and effortful processes in memory,
    Journal of Experimental Psychology: General, **108**, 356–388.
Hawkins, M. L., and Larkins, A. G. (1983). A map skills and concepts unit for the
    primary grades, *Journal of Geography*, **82**, 26–29.
Hayes-Roth, B. (1985). A blackboard architecture for control. *Artifical Intelligence*, **26**,
    251–321.
Hayes-Roth, B., and Hayes-Roth, F. (1979). A cognitive model of planning, *Cognitive
    Science*, **3**, 275–310.
Hayward, D. G., Rothenberg, M., and Beasley, R. R. (1974). Children's play and urban
    playground environments: a comparison of traditional, contemporary and adventure
    playground types, *Environment and Behavior*, **6**, 131–168.
Haywood, H. C., and Newbrough, J. R. (eds) (1981). *Living Environments for Devel-
    opmentally Retarded Persons*, University Park Press, Baltimore.
Hazen, N. L. (1982). Spatial exploration and spatial knowledge: individual and devel-
    opmental differences in very young children, *Child Development*, **53**, 826–833.
Hazen, N. L., and Durrett, M. (1982). Relationship of security of attachment to explo-
    ration and cognitive mapping ability in two year olds, *Developmental Psychology*, **18**,
    751–759.
Hazen, N. L., Lockman, J. J., and Pick, H. L. (1978). The development of children's
    representations of large scale environment, *Child Development*, **49**, 623–636.
Hazen, N. L., and Volk-Hudson, S. (1984). The effect of spatial context on young
    children's recall, *Child Development*, **55**, 1835–1844.
Hebb, D. O. (1949). *Organization of Behaviour.* John Wiley, New York.
Heft, H. (1979). The role of environmental features in route-learning: two exploratory
    studies of way-finding, *Environmental Psychology and Non-Verbal Behaviour*, **3**, 172–
    185.
Heft, H. (1983). Wayfinding as the perception of information over time, *Population and
    Environment*, **6**, 133–150.
Heft, H. (1985). High residential density and perceptual–cognitive development: an
    examination of the effects of crowding and noise in the home. In J. F. Wohlwill

and W. van Vliet (eds), *Habitats for Children*. Lawrence Erlbaum, Hillsdale, NJ.

Heft, H., and Wohlwill, J. F. (1987). Environmental cognition in children. In D. Stokols and I. Altman (eds), *Handbook of Environmental Psychology*. John Wiley, New York.

H.M. Inspectorate (1978). Primary education in England. Department of Education and Science, London.

Herman, J. F. (1980). Children's cognitive maps of large-scale spaces: effects of exploration, direction and repeated experience, *Journal of Experimental Child Psychology*, **29**, 126–143.

Herman, J. F., Chatman, S. P., and Roth, S. F. (1983). Cognitive mapping in blind people: acquisition of spatial relationships in a large scale environment, *Journal of Visual Impairment and Blindness*, **77**, 161–166.

Herman, J. F., Heins, J. A., and Cohen, D. S. (1987). Children's spatial knowledge of their neighborhood environment, *Journal of Applied Developmental Psychology*, **8**, 1–15.

Herman, J. F., Herman, T. G., and Chatman, S. P. (1983). Constructing cognitive maps from partial information: a demonstration study, *Journal of Visual Impairment and Blindness*, 195–198.

Herman, J. F., Kail, R. V., and Siegal, A. W. (1979). Cognitive maps of a college campus: a new look at freshman orientation, *Bulletin of the Psychonomic Society*, **13**, 183–186.

Herman, J. F., and Klein, C. A. (1985). The effect of travel effort on children's distance estimations, *British Journal of Developmental Psychology*, **3**, 353–361.

Herman, J. F., Kolker, R. G., and Shaw, M. L. (1982). Effects of motor activity on children's intentional and incidental memory for spatial locations, *Child Development*, **53**, 239–244.

Herman, J. F., Miller, B. S., and Heins, J. A. (1987). Barriers and spatial representation: evidence from children and adults in a large environment, *Merrill-Palmer Quarterly*, **33**, 53–68.

Herman, J. F., Miller, B. S., and Shiraki, J. H. (1987). The influence of affective associations on the development of cognitive maps of large environments, *Journal of Environmental Psychology*, **7**, 89–98.

Herman, J. F., Norton, L. M., and Klein, C. A. (1986). Children's distance estimates in a large-scale environment: a search for the route angularity effect, *Environment and Behavior*, **18**, 533–558.

Herman, J. F., Norton, L. M., and Roth, S. F. (1983). Children and adults' distance estimations in a large-scale environment: effects of time and clutter, *Journal of Experimental Child Psychology*, **36**, 453–470.

Herman, J. F., and Roth, S. F. (1984). Children's incidental memory for spatial locations in a large-scale environment: taking a tour down memory lane, *Merrill-Palmer Quarterly*, **30**, 87–102.

Herman, J. F., Roth, S. F., Miranda, C., and Getz, M. (1982). Children's memory for spatial locations: the influence of recall perspective and type of environment, *Journal of Experimental Child Psychology*, **34**, 257–273.

Herman, J. F., Roth, S. F., and Norton, L. M. (1984). Time and distance in spatial cognition development, *International Journal of Behavioral Development*, **7**, 35–51.

Herman, J. F., and Siegal, A. W. (1978). The development of cognitive mapping of the large-scale environment, *Journal of Experimental Child Psychology*, **26**, 389–406.

Herman, J. F., Shiraki, J. H., and Miller, B. S. (1985). Young children's ability to infer spatial relationships: evidence from a large, familiar environment, *Child Development*, **56**, 1195–1203.

Hermelin, B., and O'Connor, N. (1971). Spatial coding in normal, autistic and blind children, *Perceptual and Motor Skills*, **33**, 127–132.

Hermelin, B., and O'Connor, N. (1975). Location and distance estimates by blind and sighted children, *International Journal of Experimental Psychology*, **27**, 295–301.

Hermelin, B., and O'Connor, N. (1982). Spatial modality coding in children with and without impairments. In M. Potegal (ed.), *Spatial Abilities Developmental and Physiological Foundations*. Academic Press, New York.

Hermelin, B., and O'Connor, N. (1986). Spatial representation in mathematically and artistically gifted children, *British Journal of Educational Psychology*, **56**, 150–157.

Heron, A., and Myers, M. (1983). *Intellectual Impairment: The Battle Against Handicap*. Academic Press, London.

Heth, C. D., and Cornell, E. H. (1980). Three experiences affecting spatial discrimination learning by ambulatory children, *Journal of Experimental Child Psychology*, **30**, 246–264.

Heth, C. D., and Cornell, E. H. (1985). A comparative description of representation and processing during search. In H. M. Wellman (ed.), *Children's Searching: The Development of Search Skill and Spatial Representation*. Lawrence Erlbaum, Hillsdale, NJ.

Hewes, D. W. (1982). Preschool geography: developing a sense of self in time and space, *Journal of Geography*, **81**, 94–97.

Hibberd, D. (1983). Children's images of the Third World, *Teaching Geography*, **8**, 68–71.

Hill, A., Spencer, C. P., and Baybutt, K. (1985). Predicting efficiency of travel in young, visually impaired children from their other spatial skills, *Journal of Visual Impairment and Blindness*, **79**, 297–300.

Hill, F., and Michelson, W. (1981). Towards a geography of urban children and youth. In D. T. Herbert and R. J. Johnston (eds), *Geography and the Urban Environment: Progress in Research and Applications*, Vol 4. John Wiley, Chichester.

Hill, G., and Blasch, B. B. (1980). Concept development. In R. L. Welsh and B. B. Blasch (eds), *Foundations of Orientation and Mobility*. American Foundation for the Blind, New York.

Hill, M. H.(1975). Bound to the environment: towards a phenomenology of sightlessness. In D. Seamon and R. Mugerauer (eds), *Dwelling, Place and Environment: Towards a Phenomenology of Person and World*. Martinus Nijhoff, Dordrecht.

Hill, M. R. (1984). Walking straight home from school: pedestrian route choice by young children, *Transportation Research Record*, **959**, 51–55.

Hill, M. R. (1984). Walking, crossing streets and choosing pedestrian routes. University of Nebraska Studies, New Series No. 66. Lincoln, NE.

Hill, F. I. (1980). The "whole city catalogue" project: children's environmental opportunities in Metropolitan Toronto, *Childhood City Newsletter*, October 1980, 16–17.

Hills, J. R. (1957). Factor analyzed abilities and success in college maths, *Educational Psychological Measurement*, **17**, 615–622.

Hinde, R. A., and Stevenson-Hinde, J. (1987). Interpersonal relationships and child development, *Developmental Review*, **7**, 1–21.

Hintzman, D. L., O'Dell, C. S., and Arndt, D. R. (1981). Orientation in cognitive maps, *Cognitive Psychology*, **13**, 149–206.

Hochberg, J., and Brooks, V. (1962). Pictorial recognition as an unlearned ability: a study of one child's performance, *American Psychologist*, **75**, 624–628.

Hole, V. (1966). Children's play on housing estates. National Building Studies Research Paper 39, Her Majesty's Stationery Office, London.

Hollyfield, R. L., and Foulke, E. (1983). The spatial cognition of blind pedestrians, *Journal of Visual Impairment and Blindness*, May, 205–210.

Horobin, K., and Acredolo, L. (1986). The role of attentiveness, mobility history, and separation of hiding sites on Stage IV search behavior, *Journal of Experimental Child Psychology*, **41**, 114–127.

Hough, M., and Mayhew, P. (1983). *The British Crime Survey: First Report*, Her Majesty's Stationery Office, London.

Houssiadas, L., and Brown, L. B. (1980). Egocentrism in language and space perception: an examination of the concept, *Genetic Psychology Monographs*, **101**, 183–214.

Howard, I. P. (1973). Orientation and motion in space. In E. C. Carterette and M. P. Freedman (eds), *Handbook of Perception*, pp. 273–315. Academic Press, New York.

Howard, I. P., and Templeton, W. B. (1966). *Human Spatial Orientation*. John Wiley, Chichester.

Hubel, D. H., and Wiesel, T. N. (1959). Receptive fields of single neurones in the cat's striate cortex, *Journal of Physiology*, **148**, 574–591.

Huizinga, J. (1949). *Homo Ludens*. Routledge & Kegan Paul, London.

Hunter, I. M. L. (1964). Tactile and kinesthetic perception of straightness in blind and sighted humans, *Quarterly Journal of Experimental Psychology*, **6**, 149–154.

Huttenlocher, J. (1967). Discrimination of figure orientation: effects of relative position, *Journal of Comparative and Physiological Psychology*, **63**, 361–365.

Huttenlocher, J. (1968). Constructing spatial images: a strategy in reasoning, *Psychological Review*, **75**, 550–560.

Huttenlocher, J., and Presson, C. C. (1979). The coding and transformation of spatial information, *Cognitive Psychology*, **11**, 375–394.

Jacobsen, T. L., and Waters, H. S. (1985). Spatial perspective taking: coordination of left–right and near–far spatial dimensions, *Journal of Experimental Child Psychology*, **39**, 72–84.

Jahoda, G. (1963). The development of children's ideas about country and nationality, *British Journal of Educational Psychology*, **33**, 47–60, 143–153.

Jahoda, G., Deregowski, J. B., Ampene, E., and Williams, N. (1977). Pictorial recognition as an unlearned ability: a replication with children from pictorially deprived environments. In G. Butterworth (ed.), *The Child's Representation of the World*. Plenum Press, London.

Jaspers, J., van der Geer, J., Tajfel, H., and Johnson, N. B. (1983). On the development of national attitudes in children, *European Journal of Social Psychology*, **2**, 347–369.

Johnson, E. S., and Meade, A. C. (1987). Developmental patterns of spatial ability: an early sex difference, *Child Development*, **58**, 725–740.

Johnson, N. B. (1966). What do children learn from war comics? *New Society*, 7 July.

Johnson, N. B., Middleton, M. R., and Tajfel, H. (1970). The relationship between children's preferences for and knowledge about other nations, *British Journal of Social and Clinical Psychology*, **9**, 232–240.

Johnson-Laird, P. N. (1982). Propositional representations, procedural semantics and mental models. In J. Mehler, E. C. T. Walker and M. Garret (eds), *Perspectives on mental representation*. Lawrence Erlbaum, Hillsdale, NJ.

Johnson-Laird, P. N. (1983). *Mental Models*. Cambridge University Press, Cambridge.

Jones, B. (1975a). Visual facilitation of auditory localization in school children, *Perception and Psychophysics*, **17**, 241–245.

Jones, B. (1975b). Spatial perception in the blind, *British Journal of Psychology*, **66**, 461–472.

Jorgenson, D. O. (1981). Perceived causal influences of weather on affective states and behaviors, *Environment and Behavior*, **13**, 239–256.

Just, M. A., and Carpenter, P. A. (1985). Cognitive coordinate systems: accounts of mental rotation and individual differences in spatial ability, *Psychological Review*, **92**, 137–171.

Jurmaa, J. (1965). An analysis of the components of orientation, mobility and mental manipulation of spatial relations. Report of the Institute of Occupational Health, August 1965, No. 28.

Jurmaa, J. (1973). Transposition in mental spatial manipulation: a theoretical analysis, *American Foundation for the Blind Research Bulletin*, **26**, 87–134.

Jurmaa, J., and Suonio, K. (1975). The role of audition and motion in the spatial orientation of the blind and sighted, *Scandanavian Journal of Psychology*, **16**, 209–216.

Kahl, H. B., Herman, J. F., and Klein, C. A. (1984). Distance distortions in children's cognitive maps: an examination of the information storage model, *Journal of Experimental Child Psychology*, **38**, 134–146.

Kail, R., Carter, P., and Pellegrino, J. (1980). The locus of sex differences in spatial ability, *Journal of Experimental Child Psychology*, **29**, 102–116.

Kamil, A. C., and Balda, R. P. (1985). Cache recovery and spatial memory in Clark's nutcrackers (*Nucifraga columbiana*), *Journal of Experimental Psychology: Animal Behavior Processes*, **11**, 95–111.

Kamil, A. C., and Sargent, T. D. (eds) (1981). *Foraging Behaviour: Ecological, ethological and Psychological Approaches*. Garland, London.

Kapadia, R. (1974). A critical examination of Piaget–Inhelder's view on topology. *Educational Studies in Mathematics*, **5**, 419–424.

Kaplan, R. (1973). Some psychological benefits of gardening, *Environment and Behavior*, **5**, 145–162.

Kaplan, R. (1976). Way-finding in the natural environment. In G. T. Moore and R. G. Golledge (eds), *Environmental Knowing: Theories, Research and Methods*, Dowden, Hutchinson, & Ross, Stroudsburg, PA.

Kaplan, R. (1983). The role of nature in the urban context. In I. Altman and J. Wohlwill (eds), *Human Behavior and Environment*, Vol. 6. *Behavior and the Natural Environment*. Plenum Press, New York.

Kaplan, R. (1985). The analysis of perception via preference: a strategy for studying how the environment is experienced, *Landscape Planning*, **12**, 161–176.

Kaplan, S. (1973). Cognitive maps in perception and thought. In R. M. Downs and D. Stea (eds), *Image and Environment*. Irvine, New York.

Kaplan, S. (1985). Cognition and affect in environmental learning, *Children's Environments Quarterly*, **2**, 19–21.

Kashti, Y., Arieli, M., and Harel, Y. (1984). Classroom seating as a definition of situation, *Urban Education*, **19**, 161–181.

Kato, Y. (1984). Development of spatial recognition in preschool children: on Piaget's hypothesis of topological space. Paper presented to 'Forum Espace IV', National Institute of Psychobiology, Marseilles, France.

Kay, L. (1974). *Toward Objective Mobility Evaluation*, American Foundation for the Blind, New York.

Kearins, J. M. (1981). Visual spatial memory in Australian aboriginal children of desert regions, *Cognitive Psychology*, **13**, 434–460.

Keates, J. S. (1982). *Understanding Maps*. Longman, London.

Keating, M. B., McKenzie, B. E., and Day, R. H. (1986). Spatial localization in infancy:

position constancy in a square and circular room with and without a landmark, *Child Development*, **57**, 115–124.

Keil, F. C., and Carroll, J. J. (1980). The child's conception of "tall": implications for an alternative view of semantic development, *Papers and Reports on Child Language Development*, **19**, 21–28.

Keiler, G. (1985). *Lake Wobegone Days*. Faber, London.

Kelley, T. L. (1928). *Crossroads in the Mind*. Stanford University Press, Stanford, CA.

Kellogg, W. N. (1962). Sonar systems of the blind, *Science*, **137**, 399–401.

Kerr, N. H. (1983). The role of vision in visual imagery experiments: evidence from the congenitally blind, *Journal of Experimental Psychology: General*, **112**, 265–277.

Kerr, N. H., Foulkes, D., and Schmidt, M. (1982). The structure of laboratory dream reports in blind and sighted subjects, *Journal of Nervous and Mental Diseases*, **170**, 286–294.

Kerr, N. H., and Neisser, U. (1983). Mental images of concealed objects: new evidence, *Journal of Experimental Psychology Learning, Memory and Cognition*, **9**, 212–221.

Kidron, M., and Smith, D. (1983). *The War Atlas*. Pan Books, London.

King, R. D., Raynes, N. V., and Tizard, J. (1971). *Patterns of Residential Care: Sociological Studies in Institutions for Handicapped Children*. Routledge & Kegan Paul, London.

Kinsbourne, M. (1978). Cerebral lateralization and cognitive development. In J. S. Chall and A. F. Mirsky (eds), *Education and the Brain*, Chicago: Chicago University Press.

Kirasic, K. C., Allen, G. L., and Siegal, A.W. (1984). Expression of Configurational Knowledge of large-scale environments, *Environment and Behavior*, **16**, 687–712.

Kirman, J. M. (1981). Use of band 5 black-and-white LANDSAT images in the elementary grades, *Journal of Geography*, **80**, 224–228.

Klein, W. (1982). Local deixis in route directions. In R. J. Jarvella and W. Klein, *Speech Place and Action*. John Wiley, Chichester.

Klett, F. R., and Alpaugh, D. (1976). Environmental learning and large-scale environments. In G. T. Moore and R. G. Golledge (eds), *Environmental Knowing*. Dowden, Hutchinson, & Ross, Stroudsberg, PA.

Knopf, R. C. (1987). Human behavior, cognition and affect in the natural environment. In D. Stokols and I. Altman (eds), *Handbook of Environmental Psychology*, Wiley, New York.

Knotts, J. R., and Miles, W. R. (1929). The maze learning ability of blind compared with sighted children, *Journal of Genetic Psychology*, **36**, 21–50.

Korosec-Serfaty, P. (1984). The home from attic to cellar, *Journal of Environmental Psychology*, **4**, 303–321.

Kosslyn, S. M. (1973). Scanning visual images: some structural implications, *Perception and Psychophysics*, **14**, 90–94.

Kosslyn, S. M. (1975). Information representation in visual images, *Cognitive Psychology*, **7**, 341–370.

Kosslyn, S. M. (1981). The medium and the message in mental imagery, *Psychological Review*, **88**, 46–66.

Kosslyn, S. M. (1980). *Image and Mind*. Havard University Press, Cambridge, Massechussetts.

Koussey, A. A. H. (1935). The visual perception of space, *British Journal of Psychology Monograph Supplement*, No. 25.

Kozlowski, L. T., and Bryant, K. J. (1977). Sense of direction, spatial orientation and cognitive maps, *Journal of Experimental Psychology: Human Perception and Performance*, **3**, 590–598.

Kosslyn, S. M., Pick, H. L., and Farieelo, G. R. (1974). Cognitive maps in children and men, *Child Development*, **45**, 707–716.

Kuipers, B. (1978). Modelling spatial knowledge, *Cognitive Science*, **2**, 129–153.

Kuipers, B. (1982). The "map in the head" metaphor, *Environment and Behavior*, **14**, 202–220.

Kulhavy, R. W., Lee, J. B., and Caterino, L. C. (1985). Conjoint retention of maps and related discourse, *Contempory Educational Psychology*, **10**, 28–37.

Kurdeck, L. A. (1978). Perspective taking as the cognitive basis of children's moral development: a review of the literature, *Merrill-Palmer Quarterly*, **24**, 3–28.

Kyllonen, P. C., Lohman, D. F., and Woltz, D. J. (1984). Componential modeling of alternative strategies for performing spatial tasks, *Journal of Educational Psychology*, **76**, 1325–1345.

Laabs, G. J. (1973). Retention characteristics of different reproduction cues in motor short term memory, *Journal of Experimental Psychology*, **100**, 168–177.

Ladd, F. (1970). Black youths view of their environment: neighborhood maps, *Environment and Behavior*, **2**, 64–79.

Landau, B. (1986). Early map use as an unlearned ability, *Cognition*, **22**, 201–223.

Landau, B., Gleitman, H., and Spelke, E. (1981). Spatial knowledge and geometric representation in a child blind from birth, *Science*, 1275–1277.

Landau, B., and Spelke, E. (1985). Spatial knowledge and its manifestations. In H. M. Wellman (ed.), *Children's Searching: The Development of Search Skill and Spatial Representation*. Lawrence Erlbaum, Hillsdale, NJ.

Landau, B., Spelke, E., and Gleitman, H. (1984). Spatial knowledge in a young blind child, *Cognition*, **16**, 225–260.

Laufer, R. S., and Wolfe, M. (1977). Privacy as a concept and a social issue, *Journal of Social Issues*, **33**, 22–42.

Laurendeau, M., and Pinard, A. (1970). *The Development of the Concept of Space in the Child*. International Universities Press, New York.

Lee, P. C., Statuto, C. M., and Kedar-Voivodas, G. (1983). Elementary school children's perceptions of their actual and ideal school experience: a developmental study, *Journal of Educational Psychology*, **75**, 838–847.

Lee, T. R. (1962). Brennan's law of shopping behaviour, *Psychological Reports*, **2**, 662.

Lee, T. R. (1963). On the relation between the school journey and social and emotional adjustment in rural infant children, *British Journal of Educational Psychology*, **27**, 100–114.

Lee, T. R. (1968). Urban neighbourhood as socio-spatial schema, *Human Relations*, **21**, 241–267.

Lee, T. R. (1970). Perceived distance as a function of direction in the city, *Environment and Behavior*, **2**, 40–51.

Lee, T. R. (1976a). *Psychology and the Environment*, Methuen, London.

Lee, T. R. (1976b). Cities in the mind. In D. T. Herbert and R. J. Johnston (eds), *Social Areas in Cities: Spatial Perspectives on Problems and Policies*. John Wiley, Chichester.

Leiser, D. (1987). The changing relations of representation and cognitive structure during the development of a cognitive map, *New Ideas in Psychology*, **5**, 95–110.

Lepecq, J. C. (1984). Young children's spatial localization after moving, *International Journal of Behavioural Development*, **7**, 375–393.

Levine, M. (1982). You-are-here maps: psychological considerations, *Environment and Behavior*, **14**, 221–237.

Levine, M., Marchon, I., and Hanley, G. (1984). The placement and misplacement of you-are-here maps, *Environment and Behavior*, **16**, 139–157.

Lewis, D. (1976). Route-finding and spatial orientation among aboriginals of Australia, *Oceania*, **46**, 249–289.

Lewis, G. M. (1966). William Gilpin and the concept of the Great Plains Region, *Annals of the Association of American Geographers*, **56**, 33–51.

Lewis, G. M. (1967). The Great Plains Region and its image of flatness, *Journal of the West*, **6**, 11–26.

Leyhausen, P. (1965). The communal organization of solitary mammals, *Symposium of the Zoological Society of London*, **14**, 249–263.

Liben, L. S. (1981). Spatial representation and behavior: multiple perspectives. In L. S. Liben, A. M. Patterson and N. Newcombe (eds), *Spatial Representation and Behavior Across the Life Span*. Academic Press, New York.

Liben, L. S. (1982). Children's large-scale spatial cognition: is the measure the message? In R. Cohen (ed.), *New Directions for Child Development: Children's Conceptions of Spatial Relationships*, No. 15. Jossey-Bass, San Francisco.

Liben, L. S., and Golbeck, S. L. (1984). Performance on Piagetian horizontality and verticality tasks: sex-related differences in knowledge of relevant physical phenomena, *Developmental Psychology*, **20**, 595–606.

Liben, L. S., and Golbeck, S. L. (1986). Adults' demonstration of underlying Euclidean concepts in relation to task contest, *Developmental Psychology*, **22**, 487–490.

Liben, L. S., Moore, M. L., and Golbeck, S. L. (1982). Preschoolers' knowledge of their classroom environment: evidence from small-scale and life-size spatial tasks, *Child Development*, **53**, 1275–1284.

Lindberg, E., and Gärling, T. (1981). Acquisition of locational information about reference points during locomotion with and without a concurrent task: effects of number of reference points, *Scandinavian Journal of Psychology*, **22**, 109–115.

Lindberg, E., and Gärling, T. (1982). Acquisition of locational information about reference points during locomotion: the role of central information processing, *Scandinavian Journal of Psychology*, **23**, 207–218.

Linn, M. C., and Petersen, A. C. (1985). Emergence and characterization of sex differences in spatial ability: a meta-analysis, *Child Development*, **56**, 1479–1498.

Little, B. R. (1980). The social ecology of children's nothings, *Ekistics*, **47**, 93–95.

Llewellyn, K. R. (1971). Visual guidance of locomotion, *Journal of Experimental Psychology*, **91**, 245–261.

Lockman, J. J. (1984). The development of detour ability during infancy, *Child Development*, **55**, 482–491.

Lockman, J. J., Hazen, N., and Pick, H. L. (1976). Development of mental representations of spatial layouts. Paper presented at American Psychological Association Meeting, Washington DC, September 1976.

Lockman, J. J., and Pick, H. L. (1984). Problems of scale in spatial development. In C. Sophian (ed.), *Origins of Cognitive Skills*. Lawrence Erlbaum, New York.

Lockman, J. J., Rieser, J. J., and Pick, H. L. (1981). Assessing blind travellers' knowledge of spatial layout, *Journal of Visual Impairment and Blindness*, **October**, 321–326.

Loo, C., and Kennelly, D. (1979). Social density: its effects on behaviors and perceptions of preschoolers, *Environmental Psychology and Non-verbal Behavior*, **3**, 131–146.

Loo, C., and Ong, P. (1984). Crowding perceptions, attitudes and consequences among the Chinese, *Environment and Behavior*, **16**, 55–87.

Loo, C., and Smetana, J. (1978). The effects of crowding on the behavior and perception of 10-year-old boys, *Environmental Psychology and Nonverbal Behavior*, **2**, 226–249.

Lord, F. E. (1941). A study of spatial orientation of children, *Journal of Educational Research*, **34**, 481–505.

Lowenfield, B. (1948). Effects of blindness on the cognitive functions of children, *Nervous Child*, **7**, 45–54.

Lowenthal, D. (1985). *The Past is a Foreign Country*. Cambridge University Press, Cambridge.

Lukashok, A., and Lynch, K. (1956). Some childhood memories of the city, *Journal of the American Institute of Planners*, **22**, 142–152.

Lynch, K. (1960). *The Image of the City*. MIT Press, Cambridge, MA.

Lynch, K. (1977). *Growing up in Cities: Studies of the Spatial Environment of Adolescence in Cracow, Melbourne, Mexico City, Salta, Toluca and Warszawa*. MIT Press, Cambridge, MA.

McCalla, G. I., and Reid, L. (1982). Plan creation, plan execution and knowledge acquisition in a dynamic microworld, *International Journal of Man-Machine Studies*, **16**, 89–112.

McClurg, P. A., and Chaillé, C. (1987). Computer games: environments for developing spatial cognition? *Journal of Educational Computing Research*, **3**, 95–111.

McComas, J., and Field, J. (1984). Does early crawling experience affect infants' emerging spatial abilities? *New Zealand Journal of Psychology*, **13**, 63–68.

McDermott, D., and Davis, E. (1984). Planning routes through uncertain territory, *Artificial Intelligence*, **22**, 107–156.

McFarlane, M. (1925). A study of practical ability, *British Journal of Psychology Monograph Supplement*, No. 8.

McGee, M. G. (1979). Human spatial abilities: psychometric studies and environmental, genetic, hormonal and neurological influences, *Psychological Bulletin*, **86**, 889–918.

McKechnie, G. E. (1977a). The environmental response inventory in application, *Environment and Behavior*, **9**, 225–276.

McKechnie, G. E. (1977b). Simulation techniques in environmental psychology. In D. Stokols (ed.), *Perspectives on Environment and Behavior*. Plenum Press, New York.

McKenna, A. (1979). Psychology and preschool education, *The Irish Journal of Psychology*, **2**, 131–140.

McKinney, J. P. (1964). Hand schema in children, *Psychonomic Science*, **1**, 99–100.

McKinnon, J. (1978). *The Ape Within Us*, Collins, London.

McNamara, T. P. (1986). Mental representations of spatial relations, *Cognitive Psychology*, **18**, 87–121.

McReynolds, J., and Worchel, P. (1954). Geographic orientation in the blind, *Journal of Genetic Psychology*, **51**, 221–236.

Maccoby, E. E., and Jacklin, C. (1974). *The Psychology of Sex Differences*. Stanford University Press, Stanford, CA.

Magnusson, M., and Palsson, H. (translators) (1965). *The Vinland Sagas: Graenlendinga Saga and Eirik's Saga*. Penguin, Harmondsworth.

Maier, N. R. F. (1936). Reasoning in children, *Journal of Comparative Psychology*, **21**, 357–366.

Maistre, G. (1970). Propositions pour une geographie des communications de masse, *Cahiers de Geographie de Quebec*, **33**, 295–308.

Marcus, C. C. (1974). Children's play behavior in a low-rise inner city housing development. In D. H. Carson (ed.), *Man-environment Interactions: Evaluation and Applications*, Vol. 12. *Childhood City*. EDRA, Milwaukee, WI.

Marjoribanks, K., Secombe, M., and Smolicz, J. J. (1985). Cognitive maps of class and ethnic inequalities: a comparative analysis, *International Journal of Comparative Sociology*, **26**, 100–108.

Marmor, G. S. (1978). Age at onset of blindness and the development of semantics in colour names, *Journal of Experimental Child Psychology*, **25**, 267–278.

Marmor, G. S., and Zaback, L. A. (1976). Mental rotation by the blind: does mental rotation depend upon visual imagery? *Journal of Experimental Psychology: Human Perception and Performance*, **3**, 515–521.

Marr, D. (1982). *Vision*. W. H. Freeman, San Francisco.

Marr, D., and Nishihara, H. K. (1978). Representation and recognition of the spatial organization of three dimensional shapes, *Proceedings of the Royal Society of London*, **200**, 269–294.

Marsden, W. E. (1976). *Evaluating the Geography Curriculum*, Oliver & Boyd, Edinburgh.

Marsh, P., Rosser, E., and Harré, R. (1978), *The Rules of Disorder*. Routledge & Kegan Paul, London.

Martenuik, R. G. (1978). The role of eye and head positions in slow movement execution. In G. E. Stalmach (ed.), *Information Processing Motor Control and Learning*. Academic Press, New York.

Martin, J. L. (1976a). An analysis of some of Piaget's topological tasks from a mathematical point of view, *Journal for Research in Mathematics Education*, **7**, 8–24.

Martin, J. L. (1976b). A test with selected topological properties of Piaget's hypothesis concerning the spatial representation of the young child, *Journal for Research in Mathematics Education*, **7**, 26–38.

Mastropieri, M. A., and Scruggs, T. E. (1983). Maps as schema for gifted learners, *Roeper Review*, **12**, 107–111.

Matthews, M. H. (1984a). Cognitive maps: a comparison of graphic and iconic techniques, *Area*, **16**, 33–40.

Matthews, M. H. (1984b). Cognitive mapping abilities of young boys and girls, *Geography*, **69**, 327–336.

Matthews, M. H. (1984c). Environmental cognition of young children: images of journey to school and home area, *Transactions of the Institute of British Geographers*, **9**, 89–105.

Matthews, M. H. (1987). The influence of gender on the environmental cognition of young boys and girls, *Journal of Genetic Psychology*, **147**, 295–302.

Maurer, R., and Baxter, J. C. (1972). Images of the neighbourhood and city among Black-, and Anglo- and Mexican-American children, *Environment and Behavior*, **4**, 351–388.

Mayes, T. J., Jahoda, G., and Neilson, I. (1988). Patterns of visual–spatial performance and 'spatial ability': dissociation of ethnic and sex differences, *British Journal of Psychology*, **79**, 105–120.

Mays, P. (1985). *Teaching Children Through the Environment*. Hodder & Stoughton, Kent.

Meehan, A. M., and Overton, W. F. (1986). Gender differences in expectancies for success and performance in Piagetian spatial tasks, *Merrill-Palmer Quarterly*, **32**, 427–441.

Menzel, E. W. (1973). Chimpanzee spatial memory organization, *Science*, **182**, 943–945.

Menzel, E. W., Premack, D., and Woodruff, G. (1978). Map reading by chimpanzees, *Folia Primatologia*, **29**, 241–249.

Mercer, D. (1971). The role of perception in the recreation experience: a review and discussion, *Journal of Leisure Research*, **3**, 261–276.

Merry, R. V., and Merry, F. K. (1934). The finger maze as a supplementary test of intelligence for blind children, *Journal of Genetic Psychology*, **44**, 227–230.

Michelson, W., and Michelson, E. (1980). Managing urban space in the interest of children: dimensions of the task, *Eikistics*, **47**, 88–92.

Milgram, S. (1970). The experience of living cities, *Science*, **167**, 1461–1468.

Millar, S. (1971). Visual and haptic cue utilization by pre-school children: the recognition of visual and haptic stimuli presented separately and together, *Journal of Experimental Child Psychology*, **12**, 88–94.

Millar, S. (1975). Spatial memory by blind and sighted children, *British Journal of Psychology*, **66**, 449–459.

Millar, S. (1976). Spatial representation by blind and sighted children, *Journal of Experimental Child Psychology*, **21**, 460–479.

Millar, S. (1979). The utilization of external and movement cues in simple spatial tasks by blind and sighted children, *Perception*, **8**, 11–20.

Millar, S. (1981a). Crossmodal and intersensory perception and the blind. In R. D. Walk and H. L. Pick (eds.), *Intersensory Perception and Sensory Integration*, Academic Press, New York.

Millar, S. (1981b). Self reference and movement cues in coding spatial location in blind and sighted children, *Perception*, **10**, 255–264.

Millar, S. (1985). Movement cues and body orientation in recall of locations by blind and sighted children, *Quarterly Journal of Experimental Psychology, Series A*, **37**, 257–280.

Miller, J. W. (1974). Comparisons of conventional 'subdued' to vivid 'highly contrasting' colour schemes for elementary school maps: report of an experiment, *Journal of Geography*, **73**, 41–45.

Mills, A. W. (1972). Auditory localization. In J. V. Tobias (ed.), *Foundations of Modern Auditory Theory*, pp. 301–348. Academic Press, New York.

Mills, D. (ed.) (1981).(2nd Edn 1986). *Geographical Work in Primary and Middle Schools*. Geographical Association, Sheffield.

Mills, R. J. (1970). Orientation and mobility for teachers, *Education of the Visually Handicapped*, **2**, 80–82.

Minnegerode, F. A., and Carey, R. N. (1974). Development of mechanisms underlying spatial perspectives, *Child Development*, **45**, 496–498.

Mitchell, L. S. (1934). *Young Geographers: How They Explore the World and How They Map the World*, Bank Street College of Education, New York (republished by Basic Books, New York, 1971).

Moar, I., and Bower, G. H. (1983). Inconsistency in spatial knowledge, *Memory and Cognition*, **11**, 107–113.

Moar, I., and Carleton, L. (1982). Memory for routes, *Quarterly Journal of Experimental Psychology*, **34**, 381–394.

Mohr, D., Kucjaz, S., and Pick, H. L. (1975). Development of cognitive mapping capacities. Paper presented at Society for Research in Child Development meeting, Denver, CO.

Monroe, R. H., Monroe, R. L., and Brasher, A. (1985). Precursors of spatial ability: a longitudinal study among the Logoli of Kenay, *Journal of Social Psychology*, **125** 23–33.

Moore, G. T. (1979). Knowing about environmental knowing: the current state of theory and research on environmental cognition, *Environment and Behavior*, **11**, 33–70.

Moore, R. (1986). *Childhood's Domain*. Croom Helm, London.

Moore, R., and Young, D. (1978). Children outdoors: toward a social ecology of the landscape. In I. Altman and J. F. Wohlwill (eds), *Children and the Environment* Plenum Press, New York.

Moos, R. H. (1976). *The Human Context: Environmental Determinants of Behavior* John Wiley, New York.

Money, J., Alexander, D., and Walker, H. T. (1965). *A Standardized Test of Direction Sense*. Johns Hopkins University Press, Baltimore, MD.

Morgan, D. L., and Alwin, D. F. (1980). When less is more: school size and student participation, *Social Psychology Quarterly*, **43**, 241–252.

Muehrke, P. C. (1978). *Map Use, Reading, Analysis and Interpretation*. JP Publications, Madison, Wisconsin.

Muir, M. E., and Blaut, J. M. (1969). The use of aerial photographs in teaching mapping to children in the first grade: an experimental study. In D. Stea (ed.), *Place Perception Research Reports 2*. Graduate School of Geography, Worcester, MA.

Muller, J-C. (1982). Non-Euclidean geographic spaces: mapping functional distances, *Geographical Analaysis*, **14**, 189–203.

Munroe, R. H., Munroe, R. L., and Brasher, A. (1985). Precursors of spatial ability: a longitudinal study among the Logoli of Kenya, *Journal of Social Psychology*, **125**, 23–33.

Munroe, R. L., and Munroe, R. H. (1971). Effect of environmental experience on spatial ability in an East African society, *Journal of Social Psychology*, **83**, 15–22.

Murray, D., and Spencer, C. P. (1979). Individual differences in the drawing of cognitive maps: the effects of geographical mobility, strength of mental imagery, and basic graphic ability, *Transactions, Institute of British Geographers*, **4**, 385–391.

Myers, N. (ed.) (1985). *The Gaia Atlas of Planet Management for Today's Caretakers of Tomorrow's Word*. Pan Books, London.

Myers, S. O., and Jones, C. G. (1958). Obstacle experiments: second report, *Teacher of the Blind*, **46**, 47–62.

Nadel, L., Willner, J., and Kurz, E. M. (1985). Cognitive maps and environmental context. In P. D. Balsam and A. Tomie (eds), *Context and Learning*. Lawrence Erlbaum, Hillsdale, NJ.

Nagy, J. N., and Baird, J. C. (1978). Children as environmental planners. In I. Altman and J. F. Wohlwill (eds), *Children and the Environment*. Plenum Press, New York.

Neisser, U.(1976). *Cognition and Reality: Principles and Implications of Cognitive Psychology*. W. H. Freeman, San Francisco.

Neisser, U., and Kerr, N. (1973). Spatial mnemonic properties of visual images, *Cognitive Psychology*, **5**, 138–150.

Newcombe, N. (1982). Development of spatial cognition and cognitive development. In R. Cohen (ed.), *New Directions for Child Development: Children's Conceptions of Spatial Relationships*, No/ 15. Jossey-Bass, San Francisco.

Newcombe, N., Bandura, M. M., and Taylor, D. G. (1983). Sex differences in spatial ability and spatial activities, *Sex Roles*, **9**, 377–386.

Newman, O. (1972). *Defensible Space*. Architectural Press, London.

Newman, O., and Franck, K. A. (1982). The effects of building size on personal crime and fear of crime, *Population and Environment*, **5**, 203–220.

Nirje, B. (1970). The normalization principle: implications and comments, *British Journal of Mental Subnormality*, **31**, 62–70.

Norburg-Schulz, C. (1980). *Genius Loci: Towards a Phenomenology of Architecture*. Rizzoli, New York.

Nordenstreng, K. (1972). Policy for news transmission. In D. McQuail (ed.), *Sociology of Mass Communications*. Penguin, Harmondsworth.

Noschis, K. (1982). The child in the laboratory: not just conforming to prompts. In J. C. Baird and A. D. Lutkins (eds), *Mind, Child Architecture*. University Press of New England, Hanover, NH.

Nyborg, H. (1983). Spatial ability in men and women: review and new theory, *Advances in Behaviour Research and Therapy*, **5**, 89–140.

O'Connor, N., and Hermelin, B. (1972). Seeing and hearing in space and time: problems by blind and sighted children, *British Journal of Psychology*, **63**, 381–386.

O'Connor, N., and Hermelin, B. (1978). *Seeing and Hearing in Space and Time*. Academic Press, New York.

O'Connor, N., and Hermelin, B. (1983). Coding strategies in normal and handicapped children. In R. D. Walk and H. L. Pick (eds), *Intersensory Perception and Sensory Integration*. Academic Press, New York.

Okabe, A., Aoki, K., and Hamamoto, W. (1986). Distance and direction judgement in a large-scale natural environment: effects of a slope and winding trail, *Environment and Behavior*, **18**, 755–772.

O'Keefe, J. (1985). Is consciousness the gateway to the hippocampal cognitive map? A speculative essay on the neural basis of mind. In K. Oakley (ed.), *Brain and Mind*. Methuen, London.

O'Keefe, J., and Nadel, L. (1978). *The Hippocampus as a Cognitive Map*. Clarendon Press, Oxford.

O'Keefe, J., and Nadel, L. (1979). Precis of 'The Hippocampus as a Cognitive Map', and author's reply to commentaries on the same, *The Behavioral and Brain Sciences*, **2**, 487–534.

Olivegren, J. (1974). A better sociopsychological climate in our housing estates. In D. Canter and T. Lee (eds), *Psychology and the Built Environment*. Architectural Press, London.

Olson, D. M., and Eliot, J. (1986). Relationships between experiences, processing style, and sex-related differences in performance on spatial tests, *Perceptual and Motor Skills*, **62**, 447–460.

Olton, D. S. (1979). Mazes, maps and memory, *American Psychologist*, 34, 583–596.

Orleans, P. A. (1973). Differential cognition of urban residents: effects of social scale on mapping. In R. M. Downs and D. Stea (eds), *Image and Environment*. Irvine, New York.

Orzek, A. M. (1987). Innovations in ecological psychology: conversations with Roger and Louise Barker, *Journal of Counseling and Development*, **65**, 233–237.

Ottosson, T. (1987). Map reading and wayfinding, *Goteburg Studies in Educational Sciences*, **65** (whole volume).

Paivio, A. (1971). *Imagery and Verbal Processes*. Holt, Reinhart, & Winston, New York.

Paivio, A., and Okovita, H. W. (1971). Word imagery modalities and associative learning in blind and sighted subjects, *Journal of Verbal Learning and Verbal Behaviour*, **10**, 506–510.

Palij, M., Levine, M., and Kahan, T. (1984). The orientation of cognitive maps, *Bulletin of the Psychonomic Society*, **22**, 105–108.

Palisi, B. J., and Canning, C. (1986). Urbanism and social psychological well-being: a test of three theories, *Sociological Spectrum*, **6**, 361–371.

Papert, S. (1980). *Mindstorms: Children, Computers and Powerful Ideas*. Harvester, Brighton.

Parke, R. D. (1978). Children's home environments: social and cognitive effects. In I. Altman and J. F. Wohlwill (eds), *Children and the Environment*. Plenum Press, New York.

Parke, R. D., and Sarvin, D. B. (1979). Children's privacy in the home: developmental, ecological and childrearing determinants, *Environment and Behavior*, **11**, 87–104.

Passini, R. (1984). *Wayfinding in Architecture*. Van Nostrand Rheinhold, New York.

Pearce, P. (1982). *The Social Psychology of Tourist Behaviour*. Pergamon Press, Oxford.

Pearson, J. L., and Ialongo, N. S. (1986). The relationship between spatial ability and environmental knowledge, *Journal of Environmental Psychology*, **6**, 299–304.

Perner, J., Kohlmann, R., and Wimmer, H. (1984). Young children's recognition and use of the vertical and horizontal in drawings, *Child Development*, **55**, 1637–1645.

Peterson, A. C. (1976). Cognitive functioning in adolescence, *Developmental Psychology*, **12**, 524–533.

Pezdek, K., and Evans, G. W. (1979). Visual and verbal memory for objects and their spatial relations, *Journal of Experimental Psychology: Human Learning and Memory*, **5**, 360–373.

Piaget, J. (1928). *Judgement and Reasoning in the Child*. Kegan Paul, London.

Piaget, J. (1929). *The Child's Conception of the World*. Kegan Paul, London.

Piaget, J. (1930). *The Child's Conception of Physical Causality*. Kegan Paul, London.

Piaget, J., and Inhelder, B. (1956). *The Child's Conception of Space*. Routledge & Kegan Paul, London.

Piaget, J., Inhelder, B., and Szeminska, A. (1960). *The Child's Conception of Geometry*. Routledge & Kegan Paul, London.

Piché, D. (1981). The spontaneous geography of the urban child. In D. T. Herbert and R. J. Johnson (eds), *Geography and the Urban Environment: Progress in Research and Applications*, Vol. 4. John Wiley, Chichester.

Pick, H. L. (1972). Mapping children—mapping space. Paper presented at American Psychological Association Meeting, Honolulu, HI.

Pick, H. L. (1974). Visual coding of non-visual spatial information. In McLeod and Pick (eds.), *Perception: Essays in Honour of J. J. Gibson*. Cornell University Press, Ithaca, NY.

Pick, H. L., and Acredolo, L. P. (eds) (1983). *Spatial Orientation: Theory, Research and Application*. Plenum Press, New York.

Pick, H. L., Klein, R. E., and Pick, A. D. (1966). Visual and tactual identification of form orientation, *Journal of Experimental Child Psychology*, **4**, 391–397.

Pick, H. L., and Lockman, J. J. (1981). From frames of reference to spatial representations. In L. S. Liben, A. H. Patterson and N. Newcombe (eds), *Spatial Representation and Behavior Across the Life Span*. Academic Press, New York.

Pick, H. L., Yonas, A., and Rieser, J. (1976). Spatial reference systems in perceptual development. In M. H. Bonstein and W. Kesson (eds), *Psychological Development from Infancy: Image to Intention*. Lawrence Erlbaum, Hillsdale, NJ.

Poag, C. K., Cohen, R., and Weatherford, D. L. (1983). Spatial representations of young children: the role of self- versus adult-directed movement and viewing, *Journal of Experimental Child Psychology*, **35**, 172–179.

Pocock, D. C. D. (1976). Some characteristics of mental maps: an empirical study, *Transactions of the Institute of British Geographers*, **1**, 493–512.

Pocock, D. C. D. (1979). The contribution of mental maps in perception studies, *Geography*, **64**, 279–287.

Porteous, J. D. (1985). Smellscape, *Progress in Human Geography*, 9, 356–378.

Porteous, J. D. (1986). Bodyscape: the body-landscape metaphor, *The Canadian Geographer*, **30**, 2–12.

Potter, R. B., and Wilson, M. G. (1983). Age differences in the content and style of cognitive maps of Barbadian schoolchildren, *Perceptual and Motor Skills*, **57**, 332.

Presson, C. C. (1982). The development of map reading skills, *Child Development*, **53**, 196–199.

Presson, C. C., and Hazelrigg, M. D. (1984). Building spatial representations through primary and secondary learning, *Journal of Experimental Psychology: Learning, Memory and Cognition*, **10**, 716–722.

Presson, C. C., and Ihrig, L. H. (1982). Using mother as a spatial landmark: evidence against egocentric coding in infancy, *Developmental Psychology*, **18**, 699–702.

Presson, C. C., and Somerville, S. C. (1985). Beyond egocentrism: a new look at the beginnings of spatial representation. In Wellman, H. M. (ed.), *Children's Searching: The Development of Search Skill and Spatial Representation*. Lawrence Erlbaum, Hillsdale, NJ.

Prior, F. M. (1959). The place of maps in the junior school. Unpublished manuscript cited in N. Graves (ed.), *New Movements in the Study and Teaching of Geography*. Temple-Smith, London.

Proshansky, H. M. (1978). The city and self identity, *Environment and Behavior*, **10**, 147–169.

Psathas, G., and Henslin, J. M. (1967). Dispatched orders and the cab driver: a study of locating activities, *Social Problems*, **14**, 424–443.

Psathas, G., and Kozloff, M. (1976). The structure of directions, *Semiotica*, **17**, 111–130.

Pufall, P., and Shaw, R. (1973). Analysis of the development of children's spatial reference systems, *Cognitive Psychology*, **5**, 151–175.

Purcell, A. T. (1987). Landscape perception, preference and schema discrepancy, *Environment and Planning B: Planning and Design*, **14**, 67–92.

Pushkarev, B. S., and Zupan, J. M. (1975). *Urban Space for Pedestrians*. MIT Press, Cambridge, MA.

Rawling, E. (ed.) (1980). *Geography into the 1980's*. The Geographical Association, Sheffield.

Reeve, R. A., Campione, J. C., and Brown, A. L. (1986). Remembering the right locations: factors affecting young children's logical search ability, *Cognitive Development*, **1**, 239–251.

Relf, G. T., and Barrington Brown, C. (1986). *The Forest: An Orienteering Simulation Program*. Cunning Running Software, Amesbury, Wilts.

Relph, E. C. (1976). *Place and Placelessness*. Pion Press, London.

Revesz, G. (1950). *Psychology and the Art of the Blind*, Longmans Green, New York.

Rice, C. E. (1967). Human echo perception, *Science*, **155**, 656–664.

Rice, C. E., and Feinstein, S. H. (1965). Echo detection ability of the blind: size and distance factors, *Journal of Experimental Psychology*, **70**, 246–251.

Richardson, S. A. (1981). Living environments: an ecological perspective. In H. C. Haywood and J. R. Newbrough (eds), *Living Environments for Developmentally Retarded Persons*. University Park Press, Baltimore.

Riesbeck, C. K. (1980). 'You can't miss it!': Judging the clarity of directions, *Cognitive Science*, **4**, 285–303.

Rieser, J. J. (1979). Spatial orientation of six-month-old infants, *Child Development*, **50**, 1078–1087.

Rieser, J. J. (1983). The generation and early development of spatial inferences. In H. L. Pick and L. C. Acredolo (eds), *Spatial Orientation in Natural and Experimental Settings*. Plenum Press, New York.

Rieser, J. J., Doxey, P. A., McCarrell, N. S., and Brooks, P. H. (1982). Wayfinding and toddlers' use of information from an aerial view of a maze, *Developmental Psychology*, **18**, 714–720.

Rieser, J. J., Guth, D. A., and Hill, E. W. (1982). Mental processes mediating independent travel: implications for orientation and mobility, *Journal of Visual Impairment and Blindness*, June, 213–218.

Rieser, J. J., Guth, D. A., and Hill, E. W. (1986). Sensitivity to perspective structure while walking without vision, *Perception*, **15**, 173–188.

Rieser, J. J., and Heiman, M. L. (1982). Spatial self-reference systems and shortest-route behavior in toddlers, *Child Development*, **53**, 524–533.

Rieser, J. J., Lockman, J. J., and Pick, H. L. (1980). The role of visual experience in knowledge of spatial layout, *Perception and Psychophysics*, **28**, 185–190.

Rieser, J. J., and Pick, H. L. (1976). Reference systems and the perception of tactual and haptic orientation, *Perception and Psychophysics*, **19**, 117–121.

Riffle, P. A. (1969). A new approach to teaching map reading, *Educational Research*, **16**, 63–66.

Riley, R. R. (1979). Reflections on the landscape of memory, *Landscape*, **23**, 11–18.

Robinson, A., and Robinson, M. E. (1981). Mental mapping and the coordination of perspectives in young children, *Research in Education*, **30**, 39–51.

Robinson, A. H., and Petchenik, B. B. (1976). *The Nature of Maps*, University of Chicago Press, Chicago.

Rock, I. (1973). *Orientation and Form*, Academic Press, New York.

Rogoff, B. (1982). Integrating context and cognitive development. In M. E. Lamb and A. L. Brown (eds), *Advances in Developmental Psychology*, Vol. 2. Lawrence Erlbaum, Hillsdale, NJ.

Rogoff, B. (1986). The development of strategic use of context in spatial memory. In M. Perlmutter (ed.), *Perspectives on Intellectual Development*. Lawrence Erlbaum, Hillsdale, NJ.

Rogoff, B., and Waddell, K. J. (1982). Memory for information organized in a scene by children from two cultures, *Child Development*, **53**, 1224–1228.

Rosencrantz, D., and Suslick, R. (1976). Cognitive models for spatial representations in congenitally blind, adventitiously blind and sighted subjects, *The New Outlook*, May, 188–194.

Russell, J. A., and Pratt, G. (1980). A description of the affective quality attributed to environments, *Journal of Personality and Social Psychology*, **38**, 311–322.

Russell, J. A., and Ward, L. M. (1982). Environmental psychology, *Annual Review of Psychology*, **33**, 651–688.

Saarinen, T. F., and Sell, J. L. (1980). Environmental perception, *Progress in Human Geography*, **4**, 525–547.

Saarinen, T. F., Sell, J. L., and Husband, E. (1982). Environmental perception: international efforts, *Progress in Human Geography*, **6**, 515–546.

Sadalla, E. K., and Magel, S. G. (1980). The perception of traversed distance, *Environment and Behavior*, **12**, 65–79.

Sadalla, E. K., and Staplin, L. J. (1980a). The perception of traversed distance: intersections, *Environment and Behavior*, **12**, 167–182.

Sadalla, E. K., and Staplin, L. J. (1980b). An information storage model for distance cognition, *Environment and Behavior*, **12**, 183–193.

Saisa, J., and Gärling, T. (1987). Sequential spatial choices in the large-scale environment, *Environment and Behavior*, **19**, 614–635.

Salisbury, H. E. (1985). *The Long March*. Harper & Row, New York.

Sandels, S. (1975). *Children in Traffic*. Elek, London.

Sandhu, J., Richardson, S., and Townsend, R. (1987). *Directory of Non-Medical Research Relating to Handicapped People*, Vol. 4. Handicapped Persons Research Unit, Newcastle Polytechnic, Newcastle.

Satterley, D. J. (1964). Skills and concepts involved in map drawing and map interpretation, *New Era*, **45**, 263.

Schlaegel, T. F. (1953). The dominant method of imagery in blind as compared with sighted adolescents, *Journal of Genetic Psychology*, **83**, 265–277.

Schoggen, P. (1983). Behavior settings and the quality of life, *Journal of Community Psychology*, **11**, 144–157.

Schools Council Geography Committee (1979). *Understanding Maps: A Guide to Initial Learning*. Schools Council, London.

Schouela, D. A., Steinberg, L. M., Leveton, L. B., and Wapner, S. (1980). Development of the cognitive organization of an environment, *Canadian Journal of Behavioural Science*, **12**, 1–16.

Sebba, R., and Churchman, A. (1983). Territories and territoriality in the home, *Environment and Behavior*, **15**, 191–210.

Segall, M. H., Campbell, D. T., and Herskovitz, M. (1966). *The Influence of Culture on Visual Perception*. Bobbs-Merrill, Indianapolis.

Sharp, K. C. (1982). Perschoolers' understanding of temporal and causal relations, *Merrill-Palmer Quarterly*, **28**, 427–436.

Shatz, M., and Gelman, R. (1973). The development of communication skills: modifications in the speech of young children as a function of listener, *Monographs of the Society for Research in Child Development*, 38, Serial No 152.

Sherman, J. A. (1967). The problem of sex differences in space perception and aspects of individual functioning, *Psychological Review*, **74**, 290–299.

Sholl, M. J. (1987). Cognitive maps as orienting schema, *Journal of Experimental Psychology: Learning, Memory and Cognition*, **13**, 615–628.

Siegal, A. W. (1981). The externalization of cognitive maps by children and adults: in search of ways to ask better questions. In L. S. Liben, A. H. Patterson and N. Newcombe (eds), *Spatial Representation and Behavior Across the Life Span*. Academic Press, New York.

Siegal, A. W. (1982). Toward a social ecology of cognitive mapping. In R. Cohen (ed.), *New Directions in Child Development: Children's Conceptions of Spatial Relationships*, No. 15. Jossey-Bass, San Francisco.

Siegal, A. W., Allen, G. L., and Kirasic, K. C. (1979). The development of cognitive maps of large- and small-scale open spaces, *Child Development*, **50**, 582–585.

Siegal, A. W., and Cousins, J. H. (1983). The symbolizing and symbolized child in the enterprise of cognitive mapping. In R. Cohen (ed.), *The Development of Spatial Cognition*. Lawrence Erlbaum, Hillsdale, NJ.

Siegal, A. W., Kirasic, K. C., and Kail, R. V. (1978). Stalking the elusive cognitive map: the development of children's representation of space. In I. Altman and J. F. Wohlwill (ed.), *Children and the Environment*. Plenum Press, New York.

Siegal, A. W., and Schadler, M. (1977). Young children's cognitive maps of their classroom, *Child Development*, **48**, 388–394.

Siegal, A. W., and White, S. (1975). The development of spatial representations of large-scale environments. In H. W. Reese (ed.), *Advances in Child Development and Behavior*, Vol. 10. Academic Press, New York.

Siegal, I. M., and Murphy, T. J. (1970). Postural determinants in the blind. Final Project Report, Grant RD-3512-SB-700CZ. Cited in D. H. Warren, (1984). *Blindness and Early Childhood Development*. American Foundation for the Blind, New York.

Sime, J. D. (1988). *Safey in the Built Environment*. Spon, London.

Simpkins, K. E., and Siegal, A. J. (1979). The blind child's construction of the projective straight line, *Journal of Visual Impairment and Blindness*, **73**, 233–238.

Simpson, W. E. (1972). Locating sources of sound. In R. F. Thompason and G. F. Bosse (eds.), *Topics in Learning and Performance*, pp. 17–40. Academic Press, New York.

Sixsmith, J. (1986). The meaning of home: an exploratory study of environmental experience, *Journal of Environmental Psychology*, **6**, 281–298.

Smith, G. C., Shaw, D. J. B., and Huckle, P. R. (1979). Children's perception of a downtown shopping centre, *The Professional Geographer*, **31**, 157–164.

Smith, I. M. (1964). *Spatial Ability: Its Educational and Social Significance*. University of London Press, London.

Smith, L. B., Cooney, N. J., and McCord, C. (1986). What is 'high'? The development of reference points for 'high' and 'low', *Child Development*, **57**, 583–602.

Smith, P. K. (1982). Does play matter? Funcational and evolutionary aspects of animal and human play, *The Behavioural and Brain Sciences*, **5**, 139–184.

Smith, P. K., and Connolly, K. J. (1976). Social and aggressive behaviour in preschool children as a function of crowding, *Social Science Information*, **16**, 601–620.

Smith, P. K., and Connolly, K. J. (1980). *The Ecology of Preschool Behaviour*. Cambridge University Press, Cambridge.

Smith, P. K., and Dutton, S. (1979). Play and training in direct and innovative problem solving, *Child Development*, **50**, 830–836.

Smith, R. F. (1984). Artificial intelligence and its applicability to geographical problem solving, *The Professional Geographer*, **36**, 147–158.

Smith, R. P. (1957). *'Where Did You Go?' 'Out' 'What Did You Do?' 'Nothing'*. Norton, New York.

Smith, T. R., Clark, W. A. V., and Cotton, J. W. (1984). Deriving and testing production system models of sequential decision making behaviour, *Geographical Analysis*, **16**, 191–222.

Smith, T. R., Pellegrino, J. W., and Golledge, R. G. (1982). Computational process modeling of spatial cognition and behaviour, *Geographical Analysis*, **14**, 304–325.

Snyder, S. S., and Feldman, D. H. (1984). Phases of transition in cognitive development: evidence from the domain of spatial representation, *Child Development*, **55**, 981–989.

Somerville, S. C., and Bryant, P. E. (1985). Young children's use of spatial coordinates, *Child Development*, **56**, 604–613.

Somerville, S. C., and Capuani-Shumaker, A. (1984). Logical search of young children in hiding and finding tasks, *British Journal of Developmental Psychology*, **2**, 315–328.

Somerville, S. C., and Haake, R. J. (1985). The logical search skills of infants and young children. In H. M. Wellman (ed.), *Children's Searching: The Development of Search Skill and Spatial Representation*. Lawrence Erlbaum, Hillsdale, NJ.

Sommer, R. (1969). *Personal Space*. Prentice Hall, Englewood Cliffs, NJ.

Sophian, C. (1984). Developing search skills in infancy and early childhood. In C. Sophian (ed.), *Origins of Cognitive Skills*. Lawrence Erlbaum, Hillsdale, NJ.

Sophian, C. (1985). Perseveration and infants' search: a comparison of two- and three-location tasks, *Developmental Psychology*, **21**, 187–194.

Sophian, C. (1986). Early developments in children's spatial monitoring, *Cognition*, **22**, 61–88.

Sophian, C., and Sage, S. (1985). Infants' search for hidden objects: developing skills for using information selectively, *Infant Behavior and Development*, **8**, 1–14.

Spencer, C. P., and Blades, M. (1985). Children at risk: are we underestimating their general competence whilst overestimating their performance? In T. Gärling and J. Valsiner (eds), *Children Within Environments: Toward a Psychology of Accident Prevention*. Plenum Press, New York.

Spencer, C. P. and Blades, M. (1986). Pattern and process: a review essay on the relationships between behavioural geography and environmental psychology, *Progress in Human Geography*, **120**, 230–248.

Spencer, C. P., and Darvizeh, Z. (1981a). The case for developing a cognitive environmental psychology that does not underestimate the abilities of young children, *Journal of Environmental Psychology*, **1**, 21–31.

Spencer, C. P., and Darvizeh, Z. (1981b). Young children's descriptions of their local environment: a comparison of information elicited by recall, recognition and performance techniques of investigation, *Environmental Education and Information*, **1**, 275–284.

Spencer, C. P., and Darvizeh, Z. (1983). Young children's place-descriptions, maps and route-finding: a comparison of nursery school children in Iran and Britain, *International Journal of Early Childhood*, **15**, 26–31.

Spencer, C. P., and Dixon, J. (1983). Mapping the development of feelings about the city: a longitudinal study of new residents' affective maps, *Transactions, Institute of British Geographers*, **8**, 373–383.

Spencer, C. P., and Easterbrook, S. (1985). The streetwise child in geography class, *Children's Environments Quarterly*, **2**, 34–37.

Spencer, C. P., Harrison, N., and Darvizeh, Z. (1980). The development of iconic mapping ability in young children, *International Journal of Early Childhood*, **12**, 57–64.

Spencer, C. P., Mitchell, S., and Wisdom, J. (1984). Evaluating environmental education in nursery and primary schools, *Environmental Education and Information*, **3**, 16–32.

Spencer, C. P., and Travis, J. (1985). Learning a new area with and without the use of tactile maps: a comparative study, *British Journal of Visual Impairment*, **3**, 5–7.

Spencer, C. P., and Weetman, M. (1981). The microgenesis of cognitive maps: a longitudinal study of new residents of an urban area, *Transactions of the Institute of British Geographers*, **6**, 375–384.

Spiegelman, M. N. (1976). A comparative study of the effects of early blindness on the development of auditory-spatial learning. In Z. S. Jastrzembska (ed.), *The Effects of Blindness and Other Impairments on Early Development*. American Foundation for the Blind, New York.

Stankov, L., and Spilsbury, G. (1978). The measurement of auditory abilities of blind and partially sighted children, *Applied Psychological Measurement*, **2**, 491–503.

Stea, D. (1985). From environmental cognition to environmental design, *Children's Environments Quarterly*, **2**, 22–26.

Stea, D., and Blaut, J. M. (1973). Some preliminary observations on spatial learning in school children. In R. M. Downs and D. Stea (eds), *Image and Environment*. Aldine, Chicago.

Steed, V. N. (1984). Getting out in Thomas Street: an urban environmental study with 8–9 year olds in Wigan, *Teaching Geography*, **32**, 151–155.

Stern, D. (1977). *The First Relationship: Infant and Mother*. Collins, London.

Stevens, A., and Coupe, P. (1978). Distortions in judged spatial relations, *Cognitive Psychology*, **10**, 422–437.

Stiles-Davis, J., Sugarman, S., and Nass, R. (1985). The development of spatial and class relations in four young children with right-cerebral-hemisphere damage: evidence for an early spatial constructive deficit, *Brain and Cognition*, **4**, 388–412.

Stillwell, R., and Spencer, C. P. (1974). Children's early preferences for other nations and their subsequent acquisition of knowledge about those nations, *European Journal of Social Psychology*, **3**, 345–349.

Stokols, D. (1972). On the distinction between density and crowding: some implications for future research, *Psychological Review*, **79**, 275–277.

Stokols, D., and Altman, I. (eds) (1987). *Handbook of Environmental Psychology*. John Wiley, New York.

Streeter, L. A., and Vitello, D. (1986). A profile of drivers' map reading abilities, *Human Factors*, **28**, 223–239.

Strelow, E. (1985). What is needed for a theory of mobility: direct perception and cognitive maps, *Psychological Review*, **92**, 226–248.

Strelow, E. R., and Brabyn, J. A. (1982). Use of natural sound cues by the blind to control locomotion, *Perception*, **11**, 635–640.

Stucky, P. E., and Newbrough, J. R. (1981). Mental health of mentally retarded persons: social-ecological considerations. In H. C. Haywood and J. R. Newbrough (eds), *Living Environments for Developmentally Retarded Persons*. University Park Press, Baltimore.

Supa, H., Cotzin, M., and Dallenbach, K. M. (1944). 'Facial vision', the perception of obstacles by the blind, *American Journal of Psychology*, **57**, 133–183.

Sutton, S. E. (1985). *Learning Through the Built Environment: An Ecological Approach to Child Development*. Irvington, New York.

Tajfel, H. (1981). *Human Groups and Social Categories*. Cambridge University Press, Cambridge.

Tajfel, H., and Jahoda, G. (1966). Development in children of concepts and attitudes about their own and other countries. *Proceedings of the 18th International Congress of Psychology*, Moscow.

Tars, S. E., and Appleby, L. (1973). The same child in home and institution: an observational study, *Environment and Behavior*, **5**, 3–28.

Teghtsoonian, M., and Teghtsoonian, R. (1969). Scaling apparent distance in natural indoor settings, *Psychonomic Science*, **61**, 281–283.

Teske, J. A., and Balser, D. P. (1986). Levels of organization in urban navigation, *Journal of Environmental Psychology*, **6**, 305–327.

Thomas, H., Jamieson, W., and Hummel, D. D. (1973). Observation is insufficient for discovering that the surface of still water is invariantly horizontal, *Science*, **181**, 173–174.

Thompson, J. A. (1983). Is continuous visual monitoring necessary in visually guided locomotion? *Journal of Experimental Psychology: Human Perception and Performance*, **3**, 427–443.

Thornberg, J. M. (1973). Child's conception of places to live in. In W. F. E. Preiser (ed.), *Environmental Design Research*, Vol. 1. Dowden, Hutchinson, & Ross, Stroudsberg, PA.

Thorndyke, P. W. (1981a). Spatial cognition and reasoning. In J. R. Harvey (ed.), *Cognition, Social Behavior and the Environment*. Lawrence Erlbaum, Hillsdale, NJ.

Thorndyke, P. W. (1981b). Distance estimation from cognitive maps, *Cognitive Psychology*, **13**, 526–550.

Thorndyke, P. W., and Hayes-Roth, B. (1982). Differences in spatial knowledge acquired from maps and navigation, *Cognitive Psychology*, **14**, 560–589.

Thorndyke, P. W., and Stasz, C. (1980). Individual differences in procedures for knowledge acquisition from maps, *Cognitive Psychology*, **12**, 137–175.

Tinbergen, N. (1951). *The Study of Instinct*. Oxford University Press, Oxford.

Tolman, E. C. (1948). Cognitive maps in rats and men, *Psychological Review*, **55**, 189–209.

Torell, G., and Biel, A. (1985). Parents influence on children's cognitive maps and of activity ranges in residential neighborhoods. In T. Gärling and J. Valsiner (eds), *Children in Environments*. Plenum Press, New York.

Towler, J. O. (1970). The elementary school child's concept of reference systems, *Journal of Geography*, **69**, 89–93.

Towler, J. O., and Nelson, L. D. (1968). The elementary school child's concept of scale, *Journal of Geography*, **67**, 24–28.

Trickett, E. J., McConahay, J. B., Phillips, D., and Ginter, M. A. (1985). Natural experiments and the educational context: the environment and effects of an alternative inner-city public school on adolescents, *American Journal of Community Psychology*, **13**, 617–643.

Tuan, Y. F. (1974). *Topophilia: A Study of Environmental Perception, Attitude and Values*. Prentice Hall, Englewood Cliffs, NJ.

Tuan, Y. F. (1975). Images and mental maps, *Annals of the Association of American Geographers*, **65**, 213.

Tuan, Y. F. (1977). *Space and Place: The Perspective of Experience*. University of Minnesota Press, Minneapolis.

Tuan, Y. F. (1978). Children and the natural environment. In I. Altman and J. F. Wohlwill (eds), *Children and the Environment*. Plenum Press, New York.

Tuan, Y. F. (1980). The significance of artefact, *Geographical Review*, **70**, 462–472.

Tuddenham, R. D. (1970). A Piagetian test of cognitive development. In W. B. Dockrell (ed.), *On Intelligence: The Toronto Symposium on Intelligence*. Methuen, London.

Tversky, B. (1981). Distortions in memory for maps, *Cognitive Psychology*, **13**, 407–433.

Tversky, B., and Hemenway, K. (1983). Categories of environmental scenes, *Cognitive Psychology*, **15**, 121–149.

Tyerman, C., and Spencer, C. P. (1980). Normalized physical environment for the mentally handicapped, and its effect on patterns of activity, social relations and self-help skills, *British Journal of Mental Subnormality*, **26**, 47–54.

Ulrich, R. S. (1981). Natural versus urban scenes: some psychophysiological effects, *Environment and Behavior*, **13**, 523–556.

Underwood, J. D. M. (1981). Skilled map interpretation and visual-spatial ability, *Journal of Geography*, **80**, 55–58.

Valentine, C. (1914). The colour perception and colour preferences of an infant during its fourth and eighth months, *British Journal of Psychology*, **6**, 363–386.

Valsiner, J. (1987). *Culture and the Development of Children's Action: A Cultural-historical Theory of Developmental Psychology*. John Wiley, Chichester.

Vandenberg, B. (1981). Environmental and cognitive factors in social play, *Journal of Experimental Child Psychology*, **31**, 169–175.

van Vliet, W. (1983a). Exploring the fourth environment: an examination of the home range of city and suburban teenagers, *Environment and Behavior*, **15**, 567–588.

van Vliet, W. (1983b). Families in apartment buildings: sad storeys for children? *Environment and Behavior*, **15**, 211–234.

Verwer, D. (1980). Planning residential environments according to their real use by children and adults, *Ekistics*, **47**, 109–113.

von Senden, S. M. (1932). *Raum Und Gestalt Auffassung Bei Opererten Blindgeborenen Vor Und Nach Der Operation*. Barth, Leipzig.

von Senden, S. M. (1960). *Space and Sight, The Perception of Space and Shape in the Congenitally Blind Before and After Operation*. Free Press, Glencoe, IL.

Wachs, T. (1976). Utilization of a Piagetian approach in the investigation of early experience effects: a research strategy and some illustrative data, *Merrill-Palmer Quarterly*, **22**, 11–30.

Wagner, S., Winner, E., Cicchetti, D., and Gardner, H. (1981). 'Metaphorical' mapping in human infants, *Child Development*, **52**, 728–731.

Walk, R. D., and Pick, H. L. (eds) (1978). *Perception and Experience*. Plenum Press, New York.

Wallach, H. (1940). The role of head movements and vestibular cues in sound localization, *Journal of Experimental Psychology*, **27**, 339–368.

Waller, G. (1986). The development of route knowledge: multiple dimensions? *Journal of Environmental Psychology*, **6**, 109–119.

Walmsley, D. J. (1982). Mass media and spatial awareness, *Tijdschrift voor economische en sociale geografie*, **73**, 32–42.

Wanet, M. C., and Veraart, C. (1985). Processing of auditory information by the blind in spatial localization tasks, *Perception and Psychophysics*, **38**, 91–96.

Ward, C. (1977). *The Child in the City*. Architectural Press, London.

Ward, S. L., Newcombe, N., and Overton, W. F. (1986). Turn left at the church, or three miles north: a study of direction giving and sex differences, *Environment and Behavior*, **18**, 192–213.

Warr, P. B., and Knapper, C. (1968). *The Perception of People and Events*. John Wiley, London.

Warren, D. H. (1970). Intermodality interactions in spatial localizations, *Cognitive Psychology*, **1**, 114–133.

Warren, D. H. (1984). *Blindness and Early Childhood Development* (2nd Edn). American Foundation for the Blind, New York.

Warren, D. H., Anooshian, L. J., and Bollinger, J. G. (1973). Early vs late blindness: the role of early vision in spatial behaviour, *American Foundation for the Blind Research Bulletin*, **26**, 151–170.

Warren, D. H., and Kocon, J. A. (1974). Factors in the successful mobility of the blind: a review, *American Foundation for the Blind Research Bulletin*, **28**, 191–218.

Warren, D. H., and Strelow, E. R. (1984). Learning spatial dimensions with a visual sensory aid: Molyneux revisited, *Perception*, **13**, 331–350.

Waters, H. S., and Tinsley, V. S. (1987). Evaluating the discriminant and convergent validity of developmental constructs: another look at the concept of egocentrism, *Psychological Bulletin*, **97**, 483–496.

Weatherford, D. L. (1982). Spatial cognition as a function of size and scale of the environment. In R. Cohen (ed.), *New Directions for Child Development: Children's Conceptions of Spatial Relationships*, No. 15. Jossey-Bass, San Francisco.

Weatherford, D. L., and Cohen, R. (1980). Influence of prior activity on perspective taking, *Developmental Psychology*, **16**, 239–240.

Webley, P., and Cutts, K. (1985). Children, war and nationhood, *New Society*, 13 December, 451–453.

Weinstein, C. (1979). The physical environment of the school: a review of the research, *Review of Educational Research*, **49**, 577–610.

Weinstein, C. (1982). Privacy-seeking behaviour in an elementary classroom, *Journal of Environmental Psychology*, **2**, 23–36.

Weinstein, C. S., and David, T. G. (eds) (1987). *Spaces for Children: The Built Environment and Child Development*. Plenum Press, New York.

Weisman, G. D. (1981). Evaluating architectural legibility: wayfinding in the built environment, *Environment and Behavior*, **13**, 189–204.

Wellman, H. M. (ed.) (1985). *Children's Searching: The Development of Search Skill and Spatial Representation*. Lawrence Erlbaum, Hillsdale, NJ.

Wellman, H. M., Fabricius, W. V., and Sophian, C. (1985). The early development of planning. In H. M. Wellman (ed.), *Children's Searching: The Development of Search Skill and Spatial Representation*. Lawrence Erlbaum, Hillsdale, NJ.

Wellman, H. M., Rutter, R., and Flavell, J. H. (1975). Deliberate memory behavior in the delayed reactions of very young children, *Developmental Psychology*, **11**, 780–787.

Wellman, H. M., Somerville, S. C., and Haake, R. J. (1979). Development of search procedures in real-life spatial environments, *Developmental Psychology*, **15**, 530–542.

Welsh, R. L., and Blasch, B. B. (eds) (1980). *Foundations of Orientation and Mobility*. American Foundation for the Blind, New York.

West, R. L., Morris, C. W., and Nichol, G. T. (1985). Spatial cognition on nonspatial tasks: finding spatial knowledge when you are not looking for it. In R. Cohen (ed.), *The Development of Spatial Cognition*. Lawrence Erlbaum, Hillsdale, NJ.

White, S. H., and Siegal, A. W. (1984). Cognitive development in time and space. In B. Rogoff and J. Lave (eds), *Social Cognition: Its Development in Everyday Contexts*. Harvard University Press, Cambridge, MA.

Wicker, A. W. (1979). *An Introduction to Ecological Psychology*. Brookes-Cole, Monterey, CA.

Willats, J. (1977). How children learn to represent three-dimensional space in drawings. In G. Butterworth (ed.), *The Child's Representation of the World*. Plenum Press, London.

Willems, E. P. (1967). Sense of obligation to high school activities as related to school size and marginality of student, *Child Development*, **38**, 1247–1260.

Williams, P., and Jinks, D. (1985). *Design and Technology 5–12*. The Falmer Press, London.

Wilson, E. L. (1967). A developmental approach to psychological factors which may inhibit mobility in the visually handicapped person, *New Outlook for the Blind*, **61**, 283–289.

Wilson, S. (1978). Updating defensible space, *Architects Journal*, 11 October.

Wilton, R. N., and Pidcock, B. (1982). Knowledge of spatial relations: varying the precision with which locations must be specified, *Quarterly Journal of Experimental Psychology*, **34**, 515–528.

Wiltschko, R., and Wiltschko, W. (1985). Pigeon homing: change in navigation strategy during ontogeny, *Animal Behaviour*, **33**, 583–590.

Witkin, H. A. (1950). Individual differences in ease of perception of embedded figures, *Journal of Personality*, **19**, 1–15.

Wohlwill, J. F. (1985). Residential density as a variable in child development research. In J. F. Wohlwill and W. van Vliet (eds), *Habitats for Children*. Lawrence Erlbaum, Hillsdale, NJ.

Wohlwill, J. F., and van Vliet, W. (eds) (1985). *Habitats for Children*. Lawrence Erlbaum, Hillsdale, NJ.

Wohlwill, J. F., and Heft, H. (1987). The physical environment and the development of the child. In D. Stokols and I. Altman (eds), *Handbook of Environmental Psychology*. John Wiley, New York.

Wolfe, M. (1978). Childhood and privacy. In I. Altman and J. F. Wohlwill (eds), *Children and the Environment*. Plenum Press, New York.

Wolfe, M., and Laufer, R. S. (1975). The concept of privacy in childhood and adolescence. In D. H. Carson (ed.), *Man–Environment Interactions: Evaluations and Applications*. Dowden, Hutchinson, & Ross, Stroudsberg, PA.

Womble, P., and Studebaker, S. (1981). Crowding in a national park campground, *Environment and Behavior*, **13**, 557–573.

Wood, D. (1973). *I Don't Want To But I Will; The Genesis of Geographic Knowledge: A Real-time Developmental Study of Adolescent Images of Novel Environments*. The Clark University Cartographic Laboratory, Worcester, MA.

Wood, D. (1981). *To Catch the Wind: Kites, Kids and the Environment in Barronquitas, Puerto Rico*. North Carolina State University School of Design, Raleigh, NC.

Wood, D. (1984/5). A neighborhood is to hang around, *Children's Environments Quarterly*, **1**, 29–35.

Wood, D. (1986). *Doing Nothing*. North Carolina State University School of Design, Raleigh, NC.

Wood, D. (1987). Pleasure in the idea: the atlas as a narrative form, *Cartographica Monographs*, **1**, 24–46.

Wood, D., and Beck, R. (1976). Talking with 'Environmental A', an experimental mapping language. In G. T. Moore and R. G. Golledge (eds), *Environmental Knowing*. Dowden, Hutchinson, & Ross, Stroudsburg, PA.

Worchel, P. (1951). Space perception and orientation in the blind, *Psychological Monographs*, **65**, 1–28.

Worchel, P., and Mauney, J. (1950). The effect of practice on the perception of obstacles by the blind, *Journal of Experimental Psychology*, **41**, 170–176.

Worchel, P., Maunery, J., and Andrew, J. G. (1950). The perception of obstacles by the blind. *International Experimental Psychology*, **40**, 746–751.

Wright, D. R. (1979). Visual images in geography texts: the case of Africa, *Geography*, **64**, 205–210.

Wunderlich, D., and Reinelt, R. (1982). How to get there from here. In R. J. Jarvella and W. Klein (eds), *Speech Place and Action*. John Wiley, Chichester.

Wunderle, J. M., and Martiner, J. S. (1987). Spatial learning in the nectarivorous bananaquit: juveniles *vs* adults, *Animal Behaviour*, **35**, 652–658.

Yamamoto, T., and Tatsuno, M. (1984). A developmental study of spatial problem solving, *Psychologia*, **27**, 228–236.

Yates, F. (1966). *The Art of Memory*, Routledge & Kegan Paul, London.

Yonas, A., and Pick, H. L. (1975). An approach to the study of infant space perception. In L. B. Cohen and P. Salapatek (eds), *Infant Perception: From Sensation to Cognition*. Academic Press, New York.

Zannaras, G. (1976). The relation between cognitive structure and urban form. In G. T. Moore and R. G. Golledge (eds), *Environmental Knowing: Theories, Research and Methods*. Dowden, Hutchinson, & Ross, Stroudsburg, PA.

Zimler, J., and Keenan, J. M. (1983). Imagery in the congenitally blind: how visual are visual images? *Journal of Experimental Psychology: Learning, Memory and Cognition*, **9**, 269–282.

Zimring, C., Carpman, J. R., and Michelson, W. (1987). Design for special populations: mentally retarded persons, children, hospital visitors. In D. Stokols and I. Altman (eds), *Handbook of Environmental Psychology*. John Wiley, New York.

Zube, E. H. (1984). *Environmental Evaluation*. Cambridge University Press, Cambridge.

Index